Monsters, Makeup & Effects
Volume I

Conversations with Cinema's Greatest Artists

By
Heather Wixson

Edited By
Derek Anderson

www.DarkInkBooks.com

First Published by *Dark Ink Books*, Southwick, MA, 2021

Dark Ink Books is a division of *AM Ink Publishing*. *Dark Ink* and *AM Ink* and its logos are trademarked by *AM Ink Publishing*.

www.AMInkPublishing.com

This is for all the Monster Kids out there.

Never stop believing in your dreams.

TABLE OF CONTENTS

Oscar Nominated and Emmy Winning Special Effects Makeup Artist

Planet of the Apes (1968)
Invasion of the Body Snatchers (1978)
Howard the Duck (1986)
Scrooged (1988)
Nip/Tuck (2003-2010)

As the son of legendary special effects pioneer Ellis Burman Sr., Thomas R. Burman seemed fated from a very early age to blaze his own path of greatness in Hollywood, even if he nearly derailed following his destiny after high school.

My father was one of the greatest artists ever, and before he was working in California on movies, he used to create monumental sculptures back in Nebraska for the W.P.A. [Works Progress Administration]. When the W.P.A. period of the 1930s was over, since he always loved the ocean, he headed for the Pacific Ocean, got to Hollywood, and worked on all kinds of different commercially creative projects before I was born. Then, he finally got a job being a scenic artist, and that was what he wanted to do. He went to a staff shop where they had sculptors and mold-makers, and he worked as a sculptor for a while, even though he was much more versatile than that.

But my father decided that he didn't want to be pigeonholed as just a sculptor, so he went to the prop shop where they gave him his own room. He made the original mask for the *Phantom of the Opera*, the Claude Rains version. He worked on *Flesh and Fantasy*. He made the cobra in *Jungle Book*, and he also did a lot of stuff on the *Abbott and Costello Meet Frankenstein*. During that time, they were doing *The Wolf Man*, and Jack Pierce, who did not work with foam latex, came to my father. He made the foam latex appliances for Jack, and cast them for him in the prop shop because Jack didn't know how to do that.

I remember when I was little, my dad took me to the set one time, and this makeup man put a little cut on my arm and asked me why I was there. I said, "I'm with my dad." He said, "Oh, that's your dad? You know, if you're half as talented as he is, you should become a makeup artist like I am." And that was Jack Pierce. That was the first time that the idea of becoming a makeup artist was planted in my head. When I was about 13, my dad bought me a makeup case, and I ran around, putting beards on people and applying cuts and bruises. But I was never a good student, and so, by the time I got to high school, I was failing everything. So, I just ran away and joined the Marine Corps.

When I got in the Marine Corps, I got married right away and had kids. I tried to get into makeup, and they told me that it was next to impossible. So, I began doing all types of odd jobs. I worked for a sanitation company south of Venice, I moved furniture, and I parked cars at the Hollywood Palladium during the Emmys, not knowing that I would ever win one. I took on any work that I could find because I had two kids. I was pretty much living in abject poverty, and I was working in a factory down in Newport Beach where they make those roll-on lint removers (the ones with the tape on the outside).

One day, my dad called me up and asked me, "Do you have any vacation time coming?" I asked him why, and he told me that he had just been hired by Don Post Studios to sculpt a 12-foot tall King Kong gorilla for a wax museum up in Niagara Falls. He wanted me to come on and help, but I wasn't sure if I could get the time off from work. But he told me he was going to pay me five dollars an hour, which was well more than double what I was making at that time. So, I told him I'd be there, and the rest was history.

Being able to work alongside an enormous talent like his dad Ellis was already a huge honor for Burman, but he was also surrounded by some other legendary artists who would help him begin his career as a professional in the effects industry.

When I went to work with my dad, that's where I met John Chambers, Don Post, and Verne Langdon, who was another partner. One day, a makeup man stopped by when there was no one at the studio except for me, and his name was Irving Pringle. He told me that there was an apprenticeship opening at Fox. I told John Chambers the following day how I gave this guy some latex, and he told me there was an apprenticeship. He said, "I didn't know you wanted to be a makeup artist," and that's when I told him that it had always been my dream. And that's when John promised to make a call on my behalf.

I worked all week, getting sadder as the week went by, thinking, "Well, I guess that's not going to happen." On the following Monday, I was making what they call a splash mold, and John came in that morning. I asked him what happened with Fox, and that's when he realized that he had forgotten to make the call. He ran in the office, came back, he said, "They want to see you immediately because they're going to choose today." Well, here I was, covered with plaster, and it's even in my hair, so there was no way I could go over there looking like that. But John told me I had to go, so I went over to Fox, feeling bad about the state I was showing up in for my interview.

When I interviewed with Ben Nye, he gave me the bad news. There were 96 applicants for this job, and one of them was his son, so it looked like an impossibility for me to get the position. I drove home, and I felt so disappointed. When I got there, I told my first wife, Sandy, "If anybody calls, I don't want to talk to them. I don't want to talk to anybody." We were sitting there, eating dinner, and the phone rang. She answers it, and then she hands me the phone. It was Ben Nye, saying, "How would you like to come in and start tomorrow?" I couldn't believe it.

Thomas settled in as an apprentice over at Fox rather comfortably, working for the likes of Nye and Dick Smith, cleaning up offices and makeup stations, while being completely immersed in the inner-workings of the studio's lab. One day, Burman overheard a conversation that would not only change his life forever but would also have a monumental impact on the career of his friend, John Chambers, too.

Somewhere around the six-month mark of me being over at Fox, I overheard this conversation that Dick Smith was having, but I wasn't exactly sure what he was talking about. He had done some work that wasn't exactly what the studio was looking for, and Fox wanted to bring in Bud Westmore to take over, based on some work that Bud had done on *The List of Adrian Messenger*. They thought because Bud was the one in charge, that he did all those appliances and all that work, but I knew differently.

I knew that it was John Chambers who had made those appliances, but because I was an apprentice, I wasn't sure if I should say anything because my job was to clean up, not to chime in. But I couldn't help myself, so I spoke up and said, "John Chambers did it." Ben Nye asked me how I knew that, and I told him that I saw pictures of his work at John's house and some of the appliances that he made, too. Bill told me to call John and ask him if he wanted to come in and pick up a script.

I called him, and John was busy casting Spock's ears for *Star Trek*, so he told me he couldn't come in right then. But when I told him they wanted to bring in Bud Westmore, he told me that he would be right over. I didn't see John when he came in but, the following day, John drove up in front of the makeup studio just as I was stepping out the door with his little Buick Skylark. John waves at me and says, "Tommy! Tommy! It's you and me." That's when he hands me the script to *Planet of the Apes*.

At the time that 20th Century Fox was loosely adapting Pierre Boulle's novel of the same name, science fiction cinema had been in something of a downturn after the 1950s, making Planet of the Apes a huge gamble for the studio.

When *Apes* came along, science fiction was not so trendy anymore, and many of the other studios didn't have the talent to handle the makeup lab work. George Bau, who was a very talented and bright man, was at Warner Bros., and I think it was Bill Tuttle and Charlie Schram at MGM. They were contained in the studio, so when they worked on set, they mainly did beauty makeups. So, when *Planet of the Apes* came along, it changed the industry as it put the focus on makeup applications and makeup prosthetics, which hadn't been the case before.

John and I working together on *Planet of the Apes* was a great combination because John had been a maxillofacial restoration technician at Vance Hospital in Chicago, and he was a dental technician in the Army. John made teeth, and he created glass eyes, he had all of that down beautifully. What I was able to bring to the table was the fact that my father had a mask business at home, and we made Halloween masks together. We did these very exclusive Halloween masks with laid-on hair on them, even before Don Post set up his line of masks, and my father sold them at Bert Wheeler's store, Hollywood Magic.

So I had a lot of know-how when it came to making masks. I knew how to formulate the latex so that they weren't just jiggly, and they would hold their shape. Plus, I also knew how to make molds, so I was a perfect person to work with John because it was nearly impossible to find anybody who knew how to do any of those things at that time. But it was the combination of our talents that made it possible for us to be able to do what we did on such a huge scale.

Knowing the monumental amount of work ahead of them, John Chambers and Thomas Burman began work immediately on Planet of the Apes, getting everything they needed to take on what would become one of the most influential films, science fiction, or otherwise, of all time.

We started work on *Apes* on January 2nd, and I don't think we started filming until sometime in the spring [May 1967]. We had months of prep time, but it was myself and Werner Keppler in the lab, working seven days a week, 16 hours a day without a day off, all the way until the end, which was in August.

When they started shooting, it was my job to make sure that all the artists going to make up the apes had two sets of prosthetic appliances on a vacuum form. We designed it like paint-by-numbers because we were very specific about how these characters would look. We made all the colors. They didn't use anything else out of their makeup kit other than their brushes, scissors, or combs. Everything else was set up for them.

My job was to make sure that everybody had what they needed and then, every morning, Werner and I would run the foam latex, and put them in the oven. Then, we'd go about making teeth, putting hair where we needed to, and then, we'd take the molds out and open them up. Then, we'd have to do the whole thing all over again. We didn't leave there until very late at night, and we were always back there very early in the morning.

While he was thrilled to be a part of Planet of the Apes and enjoyed getting to collaborate with Chambers on the sci-fi epic, Burman had some early reservations about the project based on what he saw before the film was finalized.

After we wrapped, I got a chance to see a rough cut at the studio's theater, and that was the first time I had ever seen a rough cut before. It wasn't color-corrected. It didn't have sound effects in it. It had terrible temp music, and most of the actors wearing appliances had muffled voices. I just thought, "My God, this is terrible."

I went back, and John Chambers asked me what I thought, and all I could tell him was that the makeups looked great, and I couldn't believe that this big studio that put this film together had created something that was so chopped up and terrible. But when I went to the premiere in Westwood, and I saw it in its entirety, the movie had a completely different feeling to it, and it was brilliant. I was so proud that I had been a part of this film, and that I was able to contribute to something that would change the industry.

The success of *Planet of the Apes* taught directors they could think out of the box because everything in Hollywood had gone stale back then, for the most part. All of a sudden, everyone realized that you could take risks again. Writers could write things that they didn't think they could write before. Producers were looking at scripts a little bit differently after *Apes*, and directors realized they could push the envelope again.

It was during the second Planet of the Apes sequel, Escape from the Planet of the Apes, when Burman's apprenticeship ended at 20th Century Fox, and he set out to continue conquering the world of special effects in new ways.

After I finished working at Fox, I went to work on the movie *Hawaiians*, with Charlton Heston, of all people. Then, I did the *Kung Fu* series for a while, and I worked on the remake of *Lost Horizon*, too. One day, John Chambers called and asked me if I wanted to open up an independent studio with him because there were no independent studios back then. But, our real reason for opening an independent studio was not just to do motion picture and television work. The studio was our cover for working with the C.I.A.

The C.I.A. had been trying to figure out how these makeups were being done in the movies, especially in scenes where someone rips off their face, and it's somebody else underneath. They didn't initially realize that was achieved editorially, so they came to John Chambers. The C.I.A. wanted to know what they could do because they wanted to find ways to create quick disguises that could be put on immediately if they were being trailed by the K.G.B., for instance.

John was, of course, involved with the situation years later in Iran in 1979 and 1980, but I wasn't part of that. The C.I.A. had contacted John for some help, and he opened up a production company in Hollywood with Bob Sidell, another makeup artist who worked on *Planet of the Apes*. He wanted to make it look official in case the Iranians checked into their story around Hollywood and found out it wasn't the real deal. They even took out trade ads and posted about casting calls for this fake science fiction movie, just in case. And that became the basis for the movie *Argo*, which was a knock-knock joke that John had come up while on the set of *Planet of the Apes*.

Burman continued to establish himself as one of the premier artists in the effects industry throughout the 1970s, contributing to a variety of film projects including **Frogs, The Thing with Two Heads, Phantom of the Paradise, The Food of the Gods, The Island of Dr. Moreau (1977), Close Encounters of the Third Kind,** *and* **Invasion of the Body Snatchers (1978).**

During the '70s, my brother Sonny [Ellis Burman Jr.] and I had a shop with John Chambers, but we had to buy him out because he was diagnosed with Hodgkin's disease. Sonny and I scraped together every dollar and every single cent that we had, so we were pretty desperate after that. We took on anything and everything that came our way. We did all these films for almost no money because we were trying to get a reputation going for ourselves because we didn't have any contacts between us. We did *A Man Called Horse* with Richard Harris. We worked on *Phantom of the Paradise*, and we also did the effects for *The Devil's Rain* and *Food of the Gods*. We took on *The Man Who Fell to Earth* with David Bowie.

A few years later, I bought my brother out, and by the mid-1970s, John Chambers and I went back in one more time to do *Island of Dr. Moreau* together. After that, I did *Close Encounters, Demon Seed,* and *Prophecy* – a whole plethora of films, really. When they called me to do *Invasion of the Body Snatchers*, it was only two or three weeks before they started filming. They didn't realize how much time was needed to do all of this work. We had to go right along with the three weeks of pre-production and, then, we worked through to the end, creating all these effects.

A guy that I had hired, Eddie Henriques, he and I would rush up to San Francisco to do one of the shots. Then, we would jump on that first train back down to L.A., so we could work around the clock to get to the next thing they needed ready, and then we would head back up there and shoot out that stuff.

We were constantly moving and making everything as we went along, and I liked the pressure of not having too much time to overthink things. I work better when I have to come up with something quickly; it's like pulling a rabbit out of a hat, and I enjoy that experience more than if it's a situation where I have to put the rabbit in the hat. But I thought the director, Philip Kaufman, was brilliant, and I enjoyed working with him on *Body Snatchers*.

Back then, I was probably doing almost 90 percent of Hollywood's prosthetic work. It was around this time where a friend of mine, who was also in makeup effects, invited me to come and see a bake-off of special effects for an Academy Award. I went with him, and they had five different movies that were up for possible Academy recognition, and three of them featured the same kind of work I was doing, including their special effects.

"I realized that most people didn't understand the work that makeup people like myself were doing. That's when I came up with a whole new title – Special Makeup Effects. John Chambers didn't like it, Dick Smith didn't like it either, and the union hated it at the time, too, because they thought the term would water down our industry. To me, there was nothing at the time that I could find that described what I was doing any better than "Special Makeup Effects," and today, it's now a commonplace term.

Heading into the 1980s, Thomas realized that the industry of special effects was shifting towards a new era, as there was a booming amount of talent out there who were just getting started in Hollywood. Rather than worry, Burman found ways to keep thriving as the competition around him began to surge.

I began to see the shift in everything during the late '70s. There were people like Stan Winston, who I had partnered with for a while, plus Rick Baker, Greg Cannom, Ve Neill, and so forth, who were discovering the effects industry. And as they were discovering it, they were doing their work out of their garages, or they were starting up their own shops, and I could see everything was going to change before it even happened. Because once there was competition, it changed the whole game for everyone.

It was at the start of the decade when *The Unseen* came along. Stan Winston brought it to me. He had a partner at the time, a director by the name of Danny Steinmann whose father was a big art collector from New York, so he had a pot of money at his disposal. They had a script called, *Blood Storm*, and they wanted me to do the effects for it, telling me that they would give me a point on it. I didn't know what a point meant, but later, when I found out what a point meant, I was pretty insulted, but it was already too late.

When I read the first script, I thought it was terrible. It was about a brother and sister who had a ski resort in Aspen that had a 20-year-old young man locked up in a cage, and they had raised him since he was a baby and fed him nothing but raw meat. When he gets out of the cage, he kills women. That was their horror story. The story made no sense to me, and they decided to bring in some new writers, so I met with Kim Henkel and Nancy Rifkin. Kim had written *The Texas Chain Saw Massacre*, which wasn't a film that I necessarily had enjoyed. But I met with them, and I told them what I thought. And they quit.

Stan wasn't happy about them quitting, but I told him they needed a better story than what they had. He said, "Then, you come up with a story," and I wrote about 75 pages of what became the script for *The Unseen*. I wrote the whole premise, and they loved what I came up with and decided that was the movie they were going to make. But, then, Danny Steinmann's father refused to give him any more money because the budget had doubled, and after spending about five months on it, I needed to go find some work elsewhere, and Stan eventually dropped out, too.

Danny Steinmann finally found Tony Unger, the producer, and they made it into a movie. I never received any credit for my work, though, which I tried to contest with the Writer's Guild, but I wasn't smart enough back then to keep all my notes. I had given everything handwritten to Danny Steinmann.

So I never saw a cent from *The Unseen*, but it at least gave me the chance to realize that I could tell stories myself.

I also started looking more into Canadian productions because they had nobody up there working. The first time I realized that was when I went up to work on *Food of the Gods* in Canada. When I did *Gods*, their production company makeup trailer consisted of a 27-foot trailer, pulled by a Volvo. They had no studio, so we had to make do, and I could see they needed someone with some expertise working on all these films up there.

When I worked on *My Bloody Valentine* (1981), as well as *Happy Birthday to Me*, we did both of those films in Montreal. There was an old hockey rink that they had converted into a studio, but it wasn't converted yet, so it was just a rink without any ice in it. I taught a lot of the Canadian artists a lot of techniques, because there was no one up there who knew how to put appliances on or how to do any special makeups.

After his time in Canada, Burman found several creature features in the States to work on, the first being The Beast Within for Philippe Mora. The other project was Paul Schrader's erotic horror film Cat People, which transformed co-stars Nastassja Kinski and Malcolm McDowell into lust-filled panthers who must procreate in order to fight their werecat urges.

When Paul [Schrader] approached me for *Cat People* (1982), I thought it was an interesting movie, and it allowed me to explore the film's ideas from a story perspective. I was able to write a couple of the transformational scenes for *Cat People*, and Paul liked my ideas a lot. So, for me, it doesn't get any better than when somebody respects you as much as you respect them, and you collaborate together. It's such a great feeling.

It was on *Cat People* when I met Bari [Dreiband], who I am married to now. I had hired Bari because I didn't want the transformation of Nastassja Kinski into a cat to be heavy-handed like the transformation in *An American Werewolf in London*. I wanted it to be more feminine. Bari had a degree in Fine Arts, and I really wanted her input. She was very instrumental in doing that design. When I met Bari, I was married at the time, and I was not a philanderer. But the day I met her, it was like I had met somebody I'd known for all of my life. It was the strangest feeling, and I didn't even know why or how it happened exactly, but I quickly fell in love with her.

The thing about working with Bari is that we are completely complementary to each other. If I get an idea, she adds to it, and then she comes back with her idea. Then, I'll give her another idea on top of that to keep things going. We worked perfectly together, and we were, and still are, a match made in heaven. I enjoyed working on *Cat People* for many reasons, but Bari is by far the best reason of all.

Bari and Thomas were married in 1984, and they have been collaborating now for more than 35 years, both on a personal and professional level. Two of the most significant projects that came in during the 1980s had the Burmans teaming up with director Richard Donner on both The Goonies and Scrooged, which led to both Thomas and Bari being nominated for an Academy Award the following year.

The Goonies was a project that we inherited. Steven Spielberg had come up with the design of the John Matuszak character, Sloth, but the guy who was originally working on Sloth was very talented, but he ran into all kinds of issues. So, they called me and asked if I could go over and talk to him and to see if I could help him because Spielberg liked this guy very much. I went over and talked to him, and he told me he didn't need any help. And the last time he went in, he didn't get it right again, so they put the film on a two-week hiatus, and asked us to take over the show. So, we had to start from scratch and do everything in two weeks.

I do think the character of Sloth came out great, even though we had limited time, but a lot of that was due to John. A lot of people don't realize that, no matter what you do, what makeup you put on somebody, if that person doesn't take to that makeup and make it alive and make it real and compelling, you've lost both the makeup and the character. But John embraced all of it. He was Sloth. John and I became great friends on *The Goonies*, too. He was a character.

And I loved working on *Scrooged*, too. When they asked Bari if she wanted to be the department head, she went over and met with Richard Donner, and he told her that there were very few special makeups in the film. She believed him and brought the script home to read. She told me what Richard had said, so when I read the script, I was like, "Oh, my God. There are so many special makeups in this." As it turns out, he was just joking, and Bari had believed him.

But what was so great about Richard Donner was that he was always so open with us, and he ended up being one of my favorite directors that I have ever worked with. For instance, we had created the lost souls that were contained in the chest of the Ghost of Christmas Future. We started making these lost souls puppets, and one day, he tells me that the lost souls were out, and they were going to do it all on video. We had also made a skeletal head for the Christmas Future creature too, but Richard said they wanted to use a TV for the head, and then they were going to show everything on the screens.

I told Richard that the puppets were almost finished, and he told me to move on because they were out, so I didn't need to finish them. But I just finished them anyway, and I went over and set them up on the back of the stage. I found Richard and told him that whenever he had a moment, there was something that I wanted to show him. He eventually walked over, and I had my guys behind a table, operating the puppets. He looks at it, takes a moment, and says, "Okay. So, they're back in the movie. Now, what else do you want?"

Another big moment for me on *Scrooged* was when Richard and Bill Murray were in the makeup trailer, and they were going over the scene where Bill throws the water on the waiter who he thinks is on fire. They were going back and forth, but nothing was clicking, and here I am, at the other end of the trailer, and I said, "I've got a line." Bill turns and says, "Okay, you have a line. You're the makeup artist. You stay down there. We're talking about script right now. You just stay focused on the makeup, okay?"

So, they kept going back and forth, but they were getting nowhere. Then, they asked me what my big line was, and that's when I said that Bill should say to the guy, "I'm sorry. I thought you were Richard Pryor." Bill Murray starts explaining to me that Richard was a very good friend of his, and he thought that the line was disrespectful. But we do the shot, he throws the water on the guy, and out of nowhere, Bill goes, "Oh, I'm sorry. I thought you were Richard Pryor." I was pretty proud of that, especially since it was one of the funniest lines in the film.

But the thing I loved the most about *Scrooged* was that it gave me a chance to do both comedy and horror, where you are doing things that are silly and things you don't expect. It was a great experience, and I was thrilled when we were nominated for an Oscar for our work. I was very proud of that show.

As the '90s were approaching, the Burmans decided it was time to change things up in their professional lives, especially once they welcomed their son, Maxx, into the world, with them both wanting to work closer to home.

When Bari and I had our son, we wanted to spend as much time as we could with him, so we started to take on a lot more commercials and television work. We did the pilot for *CSI: Crime Scene Investigation*. We did the pilot for *Buffy the Vampire Slayer*. We worked on a bunch of characters for *The Tracey Ullman Show*, which was great because we only shot one day a week, on a Friday, and we had the whole week to create all the characters. Then, Tracey went over to HBO for the *Tracey Takes On* series, and we were on the entire run of that show.

For Bari and I, our focus was on trying to bring motion picture quality effects to television and raising the bar for the industry. We were allowed to do that when we did *Nip/Tuck* for Ryan Murphy. *Nip/Tuck* was the turning point for everything, and the work we did on the pilot in the surgery scene is what got the show green-lit because it was all dependent on how real these surgeries were going to look. If they weren't going to look real, then Fox was not going to give it the go-ahead.

The biggest challenge of doing television is that you rarely ever have any prep time. You get something like five to 12 days, and all of a sudden, you've got to create a 650-pound woman in a short amount of time. If you were doing this for a film, you would have six months. But, because I'd been in this industry for so long, I knew how to cut those corners, and I knew how to utilize people's talents so we could always get the job done in time. We were able to create extravagant makeups on a weekly basis, which nobody had seen before *Nip/Tuck*.

And once *Nip/Tuck* came out, suddenly everyone wanted realistic effects on their shows, including *Grey's Anatomy*. We had previously worked on *Chicago Hope*, and every once in a while, they had something that would try and push the envelope, but the medical adviser would come in and cover things all up because they thought it was too graphic. But, when they saw the success of *Nip/Tuck*, they started to up their game, and *Grey's Anatomy* followed suit. I also think our work on *Nip/Tuck* led to things like *American Horror Story* coming into play, especially because both shows have the same producer, Ryan Murphy.

When I think about it now, I feel like the most respect I have ever been shown in the industry was on *Nip/Tuck* because they allowed us to be part of the process. I even got to write a few scenes for *Nip/Tuck*. There would be instances where I saw something, and I thought, "You know, a better way to do this would be if we changed this up." And they were always open to my ideas, and I felt validated by that.

With nearly 150 credits on his resume, multiple Emmy awards for his exceptional work in the realm of television, as well as 50-plus years as an effects artist under his belt, Thomas Burman continues to find new ways to challenge himself creatively. Most recently, Burman served as a writer and producer on Making Apes: The Artists Who Changed Film, a documentary project directed by William Conlin, which celebrates the artists behind the original Planet of the Apes and explores the enduring influence it still has on the world today.

I had decided to begin writing my memoirs because people were always saying to me, "You have to write all of this stuff down – these stories are incredible." And as I was trying to write my memoirs, I was thinking about one the most enjoyable times in my career was back when I was a young apprentice. I knew Clark Gable's makeup artist. I knew Elvis Presley and Marilyn Monroe's makeup artist, and all of these people would tell all these wonderful stories from the golden age of Hollywood. That's when I realized that all of those stories are gone because those people are all dead now. And after all of these years, I realized that I have my own stories as well.

That's what set me off. I started thinking about the fact that nobody has ever told the story of what went into making *Planet of the Apes* from the point of view of the people who did the effects work. There have been a lot of books on *Planet of the Apes* in general, the production of *Planet of the Apes*, and so forth. But nobody took the time to speak to the other artists involved who have never told their stories. So, I decided to start finding out which artists were still around.

The majority of the guys they had hired on *Apes* were new to makeup, too. John Chambers interviewed them, and we gave them two or three weeks of school, teaching them everything they needed to know about doing special makeup effects. In return, we helped introduce a whole group of people who had never done makeup before to a brand new industry, and set most of them off on a new path after the film was completed.

And it inspired so many people beyond that, too. Rick Baker would not have gone in the film industry if it hadn't been for *Planet of the Apes*. It was *Planet of the Apes* that made Stan Winston decide not to be an actor and become a makeup artist. Guillermo del Toro played with action figures in his house and made a whole film on Super 8 in his walk-in closet in Mexico of *Planet of the Apes*. It was huge. It changed all of our lives, and that's what I wanted to document.

I think about that all the time, how everything completely changed for me after *Apes*. My favorite saying is, "You want to make God laugh? Just tell him your plans." Even after all these years, I still don't know how I got here. If it were ever my intention to get to this point in my career, I probably would have never made it in the first place. It's just that things presented themselves at the right time in my life, and I made the most of every single experience I had.

I feel like the most fortunate person in the world to have been able to have such a wonderful life, and I am blown away by the things I have been able to accomplish because I could never have expected it at all. I mean, I flunked the first grade, and the last grade I ever finished in school was the ninth grade. So, for me to be in the position that I am today, it's incredible, and I know how lucky I am. I'm not a very religious person, but I do believe that somebody, or something, has been keeping watch over me for a very long time now.

Thomas Burman and Wife, Bari Dreiband-Burman

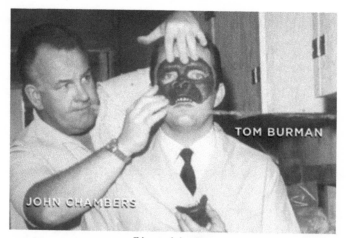

Planet of the Apes

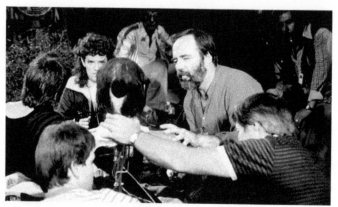

The Manitou

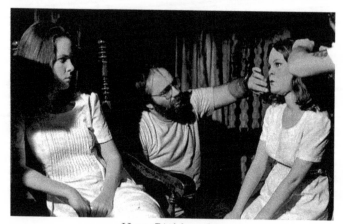

Happy Birthday to Me

The Beast Within

Thomas Burman in Action

The Goonies

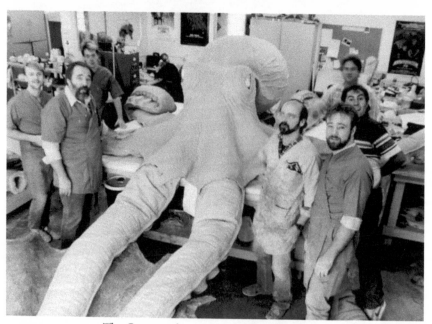

The Octopus that was cut out of *The Goonies*

Scrooged

Sketches for *Scrooged*

Conversation with…
LANCE ANDERSON

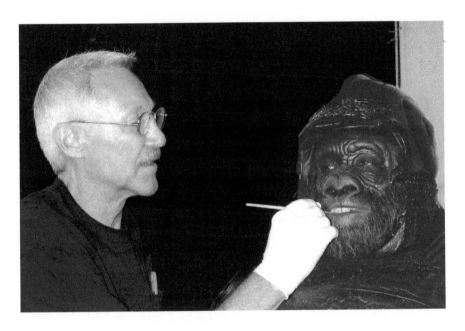

Oscar Nominated Special Effects Makeup Artist

The Island of Dr Moreau (1996)
Planet of the Apes (2001)
Dawn of the Dead (2004)
Cinderella Man (2005)

For Oscar-nominated artist Lance Anderson, his path to becoming a special makeup effects artist wasn't as direct as many of his contemporaries.

I had no idea that one day, I would get to pursue making art on a professional level. I grew up in Venice, California, and after spending a few years in the Navy, I met my future wife, Jean, at a party. Within a year we were married, and right away we had our son, David, and seven years later we had our daughter, Joni. Just before I got married, my father got me into the electrical union. It was a good-paying job, even though I had always wanted to have myself an art career. I was always painting and sculpting things in my spare time, but after 20 years of being an electrician, I didn't know whether I wanted to continue or take early retirement.

I went ahead and got my contractor's license to be an electrical contractor, and even had the name picked out for my company – Lee Electric. Then I realized, 'That's not what I want to do with the rest of my life - this is the moment where I could change my occupation and get into art.' I knew that being a fine art painter or something like that wasn't right for me because I'm not much of a salesman and I didn't want to wind up a starving artist. But I was ready to make a significant move, even though I wasn't sure what that meant exactly.

One day, I saw an ad in the newspaper that said, "Become a makeup artist." I had never even thought about that as being a career. I contacted the school where they trained people to become makeup artists and found out it was a night school. At the same time, in 1976, we moved out of Venice to Malibu to start building a new home for my family on an empty lot. I pulled a trailer onto the property and began getting the drawings and all the engineering done, all while still working full-time as an electrician.

Then, night school began, and between working as an electrician, still driving to Malibu to live in a trailer, and attending night school in Los Angeles, all of that was jamming up my time. But I was still putting a lot of energy and time into becoming a makeup artist because I knew this was the change that I needed. I was almost finished with the makeup course; we were just about to start the final section, which involved building creatures, doing facial appliances, old age makeups – all kinds of different things like that, and I was very excited to delve into everything ahead of me.

The instructor, whose name was Ken Diaz, said, "You don't need to finish the course here. Just come to my garage, and we'll start working on all of this stuff together." So, I worked with him at night in East LA in his garage, learning all the basics of prosthetic makeup and masks and everything in that field, which gave me a well-rounded start to get into makeup effects as a career.

I worked about a year doing theater and runway makeup. One day, I got a call from Ken to help work on a haunted house he was doing where the actors were going to be disfigured zombies using warm gelatin slathered onto their faces, which I could never have imagined making zombies that way before. So, when I was done with the haunted house, I went to the union to see if I could get in since I thought that's how it was done back then.

It turned out to be a catch-22 situation. A union rep named Howard told me the only way you can get in the union is if you have hours, but it was hard to get hours without being in the union. So, I continued being an electrician, and I put a pin on makeup work for a while.

Fate would intervene on Lance's behalf in the early 1980s when, out of the blue, he received a call that would forever change his life and set him on his way to starting his career in the special makeup effects industry.

I got a call from Howard, and he told me, "We received a recommendation for you for this new film because they need somebody who knows how to work with gelatin appliances." It ended up being for this film with Bernadette Peters, and Andy Kaufman called *Heartbeeps*, and Stan Winston was running it. Ken Diaz was the one who recommended me to Stan, and that was my ticket in.

I went to work over at Universal, where they were shooting *Heartbeeps*. I worked mainly in the lab, making gelatin appliances, not on set at all. It was at the wrap party for the film that Jean and I connected with Stan and his wife, Karen, and a lifelong friendship between our families was born. After *Heartbeeps*, I started working with Stan in his shop. I worked with him for a couple of years, and we did *Parasite* (1982), *Something Wicked This Way Comes*, and *The Thing* (1982).

The Thing was Rob Bottin's show, and he came over to Stan's studio asking Stan if he would help him create the Dog-Thing for the movie. Stan agreed and decided to do it as a puppet, so we did three designs. Stan, Jim Kagel and I did our own versions of the dog thing without looking at each other's designs, and we took them over to Rob to have him pick which one we were going to make. Rob picked the design I drew, so I thought it was pretty neat that we were using my design. We came back to Stan's and took a cast with my arm up in the air so that I could be the puppeteer. I sculpted the Dog-Thing with simple mechanics and assistance from Jim and lab assistant, Michiko.

I got to take the Dog-Thing to set and puppeteer it, and they put a 1930's style leather motorcycle helmet on me and set squibs off right next to my head because the Dog-Thing gets shot. They shot everything in reverse with the tentacles, so it looked like they were shooting outward. There was this gooey substance all over everything called Methocel, and it was running down my back and all over my body. I remember thinking to myself, "What on earth did I get myself into?"

Then, I worked a bit for Tom Burman on *The Goonies* and *Cat People* (1982). On *Cat People,* I sculpted the leopard's guts that had a Picasso-type arm that flipped out with a one-finger salute. I even added my mark to the gag by sculpting my initials into the entrails. There was a lot of smoke when they shot that, so you have to press pause to see them.

Later, while working at Paramount on the TV series *Star Trek*, I heard that Rick Baker had a cattle call for people to work on *Thriller,* a Michael Jackson music video. So I started working nights on *Thriller,* which meant when I finished shooting all day at Paramount, I would take a nap in the parking lot and then I'd go over to *Thriller* to do prosthetic makeups, and then I was back over at *Star Trek* in the morning. I really envied my Klingon napping in the makeup chair while I worked on him, bleary-eyed, on those mornings.

I also had the opportunity to work with Werner Keppler in the lab on *The Last Starfighter* for Nick Castle over at Lorimar, which was part of Warner [Bros.]. We started getting designs for the creatures, and I didn't have a shop at that time, so I remember sculpting and painting them at Warner Bros. and taking them home to do the mechanics in my garage. There was one that looked like an elephant and one that looked like an insect, and both of them had to have mechanical devices in them.

After that, I got a department head job on *Red Dawn,* starring Charlie Sheen, who was a good friend of my son's and still is to this day. My family was excited to learn we were going on location to Las Vegas. They weren't as excited when I told them it was Las Vegas, New Mexico though. We drove there and stayed for a few winter months in a small trailer with no insulation and a small propane tank that emptied every night so I would have to go out and change it in the cold.

After that, I worked for Entertainment Effects Group in Venice handling the mechanics for the Stay-Puft Marshmallow Man in *Ghostbusters*

(1984), plus I was back to using gelatin again to create the Star baby in *2010*, and I worked out of my garage again on *My Science Project* for Disney, too.

Now with several years of professional experience under his belt, Anderson felt like it was the perfect time to branch out on his own during the mid-1980s. He created his own company, Makeup Designs, Inc.

I opened up my shop in Van Nuys, and the first show that came in was with Michael Jackson. It was *Captain EO*, a 3D spectacular for Disney that was going to be shown at Disneyland. I designed four different characters: Major Domo, Minor Domo, the Geeks, and Hooter. It was directed by Francis Coppola and produced by George Lucas, and that's the show that got Makeup Designs up and running.

I could buy all my materials and supplies, and I even bought the building that I worked in for my entire career from just that show. This was around the time when I finally had enough hours to take the union makeup test, which I passed with flying colors. And from there on out, I just did my own thing, in my shop, for another 20 years.

After *Captain EO*, I constructed the whales on *Star Trek IV [The Voyage Home]*, but I didn't receive any credit on that because I was an outside contractor for Paramount Studios. I kept myself pretty busy, and if we didn't have a show at the shop, I would go day checking to keep things going, and my wife Jean worked at the office, too. That way we didn't have to worry about closing up shop because we were able to stay busy doing all kinds of lab work.

Around this time, Lance began not only collaborating with one of the premier Masters of Horror at the time, Wes Craven, on several projects, but his son, David, began working in the family business as well.

Wes and I had a pretty good relationship. He had a great sense of humor, and that's how he approached movie-making, with his tongue firmly planted in his cheek. Anytime you have a director that is low-key and doesn't intimidate people on the set, you have a good experience from that movie. It's just that simple. Every time I went on set for *Deadly Friend* or *Shocker*, there was no tension. It was a great atmosphere to be in, and whenever he'd make a suggestion, it was almost like he'd say it in a way where he was trying getting your approval. I loved working with him, and I miss him greatly to this day.

When I did *Serpent and the Rainbow* with Wes, that's when David really got involved in the business. He wanted to be an artist, too. I think he was waiting tables in a restaurant at the time, and when I told him about the project, I said to him, "This show just came in, and it's called *Serpent and the Rainbow*. It's going to film in Tahiti. Would you like to start building the effects and then go on set in Tahiti?"

David jumped right into it, and we worked on all these different effects and props. That's when I told him, "I'm sorry. You're not going to Tahiti. It's Haiti, actually." But he took it like a pro, and he went to Haiti all on his own. He got thrown right into the boiling hot water on that one, but they loved everything he did, and he made a great friend in Wes Craven. He got a lot of experience out of *Serpent*, undoubtedly.

I also sent David out to Maine for *Pet Sematary* (1989) to start working on the effects there, and then I came in later. I had sent him the appliance for Victor Pascow, for that big, gory gash in his head. I thought David would just put the appliance on, and maybe put a little bit of dead-looking makeup on him. But because David is so focused on details, he used all these fine brushes with blue and purple to create this beautiful makeup on Pascow. I didn't tell David to do that, so it was all his idea, and it's a work of art. It was so gorgeous.

Heading into the '90s, many people in the industry panicked over the rise of CGI and Hollywood's reliance on visual effects after the booming success of Jurassic Park, a film that Anderson worked on briefly by supplying the goat and body parts for the ill-fated snack in Steven Spielberg's dinosaur-themed adventure. But for Lance, he knew that no matter what might be popular at the time, nothing could ever replace tangible effects in the long run.

The ideal thing, I believe, is when you can have practical effects and digital effects working together. When you have a creature that's entirely digital, especially back then, everything felt exaggerated, and I think that's why you saw a lot of directors going back to embracing practical effects. They want to be able to see something in front of them more often than not.

When I was working on *The Crow*, there was a character in there originally called the Skull Cowboy, played by Michael Berryman, which got cut out of the film. The character was a specter who was to materialize like a tornado and lead Brandon Lee's character on his journey. He was going to be a mix of digital and practical effects. They only filmed him once; he was in costume standing on the steps of a church, and the digital effects of him materializing were to be added later on. I thought it sounded like a cool thing to include in the film, but after the tragedy with Brandon Lee happened, I think they decided to rewrite the ending and make the film a little more personal with the little girl.

I was initially a little upset because I thought the character looked great, but I wasn't terribly upset about it, because ultimately, they made the right decision. Besides the Skull Cowboy and Brandon's makeup, I also made several other effects. I made a couple of mechanical crows that were used for insert shots and so forth. I also created the effect with Darlene who had morphine injected into her arm, the effect when Eric has the hole in his hand, and I made a dummy of Michael Wincott for when he falls off the roof and gets impaled.

Losing Brandon during *The Crow* was such an incredibly sad experience for so many reasons, the biggest being the fact that Brandon was a great person and if one key change hadn't been made, the accident would never have happened. Originally, the scene involved Brandon's character and a guy with knives, who was going to throw a knife at him, and it would impale him in his chest. So, I made a chest harness that half of a knife could attach to. They were up in the loft, and they were shooting that scene, and I ran up there because I knew I needed to get the harness on Brandon. When I got up there, I ran up to the director, Alex [Proyas], and told him that I had the harness ready. That's when he told me they decided to change the scene, and Eric was going to get shot now instead.

So, I just stayed back, and I was still holding the harness in my hands when everything went wrong. I was probably the first one that went up to Brandon after it happened, and we all went to the hospital just as quickly as we could. The only thing that kept running through my head was, "Why did they have to change the scene? Why did they have to change the scene?" I almost felt guilty somehow, like maybe I could have said something, but there was nothing I could have said, and there was no way to predict what was going to happen. It was just incredibly heartbreaking for everyone.

After *The Crow*, Stan [Winston] called me to work on *The Island of Dr. Moreau* (1996). I was the department head for the straight makeup, and I also created the leopard guy. We shot in Australia, and it was a very troubled set from the start. There's a lot I can't talk about, but I do remember there was this rumor floating around that one of the extras in the film was Richard Stanley, the director that got fired, which I always thought was very interesting.

When I returned from Australia, I worked on *The X-Files* movie, and thankfully, that was pretty much a straight movie experience for me. It was about this same time when I did this movie called *The Hunter's Moon*, and I worked with Burt Reynolds. It was a smaller film, probably one of the later ones in Burt's career, and he had a wig on and had to stitch himself up at one point, so it wasn't anything too complicated. But I remember him talking about how he had a new book out and gave me a copy of it and signed it, which meant a lot to me. Burt seemed to be very down-to-earth, which I think was because he started as a stuntman and became an actor after that. He had some wonderful stories.

With a new century looming in the distance, Lance worked with Rick Baker on a trio of wildly different film projects, including Wild, Wild West, Ron Howard's live-action adaptation of How the Grinch Stole Christmas and Tim Burton's Planet of the Apes remake.

It was a great experience working with Rick once again. For *Wild, Wild West*, I worked on the different makeups for Kevin Kline. He was so into that character and working with these makeups. You could tell he was having a lot of fun.

On *Planet of the Apes*, I got to work on Michael Clarke Duncan, who was a wonderful, genuine person to be around. He was also really a tall guy too, so when I had to touch up his makeup on set, I had to stand on an apple box. I was always running around with an apple box so that I could be ready to jump in there whenever we had a moment.

I remember, at some point, Michael hurt himself or something like that, and we had to take him to the emergency medical center. I went with him because he was still in full ape makeup, and when we got to the waiting room, people were freaking out because his makeup scared them. But Michael was getting a kick out of all the responses – he loved it.

For *How the Grinch Stole Christmas*, I worked as a makeup artist on the set, and I did Rance Howard's makeup. He was Ron Howard's father, and he played the Timekeeper, and he was a delightful man. And when things weren't coming in during that time, I'd close up the shop and go on set to do different things including making the Romulans for *Star Trek: Nemesis*, and I also worked on Thing 1 and Thing 2 for *Cat in the Hat*.

Just a short time later, Lance and his son David would experience a changing of the guard in their family-oriented business, as Anderson decided it was time to move on from Makeup Designs. The father-son duo renamed the company AFX Studio, with David spearheading operations at the shop moving forward.

Right before David got *Dawn of the Dead*, we converted Makeup Designs to AFX, and the business became both of ours. When we landed *Dawn of the Dead*, that was David's baby; I didn't partake in the design aspects. I was more hands-on when I was at the shop.

Dave's a very creative person, and he likes to give people the opportunity to show their creativity, so he would assign different characters to different people so that it wasn't just one person's idea on every character. He'd bring in an artist to start drawing and then he would bring in a bunch of different people to do the sculpture work so that they could put their own spin on it. That way, things would materialize in such a way where they felt like they were extra special, and unlike anything you'd ever seen before.

Dawn was a huge job, and because it wasn't a cookie-cutter situation, that's how these makeups became unique and set the film apart. They weren't all just the same kind of gory-looking mess on somebody's face. They were all unique looking zombies in themselves, and I think the way we all rose to the occasion on *Dawn* is what helped make it such a successful project.

For their next collaboration, Lance and David took their industry by surprise with their efforts on Ron Howard's boxing biopic Cinderella Man, which required them to create subtle and realistic makeups for Russell Crowe and the other actors in the film who would need to step into the ring to duke it out with his character, Jim Braddock.

The challenge when you're creating special makeup for a boxing movie is that it has to hold up to what Michael Westmore did in *Raging Bull*. It set the bar, and I think *Cinderella Man* hit that standard. It had realism, and the makeup was completely consistent from start to finish. I was very proud of our work on that film, and I was even more proud to share an Oscar nomination with Dave for it. I think it was the first time a father and son had both shared the ballot together, which made *Cinderella Man* an exceptional experience for both of us.

Another show that came in for us a few years later, which ended up being important to the legacy AFX Studio for different reasons was *The Cabin in the Woods*. There were so many moving parts on that one, and it was just a massive amount of work. I got lucky on that one though, as I was working in the shop and building all this stuff that needed to be shipped away. I was just a grunt, and it was up to David to head it all up. At this point, I was getting ready to retire, and was ready to pull the pin on my career.

Even though he's stepped away from the special makeup effects industry as of late, Lance Anderson now spends his time finding other ways to fuel his endlessly creative inclinations outside of the shop.

I'm still painting all the time. I've got stockpiles of finished paintings, but because I'm not a salesman, I started collecting them, and I figure that it'll be up to David and Joni to decide what to do with them one day. These last few years have been a great time for me because I have more time to work on my 1929 Ford Model A hot rod and practicing the guitar. I'm always doing things on my own terms just for fun keeping myself busy and having a good time. I've been enjoying this phase of my life a lot.

Looking back on my career, though, I felt like I was still young enough to pursue makeup effects when I did. But when I was starting out, I quickly realized that I was considered the "old guy." Rick Baker started out when he was a teenager. Stan [Winston] started in the industry very young, too. A lot of artists did, so I didn't realize that beginning my career as an artist at 40-ish that I was starting "late." But even if I had realized it, it wouldn't have mattered anyway because this was something that I had to do.

I had always wanted to create art just for the joy of creating art, and I struggled with not being able to do as much as I had wanted to during those years while I was working as an electrician. I don't regret that I put in those 20 years, raised a family, and built a home, and did all the things I had to do. I enjoyed being an electrician because I wasn't always just stuck in one building. I had my own truck, and I drove around, did a lot of service calls, and I have always loved working with my hands, whether it was tracking down a short circuit on the job, or coming home and making my art.

So, when I think about all the things that I physically built that got on the screen, like a fat suit for Goldie Hawn to a full monster suit for *The Runestone*, and all the makeups for so many amazing people over the years, I feel so grateful that I got to pursue my dream, I traveled the world, made some wonderful friends and worked for great directors like Ron Howard and Wes Craven. Most people don't get to experience one career that they love, so for me to get to enjoy two different careers that I thoroughly enjoyed, I know how lucky I am in that respect.

I also feel lucky to have founded a studio that has truly been a family affair: from Jean working the office to Joni working on several films doing lab work, to David and his wife, Heather [Langenkamp], taking over the studio. Even my late grandson, Atticus, and my granddaughter, Isabelle, have worked in that studio. Generations have passed through those doors, which is incredible when you think about it.

Plus, watching Dave thrive as an artist over the years has been wonderful for me to see. I am so proud of him, and I couldn't be more proud that he's carrying the torch with AFX Studio, and has done a damn good job along the way.

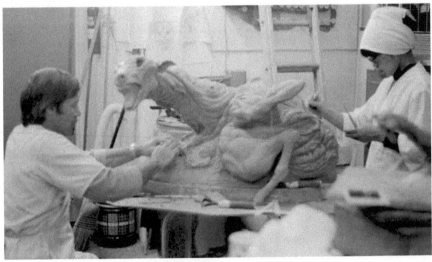

The Thing - Lance Anderson and Michiko Tagawa

Ghostbusters Crew

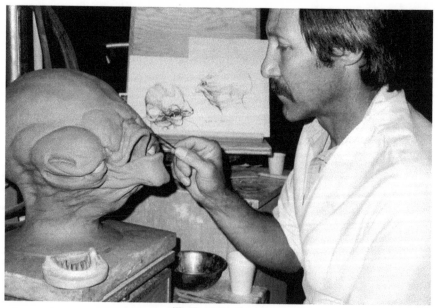

The Last Starfighter

Captain EO

Captain EO

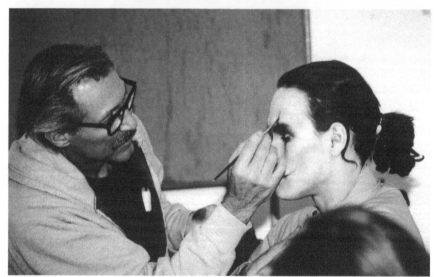

The Crow - Lance Anderson and Brandon Lee

The Crow - Lance Anderson and Brandon Lee

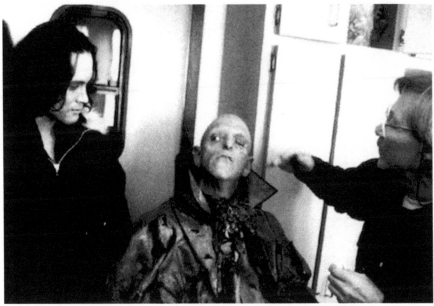

The Crow - Brandon Lee and Michael Berryman as the Skull Cowboy

The Crow - Skull Cowboy

How the Grinch Stole Christmas - Ron and Rance Howard

Garth Brooks and Lance Anderson

Garth Brooks as Chris Gaines

Lance Anderson and Stan Winston

Lance Anderson and His Hotrod

Conversation with...
TONY GARDNER

Special Effects Makeup Artist

The Lost Boys (1987)
Darkman (1990)
Hocus Pocus (1993)
Seed of Chucky (2004) - *Curse of Chucky* (2013) - *Cult of Chucky* (2017)
Bad Grandpa (2013)

For Tony Gardner, longtime special effects artist and founder of Alterian Inc., it was his love of illusions that led him to pursue a profession centered on making audiences believe in the impossible.

The start of my interest in filmmaking actually goes back to around age twelve, when I got my first Super 8 camera. I grew up in Ohio, so it wasn't like there were any resources at my disposal in regards to filmmaking. Whether it was film or makeup effects or special effects in general, none of that was even really looked upon as a career option where I lived. It was just an interesting thing that somebody else did far, far away, but it was more like a novelty or a hobby locally.

I grew up doing magic tricks, and there was one moment I remember very specifically that started me on the path to film. When I was about eight years old, my grandmother bought me a magic kit that was quite involved. It had this whole setup with a little stage that folded out, and all these cool tricks in it. I was opening it up and going through everything and the first thing that I pulled out was this black plastic card box. You put a card in it, closed the lid, and when you opened the box, the card would have magically disappeared. I didn't read the directions—I knew what it was—so I just put the card in the box, closed it, re-opened it, and suddenly the card was gone! It blew my mind.

I was so excited, I ran into the next room to show my grandmother this cool trick. I was a little too excited, and as I went running out of the room, the box flew out of my hand. It hit the floor, the bottom of the box popped out, and then the card flew out from underneath that.

My heart and my stomach completely sank. That's when I realized it was fake. Magic wasn't real. And for a while, I was completely depressed, but then I had this realization: "If I can create that same moment that I just felt for somebody else, how cool would that be?" So then I really got into magic seriously, and for me, "magic" was all about that specific moment when a trick blows your mind, when you just can't believe what you saw was real. I would do magic at birthday parties as a little kid, and there's sort of a novelty in kids doing it, where you're allowed to be weird.

Once he realized the endless possibilities that film could offer, Gardner transitioned his love of creating illusions with live magic tricks to making movies when he was a pre-teen.

My parents bought me a Super 8 camera for my birthday when I was twelve, and I started making little short films. I realized that if I wanted to film a magic presentation, I could stop the camera and then actually really fill an empty box or a hat up with stuff, and then start the camera back up, and suddenly something "magical" really did take place . . . at least on film. It all looked so much more believable on film. Film seemed to give me so many more options than reality ever did.

I started making little movies with my friends in the neighborhood and doing all sorts of crazy things: making our own versions of films we'd seen in theaters, or scenes that we liked from movies, even crazy stop-motion movies, including one with dozens of these furry things that, when animated, looked like a swarm of creatures chasing us down the street. That's when I began experimenting with makeup effects as well. I tried out a really basic version of prosthetics at age twelve, where I would mix up and tint flour paste and use that to animate the transformation of a person's skin from normal into the dry, scaly skin of some sort of creature, along the lines of stop-motion transformations on Lon Chaney Jr. in *The Wolf Man* . . . just a more affordable version.

As I got older, I was involved in a lot of different activities. I was all over the place in regards to my interests. I was the epitome of what you'd consider an ADD [attention deficit disorder] poster child back then. I played drums in a band, I played string bass in an orchestra, was doing magic, building creatures, making these short films, and was involved in the high school theater department. I was heavily involved in everything extracurricular above and beyond going to school and going to my classes—the normal academic stuff I was really supposed to be doing at that time. I also started getting involved in local community theater back then. I was doing really simple things for them, just making masks and things like that, or playing standing bass in their pit orchestra for the musicals. Nothing I was doing felt like it could ever be a career, though. They were all hobbies, in my opinion.

Despite the fact that he still saw prosthetics and mask-making as just a hobby, Gardner wasn't deterred from reaching out to several legends in the industry, fueling his desire to learn more and continue to hone his craft.

I just started writing to people I could find any information on through books and articles. I started writing to Don Post, and I ended up getting a response from Don Post Jr., who then sent me a signed Don Post mask poster. Charlie Schram and Dick Smith were two more people who were so forthcoming with information. They would write back and send detailed explanations of processes and even slides or photos.

Dick Smith sent me a signed photo of Hal Holbrook as Abe Lincoln, and I remember showing it to my friends in the neighborhood, and they were all like, "First, who's Hal Holbrook? And who's Dick Smith and who's Charlie Schram?" There was really no one to share my interests with, so I felt like I was operating in a vacuum. What was nice, though, was that I was being recommended different books through those correspondences, which I could hunt down, and that helped me continue to learn and work with whatever resources that I could find out in Ohio.

Three movies came out that changed my perceptions as someone who loved being creative. The first was *Planet of the Apes*, then *Star Wars* [*Episode IV – A New Hope*], and the final movie was *Alien*. I had seen a picture from *Alien* of the title creature somewhere, and just that one image really hooked me. I really wanted to go see the movie, but I wasn't old enough yet, so I eventually talked my mom into taking me to go see it. She hated me forever for having to sit through it, and I even made her take me back a couple more times to see it again. She'd learned her lesson, though, and would get me into the theater and then leave. I would sit in the theater and watch those three movies over and over, but *Alien* was the one that was truly inspiring; it was so original and unique.

Around that same time, I was building a really large stop-motion spider armature to animate, about a foot and a half across. But then I saw *Alien* and thought, "Why not turn that spider into a Facehugger?" I was building it up on wooden dowels and wire—just really basic, simple stuff. I built up the forms and then the skin on the whole thing with cotton and latex tinted with food coloring. It had this long tail that was wrapped around the neck and it took forever to build. I think it turned out pretty good considering I was just learning as I went and going from whatever photos were available back then.

But that's when I realized that there was really cool stuff happening in movies, and that there were resources available that made it possible to create your own versions of these inspiring creatures or characters if you put your mind to it, and then, it all clicked. There were no real directions as to how to build this stuff, just some great photos to reference. I was just figuring it all out as I went, and in hindsight, it's probably the best way to learn, because you are constantly problem-solving and you quite often end up having to think outside of the box in order to pull some of this stuff off and make it work.

Once he graduated from high school, Gardner set his sights on attending college, where he was able to continue pursuing his passion for special effects through the school's theater department.

When I went to college, *The Howling* and *An American Werewolf in London* were just coming out—two very big moments for those of us who love this stuff. I went to Ohio University, this tiny little college down near Ohio State [University], which had this really great theater department. There was no film department, so I signed up as a Theater Major and quickly discovered that the theater department was set up in this hierarchy, where the seniors got to do everything—they got to direct the plays, be in them, and just run the whole show. That meant as you went down the line, the juniors got to act or be part of the crew, sophomores were the grunts, and incoming freshmen were the grunts' grunts.

But I could do stuff that other students couldn't do as far as makeup effects were concerned. I don't know how I did it, but somehow I ended up talking the college into giving me a room in the basement of the theater building, and buying these makeup materials that I couldn't afford to buy myself to use on theater productions there. They bought foam latex, dental stone, and all this stuff that I needed in order to do prosthetic makeup. The theater department was doing this play called *Dark of the Moon* that takes place in the South, and there was this weird, creepy mountain man, an old lady with a goiter, and all this other weird stuff in it that all had to be designed and created. The upperclassmen just trusted me to make it all happen, and all of the other freshmen were like, "Who the hell is this guy?" I didn't know what I was doing, either, but I was doing it.

That's when the theater department was starting to get kudos for putting on productions that were unique and different, instead of coasting on productions that would have been simpler and easier to do. I just soaked it all in and learned a lot from watching them reach out, try new things, and take chances. I really enjoyed the experience, but I realized that Ohio University didn't really have anything that even leaned towards filmmaking. I realized that if you wanted to be a newscaster, you were in the right place, but that was as big as it got there at that time.

Coming to the conclusion that his current educational choice wasn't doing him any favors when it came to achieving his dream of becoming a professional artist, Gardner knew it was time for a big change, one that would take him clear across the country to the West Coast.

I decided to apply to USC [University of Southern California] for the simple reason that George Lucas and Dan O'Bannon had gone there. I was accepted by USC most likely due to the fact that I had a weird portfolio that was definitely different from all of the others with my Facehuggers, werewolves, and masks, but I didn't get into the film school. USC accepted me as a Fine Arts Major and told me that the cinema school was a two-year program, and that I could re-apply to the film school the following year. I was excited.

I also auditioned for the USC marching band and was accepted into the drumline. Their band camp started a week prior to school starting, so I decided to fly out a few days prior to band starting up, so I could have a look around this place called "Los Angeles" beforehand. I brought all my makeup stuff with me, including this E.T. mask that I had made back at home, which sparked an idea in regards to how I could use my extra time there before the band started. I had read that Steven Spielberg used to sneak onto the Universal lot prior to starting in the industry, so I thought I would try that, too, using E.T. as my way in the door. I was so straightforward with my approach to everything and went into it with a positive attitude; I had to try.

So, I took a milk crate, stuffed a pillowcase, and turned it into a squat body and then attached my E.T. mask to it. Then, I wrapped the little guy in a blanket and put it in a milk crate to match the scene where E.T. rides on the front of Elliott's bike in the movie. I drove over to Universal Studios, parked down the street, and then walked in through the front gate carrying E.T. in a basket out in front of me, and just pretended I knew what I was doing. And sure enough, I walked right through. There I was on the Universal lot, and then it hit me: "So, now what do I do?" I didn't really think this plan through further than the challenge of just trying to get onto the lot.

When I started my classes at USC, I realized almost immediately that I didn't really care for a single one of the art classes that I had. In a 3D Design & Composition class, we were doing these—in my opinion—really juvenile, simplistic, black-and-white paintings, and then gluing objects to them. I felt like I was back in junior high. I got so frustrated that I ended up going to all of my teachers and asked each one if I could turn my classes into some sort of independent study so that I could do something that I felt was more relevant to my interests, or I was going to go insane. Most of them agreed, but with the stipulation that I had to find somebody to be my teacher or mentor who was a professional artist within that arena, and it would be up to that person to grade my work.

One of my film classes at the time was Drew Casper's Introduction to Cinema class, and I decided I would write my class paper on the use of mechanical effects as main characters in the film industry.

I thought that I could use the paper as an excuse to interview people I also really wanted to meet. I chose Carlo Rambaldi because of his work on *E.T. [the Extra-Terrestrial]* and *Alien*, and Rick Baker, because he had just done *American Werewolf in London*. I also thought it would be interesting to interview Steven Spielberg, since he was directing films with these creatures in them as the main characters. This would give me three different perspectives that would make my paper interesting.

So, I found Carlo Rambaldi's phone number in the phone book, which in those days meant going to a local phone booth in their area and going through the phone book for information. I found his name listed and called and asked if it would be possible for me to do an interview for a paper I was writing for a class at USC. It took a while to get it organized, but a date was eventually set.

When I finally got to meet with him at his studio, his people left me in a room to wait for him. It turned out that it was his office. There were all these oversized chalk drawings up on the wall: a cat face, E.T.'s face, mechanical designs—all this stuff literally pinned up all over the walls. It was so cool. When he finally walked into the office, he seemed like someone so wise and established and comfortable in this world of film, and I suddenly felt so out of place.

I was told that he didn't speak much English, and that I'd be talking to him through an interpreter—in the end I think it was actually Carlo's son. I would talk to him, he would turn and talk to Carlo in Italian, Carlo would respond, and then an answer would come back to me. So I felt even more awkward and kind of out of place. Somewhere through the course of our conversation, though, I shared that my grandfather had immigrated to the U.S. from Italy as a little kid. All of a sudden, Carlo laughs this big laugh and starts speaking in English with this thick accent. In my head, I'm like, "You fucker."

I think he was testing me or just messing with me, but it was a great icebreaker and the conversation ended up being really comfortable, and I learned a lot from him. He shared a bunch of sculptures and showed me around. It was a really cool experience.

Gardner's quest to secure his other interviews with Baker and Spielberg didn't go nearly as smoothly, but his pursuit of both ended up leading to some other amazing opportunities.

I had gotten onto the Universal lot a few times by that point, so I knew where Amblin Entertainment was. I just went up and knocked on the door, and I talked to the people there and asked if I could interview Steven Spielberg for a paper. He wasn't there, though. I went back so many times after that, they eventually set up a real appointment.

I remember the first time I went back, they said he was off filming, and there was a kid there playing video games who seemed about my age in a side room that was set up like a mini-arcade. He and I talked for a bit and then someone came in to get him, saying he had to go back to work. It turned out to be Zach Galligan from *Gremlins*, and that's what Steven was working on that day.

I went back so many times, I literally became friends with the people in his office. Spielberg had a drum set, and I ended up re-tuning his drum set one day when I was waiting for him. I never did get him for any sort of sit-down interview for my paper, either, but I had great experiences trying. I think I got about three minutes with him when he blew in while working on scoring *Twilight Zone* [*The Movie*]. It was pouring rain and he was running behind. He ran into Amblin to grab some stuff and at least say "hello," and then we talked about Rob Bottin and cable-controlled creatures for a few minutes, and that was it.

As far as trying to meet Rick Baker, I figured out where he lived as well, and just went up and knocked on his front door in North Hollywood. An older gentleman answered the door, and as I was talking to him and explaining that I was writing a paper, I kept looking past him at this giant painting on the wall behind him. It was a gorilla head, probably about four or five feet tall—it was massive, super detailed, and looked like a blown-up photo. He eventually turned around once he realized that I kept looking past him, and he told me that it wasn't a photo, it was a painting, and that he had painted it. As it turned out, it was Rick Baker's dad, Ralph, and he proceeded to explain how he had painted all of the fine details on this gorilla.

He told me that Rick was in England filming *Greystoke* [*The Legend of Tarzan, Lord of the Apes*], and he wasn't expected back for at least a month. But I stayed in touch with Ralph. I had turned one of my art classes into an opportunity to sculpt and create some masks. I needed to find an artist to critique my class work and grade it, so I eventually asked Ralph if he would be interested in being my advisor. He was actually doing the same thing for another student at the time and said "yes."

After all was said and done with my classes, Ralph said that he really admired my attitude and my enthusiasm to go after things. He asked me if I would leave a stack of slides of my work with him because he wanted to leave them for Rick to take a look at. He said, "I'm not promoting you. I'm not pushing you on him in any way. I'm just leaving your slides with a note saying that your work is worth a look." It was far more than I ever would have expected, and it was really nice of him to do.

Gardner soon realized Ralph's gesture would go on to make a big impact, though, after Baker returned from London.

Rick eventually called me, and he mentioned the slides and the paper I was writing for school. I told him how that paper was already over, but I had another idea for a class next semester, so I still hoped to be able to meet him and do an interview. He agreed, and I ended up going to what was EFX Inc. [Baker's company] at the time.

I went into the front office there and met Rick, and he was super nice and very personable, and also kind of quiet, like me. I asked him all the questions relevant to the paper and then we started talking about makeup and special effects in general. He asked me about myself, and I told him my interests, talked about some of the masks I had made, and all my experiences at school.

He started quizzing me as to what resources I had access to work with and how I had done certain things—I felt like I was getting interviewed at the same time. He was actually writing stuff down on this little notepad, too, and I didn't really know what that implied, but the interview wrapped up, I thanked him, and I left. I was thrilled beyond belief—I had met everyone that I wanted to meet.

I went back to Ohio for the two weeks of summer left before the new semester started, and I was feeling pretty good because I met all of the people on my list, I had a plan for cinema class next year that included another list of filmmakers to meet, so I was excited to get to kick back for a few weeks. I was home for literally two days and the phone rang. I almost didn't answer it since no one else was home at the time, but when I did, it was Rick Baker. We talked for a few minutes, just shooting the shit. I was thinking to myself, "My God, why is he calling me?" Then, he finally told me that he was starting a job on a music video and he was going to need some help in the shop, somebody to run around and pick up supplies, sweep the floors, and be a runner.

He told me it was only about four weeks' worth of work, but at the end of the four weeks, he said he thought that at least I would know for sure if this was the type of stuff I really wanted to be doing or not. He knew my interests were scattered all over the place, and thought that being around the shop watching what was going on would help me figure out what I wanted to do. I agreed to the job and told him I'd be back in about two weeks when classes started.

That's when Rick said, "The job actually started two days ago, and there's someone holding your spot right now." He told me if I wanted the job, it was mine, and if not, this other guy would just stay there and be their runner. I told him I definitely wanted it and that I would be there as fast as I possibly could. I was pretty much shitting my pants at that point because I didn't think I would be working and doing anything professionally for a while, and here was Rick inviting me to be a part of the crew on a music video called *Thriller*.

Right after I hung up, my mom walked in the front door. I told her that I had to go back to California and I needed to get a flight out right away. She looked at me like I was crazy because I'd only been home a few days. I explained to her that I had a job opportunity that would last only four weeks and would be a great experience for me. I told her that school wouldn't be starting until I was already halfway through the job, and that I could handle the job and school at the same time. So she agreed to help me find my flight so I could get back out to California, and I started work the next day. I was so appreciative that my parents were so understanding and supportive at the same time.

While he may have initially thought he'd be able to balance his school and professional responsibilities at the same time, Tony quickly realized that his dream job was impeding on his ability—and desire—to continue his higher education.

At first, things were okay because the job started out with a fairly straightforward schedule and pretty standard work hours, so I could manage everything there and still get my schoolwork done in the evenings. I even kept on as a drummer in the marching band. All of a sudden, though, everything sort of imploded. My hours on the video evolved into 9:00 a.m. to late into the evening [shifts], which meant there was no time for homework or even school itself, and at that point, I just wanted to drop out.

Around that same time, Rick said that he liked how I was working out. He asked me to stay on and join the team, but with the stipulation that I had to find somebody else to take my place as a runner, which I did as fast as possible. All of a sudden, I was doing actual makeup effects work, and then I was asked to build a zombie on myself; everybody in the shop was going to be the close-up zombies in the video. What more motivation do you need to work until midnight than to build a zombie on yourself so you can be in a Michael Jackson video? That's when makeup took over as a top priority instead of classes, and I dropped out of USC.

I was excited about everything that I was working on, and learning a lot of new stuff. I was put in charge of all of the background zombie masks construction, making bladders, learning how to make molds, and even painting. After the actual filming was over, John Landis invited me to the editorial [process] during post-production, because he had heard that I was really interested in filmmaking. He was kind of a smart-ass in the best way, and I gave it right back to him, and he loved that. We hit it off great from the get-go. So, besides working on the *Thriller* video and being in it, I got to watch the process of the video coming together from the very beginning, from the design sketches through fitting teeth on the dancers at rehearsals, all the way through to post-production. I was just soaking all of this stuff in and I knew then that I wanted to be a part of this creative process in any capacity.

When *Thriller* wrapped up, Rick told me that he enjoyed having me be a part of his crew and that if something else came along again, he wanted to have me be a part of it. I was excited, but my parents weren't nearly as thrilled as I was. I remember talking to them about what Rick had said, and my parent's response was basically, "Great. You've dropped out of college, and now you don't have a job. So what **are** you doing out there?" I didn't know. I spent the next three months basically doing nothing beyond my own little art projects and masks, which I think only left my parents even more unhappy about the choices I was making.

Tony persevered through that three-month rough patch, though, and the up-and-comer would reap the rewards for his patience with a steady flow of work that has kept him consistently busy for over thirty years.

I remember after that time, Rick was offered *Starman*, and I ended up doing some prototype R&D [research and development] for an animatronic baby puppet, trying to make a flexible translucent skin, adding veins and a light source inside a test head, and all that stuff, just trying to figure out the materials and an approach. That's when I went from being that kid offered a one-time, four-week job, to having the situation turning around to the point where I spent the next four years working at EFX and getting the best on-the-job training you could ever ask for from the best person imaginable: Rick Baker.

I ended up being there for about four years, through all sorts of different shows, meeting all sorts of different people through the different projects. It was a great time. Rick took on *Cocoon* after *Starman*, but as a consultant, with Greg Cannom as the Makeup Effects Designer, and all of us already at Rick's went to work for Greg. Things were just sort of casual that way. Greg set up shop at Rick's as well, which made starting up really effortless. It was midway through this show that a friend from USC called and asked for a favor— something fairly basic, but something that ended up leading to me moonlighting on my first independent job for a few weeks.

A fellow student at USC named Brian Peck had been cast in a film, and he asked me for a dental veneer top to make him look more like a punk rocker. The director liked the finished teeth enough to ask me to come out to meet with him and talk about his lead actress' teeth. So, all of a sudden, I was driving out to meet Dan O'Bannon at his house . . . the same Dan O'Bannon that had written *Alien*. It was a total film geek moment, but I think I held it together really well.

To make a long story short, a few weeks later Dan ended up asking me to provide an animatronic puppet for the film that Brian was in, which was a low-budget horror film called *The Return of the Living Dead*. They were already shooting, and the company originally hired to do this half-corpse puppet had declared bankruptcy, but the puppet was due on set in two weeks. I was already working full-time on *Cocoon*, so of course I said, "Yes!" (Who needs sleep, right?) Fortunately, Rick was cool with me working on the half-corpse at his shop at night.

I pulled in Bill Sturgeon from Rick's to help me with the finger mechanics, and Scott Ressler helped with some of the fabrication. I had a great design to work from, too, from the amazing Bill Stout. I went on set with the puppet and ended up puppeteering the head, Brian Peck operated the jaw and read the lines on set, and I roped Bill Stout in to operate the spinal cord and the spinal fluid. I learned a lot in those few weeks, including the fact that I wasn't afraid to jump into pretty much anything.

I was asked to do some "split dogs" for a warehouse scene in the film as well, and also was asked to finish off a makeup that Bill Stout had started on Linnea Quigley, who played Trash. I did all of that stuff in the kitchen of my apartment in Hollywood. It was fun to jump around and tackle such an interesting variety of things all for the same film.

After *Cocoon*, we were all just kind of going with the flow over at Rick's, with nothing really lined up immediately. The makeup community was a lot smaller at the time, so a bunch of us from different shops would go to a pizza place in Westwood on Friday nights just to hang out and catch up with each other. The guys from Stan Winston's shop [Stan Winston Studio] mentioned that they were going to be working on *Aliens*. Given that *Alien* was one of the films that got me interested in creature effects in the first place, I knew I had to be a part of it.

Looking to continue exploring the professional makeup world outside of Baker's domain, Gardner approached Winston about coming on board James Cameron's sequel, but he made sure to get his mentor's blessing first.

The next Monday, I went into Rick's and explained to him that I'd love to work on *Aliens*, even if only for a week or two, just because *Alien* was a big part of my decision to do this kind of stuff. One of the first things I had built back in Ohio besides the Facehugger was a Chestburster. I probably would have built a full-sized costume if I had more resources at the time. Rick didn't have much going on, so he let me go work on my dream project over at Stan's.

Stan brought me in at the very beginning stages of *Aliens*, where he and Jim Cameron were just starting to figure stuff out. They set me up in Stan's makeup room in the front of the shop, and my first job was sculpting the Chestburster. It was really weird, because I was sitting in the makeup room, and through the door beside me, Jim Cameron had set up shop in the break room. Stan was in his office another door down the hall. So there's Stan, Jim, and I up in the front of the shop, and every so often, the two of them would talk from room to room to each other. It was really fun, and it became really casual and fast-paced because it was just the three of us. The banter between them was really funny, and it was just a blast to see that kind of creative dynamic.

So I sculpted the Chestburster and then was also able to mold it, core the mold, run a skin, sculpt and mold the teeth—really follow this creature through the entire process. A few weeks in, the project started to take on more momentum and more space in the shop. The scope of it was incredible. We ended up building a full-sized Queen Alien out of garbage bags, cardboard, and foam core in the back parking lot just because it was the only space we had left.

Jim [and Stan] had figured out this concept of strapping two stuntmen together on a rig inside the torso of the Queen, and he wanted to try it out and see how it would work. We all pieced this thing together and wrapped it up in black trash bags because Jim wanted the Aliens to all be black. I just thought it was so cool that they made the effort that they did to really figure it out right away, and that the director was there with us, doing it all alongside us, too. It was so impressive to see that level of problem-solving happening right in front of you.

From there, things got really busy. I bounced around on a couple different things, and so did everybody else. The Queen Alien was the priority at the time, and there was a miniature version that was going to be done animatronically to allow for faster and more controlled movements. Stan's shop was sculpting it, and then all those molds were going to go to a company called Doug Beswick Productions. Doug had done the stop-motion version of the Terminator, so he was going to do an animatronic version of this miniature Queen, as well as a small Power Loader with a miniature Sigourney Weaver strapped inside it.

Then, I don't remember what it was a mold of, but I was cutting open a silicone mold with a razor blade. I was doing exactly what you're **not** supposed to do—cutting toward yourself with a sharp blade—and as I was holding this mold with my right hand, I took my left hand and was pulling this X-Acto knife through the silicone, and somehow it caught, jumped out, and I ended up slicing my right hand open between my thumb and my first finger right down to the bone. It was this brief moment of, *What the hell?* Which was then followed by this vision of blood spraying, honest to God, for a good solid twenty feet—very Monty Python-esque.

I went straight to the ER, got stitched up, and was unable to use my right hand after that. I had no movement in the fingers on that hand for almost a month. I basically had the ability to move my thumb and pinky finger on that hand and that was it. I'd cut through a bunch of nerves and they didn't know if I'd have full mobility with that hand again or not.

Although he was unable to do much with his right hand for quite some time, Gardner still found ways to contribute to Aliens, even after Stan Winston's team left for the U.K. to set up shop to build the full-size Alien Queen.

I felt pretty bad because I had suddenly rendered myself completely useless at work. As far as the timing went, though, Stan was getting ready to send his permanent crew over to England, and he asked me if I would go with his molds for the Queen Alien over to Doug Beswick's [studio] and follow through on the work needed there. Doug asked if I would like to come on board as the cosmetic supervisor for the Queen, Power Loader, and miniature Sigourney Weaver, which was great.

I had no idea what to do as far as miniature clothes or anything like that, but I knew what sort of approaches I wanted to take towards the molds and materials for everything else. I ended up bringing in Shannon Shea and a couple other people to help me with the work and then, all of a sudden, I was kind of running a crew on my own. Doug was handling the mechanical shop and I was responsible for the cosmetic side.

We had to ship our miniature stuff out to England in advance of the live-action shooting on *Aliens*, and since Stan would be working out the paint scheme for the Queen there, we just sent the Queen out flat black and left it to the team there to paint it once those decisions had been finalized. Nobody had made a decision on what the Queen Alien's teeth were going to be, though, prior to our ship date: were they going to be black or were they going to be white? No one had an answer for me, so I took it upon myself to cast up a couple heads with the teeth clear so that they had options on whichever way they wanted to go with the color. They wouldn't be stuck having to try to paint black over white or vice versa.

And I guess when it showed up, Cameron really liked the clear look, and it stayed that way. It was one of those fortunate scenarios where something gets figured out almost by accident, which is always kind of fun, and to be a part of helping establish that look was really cool. I really felt like at that point, my short little career had come full circle from copying *Alien* to working on *Aliens*.

From there, Doug Beswick was brought onto *Evil Dead II* to handle two specific effects sequences. One was an animated sequence with Linda coming back to life and dancing, basically like a Ray Harryhausen scene, and the other was a giant demon head and tree branch that came into the house at the end and attacked Bruce Campbell. It was a great experience. There were so many techniques being used on that film that I had never seen before. It was amazing.

Doug had me sculpt a couple of different concept maquettes of this creature's head coming through a doorway. The idea was to scale up our creature head as large as possible so that you could use the real actors' faces inside this giant creature costume and have all their faces pushing through it, as if their souls were trapped within this creature's body. It went through several different approaches in regards to execution and became something massive, almost the size of a Volkswagen bus in the end, given that the face had to be on a rolling platform that was counterweighted.

One of the things that Sam realized with this thing being so big was that if the creature can't get in the door, what pushes Bruce towards the creature's mouth? The vacuum that was pulling everything in the room towards the door was suddenly blocked by the creature's giant head. Sam's solution was that a tree branch from one of the possessed trees outside the cabin would break in and help "feed" Bruce to the head. So Doug built this giant rig with a welded aluminum frame, and then Theresa Burkett and Mark Wilson came in and created soft, flexible bark over the whole thing out of sheet foam and oatmeal mixed into latex.

My time on *Evil Dead II* felt like I was part of this really cool, creative, weird art studio-type of environment, where all of these creations were being built that were completely different from one another, but they were all for the same film. Some of the techniques were really old school and some were pretty complicated. Every once in a while, I couldn't help but take a step back and go, "Wow, this is really inventive."

The more I'm talking about it now, the more I'm realizing that shows like that don't happen all that often anymore, in regards to having to problem-solve on the spot and be quick on your feet. Now it seems more like everyone sits in a dark room in front of monitors, designing and building the stuff you'll see on screen. A lot of the creative, hands-on-type of problem-solving you just had to do back then, you were forced into it because you had a problem to address and a situation you needed to come up with a solution for right away. You had no choice. Quite often now, that "thinking on your feet" experience doesn't really exist and I feel like we've lost a little bit of that excitement.

Shortly after filming wrapped on Evil Dead II, Tony spent some time just doing his own art projects, but it wasn't long before Greg Cannom pulled him in on a project he was busy with at the time, Joel Schumacher's The Lost Boys.

I remember being told that Greg was going to be using Rick's shop for *Lost Boys*, and I was renting space in there already, working on my own art projects in a back corner. Greg was okay with the arrangement, though, which was really nice of him. At one point, the workload on *Lost Boys* got really big all of a sudden, and Greg ended up asking me to help out on some stuff. I agreed, and the first thing I did was sculpt the prosthetic makeup for Kiefer Sutherland's stunt double. I had to make him look like Kiefer in his prosthetic vampire makeup, so that was a cool process.

Then, they decided that they wanted to have this little kid [Chance Michael Corbitt] be seen as a vampire, so I sculpted that one, too, which was interesting, given his face was so small and so round, and the design was so angular. There's a scene where the vampires are hanging upside down and you see their weird, clawed feet. Greg's idea was that the big toe would be opposable like a thumb, and those feet would mutate to the point where anatomically they could hold the weight of these guys hanging upside down. I thought it was a really cool idea, and I got to build these insert feet. I also worked on a vampire [Brooke McCarter's character, Paul] melting in a bathtub and a few other odds and ends. I was really enjoying the opportunity to learn new things on such a cool show.

They were filming the scene where the boys are crawling out of the cave and Kiefer reaches to grab them, gets hit by sunlight, and his arm bursts into flames. Joel didn't want shiny burn gel on a stunt guy's arm. He wanted the flames to be right on the surface of the skin and to really be able to see the flames dig into the skin. Plus, they wanted the hand to articulate, so they decided at the last minute to do an animatronic hand.

I had the hand closest in size to Kiefer's, so we cast my hand and then it was up to me to take it from sculpture through to completion, including running the foam. When we took it to the set, somebody else puppeteered it, but it was fun to actually go on the set and watch, since it was the only time I had an opportunity to go on set for the whole show. One of the other things shooting that day was a giant burning dummy of Ed Herrmann for the finale scene, which was really cool. They decided that they wanted to see him as a vampire before he was incinerated to have a more dramatic death, so Greg had built this really cool full-body puppet of the actor that would be set on fire. Unfortunately, you never see it in the final edit of the film.

There was so much to learn from on that film. Joel Schumacher is a very visual guy with a lot of really great ideas, and he would shoot a lot of footage. I learned on that one, though, that once a film got into editorial, things could change because of pacing or clarity, and effects sequences could be cut way down or get cut out altogether. It was interesting to see the effects work trimmed down to be a part of the story and not a distraction from it, but it was also sad to see some of the stuff go.

After getting to mix it up with vampires on **The Lost Boys,** *Gardner had the opportunity to contribute to two projects that were similar in nature:* **Harry and the Hendersons** *and* **Gorillas in the Mist.** *Gardner credited those years in the late 1980s as being some of the most imaginative and inspiring times he ever experienced as an artist. On* **Harry and the Hendersons** *in particular, Gardner saw the creative boundaries of special effects being pushed in very different ways.*

Rick [Baker] had asked me to come back and help finish up some stuff on *Harry and the Hendersons*. When I came onto *Harry*, they were already towards the tail end of their build. I had to fabricate a Harry head for the stunt dummy in the scene when he gets driven around and then launched off the car. I ended up casting up and assembling the dummy out of the molds of Harry's muscle suit.

Rick had this cool idea for an animatronic insert piece that could fit into Harry's under-skull, making it so you could take the animatronic mask off of [actor] Kevin Peter Hall and put it on this animatronic version of his head so that Harry could do things that Kevin couldn't do. Harry was supposed to lick a TV set, and Rick wanted him to have a long tongue like a dog's, so instead of trying to do something that could fit inside the limited space within the head when Kevin was wearing it, Rick's logic was that if we took Kevin out of the equation, there would be all of this available space to have this three-foot-long tongue that could come out and lick the TV set and pull back into the head, all in one shot. It worked perfectly, and Rick had figured out a cool way around what had initially been a very daunting problem.

The only part of Kevin that was visible when he was wearing the Harry mask were his eyes, so we had to recreate that part of his face as part of the animatronic "insert head." I sculpted the eye orbits and eyelids to fit over animatronic eyes, which was something completely new for me. I had wanted to do mechanical eyelids on the half-corpse for *The Return of the Living Dead*, so it was interesting to work with animatronic eyes and figure out clearances, closure, and tear ducts so that it all looked real in close-ups and still worked mechanically. To be able to do it on mechanics that were this precise was an eye-opener . . . pun intended.

When you're creating a makeup or animatronic character on an actor, more than half of the success of that character is the actor inside the character that's bringing it to life and making it appear realistic or believable. Kevin Peter Hall literally brought Harry to life. Harry was Kevin and Kevin was Harry, and there was so little difference between the two—it was amazing. The original design included contact lenses that were more primate-looking, but they ditched the lens idea because Kevin was so expressive and was able to do so much with just his eyes. While the lenses looked more correct for the species, Kevin's eyes added so much personality and humanity to Harry. It was fascinating to watch the character come alive.

It's unreal where your mind goes when you're watching something that is crafted as beautifully as Harry was. The suit was almost secondary to Kevin's performance, but only because everything just felt so real. It was so well-done that you didn't think of it as a suit.

For the final project he worked on with Baker, Gardner married his own love for animals with the world of special effects in some rather extraordinary ways while gearing up for Michael Apted's Gorillas in the Mist.

That was my last show with Rick. At the beginning, it was very much that same sort of relaxed family dynamic we'd had when we started on other shows, because there were just a few of us on board at that point and we had a nice amount of lead time to prototype and figure things out. I had done an exhibit for the L.A. Zoo on my own prior [to *Gorillas in the Mist*], and had established a relationship with the zoo that allowed us access to the primate area in the mornings, prior to the zoo opening.

We could sit down with one of the baby gorillas named Marcus in the mornings, which was awesome. We would sit outside of the enclosure, which had glass walls, and the animals would sit on the floor on the other side of the glass and play right in front of us. We brought the smaller sculptures with us and sculpted right in front of the animals. Marcus would put his hand up on the glass, and I could measure his palm, or even hold my sculpture up right next to his hand. At one point, I was able to sit with Marcus in his pen with him in my lap. I'm a big animal lover, so I was in heaven.

We ended up building a life-sized animatronic baby gorilla puppet based on Marcus. Even when it didn't have fur yet, and the body was just a ball of foam, you could still see this thing literally coming to life. It was amazing to watch the guys puppeteer it. I can still remember it so vividly because it felt like we were building this complete little character that was so endearing. We weren't just building an animatronic robot. There was a personality to this little guy, and it felt that way from the very beginning, which was nice.

Rick put me in charge of a prototype gorilla suit for proof of concept, where we'd be using animatronic eyes instead of the actor's eyes inside the head. It would mean that the entire face would be animatronic. We had "gorilla parts" in the shop that fit Rick already, so our approach was, "Let's build it out of stuff that already exists, make a new animatronic head, adjust a few things, and see what we get." We took it up to Griffith Park and we had Rick in the suit and were filming some footage of him jumping out of the brush at the camera and just walking by, doing a couple of different moves to see proportionally how the head looked to the body and what angle the wearer needed to be in order to pull the concept off. We learned a lot of great stuff that day, but more than anything it was fun to take Rick out there and see him running all over the place as a gorilla.

Being in charge of the prototype suit for *Gorillas in the Mist* was the first time that I was responsible for somebody inside a suit. There was a whole new set of responsibilities that came into play that I wasn't expecting. An almost parental and protective feeling kicks in when your job responsibilities suddenly include making sure that an actor is okay and safe. There was this whole serious layer added onto an experience that had previously been just "fun." The responsibility for the person inside the suit in regards to their health and well-being suddenly becomes more important than anything else, because their well-being became my responsibility, too, in addition to just getting my "creature job" done. It was another one of those moments where you go, "I really respect the people that can do this on a daily basis." It's like a prizefighter and his support team. I took my work on that one very personally and very seriously.

In the late 1980s, Gardner officially branched out on his own to form his now hugely successful company, Alterian Inc., which has contributed to hundreds of film and television projects, music videos, and commercials over the last few decades. When asked whether or not it can be heartbreaking to watch something you've worked on for months be sent off and become the responsibility of someone else, Gardner discussed how it's definitely harder for him to do so now, especially since running his own company can often leave him tied to his studio.

When you're working for Rick and watching the stuff go off to location with him, you know it's in the best hands possible, so it's not really hard to watch it go in those instances, other than just wanting to be there. It's harder now, actually, because I'm trying to run a business, which means I can't leave the shop as easily because I'm the guy in charge. Over time, you get used to watching your 'baby' go off and become part of a movie, but passing that off to somebody else can definitely be difficult.

It was funny, because after *Gorillas in the Mist*, I interviewed for the [1988] remake of *The Blob*. They had someone lined up to do the major makeup effects for the film, but they needed to bring in someone else to do some smaller stuff. I went in and interviewed for those smaller pieces, one of which was the projectionist character caught up in the Blob on the ceiling. The bulk of the effects were going to be handled by Greg Cannom, which I thought would be great because we had an excellent rapport, so that would be a blast. Then Greg had a conflict and had to pull out, so production asked me if I wanted to take over Greg's workload and they would find somebody else to do the effects that I was originally going to do.

I wasn't sure I was ready to run a shop of the size that would be needed to do Greg's workload and I didn't have a space that size available to me, either. The producers had decided to rent out a big warehouse in Hollywood for Lyle Conway's crew. They were bringing Lyle in from London to do the Blob creature itself. Production thought that they could divide that warehouse space in half, and have the creature crew on one side and the makeup effects crew on the other. With both of us in the same building, the look of everything would remain consistent. I was nervous because I had run smaller shows at other people's shops before, but I had never done anything at that level.

The schedule was really tight. I hired a bunch of friends, and we just dove in and started sculpting maquettes for each of the death scenes. About two weeks into it, I thought to myself, *Oh my God, this is a blast!* I totally loved everything about running a shop, especially the process of incorporating everybody's ideas and collaborating together. It was a lot of fun for me, and that moment was the point where I knew that I could do this, and that I wanted to do it again and again.

My wife (fiancée at the time), Cindy, was the Makeup Effects Coordinator for our side of the shop. She had come from a background in production coordinating for film, so this wasn't so different. Working together was great, especially considering the long hours, and we realized we were a good team. The two of us worked really well [together], and our skill sets complimented each other. I'm the art half and she's the smart half. We knew that if we didn't kill each other by the end of *The Blob*, we could do this. And right when *The Blob*'s extra photography was over, we got married and went off on our honeymoon.

Even though Gardner knew he would be able to work alongside his wife, he soon found out that wasn't going to be the case when it came to another business partner he ended up buying out of the company after its first year in operation.

When I was ready to start my own place, there was a co-worker I had worked with previously who wanted to team up with me. We partnered for a couple projects, *Darkman* and *Dark Angel*, and I quickly realized that I didn't want to be in a partnership with somebody else. I worked great with my wife and I'm into this because I love it, and this person seemed to have a completely different agenda. It didn't seem right on so many levels, so I wrapped up within a year's time, and then I bought him out and that was the end of it.

After *Darkman* was over, I was back on my own again. That's when we actually started Alterian proper, and boy was it a slow start-up. We decided that we would make some Halloween masks given we had some time to kill. We ended up launching a whole line of Halloween masks. We were frustrated buying masks that were thin and didn't keep their shape, and we wanted to make a few masks the way we remembered them as kids: slightly oversized and cast in really thick latex. Our little mask project grew into the Alterian Ghost Factory, which ended up becoming its own entity in its own building with its own crew. Chet [Zar] and Loren [Gitthens] went over there from the main shop and ran that for almost a whole year.

We were starting up the *Swamp Thing* [1990] TV series around the same time we were starting the Ghost Factory. We had to do masks for some *Swamp Thing* background characters, so I approached Universal and asked if they were interested in letting us do masks of Swamp Thing himself for the general public, and suddenly we had the licensing for *Darkman* and then for *Swamp Thing*, and we got into *Army of Darkness* masks after that. Warner Bros. heard about what we were doing and had us do characters for the Warner Bros. stores for a while, too, including a bunch of the *Looney Tunes* characters. We started a series of 'Ghost Maker' mask kits as well, one of which became the design for the *Scream* mask. Things were taking off, but we realized that doing these masks was full-time work, so we had to pick one or the other because we could only handle so much. We had to prioritize.

For the aforementioned *Darkman*, Gardner reunited with Sam Raimi on his very first comic book-style cinematic endeavor.

Sam had tried to set up *The Shadow* as a movie, but he couldn't get the rights, so he basically said, "Screw it, I'm going to go do my own thing." He took *Phantom of the Opera*, *The Shadow*, and a couple of other things and came up with something totally new.

In the beginning, he came to us with some designs for the main character that had already been done elsewhere, but he wasn't happy with them. He thought they were 'too gooey,' as I remember him saying. He wanted to see if we could come up with another look for the character, something a bit more "dried out," so we started out just doing character designs for him. It turned out that what he really wanted to do for *Darkman* was to have a character that was a living version of the poster art from *Evil Dead II*—which was basically a skull with regular human eyes in it. I thought it was the coolest idea ever.

We were doing the designs of Darkman in the pre-Photoshop era, so we were creating these colored pencil designs of the character with different looks, but just couldn't quite nail the image the way Sam had described it. Colored pencils tend to soften things a bit. One night at home, I just felt really inspired and I sculpted out this bust of the character and put some glass eyes in it. It was mostly a skull, with bits of burned skin and muscle here and there. I put shoulders on it and sculpted a trench coat with a high collar at the last minute, with just a rough form for the coat. I don't remember if I sent over a picture or if I showed the sculpture to him, but Sam saw that and he immediately asked me to do the movie. He went to bat for me with Universal.

I got sat down by Universal before we started and they asked me if I had ever done a makeup of this kind of complexity before. I told them I had, but I hadn't really. I just knew that I knew what I was doing, and I really wanted the opportunity. That's really the story of how all of these jobs went back then—

you were solving a problem and doing something that nobody had ever done or seen before, sometimes with no precedent. And Universal just let me go at it.

Once he began working on Darkman full-time, Tony soon realized that some of the assumptions he had made about who would be playing the titular hero (which helped inform his initial design of the character), wouldn't play out the way he expected. However, those idiosyncrasies ended up paying off in dividends in other ways.

Honestly, I had assumed Bruce Campbell was going to be Darkman. I remember thinking that Bruce's angular face would totally match up with the aesthetics of the sculpture that I had done, and we could adapt that makeup design to his face with no problem at all. But while they were in the process of casting the film, Sam came to me and told me that the studio had someone else in mind, and he said I would love him. That's when I found out it was Liam Neeson, and I remember at the time, when I was doing my research and looking him up, thinking, *Oh my God, this guy has way more of a square head and jawline, and a broken nose. What are we going to do, because he's totally the opposite of the design?* I thought we were going to have to do a complete do-over of the design from the beginning.

In the end, of course, what I thought were "issues" were the character traits that make him recognizable for who he is, so I realized that everything that I thought might be a handicap actually turned out to be a major asset to the look of Darkman. It was obviously a learning experience from that perspective, but it was really challenging, too. Prosthetic makeup is obviously an additive process, so I had to figure out how to keep that makeup as thin as possible and really dig into the skin and make it look like there was depth to the burned areas. That's when I decided that I was going to build up his entire head proportionately so that the good side looked balanced with the burned side. He ended up wearing a good half-inch of foam on the good side of his head.

That allowed us to carve into the face enough to give a sense of depth, and then use dark colors and even black around the areas where you wanted it to look deeper in the corners of the mouth and stuff like that. It was all about figuring out proportions all the time so that he looked balanced out, and not like a giant Q-tip head wearing shoulder pads.

Liam also has really big hands, and I wanted to make gloves for him so he could take the hands off and on, and we could change the stages of the dirt and bandages just by changing his gloves. Liam was really conscious of not keeping his hands up by his face a lot because his hands were disproportionate. We also built animatronic hands and forearms, so that when Darkman fought Smiley in the warehouse, and Dan [Bell] got punched by Darkman, it looked proportionate and didn't look like he was getting punched by somebody wearing a boxing glove. Liam actually puppeteered quite often, too, so that anything with the animatronic hands would also have a sense of his performance in it.

The whole experience all the way through the end was truly great. Liam had to wear that full makeup twenty-something times and he never complained once. We always made sure we had smoothies or something with protein in it for him to drink so he could look after his health. During breaks, you would see him take a muffin from craft services and pound it flat with his fist to feed it in through his teeth, because he could only open his mouth so far. He always told us, "It's not a problem. It's a challenge." I took that positive mindset with me for the rest of my career. I thought he was pretty brilliant in that way.

Around the same time he was working on Darkman, Gardner was brought on to contribute to another modern cult classic, Clive Barker's Nightbreed, becoming involved with the reshoots the producers were doing to add more gore-flavored effects to the film.

Nightbreed was a really weird one for me because we were only involved with the reshoots. The producers wanted to add a bunch of scenes, and some of them involved makeups and characters that were in the film, but we had to give them a different look. For example, there was this priest character [Ashberry, played by Malcolm Smith] that had gone to the dark side. They sent over the prosthetics from London and said that they needed me to create this character again and copy what he looked like in the film, but we needed him to look like he'd been burned for this new end scene. We had to work with David Cronenberg's character [Dr. Philip K. Decker] as well, but that was literally just—for lack of a better term—"mask wrangling," because that character just wore a zip-up mask.

There was a scene added where the killer comes into the hotel check-in area, and then the lady who checks people in finds the manager's decapitated head resting on the desk's sign-in ledger. They needed a fake head, so *Nightbreed* was the beginning of my career as a severed head in the movies. It ended up being me wearing a severed neck prosthetic, with my head up through a fake desk, with the ledger cut really well so that I could get my head up through it. We also did the scene where John Agar is being tortured and he's tied up in Christmas lights and sliced up. My experience on the show was literally only a few days on set. They were all with Clive and a really tiny crew, so it was really fun to step in and be part of the post-production process. Everybody was super nice, and I really enjoyed working with Clive.

Tony's involvement on the reshoots for Nightbreed would lead to more incredible collaborative opportunities with Barker in the future, but prior to that, Gardner once again reteamed with Sam Raimi for a third project, Army of Darkness, to handle Ash and Sheila, the main characters of the Evil Dead II sequel.

Sam already had KNB [EFX Group] working on the skeleton army, and he asked if I would like to do all of the makeup effects involving Bruce Campbell and Embeth [Davidtz], because he really loved what we'd done on *Darkman* and he really wanted me to take the same full-head prosthetic makeup approach towards Bruce's character on the film. Sam wanted us to mess up Bruce's whole body—he wanted to see Ash's limbs and head get cut off and then come back together. My thinking was that if Ash were to get reassembled and then reanimated, it would be interesting if the pieces reassembled inaccurately and were a little misaligned. Along those same lines, what if his jaw was barely hanging on, and he used a rope to tie his jaw into place, along the lines of Jacob Marley in *A Christmas Carol?* I was pitching ideas like that to Sam, along the lines of "Frankenstein meets Jacob Marley," and he thought it was an interesting idea.

To be honest, I was kind of going down the punk rock Frankenstein road with Evil Ash and Evil Sheila, whose character became my homage to the Bride of Frankenstein, which only seemed appropriate. When we got the script and I saw dialogue like, "Gimme some sugar, baby," and all of the other classic Ash lines, I knew there was going to be a chance to have some fun with this one, so I wanted to push this punk rock look a little bit.

Bruce was also giving us feedback on our work, and he was just as articulate as Sam in his vision for the characters in *Army of Darkness*. That made it really easy to just dive into everything with some confidence. Certain scenes were talked about being homages to particular old films or scenes from old films, so there was always a point of reference for us, too. There were days when it was technically super challenging, but it was one of those things where every one of those challenges was something fun. We felt like we were doing something that hadn't been done before, and so much of the weird stuff that we did succeeded because Bruce really sells it in the film. The stretching faces, the different lengths of the arms, the mini-Ashes, and things like that—Bruce just being Bruce really made *Army of Darkness* what it is.

In the early 1990s, Tony was asked to provide a zombie and a talking cat for a Disney movie that also involved cutting the zombie's head and fingers off and driving a bus over the cat. The movie didn't sound very Disney-esque, and its name was Hocus Pocus.

As soon as I read the script, I knew who had to play the zombie . . . I just didn't know his name. There were these McDonald's commercials on TV at the time with this skinny character with an animatronic moon head named Mac Tonight. He was super animated, had a lot of character, and never spoke a word. I remember thinking that if that actor could make it look easy and fun wearing a heavy animatronic head, then watching this same guy playing a gangly zombie [Billy Butcherson] with his mouth stitched shut would be amazing.

I tracked down Steve Neill, who had done the Mac Tonight head, and he happened to have a bust of the actor who had worn the head sitting out behind his garage, an actor named Doug Jones. Steve let me borrow the lifecast, and I made sure that we sculpted every character design for Billy Butcherson on that lifecast. If the studio wanted that design, they were going to need to hire that actor—it was that tight to his face. I had never worked with Doug; I just had a feeling he would be a perfect fit.

Margaret Prentice and I applied Doug's makeup every day, and every day the three of us would marvel at the sets and Bette Midler—literally everything about the film. Being on that soundstage on the Disney lot was one of the most amazing experiences. I met a really cool producer on that set, too, who was also the originator of the story of the movie: David Kirschner. It turned out that the plot of the film came from a story that David had made up to tell his daughters when they were little, and as a kid he had a cat named Binx.

In the mid-1990s, Clive Barker called upon Tony Gardner and Alterian once again to lend their talents to Lord of Illusions, Barker's feature film adaptation of his horror noir short story, "The Last Illusion." Looking back, Gardner reflected on his memorable involvement with the project.

Nightbreed led to Alterian doing all of the character designs for *Lord of Illusions*. But at the start, the production company was talking to Steve Johnson and myself about doing the effects for the film. We had to bow out after the initial design phase, as we had a conflict with a pre-existing commitment to another project that suddenly had a green light.

As production on our other project wound down, Clive's group contacted us about a nightmare sequence that they wanted to shoot some practical effects for, with people's heads melting and these weird slug-headed creatures revealed underneath. So, we were asked to come in and design and build these really cool, weird, translucent, hot-melt vinyl heads that had these stylized mechanical rigs inside them. You could see through the skin through layers of veins, and while this animatronic head pushed forward, the skin sloughed off, the eyes pushed out on stalks, and there were four weird orifices in the face that literally expanded with this black/brown slime oozing out of them. It was this really organic, disgusting, cool thing. So our experience on *Lord* was a very odd one for sure, but it was nice to have closure at the end of it, and to be able to go on set with Clive and shoot a bunch of stuff with just him and a small crew again. That was great.

One thing I don't talk about too often is the fact that Clive and I were actually going to open a haunted house on Hollywood Boulevard at one point. It was going to be in the Vogue Theatre across the street from the Egyptian Theatre. We designed it as a walkthrough experience, with a tour guide in this weird world we had created for the first part, and then you were on your own for the remainder of the experience. The rooms and set pieces were designed, and the look of all of the characters, too. We were to the point where we had storyboards for the whole backstory of the place, and had designed a line of toys based on some of the characters, and we had even sculpted one as a multiple piece model kit.

But then we got the seismologist's final report back on the building's infrastructure and were told that essentially everything needed to be retrofitted. It would have basically been smarter to tear the whole building down and start over. There were also tenants in storefronts on the front of the building that would need to get bought out. We didn't have the additional funds for any of that, so once that seismology report came back, it all just imploded. We hit all of these problems trying to find a new location in the area and eventually just bailed on it. We figured we would still do it someday, but then a couple of years later, Universal Studios started doing Halloween Horror Nights and that's when we realized there wasn't a need for our project anymore.

Around the turn of the century, Tony had to do in-depth research for his bullet-centric work on Three Kings, resulting in some inquiries from law enforcement.

In the late '90s, I was hired to provide makeup effects for a film called *Three Kings* and managed to get David O. Russell, Warner Bros., and myself in trouble before the film was over. I had been asked to create a few effects where the camera actually "went inside" an actor's body to show the damage that a bullet could do, as well as the aftereffects of that damage. This was pre-CGI, so it all had to be created practically. By the time the film was finished, I had been investigated by the FBI, Arizona State Police, and the Missing Persons Division, and had to write a press release for Warner Bros. to hand out at the gate. Turns out people thought that we had taken a homeless person off the streets of Phoenix and shot them up with a high-speed camera recording it all. We took it as a compliment and a testament to the realism of our work.

One of the actors that I was applying prosthetics on for *Three Kings* was actually a director named Spike Jonze. Spike introduced me to two musicians afterwards who went by the name of Daft Punk, who wanted to create some sort of disguise mask or helmet. We did lifecasts of the two musicians— Thomas Bangalter and Guy-Manuel de Homem-Christo—and worked out some designs in clay over their lifecasts based on some sketches that they brought out to us. The entire experience involved new materials and new processes, including LED technology, metal plating, and minor programming—all things we had never done before. Spike told them that I was the guy who could figure it out, and we just learned as we went. Best to dive in and figure things out, instead of passively standing back—you never know where that mindset might lead you.

Beyond the three different iterations of the robotic helmets, there were multiple music videos, as well as an experimental feature film called *Daft Punk's Electroma*. All of the various projects with the people at Daft Arts were super collaborative experiences, and *Electroma* was one of the first film projects where I ended up involved on the production side as well as the makeup and costuming effects. I learned a lot.

In 2003, Tony picked up the mantle for one of the genre's most beloved icons when he tackled the special effects and animatronics for Don Mancini's Seed of Chucky. The ambitious sequel required Alterian to provide three fully animatronic characters: the film's titular antagonist (voiced by Brad Dourif), Chucky's main squeeze, Tiffany (voiced by Jennifer Tilly), and their offspring, Glen/Glenda (brought to life with a vocal performance from Billy Boyd).

I was brought in on *Seed* at literally the last minute. My involvement started with a couple of really vague phone calls at first, where I was being asked if I could make a talking baby about toddler-size that could walk around. I think they were trying to suss us out. By the time I got the call explaining that they were making the next *Child's Play* movie, I was also told that it would be shooting in Romania in about three months, and they needed to have three animatronic characters built for this one. So we just hit the ground running, and without much reference material to work from other than some photos. There really wasn't time to think.

Seed of Chucky may not have been nearly the box office and critical success its immediate predecessor was, but the fifth installment of the Child's Play (1988) series was noteworthy for several reasons, including the fact that Gardner got to die on-screen as himself.

Don sprung the idea for my cinematic death on me right at the beginning. He told me that Chucky and Tiffany kill the special effects guy in the "movie within the movie," and he asked if I would be up for auditioning for it. I told him I didn't know if I'd be any good, but I was willing to do the audition. I went in and had to do the character's death scene as my audition, which was a completely different scene in that first draft of the script, with Chucky and Tiffany tying this guy down on a table and playing the game *Operation* on him while he was alive, cutting out different organs. So Don filmed me on his kitchen table acting this whole scene out on video, and that tape went to Universal. I guess I did okay, because I got hired. That audition tape is still out there somewhere. I dread the day someone finds it.

It was both good and bad playing a character in the film. Good, because I obviously had easy access to myself for lifecasting and matching up the dummy during pre-production, but it was bad once we went to film the death scene. Everything felt so fractured for me on that shoot day; we had all three puppets working in that scene. That meant that we had twenty-some puppeteers working. I was supervising them and also puppeteering on each character, and I had to rig my body so we could dismember it, then clean up, put on my wardrobe, and go shoot out another scene in character. After that, I would segue back to puppeteering. When it was over, I thought it was hilarious that we actually got through the day. That was definitely film insanity at its finest.

While he may have been under the proverbial gun that day on set, it's Tony's utmost desire to continue to live up to fans' expectations for the Chucky films, especially since he knows they're so passionate about their beloved characters.

There was some pressure, for sure, when I first came onto *Seed*, because the fanbase is huge and they're very savvy. We had to make sure we got things right with both Chucky and Tiffany, but it was trial by fire, honestly, especially on set. Every aspect of it was brand new to us, but we survived it, and we must have done okay, because they asked us back for the next two. *Curse [of Chucky]* was an experiment with Chucky wearing a "Good Guys" skin over his own, which I think we took too literally at the time. So on *Cult [of Chucky]*, I became very obsessed with making sure Chucky's look feels genuinely authentic, especially for the fans.

I had a laser scan done from an original Chucky doll, and we scanned the original clothing, too. I know that the sweater varies from film to film, but beyond that sort of gray area, I was obsessed with making sure we got his anatomy and proportions perfect for *Cult*. The studio was very supportive of that, too, and Don was of the same mindset. There were a few tweaks made for mechanical reasons, but they were minor. It was nice being able to recreate the character true to David Kirschner and Kevin Yagher's designs from the original film.

Cult of Chucky and *The Bad Batch* were two films where I was involved from the earliest stages of the script all the way through post-production, and where I was also credited as a Producer or Co-Producer on the films. Being responsible for the big picture as well as a specific department—not to mention being on set and doing makeup or performing a killer doll at the same time— hasn't seemed as nerve-wracking as I was expecting, to be honest. Your responsibility is much larger, but it seems like a natural extension of the creative process, and being a part of the production team involved with overall problem-solving is just one more aspect of helping put together a product that you can be proud to put your name on.

With over two hundred film, television, and music video credits (one of which he directed himself for Daft Punk) on his résumé, there's no denying that Tony Gardner has firmly established himself as one of the most influential and innovative makeup effects artists to come up during the last forty years in the industry. He blew genre fans' minds with his half-corpse zombie in The Return of the Living Dead, he's contributed to countless horror and sci-fi films, and worked alongside some of the biggest directors ever.

Tony also helped define the trademark look for one of the most popular electronic music acts of all time, and has even suffered cinematic deaths in his career, most famously by the hand of Chucky. Additionally, Gardner's efforts have been recognized with multiple prestigious awards and nominations, including an Oscar nomination for Alterian's work on the comedy Bad Grandpa.

While he can't really pinpoint one attribute as the key to his longtime success in a sometimes unforgiving field, Gardner says it's the problem-solving aspect of his profession that keeps him going.

Any job that pushes you creatively is definitely the most rewarding job I could ask to be involved with. If somebody tells me that something can't be done, I'm the first one in line for that job. I want to do it, I want to figure it out, I want to problem-solve. The stuff that is creatively challenging is definitely more rewarding throughout the entire process. Once you solve the process, then you have to pull it off. All of that stuff energizes me as an artist, and it was so cool that I was able to ride in on this wave of innovation in regards to practical effects in this business, where the work was literally hands-on, and the constant mantra was, "We've got to figure this out one way or another." So few jobs require that kind of thought process.

Every experience I've had doing makeup professionally, save the one year with the business partner, has been really positive. I've found that things that I've done twenty years ago are still relevant now. Something that we did with the mask business way back when came into play as we were recently making prosthetic molds for *The Mist* TV series. That tornado of our youth, trying out all of this stuff now that we're all a little older and a little wiser, we're able to put it to good use.

I just feel like I've always been a creative and collaborative artist, and even now I'm just as much of a collaborative, creative guy as I was back when I first started out. I feel fortunate that I'm able to continue doing the stuff that I'd still be doing even if no one paid me to, honestly, because I love doing it so much. Not everyone gets to be that lucky.

Moss zombie for Michael Jackson's *Thriller* music video

Return of the Living Dead

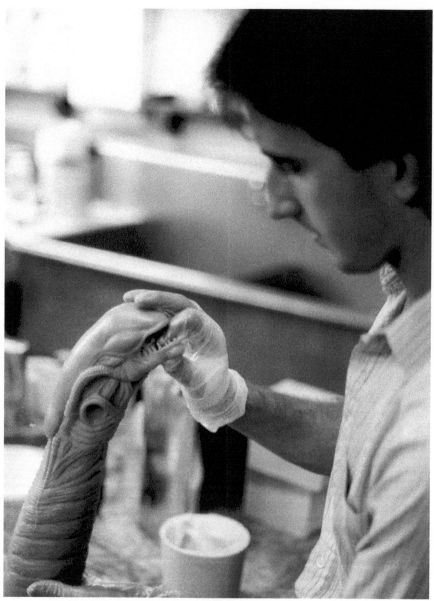

Aliens

The Lost Boys - Kiefer Sutherland

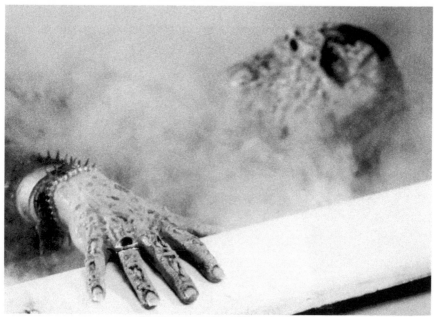

The Lost Boys - Hand Prosthetic

The Blob

Hocus Pocus – Tony Gardner

Hocus Pocus – Tony Gardner

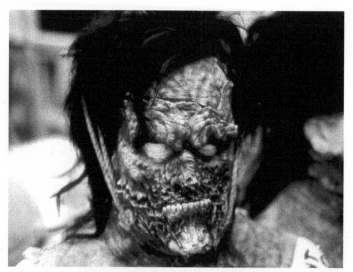

Army of Darkness - Evil Ash Mask

Shallow Hal - Tony Gardner and Gwyneth Paltrow

Hairspray - Crew with John Travolta

Geico's Caveman Character

On the Set of *Cult of Chucky*

Seed of Chucky

Seed of Chucky - Jennifer Tilly and Tony Gardner

Cult of Chucky

Darkman - Tony Gardner

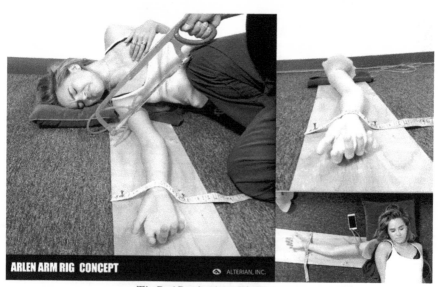

The Bad Batch - Arm Rig Concept

The Bad Batch - Suki Waterhouse

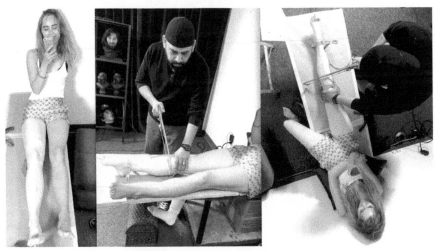

The Bad Batch - Leg Rig Concept

The Bad Batch - Jim Carrey and Tony Gardner

The Bad Batch - Suki Waterhouse and Jason Mamoa

Happy Death Day - Mask Painting

Happy Death Day - Mask on Set

Conversation with...
JOEL HARLOW

Oscar and Emmy Winning Special Effects Makeup Artist

Pirates of the Caribbean: At World's End (2007)
Star Trek: Beyond (2016)
Logan (2017)
Black Panther (2018)

Growing up in Grand Forks, North Dakota, Oscar-winning artist Joel Harlow may not have seen the glitz and glamour of Tinseltown in his future, but the one thing he did know was that he loved creating memorable characters, and fell in love with them at a very early age.

I don't know if there was a specific moment where I thought to myself, *Hey, this looks interesting. I want to do something like this,* but I had this realization while watching the original *King Kong* with my father that I wanted to somehow be involved with creating that kind of magic. Where I grew up in North Dakota, people were either farmers or athletes, so being a part of the movie-making process seemed impossible. That didn't stop me, though.

I would try and get my hands on as much material and as many products as I could to create and experiment and see what I could do to get my foot into this world of making characters that have never existed before. During high school, I worked with the theater department and they had certain challenges that needed to be overcome as far as various productions were concerned. One time, they were doing a production of *The Hobbit*, and they needed Smaug the dragon, so I built that out of chicken wire and fabric and I used a fire extinguisher as its flame breath.

And then, friends of mine who were like-minded, we would make these short films on videotape on the weekends, and all the while I was drawing and sculpting and absorbing as much as I could from the popular horror culture at the time, like *Fangoria, Gorezone,* and those kinds of publications. Tom Savini even had a book called *Grande Illusions,* and there was the Dick Smith course, too. So, all those materials opened up new, more professional ways to do things, and I fell in love.

What's interesting is that my father is a child psychologist, so a lot of people always said to me, "I bet he was really worried about what was going on with his kid who was into all this weird stuff," but he was very supportive. Both of my parents were absolutely, completely supportive and I don't think that I would have achieved what I did without their support. If they hadn't embraced my passions, then I don't think I would be here, which is why, when I was fortunate enough to take home an Oscar for *Star Trek* [2009], I gave it to them. It was just a small token of my appreciation and penance for destroying their oven and their carpet and various other parts of the house with a variety of mold-making and casting materials when I was younger. They deserved that award.

Joel's first professional break came right before he headed off to pursue his collegiate aspirations, taking him and a high school friend down to the Sunshine State to work on the micro-budget slasher movie Killing Spree, directed by Tim Ritter. It was a gig that demanded a lot of his time and ingenuity, but Harlow carried the lessons from that scrappy indie horror movie with him throughout his career.

The first professional movie job I ever did was down in Florida. This was even before I went to the School of Visual Arts. There was a friend of mine who had graduated from Red River High School a year before me, and we moved down to Florida and met with an independent filmmaker named Tim Ritter, who was doing a film called *Killing Spree*. They brought me down to design the deaths for seven of the characters, and then they all have to come back to life, too. One of them gets burned, so he comes back as a burned corpse, and I had a thousand dollars to do it all.

Somehow I did it, and if you asked me to do that today, I wouldn't have the slightest idea how to start. Whether it's quality control, or just your palate changing as far as what's aesthetically pleasing, that stuff costs money, and back then, we just didn't have it. But somehow I did it. Then, I did another film down in Florida called *Woodshop* that I don't think ever came out, and it was a case of the wardrobe department not talking to the makeup effects department, so there was some miscommunication there. I had created a makeup where this guy was melting. He had gloves that went up to his mid-forearm, and he had this prosthetic that went on his face, so it just looked like a bubbly face. But then he showed up to his wardrobe and he was wearing a tank top.

This thing only came up to his mid-forearm, and I don't know if the wardrobe department just refused to put a long-sleeved shirt on him or what the deal was, but I had to figure out how to cover his arms. I ended up going to the craft service table and getting that peanut butter and jelly mixture [Smucker's Goober Grape] that was popular for a while, and smearing that all over his arms. To my surprise, it actually blended great. I don't know what that says about the makeup, but I probably could have done the whole thing with that peanut butter and jelly stuff.

But that was one of those instances where you just have to think on the fly. You have to have your arsenal of tricks ready because you never know when you're going to need it. I needed to do something similar on *The Lone Ranger* [2013], where we had designed something that was not working because we overthought it, so we went the ultra easy route and we got the shot.

Once it came time to head off to college, Joel had to choose between going to either New York or California, but ultimately chose the East Coast as his temporary home due to his familiarity with The City That Never Sleeps.

My father was a big fan of New York, so even though I had applied to schools out in California, I ended up choosing the New York School of Visual Arts because I think some of that had rubbed off on me. We had visited New York a couple of times, but I quickly realized it's a far different place to visit than it is to live in. There were still no real makeup schools at this time, so my next option was animation, and that's what I studied at the School of Visual Arts.

There was this instructor there who taught a weekend class on makeup in Times Square, and I ended up taking that class. I believe it was over four weekends, and Jennifer Aspinall was one of the guest teachers there. And then, through word of mouth, I met Vincent [J.] Guastini out there and he was getting ready to do *The Deadly Spawn II* (a.k.a. *Metamorphosis: The Alien Factor*). So, I went over to his studio and helped sculpt this giant *Deadly Spawn* character. Of course, I was horrible. I was brand new, so I didn't have my chops yet, but I had passion, and I would go out there every day for free and just sculpt until the wee hours of the morning. Then I'd come back to my room at the YMCA on 34th and 9th to sleep, and did the same thing the next day. Some days, I was neglecting going to school at all, because I was finally getting a foot in the door in the makeup effects world.

Joel continued to carve out his career on the East Coast with his work on the Troma sequels The Toxic Avenger Part II and The Toxic Avenger Part III: The Last Temptation of Toxie, and although he didn't necessarily get paid, he did get some interesting experience out of his time spent on those films.

When I was over at Vincent Guastini's place, I had met Tim Considine, and he told me that they were looking for people to work on *Toxic Avenger Part II* and *III*. Actually, I just thought it was *Part II* at the time, because they weren't letting it be known that they were actually shooting two films at the same time. So, I went over, and I met with this gentleman in Times Square and he said to me, "If you're going to work for nothing, you've got the job." So, I got the job.

I had a portfolio of bad work, yes, but at least it showed that I knew some of the materials, and for a film like this, you can get by on that.

I signed on and then we moved up to Peekskill, New York, and we all slept in this masonic temple and we started building stuff up there. Vincent Guastini had started sculpting this devil character that I saw when I was doing the *Deadly Spawn* stuff with him, and so he passed it on to me. I remember driving up in a van—because he had to get this thing molded immediately once we got there—and I'm in the back seat sculpting on this thing so that by the time we get there, we can maybe spend another couple hours on it and then get it right into a mold.

It was pretty ridiculous. It was such a stupid way to do anything, but once again, it was one of those "let's weed them out" kind of instances where it was like, "Okay, now you've got to sculpt in a moving van." That's next to impossible, especially because this thing had all these scales on it. So that's what I did in the van as we headed up to Peekskill, New York.

Shortly after his time working with Troma, Harlow began working with Gabe Bartalos on Basket Case 2, another sequel to a beloved low-budget cult classic. Little did Joel realize that the project would ultimately lead to him uprooting his life and permanently making the move out to the West Coast.

Gabe was in charge of all the makeup effects for *Basket Case 2*, and I was one of his right-hand guys, along with Gino Crognale. We had all seen *Basket Case*, and so being able to work on the sequel under Gabe's quirky style was amazing.

Gabe designed special characters in a way that was very much a "comic book style." There was this comic book called *Plop!*, where Basil Wolverton had designed a lot of the characters, and Gabe definitely had that Wolverton type of aesthetic to his work, but could translate that look into three dimensions. I don't think that had ever been done before. When I was working for him on *Basket Case 2*, I started talking to him about going out to California. He said, "Yes, you should definitely come out to California, and you can even work in my studio [Atlantic West Effects]."

So I came out to California and my roommate and I built everything for this show that was coming through called *Happy Hell Night*, and Gabe and I went to Yugoslavia to film it. We were there for six weeks and when we were done with that, we came back and I worked for Gabe a little bit more. I eventually started to shop my portfolio around, and that's how I got a job over at Steve Johnson's XFX. I was there for quite some time, about eight years.

While working at XFX, Joel had many opportunities to continue honing his craft on a variety of projects that included numerous commercials and a wide range of film projects such as Suburban Commando, Pet Sematary II, Freaked, Brainscan, Night of the Demons 2, Species, Lord of Illusions, and the television miniseries adaptation of Stephen King's The Stand, which earned him a Primetime Emmy Award for Outstanding Individual Achievement in Makeup for a Miniseries or a Special.

There were so many projects over at Steve's when I was working with him that covered the whole gamut of effects. It was a great experience, and it was primarily me and Leon Laderach who would handle the working effects if something had to change in-camera. We did this open-heart surgery thing for this movie called *The Surgeon*, and in *Lord of Illusions*, there's this moment where the character Nix's skull comes apart and all these things shoot out of it. That kind of stuff requires a lot of in-camera trickery, and you wouldn't get to do those effects now because it would just instantly be, "That should be a CG effect. Let's just do it that way." We did all that stuff practical, and Steve was great at that.

Steve was also really great at thinking outside the box, using materials that you generally don't use for makeup: plastic bags and liquid-injected bladders—things like that. We had this movie called *Chill Factor*, where this character is running through the forest at the beginning of the film. A bomb goes off, and it's supposed to melt his clothes and then melt his skin. We were like, "Whoa, how do you melt clothes?" Since we didn't have the option for CG effects, we built the clothes out of that water-dissolving paper and pumped liquid through appliances on the actors so that the clothes melted first, and then you started pumping a different color liquid to allude to the skin starting to melt. It came out great.

Species was another interesting project because you could really see Steve's thought process at work. He never takes the easy path and would always push the envelope. I remember we were all excited to work with [H.R.] Giger because of *Alien*, which put him on the map, but I think *Species* was the first time anyone really got to experience the other side of Giger's artistic aesthetic. Sil was almost the sensual counterpart to the Xenomorph, and I remember

Steven wanted to distinguish this new creature by making it translucent and even moving in certain parts. Giger came by the shop, too, and we all got to meet him, and he would do these doodles whenever he had an idea. Whenever he'd turn around or leave the room, I remember people would excitedly take those doodles because they were considered a "Giger Original." It was a really great time to be there—so much talent on that show.

While Harlow relished all the experiences and opportunities he found while working at XFX under Steve Johnson, he realized in the late 1990s that it was time to branch off on his own, and after joining the union, Joel saw his career pivot, as he began working on larger studio projects.

As soon as I turned union, my first major film was *How the Grinch Stole Christmas*. It was an interesting thing for me to experience, because I was going from working in the shop and building makeups, effects, or whatever I needed to do, and then passing them off to union makeup artists to apply on set. For the *Grinch*, now I was getting prosthetics from, in this case, Rick Baker's shop, and I was applying all these Whoville makeups that were created by somebody else. It was a very different dynamic.

When you go onto set to apply makeups, there is a different set of requirements on you as an artist, and a demeanor that you need to adapt to when you're working in a trailer, as opposed to working in the shop. This is something that I've tried to stress to artists over the years: you can't be the shop guy when you're on set. You've got to present yourself with an air of confidence so that your actor or actress is comfortable, because you're the first person they see in the morning and you're the last person they're going to see at night. Your job involves doing something to alter their appearance, so they have to have the utmost confidence in you.

After How the Grinch Stole Christmas, Harlow came aboard two high-profile projects: Steven Spielberg's A.I. Artificial Intelligence —which Spielberg took on after the passing of the film's original director, Stanley Kubrick—and Tim Burton's Planet of the Apes (2001).

Ve [Neill] brought me on for *A.I.*, and that was a slightly surreal experience because Spielberg is an icon. Some of my favorite movies of all time are movies that he's given us, so to be able to create with him was definitely a once-in-a-life experience for me. The thing is, if I'm there on the set of a movie,

I'm there to serve the art. I'm going to do the same job on a low-budget movie as I'm going to do on a Spielberg movie, and that job is my best job possible. It was a little intimidating, but I treated it like any other film that I had been on up until that point.

With *Apes*, that film was special for a lot of reasons, even if it wasn't very well-received. Being a part of a Tim Burton film is always a wonderful time—I love Tim. I have been able to work with him a couple of times since *Apes*, and he's one of those visionary directors that if you get to work with them even once, you should consider yourself lucky. But the original *Planet of the Apes* resonated with me just like it resonated with every other makeup effects person, because it was a landmark moment in film and in effects—at least, it should resonate; if it doesn't, then maybe you're in the wrong business.

Being a part of Tim Burton's version of *Planet of the Apes*, with Rick Baker helming all the ape makeups, was a perfect storm of talent coming together. Whatever you think about that particular movie, it was still a top-notch project from both a makeup perspective and a directing perspective. And here I was, in the room doing makeups with some of the most talented makeup artists in the industry, so it was another big learning experience for me. I don't think that ever goes away. You can learn something from every project you're on, and I certainly learned a lot on *Apes*, just like I learned something on every film I've ever done.

Just a short while later, Joel began a decades-spanning collaborative relationship with Johnny Depp after working with him on the Disney blockbuster Pirates of the Caribbean: The Curse of the Black Pearl. Harlow would not only return to offer up his talents for every one of the Pirates sequels, but he was also tasked with Depp's makeup on a myriad of films, including Alice in Wonderland, Dark Shadows, Mortdecai, Alice Through the Looking Glass, Tusk, Into the Woods, and The Lone Ranger, which earned him another Academy Award nomination.

Pirates was the first time that I had met and worked with Johnny, and he's an amazing human being. He's an amazing actor, and he's a fan of makeup, so for me, as a makeup artist, you can't ask for anything more than that. He speaks the language of makeup, he knows what's possible, he knows what's not possible, and he knows when to push for an idea, and he will. If we come across something that maybe a producer or the director isn't one hundred percent on, he'll push for it because he knows the potential and he knows what the outcome can be, and he's always right.

Johnny knows how to achieve a character, and he uses every tool at his disposal—whether it's props, hair, makeup, or wardrobe. I feel very fortunate in that he had me do some of his transformations over the years, and every time I do it, it's like two buddies playing around with a makeup kit and seeing what comes out of it. There are a lot of egos out there working today that don't want to be covered up with makeup, but he will forego all of that just to give the audience a memorable experience that a lot of other people can't give them.

The *Pirates* films have been a big part of my professional life. I've had my hand in all five *Pirates* movies and I don't know—as far as the makeup department goes—anyone else that has been able to work on every film in an entire franchise. When we started the first *Pirates* movie, I don't think anyone knew what it was going to be. I had worked on films before where I thought, "This is going to be amazing," and when you see the final film, it's like, "Oh, not so much." I had that feeling with *Pirates*, where I thought it was going to be really something special, and thankfully, it turned out that I was right on that one.

Filming those movies, it's like nothing you could ever imagine. You're on an 18th-century ship, and the pirate characters are not just guys with beards and mustaches; they've got layers and layers of character to them. All of those films provided us with a real exercise in character makeup—from traditional techniques to the most complicated, sophisticated prosthetic makeup techniques you could ever imagine, like 'Bootstrap Bill' [played by Stellan Skarsgård] in *Pirates* 2 and 3.

Bootstrap is probably one of my very favorite characters that I have ever had a hand in, because I'd always been a fan of deep-sea life and creatures, and this character gave me the chance to celebrate that. It also gave me a chance to experiment with a combination of materials that you wouldn't necessarily think of in terms of makeup applications. It was a very complicated design, too. There were six different stages, and that final stage ended up being 250 pieces because of all the barnacles and various appendages.

While the intricate and wildly imaginative makeup effects might have been all Joel, he fully admits that Bootstrap Bill didn't become fully realized until Skarsgård underwent the transformative process for the role.

You can spend months, or even years, with an idea about a character, where you're building it, refining it, and bringing all the elements together, but it doesn't really become a character until it's all applied to the performer. The performer brings it to life, so it is very much a marriage between your artform and the performer. Once the makeup goes on, you get that Frankenstein moment where your creation is now alive and moving and it opens its mouth. It's like, "Oh, that's what it looks like," and Stellan was amazing.

Bootstrap was supposed to only be two stages of that makeup, because it took so long to put on. You can't pre-glue any of that stuff, because you have to apply the skin first and that has to be painted, and then each socket has to be filled with a barnacle or a mussel shell or whatever it was that would go into that slot. It was such an extensive design, but it was well worth it. Stellan wanted to go the full six stages, though. After stage two, it was supposed to be taken over by ILM [Industrial Light & Magic] and be a computer-generated effect, but he's the one that said, "I want this to follow through as a makeup, because then audiences will really get to see it." God bless him for that.

Harlow remained busy throughout the 2000s on films spanning nearly every cinematic subgenre, including The Matrix sequels, The Haunted Mansion, Skinned Deep, The Chronicles of Riddick, The Ring Two, Christmas with the Kranks, War of the Worlds, Constantine, and Domino. It was in 2009 when Joel first entered the world of Captain Kirk and the U.S.S. Enterprise for J.J. Abrams' Star Trek reboot, on which he was tasked with bringing both the Romulans and the new iteration of Vulcans to life, which ultimately led to him taking home his very own Oscar award for Best Makeup.

Going from Captain Jack to Captain Kirk, those two films couldn't be any more aesthetically different. In *Pirates*, there's a dingy quality to the work, and now you're in space, so everything is clean, everything is precise, and your makeup has to reflect that. But, as far as being involved in the *Star Trek* universe, I grew up on *Star Trek* like so many others, so I was very excited. We didn't really know what it was going to be. When I got to read the script, I was sequestered away in this little room on set. I was handling all the Vulcans and all the Romulans, but that stuff primarily played at the end of it. So we didn't see a lot of what was going on until we went to the theater when the film came out.

But it was a fantastic experience because we were building on the Paramount lot. We were in a trailer near the commissary just making Romulans all day: sculpting heads and hands and what have you. I would go in, day after day, with Richie Alonzo (who's an amazing artist who has worked with me quite a few times), and that is the type of experience that we both got into the business for. I had no idea at the time that it would lead to an Academy Award.

I hadn't really played in that world before. I had won a couple of Emmys for some stuff that I was involved in over at Steve Johnson's, but the nomination for *Star Trek* was unexpected. When the announcement came out, and I found out that I was one of those names on that list, that right there was good enough for me. I called my parents immediately, and they were so excited, and then I ultimately ended up winning the award, which was completely surreal, but I was able to take my parents to the ceremony, which made the whole experience even better.

Joel would return for the third film in the series, Star Trek: Beyond, on which he was able to live out yet another once-in-a-lifetime experience: spearheading the creation of 56 different alien species as a way to celebrate the coinciding 50th anniversary of the original Star Trek series.

I seriously doubt I will ever get the opportunity again to create the variety and the quantity of special makeups we did on *Star Trek: Beyond*. When we started, honestly, things were still in flux as far as the script was concerned, so we didn't know how many characters we were going to be building. It wasn't like they gave us a laundry list of aliens or anything, either. We would just design different aliens, and I would occasionally go in and meet with [Director] Justin [Lin], Executive Producer Jeffrey Chernov, and J.J., and they would pick out their favorites and assign them to scenes.

Of course, there were specific characters that were named in the script that we had to design too, like Jaylah, Krall, Syl, the Vulcans, and Spock, so we knew how to proceed in those instances. But it wasn't until we were up in Vancouver, and my wife, who was working with me, said, "You're at 46 aliens now. Don't you think you should have 50 aliens for the 50th anniversary?" And I thought it was a great idea. So, we made four more aliens, because we could get them into these crowd scenes, and ultimately, we ended up at 56 because there was a rising need for different scenes. And, because my crew was there and everybody was a fan, they were all bending over backwards to deliver the best-looking characters possible. There was never really a stressful moment because it just felt like a bunch of friends making characters for a pretty important film, and one that would also mark the 50th anniversary of *Star Trek*.

To this very day, after 30-plus years in the business, Harlow continues to create memorable characters and effects on some of the biggest Hollywood films, showcasing his innovative style and his endless imagination. The secret? According to Joel, there are a variety of reasons why he's still in demand as an artist after all these years.

I don't think there's any one secret to finding longevity in this business. The one thing I would tell anybody who was considering working in effects, or to those who are still making a name for themselves, would be to always keep creating, whether you're successful at it or not. If you honor the art form by treating it as an art form, then the jobs will come from that. As we're speaking, I'm in my studio right now sculpting a fish head for no other reason than just because I can.

Of course, there have been times when I haven't been working, and any time you're not working, there is a moment, however brief it is, where you wonder whether or not you will ever work again. But the work <u>will</u> come, as long as you're being true to the art form and ultimately, true to yourself. I've just been lucky. Seriously. Between the people I've met, the people that decided they wanted to work with me over the years, and the people that I've been able to have on my team, I've been really fortunate, because when you're working with other artists who love this business as much as you, they help you elevate your craft just by watching them and being around them.

When I first started out, all I did was set out to create characters, whether it was going to be in my garage for myself, or occasionally for a movie, a TV show, a play, or whatever. It was always just about creating characters, and to see what has come from that—the award and the accolades, all that business— I never anticipated that any of that could ever happen. No matter how many awards you achieve, or whatever kind of accolades you're blessed enough to win, it shouldn't overpower your desire to create.

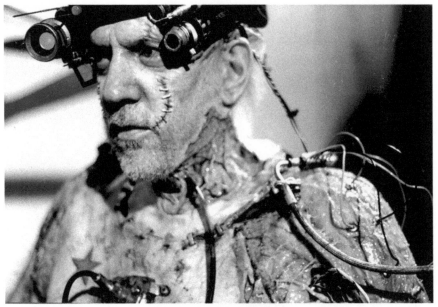

Virus - Donald Sutherland

Star Trek Beyond - Leonard Nimoy

Species 3 - Sunny Mabrey

Alice in Wonderland - Johnny Depp

Pirates of the Caribbean - Johnny Depp

Pirates of the Caribbean: On Stranger Tides - Geoffrey Rush and Joel Harlow

Pirates of the Caribbean: On Stranger Tides - Joel Harlow and Mermaid

Pirates of the Caribbean: On Stranger Tides – Mermaid Test

Dark Shadows - Johnny Depp

The Lone Ranger - Johnny Depp

The Lone Ranger - Joel Harlow and Johnny Depp

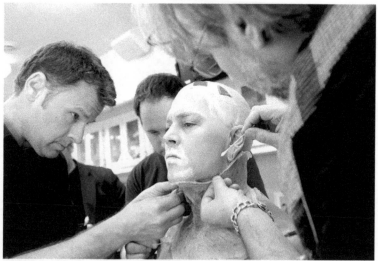

The Lone Ranger - Applying the "Old Tonto" Makeup

The Lone Ranger - Johnny Depp and Joel Harlow

Black Mass - Johnny Depp as Whitey Bulger

Star Trek Beyond

Star Trek Beyond - Sofia Boutella

Star Trek Beyond - Idris Elba

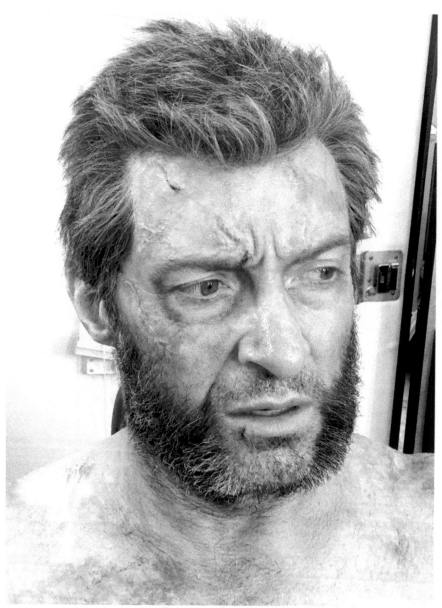

Logan - Hugh Jackman

Black Panther - Michael B Jordan and Joel Harlow

Black Panther - Joel Harlow & Mask

Conversation with…
VE NEILL

Oscar & Emmy Winning Special Effects Makeup Artist

The Lost Boys (1987)
Beetlejuice (1988)
Edward Scissorhands (1990)
Mrs. Doubtfire (1993)
Pirates of the Caribbean: The Curse of the Black Pearl (2003)

From a very early age, renowned award-winning effects artist Ve Neill knew she was destined to spend her life creating memorable characters, even if she didn't fully understand what that exactly meant in those days.

·I have always loved the idea of being able to turn somebody into something else. I don't know if it was escapism for me, or what it was, but I just thought that it was the coolest thing ever to be able to transform someone into something completely different.

I think that ever since I was five years old, I knew I wanted to be a makeup artist. My next-door neighbor, from the time I was five until I was 13, was Leo Lotito, and he was a makeup man. His daughter was my best friend and, every Halloween, we'd get made up and go out trick-or-treating. I would always want to be a witch or a ghoul or something horrible because I was obsessed with monster stuff. When I was young, I would watch the old *Universal Monsters* movies over and over, and I would make my parents take me to the movie theater and see all the scary movies that came out.

Once I got to high school, I took all the art classes, I worked on all the school plays and was the head of the makeup department there too. I loved doing all that, but I had always been told that I couldn't do it professionally because I was a woman. At the time, women were mainly hairdressers, and the men were running the makeup department. So, I just assumed that that was never going to happen for me.

When I got out of high school, I decided to go to a fashion merchandising school because I loved to make costumes. I got into that whole thing, and I started hanging out with a lot of people that did costuming and wardrobe. It was such a cutthroat business, and I didn't know if I could keep doing it. But I used to go to all these flea markets all the time too, and I had these two gay friends that owned this company called 'Glad Rags,' which was a vintage clothing store. I used to always go shopping with them where we'd go and buy all these gorgeous clothes.

They decided they wanted to open up another store, and asked me if I wanted to be their partner. So, at 18-years-old, I opened up a vintage clothing store with these two guys.

As Ve continued to prove to be a creative and stylish force to be reckoned with during the glam rock era, Neill had no idea that the world of special makeup effects would come back around in her life again soon enough.

I had gotten married pretty much a year after I got out of high school to a guy who was the tour manager for Vanilla Fudge and Dusty Springfield at that time. He introduced me to a lot of rock bands, and when I would go out picking, I would save clothes for all these popular British bands that would come into town, like Led Zeppelin. I would always save all these sparkly things for Robert Plant because he loved these sparkly little beaded jackets and things like that.

Then, this local band wanted me to make space suits for them, and they also had me doing their hair and their makeup too. I'd cut their hair, dye their hair crazy colors, and did crazy makeup on them. At one point, they asked me to make them big brains and pointed ears, which I didn't know how to do at the time. I always wanted to know how to do that, so now I have reason to.

It was at this time when I had separated from my husband and went down to the *Star Trek* convention in San Diego for some inspiration. I saw these guys walking around in these *Planet of the Apes* full-on makeup and costumes. They were great, movie-quality makeups. I went up to them, and I said, "Hey, guys. Where did you get those masks?" They looked at me indignantly, and they said, "These are not masks. These are makeups." I asked them where they got them, and they said that they had made them. That's when I asked them if they could teach me how to do that stuff.

Of course, the first thing they said to me was, "But, you're a girl." I replied with, "Yeah, I know. Isn't it fabulous?" So, a couple of the guys ended up taking me under their wing. One of them was Steve Neill, whose last name I took because I wound up staying with him for three years. We became an item, and he taught me how to do makeup. We were a great team because he didn't like being on the set and I didn't like being in the lab. So, for three years, I just started hanging out with all these effects guys. We started getting little jobs, and we'd hang out with Rick Baker in his garage. There were only a handful of us doing it back then, so we would just all cluster together. We all got to know each other and would switch up jobs if we needed to. So, that's how it all started for me.

During the mid-1970s, Neill found herself in the right place at the right time, when Hollywood had to open up their unions as a means of restocking their talent pool, and she was able to get enough days under her belt to become a fully-fledged member of the Makeup Artists and Hair Stylists Local 706 union, which is precisely when Ve's career began to skyrocket.

Fred Phillips is the makeup artist who did the original *Star Trek* TV series and *The Outer Limits*. He was very instrumental in helping me pursue becoming a union artist. In fact, before we got in the union, Steve and I would get these jobs all the time that we couldn't do, so we would call Fred up to go in and do these makeups for us.

One day, I get a call from Fred, and he says, "Hey, Ve, since I know you've done some work with Bill Shatner before, and they're going to make a *Star Trek* movie. Do you think you'd like to come work on it with me?" I almost fell off my chair at that point. I couldn't believe it. So, my first big union movie was *Star Trek: The Motion Picture*, and it was a fantastic experience because the director, Robert Wise, was a tremendous director. He'd never done anything like *Star Trek* before, but it was so beautifully done. It was such a thrill to be able to work with Fred, too.

When I went on to work on *The Incredible Shrinking Woman* for Joel [Schumacher], that all came from Rick Baker. He wanted me to be there to make sure that the gorilla always looked good, and be another makeup artist for other people, to do some of the character makeups on some of the other actors. Somewhere in the middle of the film, one of the other makeup artists walked up to me, who happened to be Fred Phillips' daughter, Janna Phillips, and she said she couldn't work on Lily [Tomlin] anymore because she was a handful.

I didn't know what to say, so I took over Lily's makeup, and that was how I started working with Lily. Lily and I got along really well, and she asked me to do *9 To 5* with her after that, and then I went and did all of her TV specials with her. The specials were great fun to do with her because they incorporated all her famous characters. I think it was something like six or seven years that I worked with Lily in all.

Neill also reteamed with filmmaker Joel Schumacher a few years later on his vampire-centric horror comedy, The Lost Boys, which ended up becoming a seminal film for fans growing up during the 1980s, and is still one of the most popular vampire films of all time.

Joel and I were kindred spirits. He was very flamboyant, so he was up for anything. Susan Becker, our costume designer, was amazing on *The Lost Boys* too. We were all on the same page and wanted to create these kickass rock and roll vampires, where we wanted everybody to want them and also want to be them. They were all completely different, so that they would appeal to different types. That way, you had your spectrum of characters there to appeal to everybody. They were all just the coolest.

Then, you have Jason Patric, who was also very sexy and Jami Gertz, who was fabulous. Plus, there were the Corey boys [Corey Haim and Corey Feldman] who were just as cute as they could be, so it was a great ensemble cast. It was just a perfect storm of talent. I don't think when it came out initially that it was a big hit. But, when *Lost Boys* came out on VHS, that's when it took off. It literally saved Warner Bros., because they were in the red when that movie came out, but by the time they put that thing out on video, it took them into the black.

It was on her next project that Ve Neill would find herself bringing home an Oscar for her stellar makeup creations on Tim Burton's madcap supernatural comedy, Beetlejuice. For the film, she transformed Michael Keaton into the film's titular "Ghost with the Most," creating one of the most inventive makeups of its, or any, time.

I had really wanted to work on *Beetlejuice* when I heard about it. Bo Welch, who was the production designer on *Beetlejuice,* came to me and he said, "Ve, I just got a script for this crazy movie, and you'd be perfect for it. You've got to get this movie." It just so happened that the production manager, Richard Hashimoto, had been the first AD on *9 To 5.* So, I called up Richard, and I asked him to get me an interview with this Tim Burton guy, who was still up-and-coming at the time.

I should have realized that I already had an in with Tim, because he had done *Pee-Wee's Big Adventure,* and I knew Paul Reubens from when he did *The Pee-Wee Show* at the Roxy. But I didn't think about calling Paul. I was more interested in production and how I was going to get in that way. So, between Bo and Richard, finally, I got an interview with Tim. When I met with him, he was working on the lot over at Culver City Studios in this old construction trailer. There were all these little sketches pinned up everywhere, with pictures of this character that looked like he was scouring trash cans. And meeting Tim himself was amazing to me. He was in his early twenties and looked like a complete freak with this crazy hair and a wrinkled shirt. I loved it. But we did our initial interview, and I think there was one more interview too, and then I got the job.

One of the first things we talked about were the characters that were in the afterlife. He wanted the people in the afterlife to have these pastel colors to them, like Necco Wafers, which are those dreadful candies that come in wax paper. But we ended up making them much brighter than that, or they wouldn't have shown up well onscreen.

Then, we started talking about the Beetlejuice character, and we got Michael in there, and started doing some stuff on him based on Tim's sketches. It didn't work because he looked too gritty, too realistic, and too creepy-looking. So, I took Michael back again, and I changed him again, but it still wasn't right. That's when Tim told me to go and do whatever I wanted to do and see what happens from there.

My thinking was, if all these other people are pastel colors, then Beetlejuice has to be that way too. So, I made him pastel yellow. Everybody thinks he was white, but his makeup base actually had yellow in it. We dyed that wig of his several different times until it finally came out like a dirty platinum blonde at the roots and, then, it became pale yellow with green tips. I put this makeup all over Michael's face, and I did these big dark circles around his eyes to make him look more cartoony, too.

I sent somebody off to a hobby store to buy me some crushed foam and some moss so I could make this guy look like he crawled out from underneath a rock. I'm going to glue all this stuff on him and make it look like he has moss growing out his face and do something really fun with this concept. Something else that was funny was that Michael wanted a fake nose for the character, but we didn't have any money to do prosthetics. My assistant, Steve LaPorte, had some swollen lips already made, so we put one on each side of his nose to make it look broken. And that's how the look of Beetlejuice came about. Tim was thrilled by what I came up with, too.

After earning her first Academy Award for makeup on Beetlejuice, Neill went on to work on yet another Oscar-caliber film, Warren Beatty's Dick Tracy adaptation, where she transformed Al Pacino into Alphonse "Big Boy" Caprice.

I love doing those kinds of character makeup. I like changing people into different people, which is why it's so much fun to do movies like *Beetlejuice* or *Dick Tracy*. That was fun because I got to sit in the trailer with Al Pacino for a few days and we tried different noses and chins and cheeks and foreheads on him to figure out his character, Big Boy.

Once we figured out the character, we did a mock-up makeup of what we had available to us. Then, John Caglione Jr. and Doug Drexler, the makeup designers for the film, went and re-sculpted everything for him. At this point, they made the prosthetics designed especially for him. Al is such a nice guy too. I would get him in the chair early in the morning, and half of the time, he would fall asleep. When he would wake up, he'd start grunting and gritting his teeth, immediately becoming this hideous guy that I had turned him into. There were a few days when I was taking spaghetti out of his lower lip after lunch, but that's a perfect example of the intimacy that's between an artist and the people that they work with. You have to be willing to step up to do these things that, in any other circumstance, you would never have to do.

After I worked on *Dick Tracy*, I did *Flatliners* with Joel, and then, I did *Edward Scissorhands*, so it was great to be working with Tim once again. And also, I was excited to be working with the lovely Stan Winston, too. When I went in to do the test makeup, that character was pretty well figured out by the time I got there. Edward's a pretty easy character to do because he's a guy with scars on his face and dark circles around his eyes, like all of Tim's other characters.

There were subtleties that needed to be worked out because we wanted Edward to be an empathetic character. One of the subtle things that I did, which I don't know that anybody knew about except for Johnny [Depp] and I, was that I would change the shape of the darkness around his eyes, to give him a different look. Like when I wanted him to look sad or perplexed, I would make those eyes have a dip in the eyebrow and go up, like that sad clown look.

Another one that was noticeable but nobody seemed to pick up on at the time, was at the end when Edward kills Anthony Michael Hall's character in the castle. I gave him a furious look with these eyes where I painted them differently, so he looked very angry. It was something that was so subtle though, where it would just be millimeters of a difference to the shape. That's why it's so important to work closely with your actor when you're developing these characters so that they can live in there. They're the ones that have to make themselves comfortable inside their character. So, it's crucial that the actors feel connected with their makeup. We help them become those characters, and every time that I worked with him, Johnny always embraced the makeup process.

I was lucky to get to work with Tim and Stan again on *Batman Returns*. They came up with the design of The Penguin together, and then I worked with Stan to hash out the makeup to make it perfect. We did a test, but I knew we were going to have to rework parts of it because I could see where the wrinkles were going to be by the way he moved his face. So, Stan had his guys go back in and make some adjustments, and that makeup came out beautifully. I just loved working with Stan. He was fantastic.

As far as everything else, they let me design all the clown makeups and the circus freaks. When it came to doing Christopher Walken, Tim wanted him to be dramatic and over-the-top. So he had this white hair, and when I would make up Chris without his wig on, he almost looked like a drag queen because he had so much makeup on. But Tim was great about letting me drive all the rest of the makeups, and because you have all these very theatrical characters, it was cool, and it all worked so well together.

Ve kept busy throughout the early-to-mid '90s making an array of memorable characters on a variety of genre-spanning projects, including Hoffa, Mrs. Doubtfire, Ed Wood, both Batman Forever and Batman & Robin, as well as two wildly different sci-fi films, Mars Attacks! and Gattaca.

Right after *Batman Returns*, I worked on *Hoffa*, which had a lot of makeups in it, and I ended up being nominated for both *Hoffa* and *Batman Returns* that next year. It was Danny DeVito who brought me on to *Hoffa*, and he actually stole me off the end of *Batman Returns* to do it. There was a slight overlap in filming, and Danny didn't want to do the film without me. Then, Greg Cannom brought me onto *Mrs. Doubtfire*. The first test that we did, we were up in San Francisco, and I let Greg lead the paint job because it was his makeup. When he was done, Mrs. Doubtfire looked more like a fat, old man than how an old lady would look. So, Greg let me do a test makeup that looked much more like an old woman wearing makeup, and that's what we ended up using in the movie.

That was one of those makeups where certain design concepts came into play. It had to look enough like something Robin Williams' character could do himself. He wouldn't have a lot of freckles and old age spots because that would complicate things, but it shouldn't look like fresh skin either. That makeup was a case of making sure that it worked in service to the story. You have to think about this character and his world and put all of those things into your makeup, because it has to look like it lives in that world. All those little things do matter in the end.

When I went on to work with Tim again for *Ed Wood*, it was an amazing film, but I had no idea if anyone was ever going to see it because it was so weird. I had a great time creating all those characters in black and white because we had to rethink how we did all the makeups. We had to do a completely different approach because black and white was such a different animal for us to be dealing with. For Martin Landau, who was Bela Lugosi, Rick did the original test makeup on him, and he looked fantastic except for the fact that he looked too healthy. So, when I did the test makeup for the camera, Tim told me I had to darken his eyes because he still didn't look sick at all.

It was funny because when Rick came into the makeup trailer, he said to me, "God damn it, Ve. I knew the minute I gave you this makeup, you were going to put black circles around his eyes." It was hilarious, and both Martin and I had to explain to him that it was Tim who wanted those dark circles. But it was such a great experience working on *Ed Wood* and getting to recreate Tor Johnson and Vampira, and all these other characters.

George ["The Animal" Steele] was such a sweetheart, too. I used to have these great Halloween parties, but this one year, I couldn't have my party, but I still wanted to do something. So, I asked George if I could make him up as Tor and I made up a whole bunch of other people as different characters, like Edward Scissorhands too. We shut down the street that I lived on, and we had people running around scaring kids, and George was wandering around like Tor. It was a blast, and he was so sweet about it.

And winning an Oscar for *Ed Wood* was a total surprise for me. I didn't even get a fancy outfit because I was convinced that *Frankenstein* was going to win since I didn't think anyone had even seen our movie. I was so shocked when they called our names, and both Yolanda [Toussieng] and I had Rick talk because we didn't even know what to say. It totally blew me away.

When it came time to reteam with Joel Schumacher once again for both of his Batman sequels, Ve was thrilled at the prospect of getting to collaborate yet again with her now-longtime friend and kindred spirit.

Joel always had this wild streak to him, so we had a great time doing his *Batman* movies. For *Forever*, Rick Baker came in and designed Two-Face, and I did the applications for him. Also, Rick made the mask for Jim Carrey's character, The Riddler, but they let me design the coloring on Jim Carrey's stuff because he was supposed to be very flashy and colorful.

Then, we split up the girls. I did Debi Mazar's makeup, and Jim's makeup artist did Drew Barrymore's makeup, and they were fantastic. They would come in at four in the morning because they didn't want anybody else doing their makeups. So, they would come in, have us do their makeup and, then sit around while we did the boys afterward. We also got to create all these cool Black Light characters that were in the alleys and that was a blast. Those makeups were so much fun, and I had the makeup trailer set up with black light so that all of the artists could see what they were doing because the colors were reactive. And when we went on to do *Batman & Robin*, I did all of Poison Ivy's makeups. That was a fun and creative challenge because she had like a dozen different looks in that movie, so we got to do a lot with her.

Near the end of the 1990s, Ve reunited with Stan Winston once again on the meta sci-fi comedy Galaxy Quest, which fit perfectly into her wheelhouse as a genre fan.

Getting to be a part of *Galaxy Quest* was the best, because it was quite literally my type of movie, especially since I used to go to those *Star Trek* conventions. I loved making all those hokey makeups on the conventioneers and Alan Rickman was such a trip. I just adored working with him. Stan gave me that head to do, and I knew it had to have a luminescent quality to it to accentuate the design.

Then, I worked with Stan when we did the lead alien, Sarris. Stan had developed a new technology where the actor could operate his mouth using this gizmo that he had attached to his tongue. There was a lot of technology that was put into effect to operate that character. Another fun thing about *Galaxy Quest* was that when we were testing Sigourney [Weaver], they were trying to give her a different look, and I suggested making her a blonde. They all looked at me like I was crazy. I knew it would work though, because Sigourney is such a beautiful woman, so I asked them to let me do a test makeup on her where we'd give her a blonde wig to see if it would work.

All I did was slightly change her skin tone to a more neutral tone and put this gorgeous makeup on her, which she absolutely loved, and then finished it off with the blonde wig. We pranced her out to the producers, and they immediately went, "Oh, my God. Okay. Yes. Go for it." And to this day, I still feel like that's the most glamorous Sigourney's ever looked in a movie. She's stunning.

Heading into the new century, Ve Neill had another opportunity to collaborate again with fellow effects legend Stan Winston on Steven Spielberg's A.I.: Artificial Intelligence where she was tasked with turning actor Jude Law into the charismatic Gigolo Joe.

We had a lot of time to work on Jude's makeup. I think we were doing R&D on that film for five or six months, off and on, and Stan and I tested so many different makeups out on Jude. We tried gelatin prosthetics on him, we tried silicone prosthetics on him, we tried foam, we worked down the line with full-face, partial-face, we tried everything.

We had just done this one makeup that was just so heavy, and I was sitting in the room with Stan and Spielberg, and I said, "You guys, you have an actor that's pretty much perfect already. Why are we covering him up? If we sharpen up his jawline, he will look like a mannequin, and it'll work great." They both agreed, and Stan went back, and he made me this beautiful, really tiny jawline prosthetic. He was concerned because he had no idea how I was going to blend it, but I told Stan to leave that to me to figure out, and that's what I did.

I just developed a way of painting Jude, layer upon layer upon layer. There were probably four different layers of makeup on there and highlights and shadowing and airbrushing. It was a lot of work, but when he was done, Jude looked exactly like a mannequin, and everyone was happy. So, we took that look and followed suit with everybody else. I also did one other character, Jane, and we used the same technique on her.

A few years later, Ve was brought into the fold on one of Disney's most ambitious projects at the time, the family-friendly adventure Pirates of the Caribbean: The Curse of the Black Pearl, which was based on the popular attraction at the studio's namesake theme parks. Not only would Black Pearl launch a major film franchise, but also gave its star, Johnny Depp, yet another highly memorable character that would go on to become a part of the pantheon of modern pop culture.

We had a rough start on *Pirates* because the studio was anxious about the way Johnny looked. Johnny and I had worked on this character, and we talked about having the dark eyes, and I said, "Well, I think we should do it like you're like a Bedouin, because they put the black around their eyes to inhibit the reflection of the sun." To me, Jack would do this to reflect the sun and the sea. I told Johnny that we were going to tan him up, make him look scruffy, and because I had a considerable trade beads collection, I found all these cool trinkets and beads and bones that we could put into his dreads.

But then, Johnny went off and did his teeth, and when he came back, all of his teeth in the front were gold and silver and the studio completely freaked out. They told him he had to lose them, but Johnny said he was keeping them, so he moved them off to the sides of his mouth as a compromise. I don't think they understood what he was going to do with that character, but after a few days watching him in action, they realized that he was onto something. And of course, Johnny was right on the money with what he wanted to do, because Captain Jack Sparrow is now so iconic.

On the second *Pirates*, when we had all the cannibals, we got to do all these cool makeups, and that was really, really fun for me. The only difficult thing was dealing with the different locations and getting to them. We were climbing up hills and going into jungles and dealing with this extreme heat while on the set, which wasn't easy. I think it was during the third *Pirates* when Johnny had already begun rehearsing for *Sweeney Todd*, and I was able to come over and work on him for that one, too. I do remember him being pretty nervous at the time.

But I think what they've done with the *Pirates* series is great, and what's even more fun for me is knowing that I was behind this character that has gone on to have a life of its own outside of the movies. I think it's so cool that people like certain characters enough that they want to emulate them and bring them back to life in their own ways. That's the greatest compliment to me as an artist.

Neill also had the opportunity to lend her immeasurable talents to another major movie franchise when she was entrusted with creating the impressively striking looks for Elizabeth Banks' character, Effie Trinket, throughout the entire Hunger Games series.

In the first film, director Gary Ross was adamant about wanting me to make Effie look ugly and scary-looking. But no matter what I did, it didn't read, for some reason. She just looked like she had too much makeup on and these dark lips. I really wanted to make her look pretty, but Gary didn't want to go in that direction, so I just followed Gary's lead and did what he told me to do. That's why, all of her looks in that first film, even though she has fabulous hair and clothes, there's still this edge to how Effie looked.

So, When *Catching Fire* started up, I asked Francis [Lawrence, director] if I could make Elizabeth more attractive. He gave me the go-ahead because to him, she's different. She's changed. She likes these kids now, so changing her looks worked perfectly in service to the story because of her change of heart. So, that allowed me to step it up and make her look pretty, and I had a ball on

Catching Fire because she had like nine different looks that I thought were all so spectacular.

With three Oscars, numerous other accolades and awards and more than 40 years of experience in Hollywood, Ve Neill is one of the most decorated special makeup effects artists of all time. Her enduring legacy includes numerous quintessential characters that have become pop culture icons and a stunningly impressive resume featuring more than 90 credits to date.

When you really love your job, and you are good at it, and you're easy to work with, those are the keys to finding success in this business. It's about being a good department head and making sure that everything runs well in every aspect of your job. I want the actors to be happy, I want production to be happy, and if there's something they need from me, I want them to know that I am going to do whatever it takes to make it happen. I think it's that mentality that has kept me working for so long now, and that's why people enjoy working with me.

I am slowing down now, though. I like doing smaller films like *A Star is Born*, and I enjoyed working with both Bradley [Cooper] and Lady Gaga. And recently, I became the Director of Education at the Cinema Makeup School. I'm working with young artists, trying to give them what they can't be taught in school, which is the experience that can only come from somebody who's been on a movie set. I want to provide them with the history of movie-making and the history of makeup. The roots and how it started and why we are where we are and how we got there. I feel that that's something that's missing in the education of these young artists these days. I want to show them all the people that I looked up to when I was starting, that made me want to become a makeup artist.

The one thing that people always ask me is, "What's the payoff for you other than the paycheck?" And I always say, "Whenever I go to the movie theater, and I see an actor become the character that I helped him become, and disappear into a role, that's my payoff." Because, to me, there's nothing quite like the feeling of satisfaction that comes from seeing a character that you helped create come to life.

Edward Scissorhands - Johnny Depp and Ve Neill

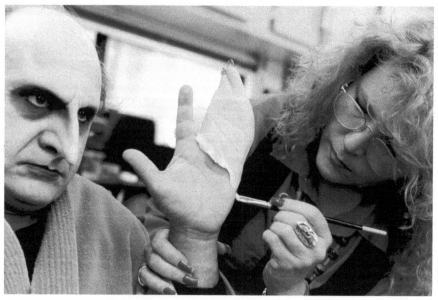

Batman Returns - Danny Devito and Ve Neill

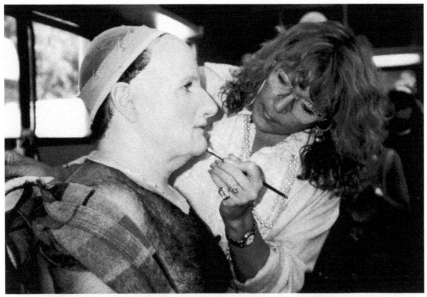

Mrs. Doubtfire - Robin Williams and Ve Neill

Ed Wood - Martin Landau and Ve Neill

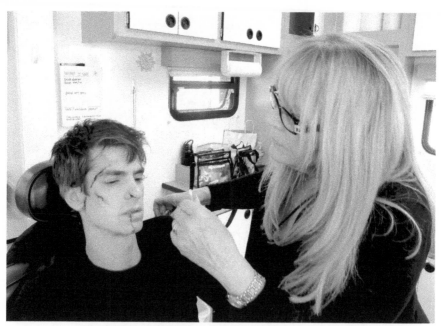

The Amazing Spider-Man - Andrew Garfield and Ve Neill

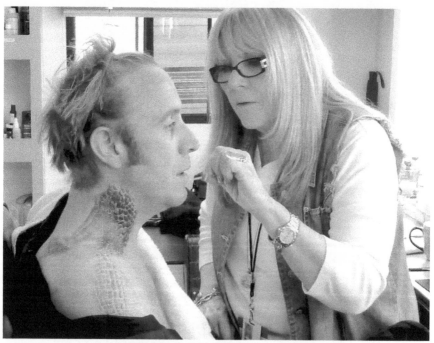

The Amazing Spider-Man – Rhys Ifans and Ve Neill

The Hunger Games - Jennifer Lawrence and Ve Neill

The Hunger Games - Ve Neill and Sam Claflin

Johnny Depp Presents 2016 Lifetime Achievement Award to Ve Neill

Conversation with...
ALEC GILLIS

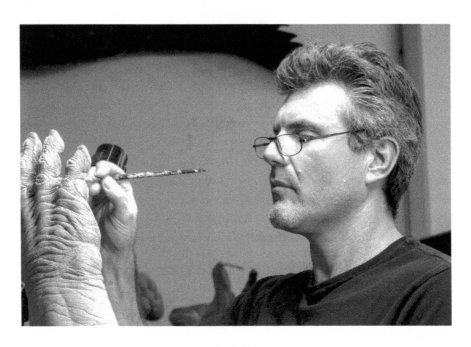

Oscar Nominated Special Effects Makeup Artist

Tremors (1990)
Alien 3 (1992)
Death Becomes Her (1992)
Starship Troopers (1997)
The X Files (1998)
Stephen King's IT Chapter One (2017)
Stephen King's IT Chapter Two (2019)

While he may not have foreseen just where his artistic tendencies would eventually take him in life, Alec Gillis realized early on that there was a creative streak inside him that was just waiting to be unleashed.

Even back in kindergarten, I knew I was a creative kid. We would sculpt things out of clay and the teacher had a kiln. So even back then I was sculpting crazy things, like little *Flintstones* houses and these weird creations. At that stage, when you get a lot of positive parental and sibling feedback, it just encourages you, and you start thinking to yourself, *Well, this is who I am.* It becomes part of your identity, and I realize now how fortunate I was, because not everyone gets that kind of parental support.

My father was in the Marine Corps, but he was also an insurance salesman and an artist, too. He was always drawing and he was very interested in special effects. My first recollection of him having a conversation with me about special effects was when I was about eight or nine and he was explaining to me how stop motion worked, and how King Kong was actually a miniature. That fascinated me.

He also told stories of people he had met in his days in New York City when he was selling insurance to people at NBC. These would be special effects artists for TV shows, as well as Dick Smith. He sold Dick Smith a life insurance policy. So he got to see life masks and clay and he had these tales about the fantastic world that these guys inhabited. That always was very, very attractive to me.

When I was around thirteen years old, I saw a magazine interview with Ray Harryhausen, and that's when I saw that one person made all these great monsters I loved. That's when it clicked with me: *This is a job? Adults do this? That's what I want to do. Why would I want to do anything else?* There was no other choice for me, really.

Before he could get busy making monsters, Gillis set out to learn as much as he could about the art of bringing creatures and memorable characters to life in front of the camera.

I started off doing animated films with G.I. Joe dolls or whatever I could find, and I even tried to sculpt in clay on their faces so I could manipulate them and what have you. There wasn't a lot of information out there when I was growing up.

There were some little glimpses behind the scenes, like a *LIFE* magazine article that showed Roddy McDowall getting his makeup applied, so I was always hungry for more information. Then I discovered *Famous Monsters of Filmland* and I spent a lot of time reading those. Any time there was any kind of a behind-the-scenes look into how a makeup or a stop-motion puppet was created, that was like gold to me.

When I was just getting into high school, there were two magazines I found: one was called *FXRH* and the other was *Cinemagic*. There were only four issues of *FXRH*, but it really went in depth about what Ray Harryhausen's techniques were, how stop-motion puppets were made, and how to create and work with molds, too. *Cinemagic* was cool because it was more fan-oriented. It was more about what amateurs were doing to attack problems, and it wasn't just about how to make a rubber mask or how to make a puppet creature—it also had camera information and thoughts about double exposure and trick photography, foreground, miniatures, things like that. *Cinemagic* gave you a total filmmaking perspective on effects and that always appealed to me. As much as I love the specifics of the technique—whether it's makeup effects or animatronics or miniatures—it's always, to me, about, "How do you incorporate that into the bigger picture of telling a story on the big screen?"

As Gillis continued to sharpen his skill set throughout high school, his hobby evolved into a career before he even knew it.

As I got better, I took over my mom's garage and turned that into my workshop. As my work improved and became more sophisticated, people began to realize I was serious about special effects. I was nineteen and a friend of my sister was working for Roger Corman. He saw what I was doing and said, "Hey, I should get you an interview with Roger because we're working on this movie called *Battle Beyond the Stars.*" I agreed, but I was really nervous because these guys were professionals and not all of my stuff was all that professional.

I asked him if I could bring a friend, just because I had met this guy recently who was five or six years older than me who was into similar stuff, and he had a great portfolio. I was hoping that might help bolster my chances. That guy, of course, was James Cameron, who back then was delivering books for a school district and had only done a short film, *Xenogenesis*, at that point.

Jim and I interviewed with Chuck Comisky, Robert Skotak, and Dennis Skotak, who were in a model shop in Tarzana at the time, getting ready to start the miniature photography for *Battle Beyond the Stars*. The movie hadn't been shot yet and it took them about six months to get back to us. I thought,

Well, that obviously didn't pan out, but then we finally got the call that they were hiring us as a team.

We commuted from Orange County to Venice every day to go work at Hammond Lumber, which was this old lumberyard Corman had purchased. *Battle* was a great opportunity for me, as I was able to do a ton of different things ranging from working with motion-control systems to building miniature spaceships, and the work was really formative for me. I loved that feeling of making a movie in a big, giant room in a warehouse. Over in one corner are the miniatures and creatures, and then you have the sculptures over there in the other corner. It's a very efficient and contained way to make a movie, and I loved it.

Battle Beyond the Stars became a springboard for my career. I got to work on a few more films, and right when Cameron was getting ready to start *The Terminator*, I got hired to work on *Friday the 13th: The Final Chapter*. Before that, I was going to UCLA [University of California, Los Angeles] film school, but I was already a working professional, and I would take the quarter off of school to work with Corman on another movie so that I could save the money up to go back to school. Eventually, it got to a point where I was saying, "Why am I doing this? How many more film theory classes am I going to sit through?" I became very aware of the gap between the real world and the world of college, and it wore thin on me. That's when I left.

But it did not hurt me in any way to not work on *The Terminator*. While I had just met Stan Winston through Jim and would probably have preferred to work on *The Terminator* at the time, I think Stan appreciated that I did not jump ship. He knew I was a man of my word and he knew he could rely on me in the future.

To work on *Friday the 13th* [*The Final Chapter*], and to do those kinds of makeup effects with that particular group, was a great experience. Originally, I started working on it for Greg Cannom, but then he left the show and Tom Savini came on. To work with Tom, who came from a completely different background and was a self-taught makeup artist, was very illuminating because I had really thought of him as a cowboy up until that point. I didn't have a real appreciation for Tom's background and what he did when he came into this industry.

Tom always had this knack for being able to problem-solve and come up with ingenious solutions. That speaks volumes about Tom's abilities as an artist. It also showed me that there's more than one way to do something, and if you get entrenched in any narrow sort of "right way" to do something when it comes to the world of filmmaking, you run the risk of limiting yourself.

Back in the '80s when Dick Smith's course came out, I had this conversation with Tom on how it was a valuable learning tool, but the downside to the course was that people considered it as the *Bible*. It was the immutable word of the great Dick Smith, and they were afraid to do things differently than how they saw it done in the course, and Tom agreed.

The thing that drives special effects, especially at that time, is that artists have to always be willing to experiment and come up with their own way to improve, to keep the craft moving forward and make it evolve. Nothing evolves if you just have a single way of doing things, and Tom was the epitome of evolving in his work. He was always coming up with something new, and I've always admired people who have that kind of rogue spirit to them.

After completing his work on Friday the 13th: The Final Chapter, Alec got the opportunity to join a makeup team led by Greg Cannom for Ron Howard's sci-fi fantasy film, Cocoon (1985). It was another project that gave Gillis the chance to learn from one of the industry's most innovative makeup artists.

In my early career, it was really awesome how with every different work situation, I was able to learn something wholly unique from that person. It was the same with Greg. He was a phenomenal artist and showed me a lot about the almost impressionistic approach to effects. He didn't over-fixate on detail, and was more interested in the overall impact of the design and how that could help those details come out.

With *Cocoon*, Greg was very bold with his colors, and he was a very gutsy guy when it came to those kinds of decisions. We did a lot of last-minute work on *Cocoon*, fixing and changing things that I honestly didn't think were going to work. Of course, because Greg is a genius, it all worked beautifully because of his ability to understand how the camera would perceive the colors. I always likened Greg to an old-school matte painter, because those guys had an amazing understanding of what would show up on film and what wouldn't, and that was a very valuable experience to me.

Alec continued to explore the realms of cinematic science fiction when he came aboard Stan Winston's crew for Tobe Hooper's Invaders from Mars, which would lead to several years' worth of work for Gillis.

By the time I got to Stan, I already had quite a well-rounded experience, from the Corman film school to working with Greg Cannom and Tom Savini. Plus, I was never pigeonholed into one job, so I had done a bit of everything. I had a very broad base, a very disparate set of experiences, and I think Stan liked that.

At some point prior to *The Terminator*, Stan basically cleaned out his crew and started over. He was never specific about it, but I think he was trying to build his legacy and he was finding it difficult to do that with guys who would always be second-guessing him. So he brought in a crop of fresh faces: Tom Woodruff Jr., John Rosengrant, Shane Mahan, and Richard Landon. I came in a little bit after that, and so did Rick Lazzarini, and we were all there to support the boss' vision.

Because of my varied background, I was able to segue over nicely to be a valuable guy for Stan, and that's when all of us younger guys got a taste of the A-level movies. It was a great, exciting time to be working for Stan. *Invaders from Mars* was a valuable experience for me, too, because it peaked in terms of creating the drones and doing those effects while *Aliens* was coming in. That was my first taste of having to handle two shows at once, and two big shows at that. While we're painting a drone over on one side, Matt Rose is off in another corner sculpting an Alien tail. Everyone just divided up into teams and tackled everything we needed to get done.

Invaders started shooting when Stan and the other guys had just packed up to go to London, and he left me behind to manage the on-set duties on *Invaders from Mars* while he took the other guys to really start getting into the build of *Aliens*. He trusted me, and that was amazing. That's one thing I took from working with Stan. The other was that nothing was off limits. If he wanted to make something, he would. It was never too big. He would always say, "We're going to figure out a way," and he'd plow into it with enthusiasm and energy. I always remember his can-do attitude to any project.

Shortly after wrapping their back-to-back sci-fi projects, Winston and his crew were given the opportunity to collaborate on a film that would celebrate the very creatures responsible for most of them falling in love with genre movies and special effects in the first place: Fred Dekker's The Monster Squad. While they weren't initially happy with Universal's decision to not grant the likeness rights to the five classic monsters— Dracula, The Wolf Man, The Mummy, The Creature (a.k.a. Gill-man), and Frankenstein's monster—they would base their characters on, their excitement far outweighed any disappointments, as Universal's decision ended up being a huge positive for them as artists.

We were all excited when Stan told us about *Monster Squad*. We were just thrilled to get that job, because who wouldn't be? At first, it was a bit shocking that Universal wasn't going to grant the rights to these characters, but at the same time, that gave us the opportunity to pay homage and still do something fresh, too. And because that was pre-Internet, we didn't have to contend with the early negativity. If we had tried to do that now, people would respond with something like, "Oh, Stan Winston thinks he's better than Jack Pierce, eh?" It was nice to have nothing hanging over us going into those designs beyond just the basics.

We flew into it by the seat of our pants. And because we were taking a chance anyway, we figured we might as well have fun with it. If you get too timid, that's probably when you're going to fall down, so we knew we had to be bold with our designs. Plus, this was also in the day when the makeup effects designer was the main creative force and you didn't have to run it through a studio where everyone has to sign off on everything. These creatures were purely the vision of Stan Winston, along with the Director, Fred Dekker. And that's how it should be.

Once production on The Monster Squad wrapped, Gillis was at a crossroads, with his mentor continuing to explore his career as a director following the release of his first feature film, Pumpkinhead.

We got to a point where we had done *Pumpkinhead*, that had turned out great and Stan was moving on to make *A Gnome Named Gnorm*. Stan had made an industry announcement that he was no longer doing effects for other people, and that he was only going to do them for his own movies that he was directing. It was the perfect display of the bravado and confidence of Stan Winston, because if anyone could have done it, it would have been Stan.

But Tom [Woodruff Jr.] and I were looking around going, *Hmm... we won't be able to work with the Steven Spielbergs or Robert Zemeckises or James Camerons anymore,* which was kind of a bummer. It would be great to see Stan get his directing career off the ground, but they were probably going to be smaller-budgeted movies where we wouldn't really have a chance to strut our stuff as much.

At that same time, Tom and I had co-written a script that was getting interest, and we thought that maybe this was the perfect opportunity to get that project going. We could bring all the creature effects back to Stan and then we could give back to him. When we pitched that to Stan, he said, "Where I need you guys most is out there making monsters." And we were like, "Well, that doesn't really fit with our overall plans." Stan saw us as the guys that did the creature stuff, and honestly, it didn't really make sense to me at the time. But I realized over the years that it was him giving us his blessing to go out there and make our own way.

We left Stan on good terms, but then a writers' strike happened and the industry geared down for a while, which put everything we had been planning on hold. That was a good lesson, actually, because we realized it's not quite that easy to just go out there and make a movie. We had to figure out how to keep ourselves going. We did a couple of episodes of *Monsters*, the Laurel Entertainment show, and we did a couple of other projects, too. We ended up having to sublet a space from Rick [Lazzarini], and it was just Tom and I working over there because there was no ADI [Amalgamated Dynamics, Inc.] back then.

Out of the blue, Gale Anne Hurd called us up and said, "I have this script called *Tremors* and I want you to look at it." We still hadn't formed a formal company yet, so we did that while we were breaking down the script and having meetings with Ron Underwood, Steve Wilson, and Brent Maddock. As things were moving forward, we were like, "Oh, this movie is really going to happen. Where on Earth are we going to build this stuff?" In the meantime, they kept asking to come and see our shop, but Tom and I would always just offer to meet them halfway because we were keeping the fact that we had no home a secret. So Marie Callender's in Toluca Lake was our go-to "office" for a while.

Once we got our first check, we put a deposit down on a building that was being built. But, of course, it never got finished in time. So we had to pull out of that. Luckily, we were able to sublet some space from Howard Berger, Greg Nicotero, and Bob Kurtzman at KNB [EFX Group]. We offered them some work, too, so we had those guys sculpting on *Tremors*, and when we found another building, that's when we were able to move. We basically had no equipment at the time, and even though *Tremors* was not a big-budget movie, we used every dime of it to get us established as a shop and buy what we needed. And that was the start of Amalgamated Dynamics. It was our first big job as ADI, and there couldn't have been a better one to start the company.

With ADI off and running, Alec and Tom found themselves returning to some familiar territory for their next project, David Fincher's Alien 3, a sequel much smaller and more intimate in scope and scale compared to its immediate predecessor, Aliens.

Alien 3 was a huge moment for us, and it came just in the nick of time, because we were out of work for seven months after *Tremors*. The fact that we inherited the *Alien* series was pretty amazing. I think the reason we got it was that they went to Stan, but he said he wouldn't do the movie unless he could direct it. So it became a fantastic opportunity for us.

In the first read of the script, I was a little disappointed that there wasn't something on the scale of the Alien Queen from *Aliens*, because we really wanted to do something big and bold. Tom and I both thought it was an odd choice that they were retracting back to the model of the first *Alien*, but that was kind of the vibe that they had going into part three. People had enjoyed *Aliens*, but they missed the spirit of Ridley [Scott]'s movie, where it was a single creature in a contained environment. It seemed odd to us to just kill off those remaining characters from *Aliens* and take it all in a new direction, and the film was certainly met with that kind of reaction when it was released, but it's cool to see that *Alien 3* has gained popularity over the years.

While in pre-production on Alien 3, the sequel's original director, Vincent Ward, departed the project, ultimately scrapping some of the initial design ideas for the film.

Vincent Ward actually left before we started building anything, so thankfully it wasn't like we had to switch horses mid-race. The ideas that were in the Vincent Ward versions of the script were much more risky than what you see now. He was taking more chances with it. He saw the Alien as a metaphor for the devil, and a lot of his influences were medieval influences. At one point, he had a woodcut of the devil with a human face on its ass, and he told us that he wanted to do that. He wanted Sigourney Weaver's face on the Alien's ass. That was a really, really risky concept.

After he left the show, a lot of those medieval influences were minimized; there are still some in there with the monks, but that was only a small part of what Vincent wanted to do. From what I heard, there was a prison movie that [20th Century] Fox liked and they thought they could try and turn it into an *Alien* movie, and now what you see is a blending of those concepts.

So when Fincher came on, it cleared the way for *Alien 3* to become a bit more of a straight sci-fi movie that fit more cleanly into the *Alien* legacy.

The one thing that I always appreciated about Fox is that they did make interesting choices in directors when it came to the *Alien* sequels. They brought in James Cameron, who had two movies under his belt. Fincher became David Fincher with the release of *Alien 3*, and then you have Jean-Pierre Jeunet, who did *The City of Lost Children* and *Delicatessen*, directing [*Alien:*] *Resurrection*. We got a chance to work with some unique talents with very strong voices on those films, and that doesn't always happen.

While Gillis may not have fully understood Jeunet's wildly evocative stylistic choices for the fourth installment in the Alien series, he had to embrace them nonetheless.

We weren't in a position to question anyone's decisions, because our job is to make the director happy and give him quality creature work that will help support his film. That's on any film, not just *Resurrection*. But I do think there were some decisions made on that one that were just a little too outside of H.R. Giger's realm, like the Newborn Alien. Of all the things in that movie, he [Jeunet] was most passionate about and had the most to say about the design of the Newborn.

Jean-Pierre had his reasons and his own logic behind why it should look like that, but it was such an out-of-left-field approach that it became this freakish sideline character and was a huge departure from the visual language that Giger established at the beginning. But at the end of the day, my job is to make the director happy. Sometimes you're doing corrective design and making the best of a situation.

At the same time they were working on Alien: Resurrection, ADI was also handling another ambitious sci-fi project, Paul Verhoeven's Starship Troopers. To Gillis, while both directors were visionaries behind the camera, their approaches couldn't be more different from each other.

Jean-Pierre is very soft-spoken, very considerate, and has this quiet sense of humor, so he was a little more predictable to manage in terms of where his passions were and his methodology. Paul is a genius of a completely different mold. He's very passionate, and when his blood boils, he lets his passion loose, and then he calms down just like that. Coming into the project, Phil Tippett warned us in advance and told us, "Paul will put you through some agony, but he appreciates that you hang with it and that you stay on the job." I just tried to remain as unflappable as possible. Paul's energy level was amazing for however old he was [late fifties] while we did *Troopers*, because we were all twenty-five years younger than him and he was outworking us all every single day.

For *Starship Troopers*, Phil's team designed those creatures, and our job was to execute and bring them into the real world. It was a much more manageable project than *Alien: Resurrection*, where we had eggs, Chestbursters, death effects, Aliens, clones, and other makeup effects, too. For *Troopers*, we were dealing with essentially three different [types of] bugs—the Brain Bug, the Warrior Bugs, and the Arkellian Sand Beetles—and then we had to create variations of those designs. Where it got grueling was on set, because of the size and weight of everything and the fact that we were out in the middle of the desert.

Alec, Tom, and the rest of the ADI crew reteamed with Verhoeven a few years later for his horror film Hollow Man, the director's modernized and deeply terrifying take on H.G. Wells' classic story The Invisible Man. Verhoeven's iteration featured Kevin Bacon in the titular role, and the project did a brilliant job blending ADI's ambitious practical effects with cutting-edge visuals spearheaded by Scott E. Anderson.

When we first read the script for *Hollow Man*, we were like, "Holy crap!" We knew immediately that this was going to take a tableful of people to pull off. The logistics of determining where the overlap between practical and digital effects was going to be were monumental. There seemed to be something on every single page. It came down to both teams having to sit down and figure out the best ways we could compliment each other. While a lot of those effects were done via a motion-capture suit, we still created a lot of skin elements and other effects to keep us busy.

One thing Paul was very specific about on *Hollow Man* was that he really wanted a lot of those gore elements to be practical. There's the scene where Kevin Bacon goes into the cage and he grabs that dog and kills it because it was barking. We were able to use a stunt dog from the movie *Michael* for that, and he just bashed around as we had a tube running out of him, squirting hot slime everywhere. And for Kevin's burns, we had makeup pieces glued to his black leotard to help out Scott and his guys.

Then you have other fully practical elements like Tom [Woodruff Jr.] in the gorilla suit. When they did the infrared scene with the heat-vision goggles, we just parked Tom under a bunch of 2K lights, where we would heat him up for about forty seconds, and then he'd run over and be hot enough to do the scene that way. Nowadays, people would probably leap to a digital solution for that, but it was so direct and straightforward to us, so we did it as a practical effect.

Something else that I thought was really cool about *Hollow Man* was how different it was from *Starship Troopers*. *Troopers* was this larger-than-life movie about bug aliens, and this was much more about horror on a human level with this creepy, crazy guy who happens to be invisible and does terrible things to other people. That intimacy creates a very different kind of movie experience, and I enjoyed that both films were so uniquely different.

While Gillis is a believer in the idea that digital effects do have their time and place, he found out on Universal's 2011 prequel to The Thing that too much digital work can not only negatively impact a film's success, but can also visually destroy one's hard work at the same time.

When we heard the movie was first out there, the producers reached out to us, sent us the script, and we read it and were like, "This is pretty good." Of course, our first question was, "Well, just how much of this version of *The Thing* is going to end up digital?" Because these days, that's just the way things go.

So, we had the conversation with the producing team, and we asked them how they saw us fitting in, and they told us that they wanted the movie to be 80% practical. My heart literally skipped a beat when I heard that. It was amazing news. The producers told us that they wanted to honor the legacy of the effects that Rob Bottin created on the original, so all the digital people would really be doing was just helping our work. We thought that these people were exactly talking our language, and that excited us.

Tom and I started designing. Everything we were doing was carefully plotted out with the input of Matthijs van Heijningen, the Director. He wanted an aesthetic that felt contemporary but still in line with what Bottin did on the original *Thing*. What struck me as how different this process was on *The Thing* was that the feeling of pure joy when it came to having effects in the movie just seemed to be lost as time went on. We would get notes that would say, "This needs to look more dangerous." They weren't interested in the subtlety of what Rob did on the original, the creeping weirdness he was able to establish. They just wanted to go from zero to one hundred, and Matthijs was stuck in the middle. He was a first-time [feature film] director and he had to pick his battles.

When we built all of our stuff and took it up to Toronto, we had an idea that something bad might be coming. But we started shooting and we all loved it, so everything was going great. There's always the safety net of digital whenever you shoot now, where they scan things just in case. It's become the standard operating procedure on any movie, so we just did what was asked of us. And I did have conversations with the visual effects guys, who were all super nice and talented, but there were the occasional conversations where one of them would say, "This effect shouldn't even be practical. It should be digital. There should be more digital in this movie." So that was always in the back of our minds.

Then they delayed the release of the film so that it could come out during a less competitive time period. But once we heard about the delay, Tom and I knew they were going to do more digital [effects] because now they had the time. If they have the time, they will continue to noodle it and overwork it, and that's exactly what happened. We saw a cut of the movie the day before it premiered and it was our worst expectations come true. But we're big boys. This happened to Rick Baker, it happened to Stan Winston, and it wasn't something we didn't wholly see coming. So that's when we put up the video of how the practical effects looked like originally, and we got a great response to that.

There was no way for Alec and Tom to not feel disappointed on the direction that The Thing (2011) took, so they decided the best way to shake off the experience was to create their own project called Harbinger Down, an homage to John Carpenter's The Thing (1982) and Ridley Scott's Alien, starring veteran actor Lance Henriksen. The duo successfully Kickstarted the project in 2013, and Harbinger Down was released in August a little over two years later. While his project management abilities had always helped Gillis in the world of special effects, they were also instrumental in helping him in the director's chair for Harbinger Down.

Everything that I've done as an effects artist was tremendously helpful to me as a director, because everything that a director does is stuff that we do throughout the course of a project anyway, so I was very comfortable. The biggest challenge on *Harbinger Down* was to do this on a low-budget schedule.

Even though we were in a contained location, we still had ten sets or so that we had to build, and we had to shoot this stuff in a timely fashion that didn't blow the budget, either.

There were days where, like with any low-budget movie, you're running from setup to setup and you don't necessarily get the coverage you want or even get to do multiple takes. You just have to go with what you get and keep moving forward. It's exhilarating, but it doesn't give you 100% control over the process.

It was an incredible learning experience and it really was the opportunity to do what Roger Corman did, which was to make a movie in a big, single warehouse. Also, what Roger did was make derivative movies, like how *Battle Beyond the Stars* was *Star Wars*, and so forth. And I love low-budget filmmaking, so what I hoped for this movie was that people who like low-budget filmmaking would say, "Wow, that was really an impressive story to pull off," even if they didn't like certain elements of it. A big part of what I wanted to accomplish with *Harbinger Down* was a different way that practical effects fans can share in the revitalization of the craft without it being backward thinking, and show them that practical arts are not just nostalgia. They can also be applied to contemporary moviemaking styles as well.

As Gillis looks toward the future for Amalgamated Dynamics, he recognizes that the key to the company's continued success for over twenty-five years is having an indispensable partner to ride alongside through the ups and downs of the business.

Having a business partner like Tom Woodruff is a big part of how my career and ADI have lasted so long. I've seen the toll this business can take on some of my friends who ran shops where they're in it by themselves, and a lot of aspects to this job can be very stressful and taxing to take on alone. The more of those experiences you have, the sooner you get to a point where you say, "Screw this. I don't want to do this anymore." The work becomes drudgery.

Beyond that, just having a partner to bounce things off of and split the load with is great because we can carry the same load twice as far when we work together. I feel fortunate in that respect. There are not a lot of people that I could have done this with. Hopefully, Tom would say the same thing.

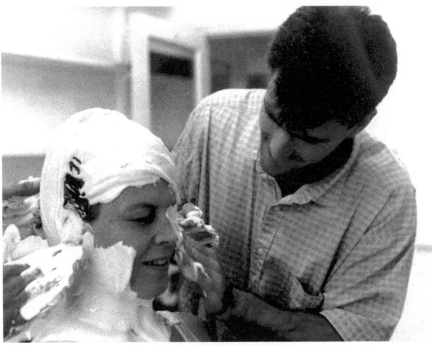

Alien 3 - Sigourney Weaver Life Cast

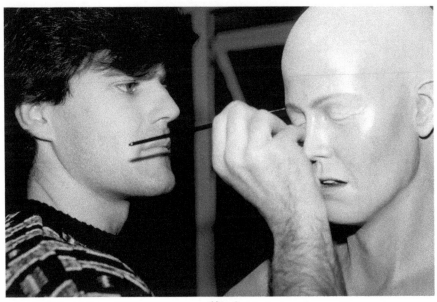

Alien 3

Alien 3

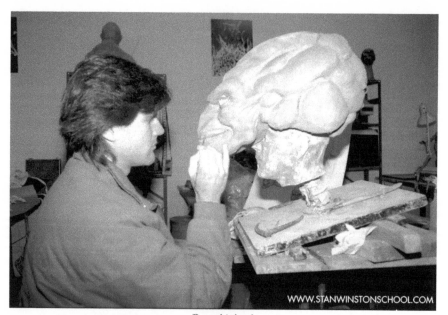

WWW.STANWINSTONSCHOOL.COM

Pumpkinhead

Tremors - Tom Woodruff Jr. and Alec Gillis

Wolf

Starship Troopers

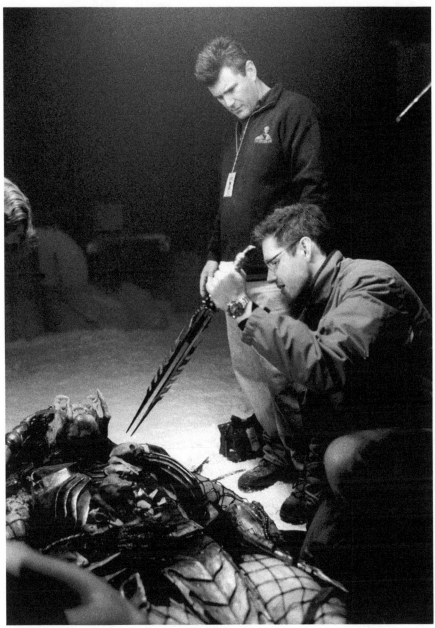

Alien vs. Predator

Alien vs. Predator

Hollow Man - Tom Woodruff Jr. as the Gorilla

The Thing (2011)

The Thing (2011)

Conversation with...
JIM McPHERSON

Special Effects Makeup Artist

Matinee (1993)
Stargate (1994)
The Nutty Professor (1996)
Men In Black (1997)
Planet of the Apes (2001)

A renowned sculptor and character designer, Jim McPherson's fascination with iconic monsters and creatures developed at an early age when he discovered the classic television series The Munsters.

When I would watch *The Munsters*, that's where I saw things that would influence me very early on. It's where I saw, to me, Frankenstein, it's where I saw a version of Dracula, and I think that's when I started to realize there was makeup involved with these characters. It made a huge impression on me. I also remember finding this Universal Monsters version of [the card game] "Old Maid," and there were a lot of monsters in there that I didn't know. It really sparked my creativity, and I can remember being in school, and when we would be asked to draw something, I was always drawing Frankenstein.

I always loved drawing though, and there was a lot of drawing in my childhood. I also had these different sculpted toys that left a huge impression on me. Soon after that, there were these model kits of all the monsters, and I had to get those and build all of them too.

After high school, I moved to New York. I was doing props for Broadway and for commercials which kept me busy doing more mold making and more sculpting. I thought about pursuing illustration for a time, because I was drawn into the world of comics, but I really wasn't enjoying it, so I decided to switch my focus to sculpting when I was in college. I also started working for a puppet workshop in Rhode Island during my college days, where they showed me how to sculpt in plasticine, how to make molds and things like that.

That's when I started looking at all these magazines, like *Famous Monsters [of Filmland]* and *Cinefex*, and I began reading about all of these great artists. I remember seeing Rick Baker in *Famous Monsters*, and that article really stuck with me. That's when I realized that what I really needed to do was to get my portfolio together, because I felt like this was something I seriously wanted to pursue.

As he continued to work on various professional projects in New York City, McPherson ultimately decided if he wanted to continue seriously seeking out a career in sculpting, it only made sense for him to head out west to Hollywood.

One of my best friends is Kevin Lima and he had left to study out at CalArts (California Institute of the Arts). He had been doing some freelancing while still in college, and one year, he came back out to work in a costume shop in New York. It was basically Kevin who told me that I needed to get out of New York and offered to help me get things going in California.

The West Coast was where it all started to come together for McPherson on a professional level, where small jobs and initial contacts led Jim to bigger and better gigs.

I was really lucky because when I came out here, a friend of a friend secretly gave me a list of phone numbers. The first place that I got hired was over at the Burman's [Tom and Bari] and they were training me to make peachstone molds and appliance molds. I worked on *Howard the Duck* and I worked on the molds for four stages of appliances we needed to create for the Dr. Jenning character. I also sculpted his body padding and the little vertebrae bones that are sticking out of his shirt for about two seconds in the movie. I also made the molds for the teeth, cast up the teeth, made some bald caps for Jeffrey Jones, and then molded some of the appliances and body padding, too.

I was at the Burman's for about three or four months, and during that time, we worked on *Howard the Duck*, an episode of the *Monsters* series that began in the 1980s, and then Matthew Mungle and I worked on one of the Mickey Spillane commercials with the pull-off masks. They even had us come out to South Carolina so we could do a life cast. When we got there, Mickey picked us up in a pick-up truck at the airport and it was kind of surreal. Everybody in town knew him, and he was the most famous person in the town. We got to talk about comic books that day, because he wrote *Sub-Mariner* and still had friends who worked on comics, and that was a really interesting experience for me, as a fan of those stories. It also proved that you just never knew who you'd end up meeting because of this job.

After wrapping up his time with the Burman's, McPherson ventured out in search of more work at the insistence of Matthew Mungle, who believed Jim would immediately hit it off with industry veteran Mike McCracken and his son, Mike Junior. Mungle's senses were right on target, as not only did Jim start working for them almost immediately, but the elder McCracken would become a key figurehead in his burgeoning career, as McPherson continued to pave his way in the world of special effects.

I had started working with Mike for something else, but I remember that we very quickly segued into doing *The Kindred*. For that one, Matthew did the Amanda Pays transformation and Mike did the maquette and sculpted an immobile posed embryo version of the Anthony monster that you see in the jars. His son-in-law, Jeff Kennemore, sculpted a neutral pose of the Anthony character that was going to move in the jars, and Mike Jr. sculpted the cat-looking thing that's on the desk in the scene with Rod Steiger. I also sculpted the little puppet that's in the rearview mirror, which I puppeteered and I still have to this day. I also ended up doing a bunch of rigging and doing a lot of gags for *The Kindred*.

We shot some of it in an abandoned hospital, but we did use stage two at The Culver Studios too, where, I believe, parts of *Citizen Kane* had been shot. They built a house on the stage, and the floors were slanted, so with all of the slime we were using on all the monsters, it was getting everywhere. There was actually like a swimming pool pit that was covered with mud that Anthony would come out of that we had people down in that water. It was a very gooey, very slimy experience for all of us, and it got worse the longer we were there. It was definitely a gooey trial by fire with *The Kindred*.

McPherson continued to find more projects to contribute to as he kept his nose to the proverbial grindstone. The first project had him collaborating with James Cummings for Slumber Party Massacre II, where he was tasked with taking on creating some of the body parts that get hacked off throughout the sequel. And on the second project, Jim found himself rigging one of the most memorable moments in Wes Craven's The Serpent and the Rainbow.

Lance Anderson brought me on for *Serpent*. Jim Kagel had sculpted the zombie girl, and I had to rig the snake that comes out of that zombie girl's mouth during the nightmare scene. I had to reinforce the mouth, and stretch the skin, so that the snake could go through. I didn't go to Haiti, but I guess it worked because it's in the movie. We also worked on *Moonwalker* right around the same time too, and Michael Jackson came to the shop one day, which was a pretty unexpected event.

It was right around that time when McPherson found himself extremely busy, between working over Stan Winston's shop for both Leviathan and

Alien Nation, and then also being hired by Mark Shostrom for Don Coscarelli's Phantasm II.

When I was working for Mark on *Phantasm II*, I was mostly making molds and I also helped do a lifecast of Angus Scrimm. I did work on a creature that comes out of the Tall Man's forehead, but I found out like 25 years later that the guy that did the mechanics, Dave Barton, resculpted it. What I mainly remember about *Phantasm II* is that there were a lot of late nights, and there were a lot of talented artists that came together on that one. We all worked very hard.

Very soon after that, Rick Baker brought Jim on board the ambitious effects showcase, Gremlins 2: The New Batch, where he joined more than 75 other artists in helping bring Joe Dante's madcap sequel to life.

I was excited to get called in for *Gremlins 2*. I had been sending Rick my artwork, so when they were staffing up, he called me in. Steve Wang was the sculpture supervisor and he was blocking out entire puppets, and then working on the head and then the body. They would pass the arms to me and I did at least four sets of arms, with the last two being attempts to get the mechanics to actually fit in the arm.

At some point in the process, Steve said that he was going to explain to me how to sculpt like he does, since I was helping him, and he shared some techniques that he used to do these scale patterns. So, I ended up doing a lot of detailing. I also detailed the arms and fingers for Matt [Rose]'s character, Lenny. I also created a maquette for the George Gremlin.

I recall Rick talking with Joe Dante about the Daffy gremlin, and then they decided there was going to be Lenny and George. Rick said to me that the gremlins should be like the Warner Bros. cartoon characters somehow. In my mind – because I didn't have the internet or any real reference – I knew that in the Warner Bros. cartoons that they had this little gangster who was like Edward G. Robinson, even with the hat, who had a sidekick that was a lot like Lenny, so it seemed perfect.

When Rick saw what I had done with the George Gremlin, he wanted to see what the Mogwai version would be like. I sculpted a Mogwai and he thought it was interesting, and then I continued to just do maquettes with different characters even though they were going to be assigned to other people. I have some feeling he might have been trying to light a fire under me to push me to design something awesome, which I feel like I did with George.

Over the next few years, Jim would go on to join the crew working at Tony Gardner's Alterian Studios and lent his talents to a handful of genre-spanning films, including Army of Darkness, The Addams Family, Swamp Thing, Mom and Dad Save the World, Psycho IV: The Beginning, Super Mario Bros., and Cast a Deadly Spell.

I think the first thing I did over at Tony's were the mutant masks for *Swamp Thing*, and then he had me work on the bear rug for *The Addams Family*. I also sculpted the final stage Mrs. Bates for *Psycho IV* and I sculpted the Ash likeness for *Army of Darkness* too. That one we had to move very quickly on, so it was a tricky project for us. I also did some maquettes for *Sleepwalkers* and worked on *Cast a Deadly Spell*, too. We made the gargoyle, and I think we maybe had three or four days to sculpt the body. I ended up splitting the project with Brian Penikas, where I did the front and he did the back. It came together great in the end, though.

I also worked on the Bulldogs for *Mom and Dad* at Tony's, and I had three days apiece for those. I made little blenders for the bulldog's eyes throughout the night, snipping the eyelids and making them thinner so they would fit on the mechanics, doing all the final gluing, and going to set. We really went through the wringer together on that one, too.

McPherson continued to keep busy throughout the 1990s, working on several high-profile projects like Batman Forever, Stargate, Men in Black, Stuart Little, The Nutty Professor and How the Grinch Stole Christmas as well as a handful of films that would go on to become cult classics – Matinee, Escape from L.A. and Deep Blue Sea.

For *Matinee*, we created the Mant/Ant costume and the puppet. When I was working during the design phase of *Matinee*, Joe said to me, "I want it to be bigger than *The Fly* but smaller than *Return of the Fly*, because that's just too big. So I based Mant on the look of *The Deadly Mantis*, which was a puppet on a track that Chris Mueller had sculpted. My feeling was that the Mant should look like if Chris Mueller was moonlighting for William Castle back in the day. It's strange, because the quality of the Mant is a criticism I hear a lot, but the style is very, very similar to those old movies, and that's what we were going for.

But I did get to make myself up and be in the trailer for *Mant*, which I think you can only see on the Laserdisc for *Matinee*. I had to do 18 sit-ups on a wheeled hospital gurney which wasn't as easy as it might sound, but Cathy Moriarty did tell us that she was very impressed with our work, and that really meant a lot to us. And Rick submitting my name for credit as the Mant/Ant designer was a pretty big deal for me, and I was very grateful to him.

When we were on *Batman Forever*, we worked on Jim Carrey's The Riddler character. We based his look on the Brian Bolland comic book Riddler, where he doesn't look like he has eyebrows. Matt [Rose] did the initial mask and the eyebrow covers. Something that most people don't really know about *Batman Forever* is that the background people were supposed to look like *Dick Tracy* type people and I made a lot of generic pieces to fit on different actors – chins, ears, foreheads, noses.

Also, in that final shot of Jim Carrey in the asylum, he originally looked a lot different, almost like The Elephant Man. But for whatever reason, we had to go back in and redesign his look. Initially, I did a drawing with a question mark on his face, where his chin was the dot of the question mark. It was done very quickly but Rick said it was too literal, so I went back in and we kept the look of asymmetrical head and a bigger chin, so it really sells the look when he did that Thinker pose after his head melts.

When *The Nutty Professor* came in at Cinovation, Rick wanted me to sculpt figures that we could animate in the computer, which I had never done before. Initially, I did a ton of storyboards for Rick, where he told me to just keep coming up with all these different ideas, and I also sculpted a whole bunch of the Klump transformation figures. There were these maquettes where all the weight of his body was moving from one side to the other and they were very cartoonish, but Rick just told me to go nuts with them, so I did. Like one of them had one side which was a skeleton, and the other side was a double-weighted Sherman Klump. Eddie thought they were pretty funny when we did our presentation, so it was great to get that kind of feedback from him.

Then, they set me up with this 'Elastic Reality' software where I could actually animate these things, and do all sorts of crazy things with these characters. That was the first time I had ever really used a computer for work. I created the effect where his face drops down on a lectern when he was giving a speech at the end of the movie. I also did the giant foot, the giant hand and I sculpted the Klumpzilla makeup, too. We did a lot of wild design work on *Nutty*

Professor that really wasn't being done all that much at the time, so I'm very proud of the work that we did on that film.

For Barry Sonnenfeld's *Men in Black*, McPherson was tasked with helping bring to life two wildly different aliens, Mikey (who also appeared in Will Smith's "Men in Black" music video) and Chucky, the bartender who has a miniature alien inside his head controlling him from an internal cockpit.

Men in Black was tough because Barry wasn't really comfortable with sci-fi. He didn't always know what he wanted, which meant we did a lot of trial and error, and it sometimes took forever just to get Barry to sign off on anything. Before they hired Rick, Barry had had six months, at least, where he was working with illustrators, so when we were getting started, they sent all this stuff over because they thought we could use it for *Men in Black*. And when this pile of stuff showed up, it was all fantastic. There was so much amazing work that had already been done, like these crab creatures that had 400 arms that I thought were incredible. There was some really well-drawn, really imaginative work done on *Men in Black*.

The two characters that I worked on were Mikey and Chucky. Essentially, what happened was Rick had a script and Mark Setrakian and I were meeting with him, and the direction read something like, "He lifts the chin and light comes out." Rick didn't like that idea, and he had a meeting with Barry the very next morning, so he put it on us to come up with something. It was Mark's idea that this alien should have foot pedals and it should be like this creature moving this guy around. We kept coming up with ideas on how we could make this something that was really fun and different, and I did a concept drawing so that we could get Barry to sign-off on the idea. So I tried to make it like this cute gray alien with big eyes and little pupils. It was not my finest moment as an artist, but Rick took it, he showed it to Barry the next morning, and Barry ended up really liking it.

We did a lot of work on *Men in Black*, but I think we did even more on *The Grinch*, which was such a huge project for us. I remember that Rick had to redo the character of The Grinch so many times because initially Jim Carrey really didn't want to wear any appliances. They wanted to see what that looked like, so we kept minimizing it until it was almost nothing and then everyone realized it didn't look very good that way. Jim really thought he could do it with his own face. He had to see it proven that just a very minimal thing wasn't going to work for that character, and then Rick was able to bring it back to how you see that character now in the movie. I remember the Whos were an issue for some time too, because production thought the characters looked "too rubbery," but I always thought that those early test makeups were gorgeous.

Jim continued working in Hollywood throughout the 2000s and in the 2010s, and even spent time at a variety of entertainment companies including SEGA and Walt Disney Feature Animation. These days, McPherson spends his time utilizing his immense creative skills as the 3D Art Director and Lead Modeler at Gentle Giant, one the biggest retailers for high-end collectibles known for the amazing likenesses they are able to capture with their stunning three-dimensional creations. Gentle Giant also does design work for Hollywood productions and private clients as well, allowing Jim the opportunity to continue to flex his creative muscles in a variety of ways on properties like *Alice in Wonderland*, DC Comics and even picnic basket enthusiast Yogi Bear, as one of the company's Lead Digital Sculptors.

I'm so grateful for everything that I've been able to do, even now at Gentle Giant. I think the reason I was able to work as much as I did was because of meeting people like Matt [Rose], Steve [Wang], Mitch [Devane], Norman [Cabrera], and a lot of other people, too. There are many people who were generous enough to stop and help me throughout my career, and I will always appreciate that. When I think about it now, I was always drawn to toys and characters as a kid that had some type of sculptural element to them. I found them to be fascinated by how they looked, especially this doll called Captain Action, which was basically like a doll that had all these appliances that could change him into other characters.

I just never knew that these things that I was so fascinated with back then would turn into my career, and helped form the things I have done and the type of work that I am still doing to this day. I probably could have taken a more direct route out to California had I known, but I think it's so great that all these things I wanted to do as a kid, I've had the opportunity to do them, and more.

Gremlins 2: The New Batch - Jim McPherson

Gremlins 2: The New Batch

Jim McPherson with *Gremlins 2* Design

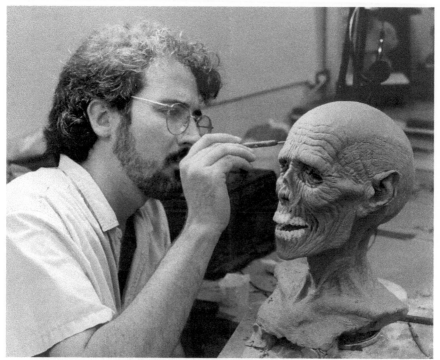

Psycho IV: The Beginning - Mother

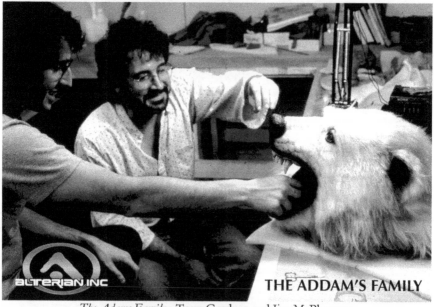

The Adams Family - Tony Gardner and Jim McPherson

The Adams Family

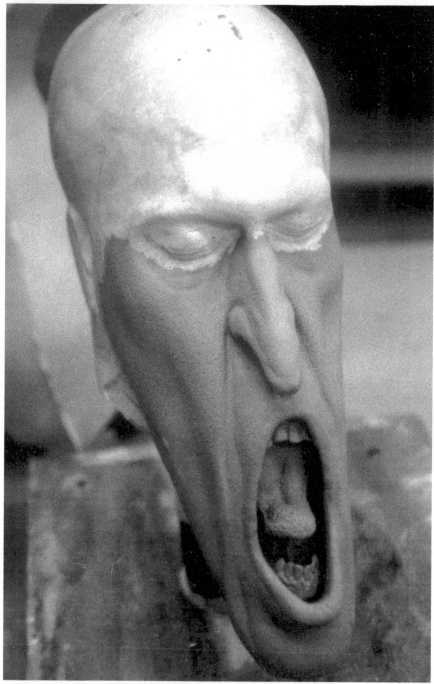

Army of Darkness

Army of Darkness - Bruce Campbell

Army of Darkness - Bruce Campbell

Matinee

Matinee – Jim McPherson

Batman Forever - Jim Carrey

The Nutty Professor

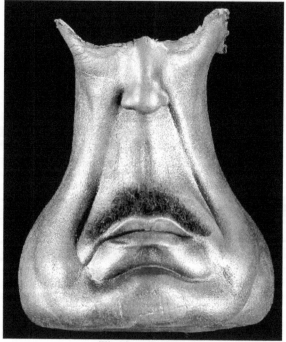

The Nutty Professor

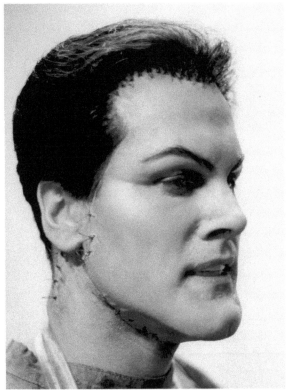

Escape from L.A. - Bruce Campbell

Escape from L.A. - Bruce Campbell

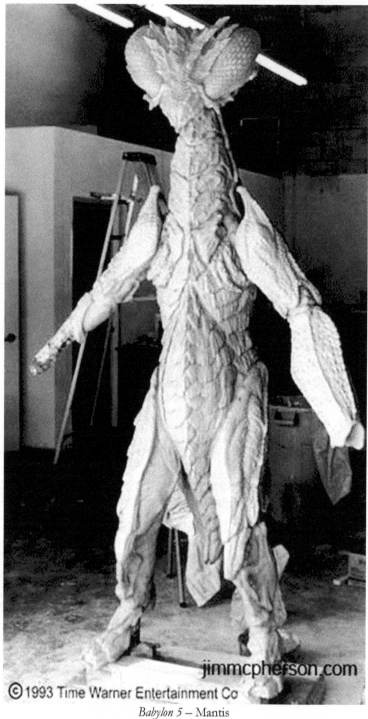

Babylon 5 – Mantis

Planet of the Apes

Conversation with...
HOWARD BERGER

Oscar and Emmy Winning Special Effects Makeup Artist

Day of the Dead (1985)
Evil Dead II (1987)
Scream (1996)
Kill Bill: Vol 1 (2003)
The Chronicles of Narnia: The Lion, the Witch and the Wardrobe (2005)
The Walking Dead (2010)

Between his deeply-rooted adoration of movie monsters, his father's work in the filmmaking industry and growing up in Southern California, Howard Berger seemed fated to walk a path of greatness in Hollywood from a very early age.

I grew up in the Valley, and my dad owned a post-production sound company and, because of his interest in movies, that just led to my interest in cinema over the years. My mom was a teacher and also an artist, so I think I picked up some stuff from her as far as the artistic stuff goes.

And early on, I just fell in love with monsters. The first horror movie that my dad ever showed me was *The Thing with Two Heads*. That was the film with Rosey Grier, Ray Milland, and Rick Baker did this great two-headed gorilla in the movie. Between that and the classic monsters – *Creature from The Black Lagoon* is an all-time favorite of mine – and finding the monster model kits, too. I think it was around the age of eight when it all culminated for me.

Because my father was in the industry, he was friends with a lot of the people at the studios, especially publicity people, and he was able to get me photos, all of the press packets from these horror and sci-fi films, like *Planet of the Apes* and *Godzilla*, and I still have all of those photos in scrapbooks. When my dad took me to see *Planet of the Apes*, that lit a fire in me, and nothing was going to stop me from making monsters.

There used to be a film festival in Los Angeles called Filmex, and we went to it one year, over at what is now the El Capitan Theatre, but at the time, it was called The Paramount. We sat there enjoying six hours of movies, clips, and all this behind the scenes footage. Doug Trumbull was there to talk, as were some of the animators from *King Kong*, and I thought it was all very fascinating.

Both of my parents were supportive of my weird fascination with all this stuff. For a while, they thought it was just a hobby, but at some point, it turned, where I was really into collecting masks and experimenting with makeup, and they realized I was serious. I just kept experimenting nonstop as a kid and as a teenager with anything that I could get my hands on. It was just all about monsters and makeup and movies.

It was at age 13 when Howard would get the encouragement he needed to continue his pursuit of becoming a special effects artist when his father arranged for him to visit one of the leading artists in the industry at the time, Stan Winston.

I was living up in Northridge at the time, and I was only about three miles from where his shop was located. One day I packed up my drawing book and my sculptures and walked all three miles over to Stan's shop to show him my work. I remember knocking on the door, and Stan let me in, sat down with me, and went over everything that I had brought to show him. He was rightfully critical of my work, which was very helpful for me and also mind-blowing for me as a kid, because here was Stan Winston looking at all these things that I had created.

After that, he let me take a look around the shop, and they were working on *The Exterminator* around that time. I can remember everything about the shop from that visit still; the way it looked, the way it smelled. It was the first shop I had ever visited, and it hit me so hard. Stan told me that day that I could keep visiting him and the shop, but that I had to keep my grades up and get all A's and B's on my report card. Every time I wanted to go and visit, he'd ask me if I had my report card to show him and, boy, I always made sure I was always getting A's and B's because I wanted to be there so badly and because I didn't want to disappoint Stan either.

I began hunting down all these other artists, too. I went to this convention they used to have at the Marriott by LAX, which was like a science fiction/horror/fantasy convention. I went to see Ray Harryhausen, and there was also this guy named Rick Baker there talking about makeup. He was promoting *The Incredible Melting Man*, and he had just done the *King Kong* remake and *Star Wars*, which hadn't come out yet. I just thought he was the greatest. When it came to picking my heroes, it was all about Stan, Rick and Dick Smith for me.

As I got older, all I really wanted to be doing was special effects, and Stan told me that my education was the most important thing and that he'd put me to work after I graduated. So as soon as I finished high school, I applied for a job with Stan and true to his word, he hired me, and that's when my career began. And I've been doing this now for over 37 years, and it's been such a great ride.

To Howard, he felt like he came up in the special effects industry at the perfect time, as it gave him the proper foundation to continue to thrive as an artist working in Hollywood for decades to come.

When I think about it, the experiences that my generation of artists had will never happen again for anybody in this industry. We had amazing leadership, and we had to take it one step at a time. Stan always told us, "You've got to crawl before you can walk." These days, it feels like there's a lack of patience with new artists, and people need to take their time and learn as much as they can from experienced artists who have been there for decades.

There is a whole generation of artists – guys like Craig Reardon or the Burmans – who all have amazing stories about being thrust into these high-pressure situations to make them better at their jobs. Their bosses forced them into taking the reins, and they became leaders because of it. This business is a team effort as well, and you need to be prepared to jump in wherever you're needed. When I started as a mold maker, I was so happy to be doing whatever I could do to help facilitate the needs of my boss and the projects we were working on. Over time, I moved on to the foam department and continued to hone my skills as an overall general lab guy. That's how I was able to gain longevity in my career.

Stan brought me on when he was doing *Invaders from Mars* and *Aliens*, and then we got into *The Monster Squad*, *Predator*, and *Pumpkinhead*, which was the last show I worked on at Stan's. I remember when we were on *Aliens*, we were like, "Who's going to see this movie? It's been so long since *Alien* came out." Building the Queen Alien suits and all this other crazy shit was cool, and we had no idea that the movie would ever be a hit. It was the same for *Predator*. Boss Film had been handling the creature initially, and production decided to start over from scratch when it came to the predator.

One day, we were there working on *The Monster Squad*, and all of a sudden, Arnold [Schwarzenegger], Joel Silver and John McTiernan came into the shop with Stan, and I was pulled off *Monster Squad* with Bob Kurtzman, Matt Rose, Steve Wang, Grant Arndt, and Shannon Shea and put into another shop to handle *Predator*. We had a month and a half to build the creature suit. We received the design, which Steve Wang was heavily involved with, and started building this creature suit.

Shannon and I ran the foam rubber, Bob sculpted the hands, John Rosecrans sculpted the feet, I think I sculpted the armor on the arms, and it was Steve and Matt who were managing everything. They went to Mexico to shoot and then we had two weeks in Culver City on a green screen. It was so difficult for us to tell if it was going to work. We had no idea how the film was going to be until we went to the cast and crew screening at Fox, and it turned out great.

To this day, I still remember the last night I ever worked for Stan. My mother had been sick, and I was afraid she was going to pass. I was also afraid of letting Stan down too, but I knew I needed to go, so I left early, and my mother did pass away later that night. I remember the next morning, Stan called me and told me he wanted to come over and sit Shiva with me, which he didn't have to do, but he did anyway.

Stan was always great that way. He was always an excellent boss and leader. He was a father-figure to a lot of us as well, and he always took care of all of us. Stan was also an excellent educator, and that's a big reason why the crew that has come out of his shop have all gone on to become amazing artists. Most of us aspired to be just like Stan, so we always wanted to do our very best.

After his time at Stan's, Berger ventured out to work for other esteemed shops and artists in Los Angeles, spending a significant amount of time working for the likes of one of his heroes, Rick Baker, as well as Kevin Yagher and Mark Shostrom.

I ended up working for Rick Baker on *Harry and the Hendersons*, which was terrific. It was just a handful of us in the very beginning, and it kept growing and growing because we needed more people. I got to see how Rick did things and how he worked as an artist and as a leader.

I also worked over at [Kevin] Yagher's for two years, starting as a mold maker and running foam, then I graduated to being a shop supervisor. Shortly after that, I started going to set, and Kevin had me going to *Child's Play* and *Nightmare on Elm Street 4*, both of which were amazing sets to be on. Kevin was very generous as a boss, and I learned a lot about being resourceful from my time with him.

I worked on *Evil Dead II* for Mark Shostrom, and I think we all were of the same opinion going into it that it was pretty ridiculous, the things that Sam [Raimi] wanted to do. At the time, we thought it was pretty silly, but it turned out to be one of the most beloved cult films of all time, which proves you can never tell what's going to connect with audiences, and what won't. But *Evil Dead II* was one of the most challenging films I've ever been a part of, and I'm so proud of what we were able to do on it.

It was in 1988 when Howard, along with Greg Nicotero and Robert Kurtzman, decided it was time to blaze a new path in special effects, and the trio created KNB EFX, which has become one of the most prominent and well-respected companies in the industry over the last 30-plus years.

I don't remember exactly what inspired us to start KNB, but we were all having dinner one night, and I said to Greg and Bob, "You know guys, maybe we should take a stab at starting a new company or something." In my eyes, we didn't have anything to lose. We didn't have any money, so we just went for it. We ended up landing a smaller movie where we got paid next to nothing, but it got the ball rolling, and we've been going strong ever since.

When we started KNB, we took all of the people that we had worked for and worked with and picked our favorite attributes from them. I pulled a lot of stuff from working with Stan and applied it to how KNB should be run, which suited us quite well. Between the three of us, and each of us had our own strengths and interests, too. Greg handled all of the business aspects, Bob handled the artistic stuff, and I handled the running of the shop.

We started off getting jobs based upon the fact that we were less expensive than a lot of other studios, and then things started to change when our clients saw how capable we were, and so word spread fast about KNB. We were inundated with all these small horror films that started to add up. Greg would take one, then I'd take one, and Bob would take one, but all three of us would be involved in all of the decision-making. And that is something about KNB that follows through to this very day. We still believe that nobody cares more about your business than you, and we live by that.

Our reputation just grew and grew, and we always felt like the buck stopped with us. All three of us would try to bounce around so we could always be on set for different projects, which meant that none of us got any sleep. We still facilitated the productions, and we were always visible on set because that was an important part of our identity as a studio. Not too long ago, we did a film with Seth Rogen called *This is The End*. I went to set for it, and Seth walked by and said, "I can't believe we got Howard Berger sitting on our set. This is amazing." But that's what I do. When you hire us, we are there every step of the way, and I think filmmakers appreciate that.

KNB were an integral part of several notable horror projects during the late 1980s, including The Horror Show, A Nightmare on Elm Street 5: The Dream Child, Halloween 5: The Revenge of Michael Myers and Bride of Re-Animator for director Brian Yuzna.

I love the work that we did on *Bride of Re-Animator*. That makeup is great, and I'm still super proud of it. That was Bob [Kurtzman], Brian Wade, and myself; we sculpted everything. Bob and I sculpted the suit, Bob sculpted the facial stuff, and Brian Wade did the hands and feet. It was half a suit, makeup, and different appliances, so it involved all this crazy shit.

Kathleen Kinmont played the Bride, and we had very little time and money to do it. Brian Yuzna split the film between us, "Screaming Mad" George and John Carl Buechler, and we handled anything that was Bride-related. It was a super exhausting shoot, too. Bob and I did the makeups on Kathleen, and it took four hours every day, plus two hours to clean her up. We only had the time and money to run three suits over six days of shooting, and after the first day of using a new suit, we had to be very careful, because we had to use it the next day.

We tried to get them to schedule it, so Kathleen could have a day off in between suits because they were so harsh on her skin, but it couldn't happen. So, here's this young actress who we were torturing as we were gluing her into this shit day in and day out. And aside from the makeup, we all had to make all the body parts and all of the dummies, too. Looking back on it now, I am still super happy with how it turned out, even though it was such a hard shoot for everybody.

*The team at **KNB EFX** found their mettle tested once again when they were hired onto Sam Raimi's Army of Darkness, which was yet another enormously ambitious sequel that utilized a massive amount of special effects and movie magic that still delights horror fans to this day.*

I feel like it was on *Army of Darkness* where we proved ourselves to Sam, and we showed a lot of people in the industry just what we were capable of. Originally, Sam had just done *Darkman* with Tony Gardner, and he had wanted Tony to do the entire show. It was Sam's producer, Rob Tapert, who thought it would be a good idea to bring us on, so Tony handled everything to do with Ash and Sheila, and we were in charge of everything else.

We made a plan and started building because we knew we were going to need to make sixteen mechanical puppets on speed rails, and we would be down in these deep trenches handling everything while they were shooting. We also made the pit monster, which was played by Bill Bryant. A fun story about that creature is that initially, Sam didn't like the design, but we went ahead and built it anyhow.

We dressed Bill up as the monster and had him stand on a board like he was a mannequin. Sam comes in to take a look at it, and as he starts talking about the creature, Bill lunges at Sam, and Sam jumps back and screams. He was like, "Oh my god, it's the most terrifying thing I've ever seen. This has to be in the movie!" So, we were able to sell the creature by scaring Sam.

The three of us were working around the clock, seven days a week. We had just opened up a new shop, it was 3500 square feet, which was nothing, but somehow, we were able to produce all of this stuff for *Army of Darkness*. Then, we took it all to the desert during the summer and just went for it. Sam storyboarded everything in the movie, so it was never a question of what we were doing, it was a question of how much are we putting into each frame.

It took a lot of coordination, and we shot the hell out of everything, with the second unit running concurrently. We'd bounce back and forth, Bob on the first unit, me on the second unit, and then we would switch. We shot a lot of video on that show, and I look back at the behind-the-scenes, and it's just totally insane. Sometimes you bust your ass and work so hard on things, and then you see the movie, and it's not even in the movie. But Sam always uses everything, and *Army of Darkness* embraced all of the effects, and everything still holds up. It was one of those movies where you push yourself and end up extremely happy with the results.

Howard and his compatriots at KNB followed up their ground-breaking efforts on Army of Darkness with their work on several more horror sequels including Jason Goes to Hell: The Final Friday and Wes Craven's New Nightmare.

When we did *Friday the 13th [Jason Goes to Hell: The Final Friday]*, Adam Marcus directed it, and Sean Cunningham gave him carte blanche, which was great. Adam always had great ideas too and had a very specific vision as to what he wanted. I was on set with him every day, but that was Bob's show. We ended up making a lot of crazy shit, and Bob always had a tendency to do that; build stuff without letting us know until we show up. But as long as it got used, we were super happy.

We took a different approach to this one, too; we didn't treat it like a horror franchise film. We spent a lot of time making everything very innovative and cool. All of the puppet heads and replicas were executed beautifully; we spent a ton of time on all of them, and I think it shows in the film.

With *New Nightmare*, we had already worked on so many of them, so it felt very comfortable for us to return to the series. I had applied the Freddy makeup on *Part 4* for Kevin Yagher, which was an awesome experience, plus I did some other stuff with Robert Englund as Freddy for publicity things, too.

One day, Wes Craven called and said, "Hey, we're going to do this *New Nightmare* film, and I want you guys involved." We were pushing to do Freddy too, but they brought on David Miller who did the original Freddy makeup, so we handled all of the other work. We built a bunch of Freddy puppets, all this transformation stuff, and tons and tons of different effects for that movie. It was fun to go back into that world and come up with this mechanical Freddy hand that we built. I puppeteered it, and it was the first time I had been part of a motion-control shot. Bill Mesa was the FX supervisor on it, and it was me puppeteering it, running through the set and knocking shit over. It was so much fun to control that hand.

Everybody in the shop was involved with building everything for *New Nightmare*, and Wayne [Toth] and I handled all of the set work. It was so enjoyable to go back and work with Wes again because a big part of the excitement of this business is whenever you get to go and work with your friends. And Wes was always so loyal, so it felt great to be back on set with all of our *Nightmare* friends making this movie.

Craven's loyalty to the KNB crew would pay off yet again just a few years later when he hired them to come aboard an original slasher film that was called Scary Movie. Little did Howard, or anyone else at the time, know that the project would go on to give birth to a brand new franchise that would forever change the landscape of the horror genre.

When Wes approached us to do *Scream*, it was still being called *Scary Movie* at the time. Kevin Williamson wrote the script, and I will admit that when I first read it, I didn't like the script all that much, just because I felt that it read as a rip-off of all these things in horror that I had worked on.

Another issue was that I couldn't get a grip on was what the killer looked like. We did a bunch of artwork, and it just wasn't hitting the right way, and I was getting frustrated. So how the mask came about was that they were location scouting and Wes took a photo out a window, and later he looked at the photo and in one of the corners was this mask. He thought it was cool and wanted to go in that direction. He brought it to us, and we ended up redesigning it to some degree to avoid any copyright infringement, and Bob sculpted the masks, all different.

Throughout the course of the movie, the mask changes because Wes wanted a version, Bob Weinstein wanted a version, somebody else wanted a different version. So that's why there are different versions. Bob was handling the first block of shooting up in San Jose, which was the Drew Barrymore scenes, and then I went up to do the rest, and it was all night shoots.

Honestly, I didn't believe in the project at all and wasn't expecting a lot to come out of it either. So, when it was released, on December 21st of all days, I thought, "This is the dumbest time to release this movie, and it is going to bomb." But it did six million on opening weekend, and then it did eight million the next weekend, then ten million, and it kept going after that. And when I went to see it, and I was like, "Holy shit, this turned out really great." Wes took this unconventional idea and made it into this entertaining and thrilling movie. He had created something unique and raised the horror genre to a whole new level while doing so. Plus, Wes made more money than he made in his entire career on *Scream*, which was good for him. I was happy for him, and we enjoyed coming back for *[Scream] 2* and *3*.

It was also during the 1990s when Robert Kurtzman and the team at KNB would branch out a bit, with the action/vampire hybrid From Dusk Till Dawn.

Without a doubt, *From Dusk Till Dawn* was some totally crazy shit, where everything about it felt like no holds barred filmmaking, and all went full-tilt boogie while making it. During *From Dusk Till Dawn*, Greg and I would literally sleep at the stage because there was no downtime. It was a non-union film, and we got our asses handed to us, but in a good way. We did some amazing creative work, and I think it's a big part of why people love that movie as much as they do.

Dusk came about because Bob Kurtzman had an idea, and he realized he needed a real screenwriter to flesh it all out. We knew Quentin socially at the time; he wasn't "the" Quentin Tarantino yet, as he was still working at the video store. So, KNB wrote a check for $1500 to pay Quentin to write the screenplay. It was the first time Quentin had been paid to be a writer, and this was before he had made any movies of his own either. The deal we made with him was that we'd pay Quentin to write the script, and if he got a movie going, we would do the makeup for the movie for free.

Then, *Reservoir Dogs* came along, and we ended up doing all the effects for him free. When it came out, Quentin was suddenly the king of the universe, and people started wanting to look at other scripts he has done, and one of them was *From Dusk Till Dawn*. One thing happened after another, the movie got picked up, got sold, and Miramax was going to do it. Robert Rodriguez had just finished *Desperado*, and Quentin was going to work with him, and it all came together quickly at that point.

It was total guerilla filmmaking though, and no matter how hard we tried, we could not stay ahead of Robert Rodriguez. The crew call was at 7 A.M., and we were rolling at 7 A.M. We would do an enormous number of setups every day, like rapid fire. Greg and I decided to break it up where he would be on set next to Robert, and I would be in the back room. We shot out all the Titty Twister scenes over six weeks, and I still think we came up with some of the coolest shit we had ever done during that time.

When Bob was first trying to get the movie going, he had storyboarded the entire film, so we gave Robert all of those boards, and he utilized them as his blueprints for the film. On set, it was Wayne Toth, Norman Cabrera, Gino Crognale, and myself and the four of us were doing all the makeups for the entire movie.

We had a crew helping us get people suited up, but the four of us were each doing twelve makeups a day, working like dogs and we never had any downtime. But it was great, the energy was so magnificent on that set, too. Sadly, it was one of the last times that Greg and I were on set together, from beginning to end. We then got so busy that we would always have to split up, but it was a great partnership on that set.

KNB continued to remain a constant presence in Hollywood throughout the late 1990s, contributing to a variety of film projects including Vampires, The Faculty, A Simple Plan, Very Bad Things, The Green Mile and were the masterminds behind a pair of ambitious remakes from Dark Castle Entertainment – House on Haunted Hill and Thir13en Ghosts – as well as the nautical horror movie Ghost Ship.

House was more so Greg than myself, but I did do some time on it. For *Thir13en Ghosts,* I went to Vancouver and shot it. Greg had the idea to bring Bernie Wrightson in to do the concept artwork, so he did a slew of drawings for *Thir13en Ghosts* that were incredible. The first couple of scripts were very different from what you see in the movie, as some of the characters were different. I think The Hammer and The Breaker were always in there, but there were other characters, too.

There was a War Ghost that we were designing and a bunch of other things, and Norman Cabrera was our key artist for that one, and he designed a couple of the ghosts and did a majority of the sculpting. Once the director approved them, we went ahead with building everything. It was a fun project, and I had hired Craig Reardon to go up with me to Vancouver.

Up there, I also hired some Canadian makeup artists like Leanne Podavin, who did The Jackal and The Big Baby, and then there was Mike Fields and Charles Porlier as well. Aside from the makeup, I remember we had to do all these other gags, like people getting crushed in the glass wall, and a guy getting severed and chopped in half. If I were to do it all again, I would have designed things a bit differently, but it all went very well.

There were things about it that I had a hard time wrapping my head around because of the way the script was written. I remember being on the phone with Joel and talking about when the lawyer gets chopped, and we ended up revisiting that concept in *Ghost Ship*. A lot of the stuff hadn't been done before, and we were trying to come up with something fresh and interesting. The guys at KNB and myself worked really hard and very quick but had a blast doing it. We just knocked it all out, and did all of the makeups as quickly as we could on set.

I do remember waking up one morning and when we got to set, nothing was going on. Someone came up to me and said, "Didn't you hear? There was an accident at the World Trade Center." We turned on the radio, and that's when we heard about the attacks. We finished, but it was a weird and sad day, and then none of us could get out of Vancouver. We ended up waiting for about a week and then rented a car so that we could drive from Vancouver to Seattle. We were on the first flight, since the attacks, to LAX. The plane was dead silent; no one said a word, and the L.A.P.D. was there when we landed, with guns. It was a very strange, surreal event.

As their studio headed into the new millennium, Berger and Nicotero both realized the importance of diversifying the work they were doing at KNB was more critical than ever, especially since the world of filmmaking was shifting.

We learned very early on that we had to diversify, so being able to adapt to the changes in Hollywood was easy for us. We could do special props, we could do special prosthetics, animals, design work, anything really. We never pigeonholed ourselves into what we were proficient at, and we have always tried our best to have people working with us at the shop who could do a multitude of things.

Around that time, Greg and I did a lot of hunting for work, and we found some great projects to work on. There was *Wild America*, which was all animals, and we also did *Cabin Fever*, which was a favor to David Lynch. We had worked with David before on *Mulholland Drive*, and David called us up about a young assistant of his who wrote this script, and he was going to put his name on it as a producer. I read it, and I told Greg that I thought the script was interesting and we could do it for very little money.

Garrett Immel, who still works with us at KNB, wanted to do *Cabin Fever*, so we put him on it, and he did all the prep work and went to location by himself. That was a big lift for Eli because Eli hadn't done anything before *Cabin Fever*, so I feel like KNB certainly had a hand in Eli's success. The movie ended up being great too, and we loved the work that Garrett did for us. That led to us taking on *Hostel*, and I think we did a few other things with Eli later on.

We were able during that time to always stay busy, and I think it stems from Greg and I having different interests. We don't cross over too much. When we did *Chronicles of Narnia*, Greg was doing *Land of the Dead*, and we were also doing prep for *Sin City* at the same time as well. Even though we are often on opposite ends of the world, we always keep in touch and know exactly what the shop is up to. It's always a constant flow of information between the two of us, which is another reason why we've been able to thrive as a studio.

It was on the aforementioned The Chronicles of Narnia: The Lion, the Witch, and the Wardrobe, where Howard would take home his very first Oscar award for his incredible special effects creations that helped bring Aslan, Mr. Tumnus and numerous other fantastical characters created by author C.S. Lewis to life for the big screen in December 2005.

We were brought into *Chronicles of Narnia* because of Richard Taylor [from WETA]. He was supposed to do *Narnia,* but Peter Jackson was getting ready to start *King Kong*, so Richard went to Andrew [Adamson, director] and said, "I'm not going to be able to do *Narnia,* so I recommend you talk to Howard Berger." They had been talking to Kevin Yagher and Stan Winston as well when they came to me.

I was a fan of the *Narnia* books and was extremely excited about the project. Andrew had the artwork for the entire film up on his walls, and when we met, he walked me through the film visually. I didn't know what to say, it was pretty spectacular, and it took about six months before they called and hired us. I had been courting them the best that I could with whatever they needed, and I remember getting that phone call from Andrew welcoming me to *Narnia*. I was so out of my mind with excitement. I went home from the set of *Lemony Snicket*, and my kids and wife were there, and said to them, "Guys, we're going to go to New Zealand."

We ended up getting all the design work that Richard Taylor had done prior, and at first, it was difficult for Andrew to let go of some designs, but they were not possible to do physically. That's when we got into VFX. It was one of the first times that I had worked with VFX very closely. It was a hell of an adventure. And then, when it was over, I was so sad, because I missed being in the world of Narnia so much.

But when we heard that we were nominated for the Oscar, I knew I was going to have a lot of fun over the next month until the ceremony, so I just needed to remember to stop and take it all in. Going to the Oscars was amazing in itself, but then winning was even more amazing, and it was one of my most favorite nights of my entire life. I was so grateful that I was able to go back to work on the second and third *Narnia* films, too.

In the mid-to-late 2000s, KNB EFX was also involved with several notable horror and sci-fi projects, including The Hills Have Eyes remake, The Tripper for actor-turned-director David Arquette, Spider-Man 3, Hostel: Part II, Transformers and both Grindhouse films for Robert Rodriguez and Quentin Tarantino.

I would say that there is a shorthand that Greg has enjoyed with both Robert and Quentin over the years, so doing *Grindhouse* was a total blast. The first one we shot was *Planet Terror*, and then *Death Proof*. Greg started thinking about *Death Proof* early on because that car accident scene was so intense. Quentin wanted to do things that had never been done before, so we needed production to be on the same page with us. It wasn't just a one-off, getting the actors in for life casts. The girls kept coming back into the shop, and we kept painting the bodies so that they could match the scene perfectly.

And it was Greg who figured out the whole car accident thing and brought it to life. It was extremely complicated because of the way Quentin wrote it, so he wasn't sure if we could pull it off. But it was Greg who masterminded it all. For *Planet Terror*, Robert wanted it to be huge and over-the-top in our approach. I think between Greg, Kevin Wazner and Scott Patton, they brought all that stuff to life.

With Robert, things can be a little more fluid when he's shooting, and Quentin is someone who is very dogmatic about what's on the page. And with *Planet Terror*, they spent a lot of money and shot a lot of takes, and all of that work was pretty much Greg, he worked so hard on that one.

A short time later, Howard was presented with the opportunity to collaborate with visionary filmmaker Vincenzo Natali for his sci-fi/horror mash-up Splice, which wasn't without some complications, but Berger rose to the occasion.

I had been on a show in Chicago, and producer Steve Hoban reached out to me, as I had done a *Ginger Snaps* movie with him. He told me that he was getting ready to do a movie with this up-and-coming experimental filmmaker, but they were having trouble with the creature stuff, and he wanted to know if I could come in for a day.

So, I went up to Canada and met with Vincenzo Natali and Bob Munroe, the VFX supervisor, and they had been going down the road for months with another effects artist. I looked at everything and asked them when they were shooting. They told me they were shooting in two weeks, and I said, "No, you're not." They had nothing there whatsoever, as everyone had been so enamored with talking about skin textures and what have you, that they neglected to build anything. The good thing was that all of the design work had already been done and there'd been a lot of sculptural work done as well, which was all excellent stuff. So, they went ahead and hired KNB, and we hopped on it ASAP.

I went home after, right before Christmas, and we started going crazy prepping everything, and it was a very difficult project because Vincenzo was so specific. But it would've been a disaster on set otherwise if we hadn't intervened, and we were able to come on board and clean up a very large mess and brought it all to life within the timeframe they needed. I think what helped was that on *Splice* there was this strong marriage of a talented director, great VFX people and what KNB was able to bring to the table. It was a seamless process.

With decades of experience in the world of special effects, there is nothing that Howard Berger hasn't accomplished during his esteemed career, and yet, he's still going strong to this very day. Between his multiple award nominations for his work in both television and film, getting to work with his professional heroes and establishing himself as one of the premiere effects talent, as well as getting to enjoy some time on screen in various minor roles, including a caged gorilla on Tim Burton's Planet of the Apes remake, Howard credits his longevity in this business to one thing: enthusiasm.

We still love what we do. We wake up every day and still enjoy everything about our jobs, and both Greg and I like to stay involved with everything going on at KNB. When we're not on set, we're at the shop. We are always available when we're needed by our team or by production. And something else that is important to both of us is that at the end of the day, we are both a huge part of the team at KNB, so we are involved with everything. My father always said, "No one cares more about your business than you," so I live by that. That's been the key to success for us at KNB.

I still get enthusiastic about things we make, and we have such a great team of artists and techs at the shop, it's exciting seeing their work come together. That thrill is still there for us, and even when the deadlines are tight, we are still having fun. For the past eight years, I've been serving as a department head on different shows, and it has made me a better artist, a better boss, and a better leader. I've had to go outside my comfort zone often, which is important to me to help me continue to grow. At the end of the day, I'm still that kid who fell in love with monsters and makeup, and I still love them as much now as I did back then.

Howard Berger and Greg Nicotero

Day of the Dead – Bob Matin of Fangoria, Tom Savini and Everett Burrell

Evil Dead 2

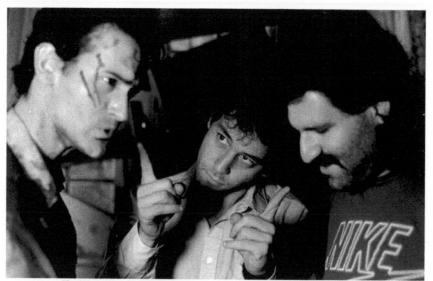

Evil Dead 2 - Bruce Campbell, Sam Raimi and Howard Berger

Creepshow 2 - Mike Trcic and Howard Berger

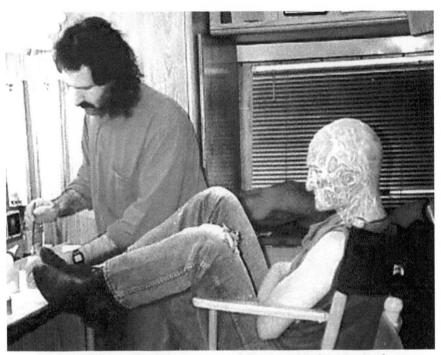

A Nightmare on Elm Street 4 - Howard Berger and Robert Englund

Kill Bill: Vol 1

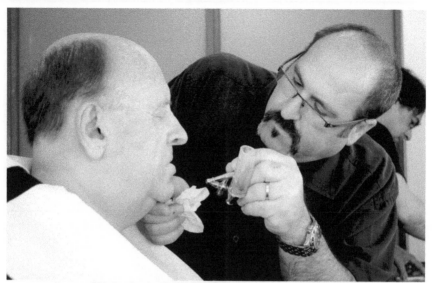

Hitchcock - Anthony Hopkins and Howard Berger

Anthony Hopkins as Hitchcock

Hitchcock - Anthony Hopkins and Howard Berger

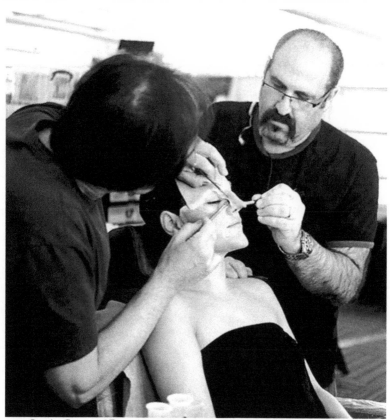

Oz the Great and Powerful - Mila Kunis Makeup with Peter Montagna

The Amazing Spider-Man 2 - Howard Berger and Chris Cooper

The Amazing Spider-Man 2 - Jamie Foxx Makeup with Peter Montagna

Deepwater Horizon - Howard Berger and Mark Wahlberg

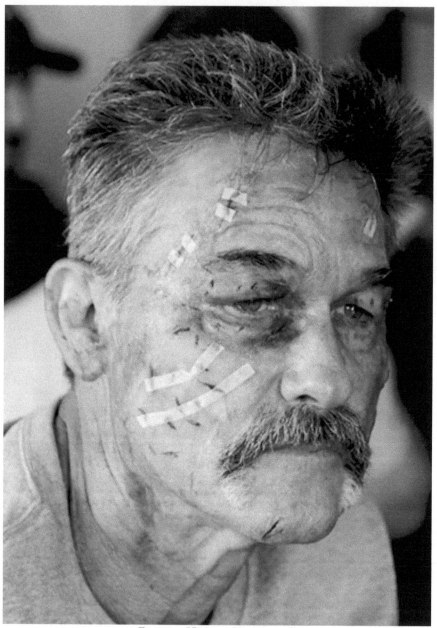

Deepwater Horizon - Kurt Russell

Patriot's Day

Dick Smith and Howard Berger

Conversation with...
TOM WOODRUFF JR.

Oscar Winning Special Effects Makeup Artist

Pumpkinhead (1988)
Tremors (1990)
Death Becomes Her (1992)
Starship Troopers (1997)
Zookeeper (2011)
Stephen King's IT Chapter One (2017)
Stephen King's IT Chapter Two (2019)

Growing up in Williamsport, Pennsylvania, the world of Hollywood seemed like a distant dream to Tom Woodruff Jr. But what began as a childhood hobby quickly evolved into something much more as he became fascinated by how movie monsters were made.

None of this was planned. When I got started in all of this, it wasn't anything like it is today. It was really kind of an offbeat idea, and even as a kid, I only had a couple of friends that used to like watching these movies, too. There was a monster magazine available at that time, *Famous Monsters of Filmland*, but it was the only thing you could find. For all of us, it was something that was cool, but for me, it struck a chord creatively because I wanted to figure out how to duplicate those things I'd seen in different movies.

I remember this journey of trying to find how to get my hands on makeup supplies and makeup materials, and it was really difficult because it was a time when it was virtually unknown outside of the industry. I was also living in a very small town back east, and so makeup effects were basically unheard of. When I finally found a local pharmacy that said in the Yellow Pages that they had theatrical makeup, I thought, *This is it*. I thought I hit a gold mine.

My mom gave me a ride over, and because I was a kid, I had this fantasy that I would walk in and there would just be racks and racks of foam appliances and materials that I had read about in *Famous Monsters of Filmland*. When I got there, it turned out that all they had was a little glass case with a couple of sticks and greasepaint for sale. It didn't deter me. I bought a couple of old-fashioned sticks, greasepaint, and some spray paint and went home with some spirit gum, too.

When I went home, I tried to figure out how to duplicate a Wolf Man makeup on myself. Lots of times, because it was me trying to work with a mirror on myself, it was less than satisfying. Sometimes I would even do makeups on my own hand, because it was something that I could see very easily and play around with, and that helped.

As he continued to pursue his interest in makeup effects, Woodruff Jr.'s parents were generally supportive of his interest in the creative arts, but it was more his own belief in wanting to do effects professionally that kept him going throughout his childhood.

I had a feeling when I was ten years old that this was something I just had to do. I didn't think of it in terms of a profession or in terms of making money, because at that age, kids just have this kind of acceptance that there is always food on the table and there's always a roof over your head. You don't think about how you need to approach life as an adult and be responsible for yourself. I did think of it as something I wanted. I wanted to be those guys working in the movies. I wanted to be the guy putting makeup on actors, and I wanted to be the guy creating monsters and working on monster movies.

I always thought my parents were supportive, but they were supportive in a much less involved way than parents are today. For me, it was a much more pure method of me finding out what I really enjoyed, what things I had a knack for, and what things I had an interest in learning more about. They never dissuaded me, nor did they artificially prop me up, either. It was just that they had accepted that I was at a point of my life where I was learning different things and trying to find my way, and I had a career goal. It was their way of giving me some time and some space to figure out what I would want to do or what I wanted to try to do, but I already knew monsters were "it" for me.

On his quest to gain as much makeup effects knowledge as he could, Tom reached out to one of the great pioneers in the industry, John Chambers, for guidance and feedback on his work.

Through various means, I was able to contact John Chambers, who was the makeup artist behind the original *Planet of the Apes* movies. When I was in college, a friend of mine said, "We should go out to California and look for a summer job." I thought, *Wait, what? Go out there and do what?* I had never even heard of doing something like that, so going out to California was our adventure during the summer of 1978.

When we came out here, I met John Chambers in person and he sent me around to meet a bunch of these makeup artists that I had read about so I could speak with them and get to see their labs. It was a really amazing time to get out of my small town back home and step into these environments that I always thought about, always pictured, and always imagined. It was really a big thing in my life, and the fact that John Chambers was so open, and immersed me in all of this in a very comfortable way, was something I'll never forget. After that summer, I went back to school and finished out my college days on the East Coast.

The next time I came out here was right after I graduated in 1980. I came out and loaded all my stuff in the car and drove out here by myself. It was really tough because it was in the time of a really big writers' strike and the whole town was shut down. I remember John Chambers saying to me, "You know, there are makeup artists that have worked out here for twenty years that are losing their homes because they don't have work right now." So that really made me think. It was tough. People who have been struggling for work do not want to see somebody new in town that's looking for work, so I think I lasted for a couple of weeks, and then I headed back east.

Once things began to get back to normal in Hollywood, Tom decided it was finally time to make an official move across the country, and John Chambers was once again instrumental in helping him get established on the West Coast.

After I got married, I finally made the move out here in 1982. When my wife and I moved out here, we found an apartment and again, John Chambers was integral in that. Because we were from out of state, we had a hard time finding someone who would lease to us. They didn't know if we'd be able to find work or not, so John talked to somebody he knew and told the landlord that he was my uncle. He put himself out there for me in a way he didn't need to, but I was grateful that he did.

Thankfully, I got a job right away, and my wife found a job right away, too. I was selling cameras in a store in North Hollywood. I had a day off during the week, and on those days, I would call John and spend some time with him, or he would set me up to go see some other people. That's how I got to meet Tom Burman, [Stan] Winston, and eventually Allan Apone, who owns Makeup & Effects Laboratories. I would go around to all these places, and I had this meager portfolio of my work to show them, but that was it. I had to show them that I had some ambition and I was willing to try new things and would be willing to put in the work to become a better artist.

I finally got a call from Makeup & Effects Lab. They were crewing up for a movie called *Metalstorm: The Destruction of Jared-Syn,* which was a 3D science fiction movie. To me, it didn't matter what the movie was, I just wanted to go to work. I put in my two-week notice at the camera store and I was gone. So, in November 1982, that's when I finally became a legitimate, working, paid contributor to the makeup industry.

It was such an unbelievable feeling for me to walk into a shop, and that's what I was going to be doing every day for the next few months. The thing that I always thought was so great about Makeup & Effects Labs was that it was a time when I got to go in there as basically an unknown, but I was turned on to things and shown things and taught things. We got a chance to do everything, and I quickly realized that I had talent for it all.

For that first show, I learned how to sculpt creatures. I sculpted some appliance makeups, too. I did my own mold, I ran my own foam rubber, I did all my own painting, and then I went on the set and applied them to the actors. It was incredible to have so many opportunities in one film, and to learn so much in just four or five months. It was a great time.

Following Metalstorm, Woodruff Jr. didn't have to wait too long for the opportunity to work for another giant in the world of modern special effects, Tom Burman.

After *Metalstorm*, it just felt like the show was over so suddenly, and you're starting back at square one in terms of trying to line up work and keep things going as an artist. Luckily, it wasn't long until I got onto my next show. Tom Burman, who I had met through John Chambers, brought me onto his crew for *Star Trek III* [*The Search for Spock*]. It was one of those mind-blowing things for me, because Tom Burman was such an important part of the original *Planet of the Apes* makeup, along with John, and now here I am working with him in his shop.

It just felt like there was some kind of predetermined path that I was following, and it all felt so right. I learned a lot on *Star Trek III*, too—I was sculpting and making molds, and I was learning rubber and casting and painting, too. It was all very fulfilling. Before that was over, we started working on [*The Adventures of*] *Buckaroo Banzai* [*Across the 8th Dimension*], so to be a part of the *Star Trek* franchise and this great cult film so early on in my career was really cool.

As he continued to establish himself in Hollywood, Tom began to notice a shift in the industry as filmmakers began embracing the possibilities that special effects afforded them on their ambitious cinematic endeavors. While it was a time of great creativity in his chosen profession, many artists found themselves pigeonholed by their artistic specialties rather than being allowed to flourish as general artists, which had been the industry standard for so long.

The timing was so different back then. We were all doing everything in terms of the different specialties within the world of special effects, so there were always general artists who could jump in at any given moment to help out on anything. But as makeup effects started to grow, I noticed this shift happening to this more segregated artistic approach, where people's strengths were the only kinds of work they were given to do. What was starting to fall away were the general artists, and it's incredibly important to have those kinds of people working with you, because they can bring so much to the table. That's why I was always happy to jump into anything and everything—I wanted to know how to do it all.

Shortly after contributing to several projects for Tom Burman, Woodruff Jr. found himself working for another legend that John Chambers had introduced him to, Stan Winston, who was gearing up for an ambitious science fiction film by James Cameron that promised to push the boundaries of special effects in unprecedented ways.

For *The Terminator*, it was once again a case of being in the right place at the right time. Stan had a pretty well-established career by then, and had even received a few award nominations. He had a name, but I do think it was *The Terminator* when people sat up and took notice of what Stan could really do. When he started to build his crew for it, we were all new to him. We were all young kids and he was a very energetic, engaging, and creative person to work for, especially during that time in my career.

Jim Cameron was also certainly an unknown force at that time. He had been around working on different things, but no one knew him as the director we know him as today. So it was exciting to be part of that open playing field, with all this rising talent coming together, and to be instrumentally involved in bringing in ideas and techniques that no one had ever dared to do before. Also, I want to mention the script for *The Terminator*, because I can still remember the first time I read it and how I just couldn't get over how great it was. I knew it was going to be a great movie. I knew it was going to be a good story, visually. But, of course, I had no idea what it was going to become.

When we started *Terminator*, we had one little shop, and then, all of a sudden, we had to rent another small unit in the same complex, and then we had to rent a third one. It just kept growing and growing. When you're in the middle of something like that, you don't really have a feeling for how vast it is until it's over and you can give it all a little perspective. You just concentrate on everything that's surrounding you and just keep pushing forward.

The Terminator was certainly the biggest show I had been a part of up until that point, and the work we were doing was expanding the world of special effects. Suddenly, anything was possible, and it was really an exciting time to be a part of this industry. There's almost an energy that happens when you're on a set like that, where everything is so innovative that it just takes over, and it's a very positive vibe.

Obviously, this wasn't going to be a movie where we were going to be able to put a guy in a robot suit and just let him walk around. That was the approach that everyone had been using up until that point, but I don't think there's any way that [the Terminator] would have been as effective as it was had the endoskeleton not been created and James had gone a different direction with the look of the Terminator.

Something else I always thought was very smart of James was to not reveal the secret about Arnold until we're deep into the movie; it's such a great, *What the hell **is** this guy?* moment that does an excellent job of bringing the audience right into Sarah [Connor] and [Kyle] Reese's nightmare as they try to outrun this thing. That was really smart thinking on his part.

What also sells the effects even more is how the design looks like it really could be existing inside of Arnold's body, because of the way he was built and how we did all the appliance pieces for him. James, Stan, Arnold, and every single person who worked on *The Terminator* found a way to make everyone believe that Arnold really was this unstoppable mechanical monster, and very few sci-fi films of that era were able to leave such a lasting impact. It was hard to not recognize that James was a really forward-thinking filmmaker and this was a movie that was going to get a lot of attention.

Tom once again found himself on the set of a James Cameron film a few years later when the visionary director hired Stan Winston and his talented crew to tackle the gargantuan effects needed for his lofty sequel Aliens.

There was a good amount of time for us between working on *The Terminator* and *Aliens* for Jim—we had a few more films, like *The Vindicator* and *Invaders [from Mars*, 1986], that we worked on first. But I remember when *Aliens* came in, we only had a couple of months to work on it, so we were definitely feeling the pinch.

I also remember that we were griping and joking with Stan because at the same time we were doing *Aliens*, Rick [Baker] was over working on *Harry and the Hendersons*, and they gave him something like nine months for that show, where we had only something like six months for *Aliens*. Of course, we got it all done, and sometimes I think it's better when your schedule pushes you like that. I thrive on that kind of energy because it forces you to keep moving and working. There's no time to second-guess anything, and that's something I enjoy when I'm on a deadline.

And the thing is that, whether you're working on *Aliens* or any other show, there's never enough time. You could have six weeks, six months, or a year, and it's never going to be enough time to get everything exactly perfect. That's when you have to get creative.

Soon after completing Aliens, Tom also contributed to what would become yet another dream project for him, Fred Dekker's The Monster Squad, which gave the entire crew the opportunity to pay homage to the Universal Monsters so many of them grew up loving and wanting to create in the first place.

It's hard to even describe what it was like to be a part of *Monster Squad*. We had just come off of *Terminator* and *Aliens*, and I remember thinking to myself, *Man, how is it that this job just keeps getting better and better?* It was amazing. And even when we found out that Universal would not be granting the license to duplicate their characters, it didn't kill our enthusiasm at all. In fact, it was very exciting to think about the prospects of doing something new on all these classic movie monsters.

Stan broke the show down, and he assigned out the characters. I don't remember at that time if any of us lobbied for a particular character, but I do know I was thrilled when he said I could do the Frankenstein monster. For me, though, an even bigger thing was to get Stan's support for me playing [Gillman, based on] The Creature from *Creature from the Black Lagoon*. I always thought that making monsters was amazing, but being able to make them physically come alive and play them myself was even better. There was no end to the amazing things in my life. I was constantly getting to live out my dreams that I had since I was just a kid.

Monster Squad was nice because Stan was totally in the role of director over us. He actually turned the design of the creatures over to us. There were four of us—Shane [Mahan], John [Rosengrant], Alec [Gillis], and myself. We started doing sketches and we had these design meetings, and when we got something to a certain level, we would show Stan and he would approve it. It was a great testament to Stan and his ego, because he really let us be the ones driving how these creatures would eventually turn out.

Even though I was playing the [Gillman], it was nice to be able to go on the set and help apply the Frankenstein's monster makeup to Tom [Noonan], too. He was a great guy. Stan and a makeup artist named Zoltan Elek did the application to Noonan's face, and I was able to do his hands.

Tom continued working at Stan's shop over the next few years, helping bring to life various creatures and characters on Alien Nation, Leviathan, and Pumpkinhead, the lattermost being directed by Winston, with Woodruff Jr. once again getting the opportunity to have some fun while playing the titular monster for his boss. Shortly after those projects, the timing seemed right for Tom and longtime collaborator Alec Gillis to step out on their own.

There were two things that developed, and it just seemed like the timing was right. As we were wrapping up *Leviathan*, Stan had lined up his next movie that he was going to be directing, *A Gnome Named Gnorm*. Shortly before that, Alec and I had done a short film of an idea we wanted to do, which was similar to the *Tales from the Crypt* anthology stories. We wanted to have these three weird stories introduced by this demonic character who works in Hell. We shot that and we were sending it around, and as soon as we got back from *Leviathan*, there was some interest in this thing from Producer Max Rosenberg, who ironically was the Producer of the original *Tales from the Crypt* movies.

So, we just thought at that time, "Okay, Stan is at a point now where he's firmly going to be directing things, and he doesn't really need us because it's not going to be a huge show." He had said after *Pumpkinhead* that he was going to start focusing more on directing and not taking on all of the shows like we had been doing for the last five years. The thing is, Stan would never dismiss us. Never. But we had this opportunity and we thought, "We should go for this, and at the same time, we can also help lighten Stan's load." That way, we weren't jumping ship to do our own thing. We were jumping ship to help Stan, and he gave us his blessings—we left on very good terms with him.

Obviously, the movie never got made, but there we were, out on our own, and that was kind of a shock because for the first time it was up to us. Alec and I were both wholly responsible. It was like when I first moved out to California and was responsible to find my own work. It wasn't like sitting and working with Stan and having work delivered to you on a constant, daily basis.

We got to do makeup on Mary Woronov's character for the movie *Warlock*, and we did a couple episodes of a TV show called *Monsters*. We were barely getting by, honestly. But then we were contacted by Gale Anne Hurd, and she said she had gone to Stan with this low-budget project and Stan had told her, 'Well, I'm really kind of tied up with my own thing right now, but go talk to Tom and Alec.' That's how we got involved with *Tremors*. It was a great project, but it was also the show that jumpstarted ADI [Amalgamated Dynamics, Inc.], and got us off and running as our own company.

While Ron Underwood's Tremors was just as ambitious as many of the other big creature features Tom had worked on previously, the horror comedy came with a much smaller budget, which meant that he and his business partner, Alec, were going to have to get really creative with the Graboid creatures lurking beneath the soil of Perfection, Nevada.

Tremors was a very low-budget movie, and we had to find a way to just muscle things around from inside these pits that were dug in the desert for us with big, long aluminum poles and cables. Somehow, it all worked. It certainly worked for the level of the movie, and what was interesting about it was when we got the script, I could just tell that *Tremors* was going to be a fun movie because it had that fun approach to the monsters.

Also, when I saw the script, I immediately recognized one of the names, S.S. Wilson. That's when I remembered he had written a book about stop-motion animation, and just for the hell of it, I picked up the phone book and looked at his name, and here he was, living in Reseda, California. I called him up and I said, "Well, I just got this great script, and I hope I get the job because I'd really love to work with you. Oh, and do you have any more of those *Puppets & People* books by any chance?" He laughed and said, "Funny enough, I've got a couple left in the garage. I'll bring you one." S.S. and I had a shared enthusiasm about stop-motion creatures, and Director Ron Underwood and Producer Brent Maddock brought so much to the movie, too, so *Tremors* really felt like a big family-made movie. Everybody seemed to work so well together, and we all appreciated each other's enthusiasm.

Although the original Tremors was not an initial financial success for Universal, the studio moved ahead with several sequels over the years, with Woodruff Jr. and Gillis handling the practical effects on several of them.

I was bummed that *Tremors* didn't do well when it was first released, but I guess I should have realized that [would happen] because it was such a unique take on monsters at that time. If you have a film that crosses genres the way this did, it's tough to sell. I remember that Universal was in this weird position of knowing that everybody out there wanted a sequel, but they couldn't put in the money to do one theatrically. They were smart, though, and realized there was still a way to make a sequel that was going to be profitable enough to make it worthwhile, so they embraced the idea of doing direct-to-video sequels, most of which we were involved in.

We worked on the first three *Tremors,* but by number three, that family feel of the production company was gone. The meetings we had on that *Tremors* [*Tremors 3: Back to Perfection* (2001)] were a struggle, and it was so low-budget, too. New producers were involved and everything felt very different. That's when we knew we were done working on them.

In the early 1990s, both Tom and Alec had an opportunity to return to the Xenomorph universe with David Fincher's Alien 3. ADI was in charge of bringing the titular villain to life for the sequel, and Tom was given the opportunity to do more creature performance work at Fincher's request. While Alien 3 did fairly well financially, it received very mixed reactions from critics and fans upon its release.

Both Alec and I came into *Alien 3* excited to be back working with these creatures, and we were also excited because of David Fincher and everything he brought to it. Looking back now, I guess a lot of people didn't get what he was trying to do. People were blind to what *Alien 3* was all about, because they had just come off of this big action-packed movie with tons of Xenomorphs, and the notion in Hollywood is that you have to go bigger and bolder when you're doing a sequel. *Alien 3* wasn't that at all. I loved that David decided for *Alien 3* to go back to doing just one creature, but I don't think audiences back then were expecting that.

Over time, though, it seems fans have come to appreciate the intimacy of the story, and I loved being a part of that on both sides: the effects and [playing the] creature. People come up to me at a lot of these conventions that I do and they say to me, "I hated *Alien 3* when it first came out, but now, it's one of my favorites." Time can always help you find a fresh perspective.

Aliens 3 was probably the last movie that I did any real sculpting on, though. By the time we did *Death Becomes Her* [which also came out in 1992], we had to start bringing in specialists because there just wasn't the time for me to run the company, make sure things were being done, and be able to sit down and do any of the artistic work, too. That was tough, because that was always so much fun for me. I'm lucky if I touch any clay once every three or four weeks when I work on projects. I still do small projects of my own at home because I enjoy doing them, but it's a whole different thing to be able to do it today while I'm at the shop.

Another 1990s science fiction project for ADI that has gone on to become a modern cult classic is Paul Verhoeven's Starship Troopers which pitted soldiers against "Arachnids," an insectoid species of aliens hell-bent on exterminating the human race. While ADI was tasked with the practical effects on Starship Troopers, Woodruff Jr. saw the unlimited potential visual effects brought to the table to take Verhoeven's bold vision to another level.

I always felt that *Starship Troopers* was successful the way *Jurassic Park* was successful, in combining the world of digital creatures and practical creatures by taking full advantage of both approaches. When I first started out in this business, I had a list of heroes I wanted to meet and work with. Phil Tippett was one of those guys. Here's a guy that was probably every bit the animator that Ray Harryhausen was, and because of *Jurassic Park* and where that pushed [things], he was the guy that made the jump from traditional hands-on creature animation to digital animation. He was always the best at it and always knew how to make things right, how to make them look good, and how much time it really took to do it the right way.

When *Starship Troopers* came along, we were more than ready. We immediately saw it as an opportunity to do a big creature movie that, had there been no digital [effects], could not have been made. It would have been impossible to tell the story with the scope that the filmmakers chose to use without digital effects, and Paul had such a specific vision that it made everyone's job so much easier on that show.

Starship Troopers also gave us the opportunity to do the level and scope of work that we wanted to do, like what we had done earlier in our careers. Things have gone downhill in terms of how involved we are in movies with a few occasional upbeats along the way, but that scope of work just isn't happening anymore, at least in the practical effects world. It was a rare opportunity, and we loved it.

ADI returned to the world of science fiction later that year with Alien: Resurrection, and the team was also involved with the big screen debut of The X-Files television series, which was released in theaters in 1998 and gave Tom another opportunity to step inside a monster suit.

X-Files was an interesting show for us. On one hand, I got to play the alien in the movie that they thawed out of the ice containers. That was great, and any time I can be in a monster suit, I'm always happy. But on the other hand, the production process itself wasn't always a lot of fun for us.

It started off great, though. We got to meet [*The X-Files* creator] Chris Carter, who was a really nice guy, but I had never watched *The X-Files* series, just because I didn't feel I ever had the time to get hooked on a TV series. So, I didn't know the world that well. The big thing that we didn't know going into this was that these guys came from the TV world of *The X-Files*, where the producer is in charge, and we had come from the world of film where directors are always in charge. We always worked with the producers and with the production crew, but at the end of the day, we still always took on the director's point of view.

For us, film is the director's medium and we always wanted to be attentive to the director at the expense of anything else. On *The X-Files* movie, we had it backwards. We would work with [Director] Rob [Bowman] and he would say, "Oh, I want to see this and I want to see that," and we would put those things into it. The producers would then give us some notes and we would do what the producers were asking, but if there were any differences, we would always defer to the director. So there were a couple of times where we just didn't understand why the producers were so unhappy with things that came to set, and in one case, we even let the size of the embryo inside of a frozen caveman become an issue.

It all came down to them feeling like we weren't honoring the construct of the way television was, which was the producer's medium. We were still working within the production medium, so there was a little bit of a glitch for us when it came to getting things off and running on that show, but once it was underway, it all went fine and we were happy with the results. And I think the film came out incredibly well, too.

Just a few years later, ADI had the opportunity to re-team with visionary filmmaker Paul Verhoeven for Hollow Man, his modernized take on H.G. Wells' The Invisible Man that did a brilliant job of marrying practical and visual effects, much like Verhoeven's previous film, Starship Troopers.

Hollow Man was another great example of a movie where the digital effects were working hand in hand with practical effects, and they complimented each other perfectly. For example, after Kevin [Bacon] is turned invisible, his team makes this rubber mask to put over his "face," and that gave us so much to work with in terms of the expressions, particularly this one mask we sculpted with this creepy expression to it. That look had this bizarre quality, and to me, what really sold *Hollow Man* as a concept and made it cool was when he would take the glasses off or open his mouth, and you could see hollow rubber skin all the way to the back of his head. That just made it so compelling and realistic.

Being a practical effects guy, I know there's this mentality out there that when it comes to practical and digital, one of those ways is better than the other. To me, it's not about one or the other. The truth is, there is no way to really quantify what technique is better for all cases anymore. When you're building a house, what is more important, a hammer or a saw? It all depends on what you're trying to achieve. That's where people get lost and swept up in the frenzy of an Internet discussion or an online battle. Both can be equally effective in different circumstances.

While they have always embraced the possibilities of digital effects when trying to bring creatures and monsters to life, Woodruff Jr. and Gillis learned a painful lesson while contributing to the 2011 prequel to John Carpenter's The Thing (1982), itself a landmark film in the world of special effects.

When you talk about the original *The Thing*, the creature effects were one of the most important aspects that became a driving force to compliment the human performances. So, for this version, that's the way it was presented when it was brought to us. The producers said, "We came here because we want this to be very much like the first movie, except let's do the digital stuff to assist what you're doing practically with the effects."

The idea was that we were all going to be working together and the digital effects were going to support the practical effects, but the practical effects were going to drive the way the creature was being done on-screen. But, by the end, everything that we had done—and I mean **everything** that we had done—was covered with this layer of altered digital effects. I don't know if "frustrated" would even begin to describe how we felt.

But we were also frustrated on a basic level because a lot of creative work that went into what we did on *The Thing* [2011] was completely lost because digital effects were misused. It also seemed like it was this deep, dark secret that was never revealed to us until we literally were driving in the parking lot to go to the screening of the movie three days before it hit theaters.

That was like a kick to the stomach, and we were left wondering if our work was so bad that they had to replace everything. We realized after seeing the movie that it wasn't that at all. It ended up being that somewhere along the line, the choice was made to create, or recreate, everything as a digital effect. I think that decision drove the core audience away, and I'm sure the studio was hoping that it just wouldn't matter. People would go see it because it said "*The Thing*" in the title, and it didn't matter how the effects were done.

Alec had this idea, and he said to me, "Look, we've got all these behind-the-scenes and on-set videos that we shot ourselves that show the kind of work we really did on *The Thing* [2011]. Let's put it up on YouTube." That's when we created the studioADI channel. It started off with us trying to reach out to the fans of *The Thing* [2011] that didn't know where to go with their frustration as to what happened with the effects on the new film. It wasn't so much about proving it wasn't our fault, but it was about us saying, "Look how it could have been and how we wanted it to be." We wanted to show that practical effects were still relevant, even today.

*Shortly after **The Thing** (2011), both Tom and Alec Gillis decided it was time to explore their creativity in other avenues while still keeping true to their love of practical effects and monsters.*

Fire City: End of Days came about because the writers and producers approached us to see if we'd be interested in helping them out. They said they had very little money in their budget, but they wanted to create this creature for what was basically a teaser highlighting what they wanted to do for this whole series of films they had planned. They gave me the script for the first one, and it was page after page of monsters and creatures and demons. I immediately recognized that they had to find a way to do this, but in a pared-down way, so it feels big and gets people excited, but also doesn't cost millions of dollars, either.

I remember thinking to myself after I read the script, *Man, it would be great if this becomes a movie in three or four years, and it would be wonderful to be connected with it from the very beginning.* So, we built the creature you see in the short, and I got to play the monster, too. The next step was to do a simplified version of the movie through crowdfunding that was going to basically show what the world of *Fire City* was like. They came up with this idea for a prequel, and I knew it was something I really wanted to direct. We had some long talks and these guys decided that they would first do a short film as a test called *Fire City: The King of Miseries.*

To their credit, they put up the money to have this thing made, we shot this short, and they were sold. They were very happy, and that's when we officially went forward with the crowdfunding so we could raise the money, and we were able to create the feature film, *Fire City: End of Days.* When it comes to what originally got me interested in film in general, it's always been characters and their relationships. And to me, there's this whole relationship between the main demon character and this little girl in *Fire City* that I absolutely love. That alone was enough for me to want to direct the project—it had nothing to do with the creatures.

Over the thirty-plus years he's been professionally working in Hollywood, Woodruff Jr. has been able to live out many of his dreams, whether it's making creatures and memorable effect gags, getting to perform in a creature suit, or even directing. He's collaborated with iconic artists and filmmakers throughout his career, and the company he founded with Gillis in the late 1980s continues to stay busy on film and television projects to this very day. Tom credits a lot of the successes he's shared with Gillis to the strong partnership they forged back when they first started working together under Stan Winston.

Although we're very different people, Alec and I have similar backgrounds. He grew up as a kid working out of his garage in Arizona doing masks, makeup, and stop-motion, and when I was a kid, I was growing up in Pennsylvania working out of my parents' basement doing the exact same things. We were born of the same stock, but when we got together at Stan's, it seemed like we had the same sensibilities in terms of not just monster-making, but also in how the monsters would end up moving and performing on set.

When we got interested in doing our own short films, we both wanted to be directors and we figured that if we just hooked our wagons together, it would be great to have the support of somebody that isn't just there to say "yes" to everything you say, but can offer a different point of view in a very respectful way. One of Alec's gifts, besides being artistic, is that he's a great communicator. He has a great way of balancing out the good and the bad of how you choose to look at everything.

There have been so many times over the last thirty years where one of us will get off the phone after having a bad experience with a producer or just general problems, and then we can just talk about it and work it out ourselves. To have another voice to help keep things in perspective so that you can still move forward, do a good job, and make great monsters, is the absolute best resource you could possibly have.

I'm not sure if I have any definitive answers as to why I've been as fortunate as I have been throughout my career, but a lot of it comes down to something [artist] Don Post once said to me. He told me, "It's great that you young guys come out here and you want to make monsters, but you always have to remember, things always change, so you have to be prepared and be just as willing to change, too."

It was great advice, but I just don't think we'll ever see an end to monsters. There isn't really money in doing special effects anymore, so we keep working despite it. You just have to realize that you have to roll with it.

Something that stayed with me from that very first time I came out here, was that I found out that something like a writers' strike can completely crush a person's lifestyle, even if you're not a writer. I never became part of that lifestyle. I was always smart. It was always about keeping things working at home, keeping the shop in place, keeping the shop open, and not being so cavalier about the work you are doing. I've been fortunate because I've gone through a good portion of my career now just trying to make sure I'm still that kid who fell in love with all this stuff in the first place. I make the decisions based on that kid's excitement and that kid's love of the world of monsters.

Aliens

The Monster Squad

Pumpkinhead

Pumpkinhead
Alec Gillis and John Rosengrant give *Pumpkinhead* (aka Tom Woodruff Jr.) a Drink

Tremors

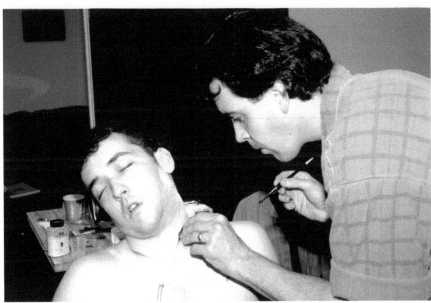

The Grifters - John Cusack and Tom Woodruff Jr.

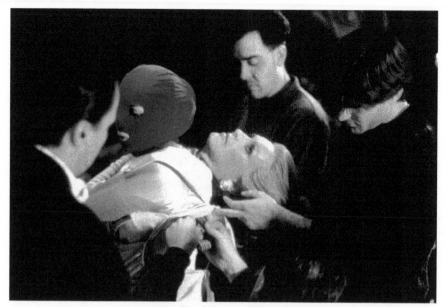

Death Becomes Her

Wolf - Alec Gillis, Director Mike Nichols and Tom Woodruff Jr.

Wolf

Hollow Man - Tom Woodruff Jr. as Isabelle the Gorilla

Bedazzled - Tom Woodruff Jr. as Biggest Devil

The Tonight Show with Jay Leno
Kevin James and Tom Woodruff Jr. as Bernie the Gorilla Promoting *Zookeeper*

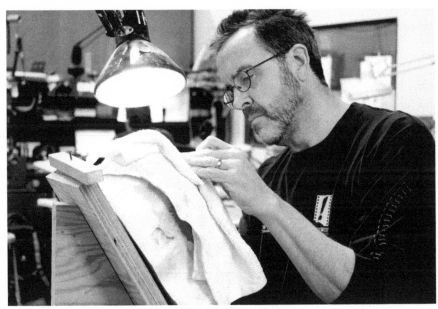

Tom Woodruff Jr. at Work

Conversation with…
"SCREAMING MAD" GEORGE
(JOJI TANI)

Special Effects Makeup Artist

Big Trouble in Little China (1986)
Predator (1987)
Society (1989)
The Abyss (1989)
The Guyver (1991)

A multi-hyphenate creative maelstrom in both Hollywood and Japan, "Screaming Mad" George is truly an artist in a class of his own, with a career that has spanned the world of punk rock, music video and feature filmmaking. But for George (born Joji Tani), one of his earliest aspirations was spawned from his love of Japanese comic books.

One of the first things I can remember wanting to be was a cartoonist. I was heavily into Japanese comics, and I started to draw my own comic book and characters myself. When I was little, I went to this international school and then my parents removed me from that school and sent me to a local school so that made my learning delayed a little bit. There were differences between the styles of the two schools, where I couldn't adapt as quickly as everyone had hoped I would, and I didn't understand quite a lot of stuff that was going on in class.

So, what I did to keep busy was to just keep drawing. But as I started to try and create the stories for the comics, I was having a lot of trouble. I could come up with the ideas, but I could not finish them. That's when I realized I was much better with illustrations than with stories. And when I was in junior high, I would go to the library when I had free time and that's when I first encountered Salvador Dali. My life completely changed when I saw his paintings.

When I was still in junior high, I started doing oil paintings and when I got to high school, I was painting even larger oil paintings. I had decided that I wanted to be a painter, and after I graduated from high school in Japan, I moved to New York. For the first year, I studied English, and by the second year, I got into the School of Visual Arts in Manhattan. It wasn't easy, because the first time I took it, I failed the TOEFL (Test of English as a Foreign Language) exam. But when I showed the faculty my painting portfolio, they decided my work was good enough to let me in. So, I was very lucky.

Despite still struggling with the English language, George's work propelled him beyond any barriers and left a resounding impression on his teachers, which put his education at the School of Visual Arts on an early fast track.

When I was a freshman, everything I was learning in my classes was very elemental stuff. In the middle of the semester, we had an assignment where we had to paint a self-portrait, and my painting was of my face split in half, with all this skin and eyeballs hanging, and the skull in the middle. When my teacher looked at it, he said, "You don't need to be in this class. You need to be in the second year workshop." So, in my second semester, I went onto the second year of school which was great because they gave me a lot of space where I could paint anything I wanted.

I had finished another huge painting, and somehow, it got into the end-of-the-year show in school. It was odd because I was technically a first-year student and, usually, those end-of-the-year shows were more for the graduates. But I was so happy that I got picked. During my second year, I found out that I had been awarded a scholarship which was amazing because I didn't apply for the scholarship or anything. It was great to be able to just keep painting more and more.

Even as he continued to express himself artistically with a canvas and brush, George was ready to explore other ways to tap into his creative side, and from his desire to create his own style of living, breathing art, his band Disgusting was born during the late 1970s.

I remember there was this girl in my class, Julien, and she played Ragtime guitar. I had been trying to learn the Ragtime guitar at the time, and asked her if she could help me get better, and we just started playing together, which led to us becoming a band. We started finding other people to join Disgusting, which was our first name, and all of this was happening right in the middle of the punk movement, which was very cool. For me, the idea of stage performance was that it was a very expressive way for me to be creative. Painting as an artform is very stiff because it's just this one perspective of this one image. But, with live performance, you're adding in that movement and you can tell a story.

When I was performing, I wanted to do something that was very shocking, so I remember that during one of the songs, I pulled up my t-shirt and I pretended to split my stomach, with my guts and all this blood is falling down right in the middle of everything. And then, I wrapped my neck with the guts and kept on singing. For the last gag, I made a fake penis with blood inside, which was really just red paint inside of a condom. But I would strap on the fake penis so at the end of the show, I would open my zipper and castrate myself with huge scissors. I really wanted to give people a lot of theatrical gore.

At the time, a lot of punk music was about wanting to die young, where musicians wanted to destroy themselves, and I wasn't really keen on that idea.

That felt too real to me, and that wasn't what I enjoyed. To me, everything was about theatricality and surrealism, and if you act it all out realistically enough, you can still give the audience the same kind of impact, and take things even further, which is how I realized just great special effects could be. And I definitely did not realize it at the time, but that was the beginning of my special makeup effects career.

"Screaming Mad" George continued to perform in New York's punk scene, eventually changing the band's name from Disgusting to The Mad, and he also adopted a new performance style to go with the group's new moniker.

For The Mad, I became the front person and lead singer. I created most of the concepts and the music, and every show, there was something different that would happen. What we were doing was more surreal than anything else, so it became about creating something that was bizarre and weird rather than it was to do all this blood and gore.

After he graduated from the School of Visual Arts, and Julien set out to join The Cramps, George decided to not only change up his band name from The Mad to IRRATIONAL, but he also decided to switch up the music style as well.

That was around the time when I started making full body suits. After I saw Dick Smith's work on *Altered States*, which was a suit of muscles and veins from head to toe, I said, "Oh, I have to make this." So, I sculpted and made the suit, and had to figure it all out for myself because there were no schools around for this type of thing. But I began to realize that I had to start making some money because the band wasn't making any money, and so that's when I decided to shift my career towards becoming a special makeup effects artist.

I made a 15-minute short film that was five of our songs that I knew I could do specific special effects sequences for each song. It was a portfolio piece, basically, and I started sending out these videos to see what would happen. I sent one of the tapes to my friend, Shinji Nakako, who was a Japanese journalist that had been writing about special effects. He was a friend of Rob Bottin, Rick Baker, Steve Johnson – a lot of famous effects artists. He passed it on for me, and that's when I decided to go to Los Angeles to meet with the big guys.

When he ventured out to the West Coast, George wasn't sure exactly what would come of his trip, but he quickly found an opportunity to start making a name for himself in the industry alongside some legendary talents.

One of the first people I talked to was Rick Baker, and I asked him if I could work for him for free for a year, because I knew I needed to get my foot into the business. I had the support of my father, so I just wanted the chance to work for the best. At first, Rick wasn't really into the idea, but I kept pushing, and eventually he said yes. So, I went back to New York to get ready and I moved to L.A. a few months later. But, when I got there, Rick had decided to take off for a year and was handing off *Cocoon* to Greg Cannom. I didn't know what I was going to do, but Greg was great and allowed me to work on the film with him, so that's how I got my official start in the makeup effects industry.

Of course, I wasn't doing any creative things on *Cocoon* because I was just starting out. So, I was sweeping floors, helping everyone mix polyfoam and silicone, just the everyday work that needed to get done. One of my main responsibilities was that I had to buy materials, which was great because I started learning about all these different materials and where I could get them, because I had no idea.

Because I was working for Greg for free, I was only working on *Cocoon* three days a week, so I asked him if I could come into the shop on the other days to work on my own projects. I wanted to keep doing creative things, and Halloween was coming up, and I wanted to make something to wear. Greg agreed to let me do it, but I think he was expecting me to make some small appliances or masks, but I was making a full body monster suit. I did my body cast, and everyone kept telling me there wasn't a way to make a full body monster suit, but I did it. I ended up taking over 10 feet of space working on it, and I'm sure Greg was surprised, but I don't think he was going to tell me to stop at that point either.

What really helped me was that I was at this shop around all these skilled professionals. Everything I was doing at that time was self-taught, but just by watching all those people, I learned so much. I could see all the things that I was missing to succeed in making molds or sculpting or even mechanics. Everybody was so helpful, and that year, I went to the big effects industry Halloween party, and I won one of the categories because of that full monster suit.

Once Cocoon was wrapped, George found himself at a crossroads, as he wasn't sure just where his career was headed next. Rick Baker wasn't crewing up for any new projects just yet, and he began to get nervous about his prospects. But it ended up being his impressive Halloween costume that led to him being contacted by another effects legend, Steve Johnson, who ultimately brought George into the fold at Boss Films for an upcoming project.

When Rick said he wasn't going to need anyone for a while, I was nervous, because I didn't know what I was going to do. Out of the blue, I got a call from Steve Johnson who told me he liked the monster suit I had built and watched my video, and wanted me to come in for something because of my sense of surrealism. That ended up being *Poltergeist II*. When I started though, they were still wrapping up *Fright Night*, so I painted some lenses and background stuff, and got to go to set as a puppeteer for the bat creature's eyes. And we started *Poltergeist II*, Steve made me in charge of the vomit creature. I couldn't believe he put me in charge of something like that. It was just amazing.

My biggest worry was that I just didn't want to disappoint Steve, so I was always working as hard as possible and really put my everything in my work. And in the end, I think the vomit creature came out really well. I was so happy with it. Then, Steve put me in charge of Carol Anne's transformation sequence, and he had this idea of doing a motion-controlled skull that I had to make a series of heads that would gradually become Carol Anne's face. We managed to pull it off as a morphing technique, and it worked great. This was way before CGI came along, too.

And then after *Poltergeist II*, we went right into *Big Trouble in Little China*. Steve put me in charge of designing and finishing up the flying eye. So, I did the design on it and Jim Kagel, who's really a super sculptor, he was the one who did the sculpture of it. I also got to paint the flying eye and directed 20 puppeteering shots for it for the second unit photography.

"Screaming Mad" George continued working at Boss Films for the next few years on various projects during the time when projects like Hunter (the original title of Predator) and The Lost Boys came into the studio. Eventually, due to a series of unfortunate circumstances, both films would end up heading out to other shingles, which caused a major shift over at Boss at the time.

I was in charge of a Chevrolet car commercial that had a bunch of aliens in it when *Hunter* came in, and I just remember everyone was always quite busy. There was always a lot going on, and I remember how bad I felt for everyone, especially Steve, when *Hunter* ended up going over to Stan Winston's. They did a tremendous amount of work, and it all just went away. What's funny though is that Steve Wang, who eventually helped create The Predator at Stan's, had actually been at Boss Films too, working on the creature's legs.

Then, when *The Lost Boys* ended up somewhere else, Boss practically closed up their monster shop. My last job for them was on this laserdisc project that was all about special effects, where it had interviews with Dick Smith and Rick Baker, and it showed people how to make all kinds of stuff. I showed people how to make a mechanical mask, and after that, I had to figure out what was next.

With a handful of impressive credits on his resume, and his creativity thriving at a time when horror and sci-fi filmmaking wasn't afraid of taking risks, "Screaming Mad" George really began to come into his own during the late 1980s.

After I left Boss (Films), I did some sculpting work on *Spaceballs* and then the next film to come along was *Arena*. They called me in to design these alien creatures, and unfortunately, only one of my creature designs was picked. But I asked if I could be the one to make my "Sloth" alien over at John [Carl Buechler]'s shop, and they agreed to let me do it, since John was handling everything else.

It was around that time where I realized I needed to have my own company and find a shop to rent, and I ended up renting out a space in the back of Burman Industries, Inc., just in time for *Nightmare 4*.

For Renny Harlin's A Nightmare on Elm Street 4: The Dream Master, producers reached out to a variety of special effects talents to handle the sequel's ambitious amount of practical effects work which included everything from creating multiple versions of Freddy Krueger – including his resurrected form and a 20-foot-tall chest – to crafting a "soul pizza" that contained tiny versions of the Springwood Slasher's victims to what would arguably become the film's most jaw-dropping moment: the transformation of workout fanatic and hater of bugs, Debbie (Brooke Theiss), into an oversized cockroach.

I'm still not sure how it even happened, thinking about it now. I just remember I got the script and they were bidding out all the different effects sequences. I knew I wanted to do the roach sequence and they gave me some basic storyboards to work from. I met with Rachel Talalay and Renny Harlin, and I guess they liked my way the best. It was a lot of work, but it all went really well.

Brooke was such a great person and so easy to work with, too. She never complained about anything. She was having a good time even when we did her full body cast, and that's really her inside of that roach suit at the end. She didn't have to be inside of that suit, but she wanted to do it. That's how much she enjoyed it, even though we put her through a lot.

The first thing we did was the bench press sequence, where her arms break. We placed Brooke inside this fake body, so it's just her shoulders and her head showing, and it was pretty uncomfortable for her inside that body because she was just stuck in there for a while. We had to use a hot melt skin for her arms when they are breaking, and then, the second sequence was the bug arms which weren't hard to do. But the scene where her face is in all that goo – oh, my god. It was really amazing how she dealt with all that ultra slime everywhere, because it's not an easy thing to deal with. It was great, and it ended up being this very, very cool moment in the film and a great showcase for me, too. I was really lucky that I was the one who got to do the roach shot because everyone still talks about it.

"Screaming Mad" George continued to keep busy on other projects after Dream Master, including the B-movie cult classic Curse II: The Bite, when a chance meeting with Brian Yuzna would lead to him taking on another project that would catapult George's work into the limelight yet again.

I had been in talks with this Japanese company about directing this script I had called *Animus*, but because I hadn't directed before, they weren't sure about me doing it. So instead, they asked me to get involved in this movie called *Society* and had me meet with Brian [Yuzna], and we hit it off immediately.

That first time we sat down to talk about the movie, his biggest problem with the *Society* script was that it was a very gory ending where it ended in a complete bloodbath, and Brian really didn't want to go into that direction. He thought we should do something different, and that's when I asked him about using Salvador Dali as our inspiration for the effects.

It just felt like if we weren't going to do this whole bloody mess, then why not try and do something very surreal, very gooey. Almost like what Rob Bottin did for John Carpenter on *The Thing* (1982). We knew the easy way would have been to just go with all the blood and the gore, but we thought taking this route would be far more interesting. So, I came up with a bunch of weird and surreal stuff and, as long as it fit into the movie's story, it was a go. Our budget was limited, but I still got to do everything I wanted, and I feel like there's a lot of me in that movie. Putting all of that weirdness out there was like putting myself out there, and it's a shame it didn't do better in the U.S., because I think it's a really great film.

After finding their groove together on Society, George would reteam with Yuzna for his twisted sequel, Bride of Re-Animator, which he still enjoyed working on, even though his creativity was a bit more reined in this time around.

With *Bride*, Brian wanted to do more of a classic sequel but with a newer approach, but always keeping a sense of classicism to everything, so I didn't get a lot of opportunities to go too far with anything. He had KNB doing the Bride makeups, so I got to create all the failed experiments, and that's where I got to go nuts. I liked *Bride of Re-Animator*, and enjoyed working on it, but I definitely had more room creatively on *Society*, which is why I think I enjoyed working on that one so much.

It was during the early '90s when George would get the opportunity to flex his directorial muscles on his first feature film, The Guyver, which he co-directed alongside another effects legend, Steve Wang. Based on the Japanese manga series, the story follows a government agent (played by Jack Armstrong) who stumbles upon alien technology that is able to transform him into a super powerful human/alien hybrid who kicks all kinds of bad guy ass (which happens to include none other than Mark Hamill). Even though "Screaming Mad" George was confident in his abilities to be able to bring the visual aspects of the story of The Guyver to the big screen, he discussed how Wang became a crucial partner for him as they embarked on the project together.

I had made those short videos years ago for my video portfolio, so I knew I could handle that even if I wasn't that experienced. But Steve, he had done more action directing with his own projects before this, so I thought he was someone who could do all of that really well. Plus, when it comes to creating high quality masks and everything, Steve is the best. When I was first approached for *The Guyver*, it was actually them wanting me to do all the effects work, but I convinced them that I could direct it, too.

So, as we were working on it, I knew Steve was going to be the one who could really do the action in *The Guyver* very well. He knows so much about action movies, and he could always see the best way to get these scenes in-camera, and because I realized that being a director was going to be a lot of responsibility, it was great to work with someone who could split the workload with me, and we'd have fun doing it. He'd direct the action scenes and I'd take on the effects scenes, and it worked out great. The suits and the creatures were all very high-quality, which only made the movie even better.

Having Mark (Hamill) involved with *The Guyver* was a great help too. "Everyone who worked on the film were all very professional, and there were no egos on that set, but he just understood everything we were trying to do, and somehow made it all better. Plus, being a first-time filmmaker, to have someone like Mark working on your film is so helpful. But I think Steve and I both learned a lot from that film.

Even though he was able to enjoy being at the helm of a feature film for ***The Guyver****, "Screaming Mad" George continued to find a great amount of success in the realm of special makeup effects as the 90s rolled on, including films like* ***Tales from the Hood****,* ***Progeny****, and* ***Children of the Corn III: Urban Harvest****. But it was early in the decade when George would connect with one of the most famous cinematic time travelers of all time – Alex Winter, who portrayed Bill S. Preston, Esquire in both of the* ***Bill & Ted*** *movies – for the oddball comedy,* ***Freaked****, which was in many ways a spin-off of the MTV sketch show* ***The Idiot Box****, which Winter also had a hand in creating.*

Alex Winter and I met at a gallery opening that had a lot of low-brow art and pop-surrealism pieces. There was lots of weird stuff, I remember, and it felt just like what you'd find on the L.A. art scene at that time. There were a ton of people there, and I remember Alex and I met, and he was telling me about this film he was developing called *Freaked*, and he was going to have the Butthole Surfers in the movie and doing the music. I am pretty sure at first it was supposed to have more horror stuff, because he wanted to make a really fucked-up movie, and he wanted to have me to design all the characters.

When I read the first script, it surprised me. It felt so underground, and so out there, I just didn't think that movie was ever going to get made. I guess Alex started to understand that, too. He got together with Tom Stern (who was also behind *The Idiot Box*), and so by the time he finally finished his final draft, he was able to get Fox interested in it. I did all the initial design work, but then things started to get changed around a lot and it felt like the movie was trying to be more mainstream. Especially when he started meeting with all the producers. And then, some other companies got involved with the creatures too, which at first I wasn't sure about, since I had been designing from the beginning. I realized though that it was actually a very big job for just one company, so I think it was a very smart decision to get other companies involved. There was a lot of work to do on *Freaked*, and I am happy with how everything turned out.

Even though he continued to work on features, George also began to showcase his talents in the world of music, as he collaborated with a proverbial "Who's Who" of nineties rock.

I met this photographer named Dean Karr who is a really incredible artist. He was doing CD covers and promotional pictures at the time, and he began directing promotional videos too. I can't remember what his first video was, but his second one was for Marilyn Manson's *Sweet Dreams* video, and I was hired to do some of the makeups on Marilyn and a few other things too. And after we did the *Sweet Dreams* video, Dean was going to shoot *Antichrist Superstar* album cover and all the inside promotion photos. He asked me to come with him to do Marilyn as the worm that starts hatching and turning into this demon angel, with this cracked body. So, I did all that makeup.

The only thing is that, because this wasn't the movies, this kind of work is something you usually don't get the credit for. So, many people are surprised when I tell them that I worked with Marilyn, or that I worked with Dean a lot as he was getting more and more music video jobs. That work kept me very busy – I did the beating heart at the beginning of Nine Inch Nails' *Closer* video, I worked on several Ozzy Osbourne videos, and I worked on the *Make Me Bad* video for Korn, with the bug crawling under the skin. I also made a bunch of masks for Slipknot over the years, too.

As he kept himself busy on the music video front, George was called back to Japan to take care of his father, which provided him with the opportunity to re-establish himself professionally through various new projects and through teaching new generations of artists as well.

When I came back to Japan, I directed a few music videos for a band over here, and there's also a famous baseball player who likes to wear masks, and so I reworked one of my old masks for him to wear, which was a big thing with their fans. I wasn't really looking for special makeup jobs, so I started teaching and just became more laid back. I'd also been working on some projects for myself, just because I wanted to be creative again without restrictions, like I was doing in high school. So now, I'm the boss. Before, directors were always the boss. But now I only have to answer to myself.

And, it's not that I don't want to do any makeup effects or anything. If somebody asked me to do effects, if it's interesting, I'll do it. But I'm not really going around looking for jobs right now. I like doing different things, so I'm okay with just doing whatever I like doing right now.

While there's no denying that "Screaming Mad" George's work as an effects artist is truly in a class of its own, he's proud of the fact that he's been able to establish himself creatively in other fields as well throughout his entire career.

There are so many people out there who might only think of me as just a special makeup effects artist, but I've been lucky to have done a lot of different things. I was a punk band guy. I used to make industrial gothic music. I'm a painter. I'm a director. And I still want to direct – I'm still working on the script for *Animus*. I think I just want to keep doing things I enjoy, and wherever it takes me, I'm happy to go there.

Screaming Mad George at Work

A Nightmare on Elm Street 4: The Dream Master

Society

Sea Creature

Screaming Mad George with one of his sculptures

Screaming Mad George's Band - *The Mad*

Conversation with…
BARI DREIBAND-BURMAN

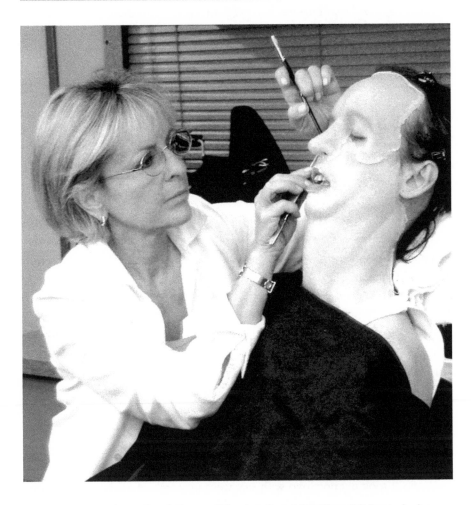

Oscar Nominated and Emmy Winning Special Effects Makeup Artist

Cat People (1982)
Howard the Duck (1986)
Scrooged (1988)
The Bodyguard (1992)
Nip/Tuck (2003-2010)

Bari Dreiband-Burman, an Oscar-nominated and multiple Emmy Award-winning artist who has worked in various mediums throughout her four decades in Hollywood, helped raise the bar for photo-realistic practical special makeup effects in Hollywood. Alongside her husband, Tom Burman, they transformed a character on the pilot episode of Ryan Murphy's series Nip/Tuck, and it was their work on this groundbreaking series that changed special makeup effects on television, with the Burman's consistently leaving viewers' jaws on the floor each and every week with their mind-blowingly lifelike creations.

And while her successes on Nip/Tuck would come some 20 years after the start of her career, it seems like Dreiband-Burman was always destined for creative greatness due to the unique interests she had early in life, as well as her passion for blazing her own trail in entertainment.

For as long as I can remember, I have always loved anatomy. The human body is simply the most miraculous thing ever—think about how amazing it is that you wake up every day, and you walk around, and do all these things with your body and mind, and it all just works together. It has always been something that is completely amazing to me.

I come from a fine arts background too. My family were painters, and I have a degree in Fine Arts from California Institute of the Arts, so I thought medical illustration would be perfect. Unfortunately, that ended up being too much of an emotional experience for me. I would work with this plastic surgeon who would do pro bono work for children, and I'd have to see these children in horrible situations. It just wiped me out. The thing that I kept thinking was that I needed an art-oriented job that had nothing to do with my family, because I wanted to have my own identity and create my own world. And to me, Los Angeles is music and film.

So, I took my portfolio with me, went in search of a job, and I became one of the first women scenic artists at NBC. They were somewhat pressured to hire me—they didn't want to hire me, but they couldn't say no, because my work was good. They wouldn't let me do any art; they'd just let me hand them five-gallon drums of paint. It was cool with me because I was just starting out. During my breaks, I would just walk around and try to find out what art-oriented work that I could do by myself because I have always liked to work by myself.

I was never a makeup fan. Having come from a fine arts experience, makeup was just not my world. But one day at NBC, I popped my head into

The Tonight Show room, and saw somebody applying makeup to a face themselves. I thought to myself, "I could definitely do that. I could easily switch from oils to pan sticks." I didn't know anybody in the business, which is what I liked. Michael Westmore was teaching a class at the Valley College, so I took a class. During this time, I was also a freelance illustrator. I would do cartoons and illustrations and eventually, I became a cartoonist for *Penthouse*. They were putting out this magazine called *Viva*, which were all male nudes. The west coast editor was a woman, and she became one of my best friends. Then, I went from cartoons and illustrations to doing makeup on models, and at some point, somebody suggested that I should go over to Universal Studios. So, that's what I did.

While she initially had some difficulties picking up Universal projects that revolved around applying straight makeup, Bari was able to eventually break her way into the ultra-competitive field, and found great success in that department over a number of years.

At that time, most effects people were inherited into the business, so they didn't come from my world, which was sculpting and painting. There weren't a lot of women working there back then either. I started in 1976, and they would put me on anything that wasn't straight makeup. It was really hard to get into it, because there was some nepotism in the makeup department. But then there was an open period where Universal let women in for a small window of time, and I was accepted, and I worked there for three years.

I did the TV movie *Women in White*, and then I went to Vegas and did the series *Vega$*. Then I came back and did *The Border* with Jack Nicholson. He had already done *Five Easy Pieces* and *The Shining*, so he was well-established as an actor. I remember that it would be four in the morning, and he loved to tease me because he knew I didn't like scary things. But he was absolutely wonderful.

When I was starting out, I was so happy to be a freelance artist because of the freedom, but at Universal, there were benefits and healthcare, and that was incredible. You didn't ever have to beg for the check like you sometimes had to as a freelance artist. But one day, I was working really late on a Friday night, and I didn't get out until two in the morning. I went to my car, and it had been vandalized. They took my makeup cases, they took everything. I was devastated. I went to the department head and they said, "Well, that's the way it goes." That's when I thought to myself, "Okay, I guess I'm open to other avenues now." And sometimes, it takes a terrible situation for you to realize you need to make a change in your life.

I probably never would have left Universal had it not been for that night. When the work is good and you're happy, you don't want to change. And so after my experience at Universal, I went over to Warner Brothers and I think Leo Lotito Jr. was the department head there at the time. I worked on *Bring 'Em Back Alive* and I did *Falcon Crest*, too.

It was around this time that Bari would have a meeting that would forever impact her life, both professionally and personally, when she decided to show her work to Tom Burman, who she shared an immediate connection with.

Back when I was at Universal, this makeup artist there used to always tell me that I needed to show my work to Tom Burman, because they thought he would love my work. So, after I came back from working on *The Border* in Texas, I took my portfolio over to Burman Studio. When we met, I felt like I was immediately tuned into Tom; he was just wonderful.

He was just starting up on *Cat People* (1982), so he was looking to create a feminine approach towards Nastassja Kinski's transformation. I agreed to come on board, and we've been together ever since. I still wasn't really a makeup effects fan at that point though. I appreciated the art to it, but I always approached everything from a sculptural point of view. When we did the head cast for Nastassja Kinski, we discussed how you could take a woman's face and morph it organically into a cat. So that's how I approached it, with four or five different clay sculptures of how she anatomically morphs into this cat creature.

I know in a lot of instances, makeup people look at other makeup artists' work, but for me, Michelangelo and Da Vinci were my gurus. These contemporary effects artists are truly doing great work, but my heroes were different than their heroes. So, I don't think I ever got nervous in my work because the things that were inspiring me as a makeup artist were so different from what was inspiring everyone else.

Tom and I continued working together and then we got married. For my nature, I couldn't be with someone that didn't understand my work. I take it so seriously and I'm so passionate about my art that if I couldn't share it and wrestle with it with someone else, I just couldn't be with the person. I couldn't be married to someone that I couldn't share my art with. That's one of the many reasons I'm grateful for Tom.

Dreiband-Burman continued to collaborate with her spouse on a variety of science fiction projects including the adventure comedy The Adventures of Buckaroo Banzai Across the 8th Dimension and Star Trek III: The Search for Spock as well.

Honestly, *Buckaroo Banzai* was a bit of a nightmare. It was so disheartening because W.D. Richter, the director, had a lot of problems during production on that film. Our initial makeups were supposed to take three hours. They were these beautiful, multi-faceted, twelve-piece applications, and then on the day, they told us we only had 30 minutes to get people into their makeups, so we had to make everything as a mask.

We were broken-hearted because we had put so much into those makeups, and now we had to go with what we felt was a cheap route. So, artistically, *Buckaroo* was a depressing project. But it takes things like that to make you realize, "I will not let this happen again." At the time, I was still too green to be able to stand up for something. But I think as you get legs in the business, and as you get a stronger reputation and the respect that comes along with that, you just learn how to say no sometimes.

I enjoyed working on *The Search for Spock,* even though I wasn't a Trekkie. I was aware that I was working on a property that was revered, but I didn't really have any pressure on me because of that. We worked on the Klingons, doing the forehead appliances, and I think the way we were able to change those appliances and how the foreheads looked more natural was a great step forward for those characters. We did some beautiful work on that film; it was great.

For their follow-up project, Dreiband-Burman and her spouse headed to the Goon Docks in Oregon for the 1985 family comedy The Goonies, which was being produced by Steven Spielberg and directed by Richard Donner. The Burmans were tasked with bringing the lovable Sloth character to life, with the assistance of John Matuszak who would be underneath the extensive practical makeups. Little did she know at the time, her efforts on The Goonies would lead to multiple collaborations with Donner on several of his future projects.

I love Richard Donner. I think that he's a wonderful person and collaborator, and I have always enjoyed working with him. Originally, Craig Reardon had three months to do *The Goonies.* One day, we got a call, because he wasn't able to deliver on the show. Where he had three months to work on everything, we literally only had just nine days—all while people were closed for Christmas, too. We quickly had to take a non-working situation and make it into a working thing, which included an animated head with servos and those kinds of complexities.

I definitely would not call *The Goonies* a leisurely experience whatsoever, but that thrill of trying to make this impossible deadline was very exciting. And John Matuszak (who played Sloth) was a trip. He was this six-foot-seven, huge, hulking man. When we would get him ready, I would work on the front. They would put up apple boxes for me in front of John, and then Tom and his brother Sonny [Burman] would do the back. John was also a bit of a party guy, and I remember one day he came in with a bit of blood on his knuckles at four in the morning. Who knows what he got himself into.

We wanted to make sure that Sloth had a lot of empathy too, because the character was counteracting his size and his massiveness in the eyes of these kids. I think that our makeup and John gave Sloth a lot of heart, and that made him feel like magic on the screen. The real bliss in makeup is when you're doing something that you know is your best makeup. A problem you can run into as a makeup artist is if the actor inside the makeup isn't able to bring it to life. It doesn't matter how good the makeup is if the performance isn't there.

But John was wonderful; he would visit us afterwards at our studio from time to time. He used to have to bend over to come into the studio door and when he would walk in, he would yell, "Where's my little buddy?" And his "little buddy" was Tom, of course. John really was such a great guy.

Before re-teaming with Donner on several other films, Dreiband-Burman utilized her talents on films like Throw Momma from the Train and The Running Man, designed the makeup for the Dr. Jenning character in Howard the Duck, and was the creative force behind the look of "The Supreme Leader" villain in Francis Ford Coppola's 3D short film Captain EO, which featured Michael Jackson in the titular role, and Anjelica Huston as his nemesis in the project.

I've worked on a lot of great projects, but *Captain EO* has always been one of my favorites. The first person that was going to play the Supreme Leader was Shelley Duvall, but she didn't want to be encased in makeup, so she quit. Then, Anjelica Houston came on board, and she didn't want to be encased in makeup either. It was at that point where I said, "Okay, I think it's time for me to redesign this thing." I wanted to make her this evil witch in black and white, with Michael Jackson's character in color as a contrast, and then when she transforms at the end, it's this really dramatic change. I thought it all came together beautifully, and Anjelica was simply fabulous to be around.

In the late 1980s, Richard Donner reached out to Bari and the Burman Studios once again for his darkly comedic take on Charles Dickens' A Christmas Carol. Donner's new adaptation, Scrooged, featured Bill Murray encountering ghosts, ghouls and specters as he learns (quite literally in some instances) the true meaning of Christmas spirit over the course of a day. When Donner approached Dreiband-Burman, he mentioned it wasn't going to be a "big show," but after looking over the initial script, it became very evident that Scrooged was going to be heavily reliant on practical effects to bring Donner's vision to life.

I was always excited to get a call from Richard, because he's so much fun to work with. When we talked, he told me that he had a script he wanted to send us, but it was a show with no makeup in it. Tom and I read it over, and we both realized that this was going to be an incredibly effects-heavy movie—essentially the opposite of how Richard saw it. We went back and forth with him, and then he realized the possibilities with these different ghosts, and how much effects could play into the comedic aspects of the script.

He gave us total freedom, too, so we had a great deal of fun working on *Scrooged*, and Richard really trusted us on the characters. In an interview that we did for our [*Planet of the Apes*] documentary, he said, "The thing about the Burmans is that if you're working with the Burmans, you never have to worry about their work. That way, you can focus on everything else, because you know they've got it covered." He knows that we listen to what he wants and then we make it happen.

And when it comes to Tom, his strength is inventing. He's not a person that would want to do the same thing every day, and this really allowed him to go all out and try so many different things. Between the Christmas ghosts, Frank's boss [played by John Forsythe], Buster Poindexter as the cabbie, and then a bunch of other gags, we were pretty busy on *Scrooged*. It all paid off though, because we were nominated for an Oscar because of our work, and that was thrilling.

It was very exciting to go to the Oscars, especially since I was able to take my parents to the show. It's always wonderful to be acknowledged for your work, and I was very proud that we were being recognized for doing such a wide selection of makeup, which doesn't happen very often. To me, when you get honored in any way for your work, it really puts a value on your art, at least from a personal perspective. It's why we worked on *Nip/Tuck* for seven years, it's why we worked on *Grey's Anatomy* for twelve years. Respect and loyalty are a big deal to me.

Bari continued working on numerous film projects throughout the 1990s, including Avalon, which Dreiband-Burman cites as one of her favorite makeups ever— "that film allowed our makeup to tell the story." Her other 90s credits include The Godfather: Part III, Dead Again, Wayne's World, Last Action Hero, Body Snatchers (1993), The Mask of Zorro, The Rage: Carrie 2, and many more. But it was at that point in their careers where she and Tom felt like it was time to take the Burman Studios in a different direction.

I'm a practical person. Whenever we were working on different films, we were always having to go away to these different locations, and that was hard to do because of our son, Maxx. It was around the time he was nine years old where I decided it was time to start doing television, because it meant we could work locally.

Everyone thought we were crazy, but I wanted to be able to pick Maxx up from school, have dinner together, and be able to have some semblance of a quality family life together. But many other effects people thought we had lost our minds because TV was nothing at that point. We didn't have a reputation back then either. But we were able to bring feature-quality makeup to television, week in and week out, and that's how our reputation became so strong. And subsequently, you immediately saw this shift in effects in all these different shows.

We worked a lot with Tracey Ullmann, who is just a dream to work with because she loves makeup. She loves the process, she loves how it can exaggerate a character, and she always enjoyed the process. We briefly worked on *The X-Files*, but that wasn't a good experience at all, which was unfortunate because it was a show I was very excited to work on. We did the *Young Indiana Jones* series doing some old age makeups, but then once we started working on *Chicago Hope*, we noticed that we suddenly became the go-to shop for all these different medical series.

Once we began to show what we could do with *Chicago Hope*, that led to more opportunities, like *Grey's Anatomy*, because the same producers for *Chicago's Hope* did *Grey's Anatomy*. We did twelve seasons there. It was wonderful. But it was when we began working on *Nip/Tuck*, when our work began to be recognized on an entirely new level.

Created by Ryan Murphy, the creative force behind recent series like American Horror Story, American Crime Story and so many more, Nip/Tuck became a pop culture touchstone in the early 2000s during its six-season run on the F/X Network, and forever transformed the landscape of cable television series.

It absolutely changed television. Nobody had wanted to do it when Ryan was trying to get it going – either because his approach to the world had some camp to it, or the fact that it also dealt with serious issues as well. They asked us to come and do the pilot episode, which Ryan had hoped would win over potential networks.

Tom initially didn't want to do it because it was shooting down in San Diego, but because it was going to be dealing with creating photo-realistic anatomy, I really wanted to do the pilot. Eventually, I was able to convince Tom that we should take the job. I immediately liked Ryan too, especially because he would shoot our work very closely. I'm a real detail fanatic, and not many directors know how to shoot effects like Ryan does.

So, for the pilot, there was a character that we had to transform on-camera, and Ryan kept telling us that we needed to wait. It was around eleven o'clock at night and he came up to us and finally said, "You have ten minutes to get this entire transformation done." Tom and I just looked at each other, because everyone had been there for so long already, so now the pressure was really on both of us to pull this off.

I can't exactly remember how the sequence went, I just remember Ryan was shouting while he was directing, and Tom was crouched under the table making all these things work as Ryan would yell the next thing to do. We ended up doing six stages of makeup effects all in one take though. When Ryan said to cut, the cameraman looked over and said to him, "Oh my god, did you see that?" It was like a ballet; it all just came together beautifully.

We were over at Paramount one day, and one of the producers was walking with Tom and I downstairs. She told us that the reason the show was greenlit was because of that scene. It all rested on our work. I just thought it was really classy for her to even say that, because producers aren't always so generous with their praise.

But Ryan gave us so much freedom, trust, and respect on that series, and he let us do what we wanted to do because we never limited him on how he shot things. You can't fool Ryan. Everything has to be beyond perfect, and we did that for him. I begged Ryan to let me do the Carver mask in season two, because it had to be disturbingly perfect. It couldn't be a store-bought prop mask either, so that mask became a personal mission of mine.

There wasn't anything that I didn't love about working on *Nip/Tuck*. Everything about that series was pure art, and no one had seen a television show quite like it at that point either. It was a real showcase for our work, and the fact that we won an Emmy for that pilot was a great affirmation that the work we were doing was just that ground-breaking. In fact, there was an episode where they wanted to have a dog undergo plastic surgery, so we had to duplicate this dog. It ended up being so photo-realistic that the Humane Society came in one day because they thought that we were using a real dog. But doing our very best work for Ryan was always deeply important to both of us.

After more than 40 years in the industry, Dreiband-Burman's desire to keep creating hasn't slowed down one bit. A brilliant sculptor and painter whose work has always stood out amongst her peers, she credits her unwavering enthusiasm for the creative arts and a strong collaborative spirit with her husband Tom as two of the reasons why she has so thoroughly enjoyed her career over these past four decades.

I love working with Tom. He comes from a completely different background than I do. My family worked in fine art, and his dad was a prop man who also made these amazing monumental World War I sculptures in Nebraska. He worked on all these horror films too, before we even met. But the thing about those differences is that I have never put my passions on him. And he's never imposed his passions on me either.

When we would do prosthetics and other artifacts, watching them come to life was always fascinating for me because Tom was more of a storyteller in his work. One of his many strengths is that he is really good at inventing and creating effects work. I'm more focused on the details of photorealism, anatomical design, painting, or art you would see in a museum, and all these fine details that I feel need to be obsessively perfect. Ultimately, we're both good at two very different things; what I'm really good at is not his strong suit, and what he's really good at is not my strong suit. We complement each other perfectly in that regard. I'm always caught up in the moment of the effects, and he's thinking about the whole story.

Honestly, I know that I am probably very different than most of the makeup effects people who came up around the same time, too. For me, the appeal of the work comes from a different place, and I think the one thing that I have always carried with me that is really important is to treat every time I do makeup is like it's the very first time. I still get giddy, nervous and excited—it doesn't matter whether I've been doing it for forty-some-odd years or not.

I also think a big thing about working in this industry is to keep your ego in check. You've really got to concern yourself with being the best person you can be, and never lose sight of why you're there in the first place. I'm there to collaborate with the director, the writers, the actors, and if everybody is giving a hundred and ten percent, then it's bliss for everyone involved. That's movie magic.

The other thing I always tell people is, even when you don't realize it, opportunities come at you twenty-four-seven, continually. You have to constantly be paying attention. When I was at Universal and I was devastated about my car situation, my equipment and the disloyalty, I could have just stayed there. But that was my opportunity to do something different, and look at what happened. To me, we all have a certain window of time on Earth, so what do you want that to look like? Seize any opportunity you can, and pay attention, because the situation may not fit your picture at the moment, but it just might be even better in the long run.

Tracey Takes On - Tracey Ullman and Bari Dreiband-Burman

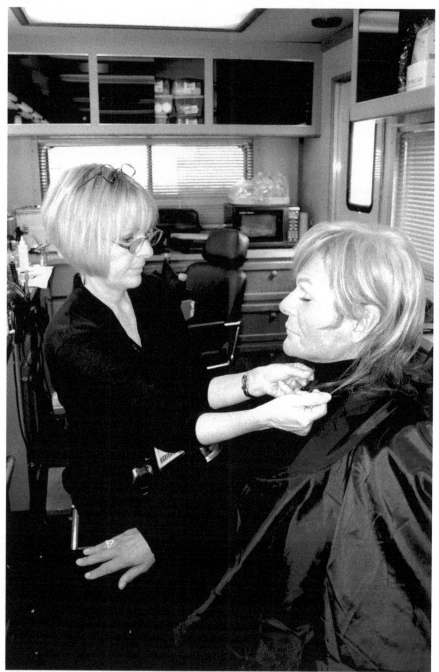

Bari Drieband-Burman at Work

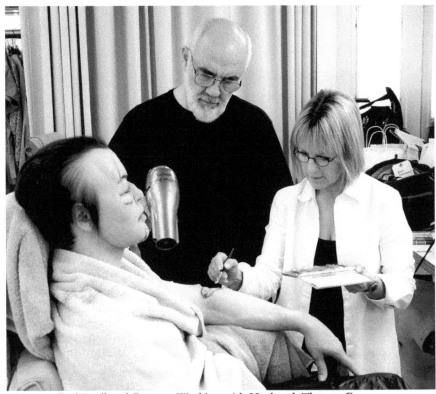

Bari Dreiband-Burman Working with Husband, Thomas Burman

Conversation with…
PATRICK TATOPOULOS

Special Effects Makeup Artist

Stargate (1994)
Independence Day (1996)
Godzilla (1998)
Underworld (2003)
I, Robot (2004)
Silent Hill (2006)
Underworld: Evolution (2006)
Underworld: Rise of the Lycans (2009)

A triple threat artist who spent his first 30 years living overseas in France and Greece, designer/director/special effects master Patrick Tatopoulos was inspired to follow his creative instincts from a very young age, a fascination that would carry him to places he never dreamed possible.

When I was a small kid, I remember hanging out with my grandfather on Sunday afternoons, sitting by the river, and watching him paint. I didn't necessarily think, "I want to do this exactly," but when I watched him, I saw his passion and technique, and as I grew up, I turned out to be a very artistic kid.

What really got me going were creatures. I would start to sketch out creatures, monsters, severed heads – things like that all the time. When I was in school, my teachers would see these drawings and be like, "Is he okay at home?" But I was a very happy kid and had a great family. It just so happened that I was fascinated by these very macabre things, so once the teacher understood that this was just something I liked without being weird about it, everything was okay.

The movie that got me the most was [F.W.] Murnau's *Nosferatu*. That was life-changing for me because of how spooky and eerie that figure was. That was when I decided to buy clay to sculpt my own creatures. I let them dry and painted them. A good friend of mine took pictures of them, and I tried to get in touch with Rick Baker and other great artists that I had learned about in Hollywood, but it was hard to get an appointment with any of them to show them my work.

After I passed my exams, I started to work for sports magazines and other places doing little sketches and doodles. Then one day, I decided to move to Greece from France to start a new life. In Greece, I became the only person who was working with an airbrush at the time. Airbrush was still a new tool, and I became this rock star in Athens because I was using the airbrush better than anybody else. I got a lot of work painting on the side of vans and fun art projects like that.

Eventually, I decided it was time to take my portfolio and head to Los Angeles. My suitcase got stuck in Amsterdam, and so I landed in L.A. without a portfolio. It was a disaster. Here I am, standing on Hollywood Boulevard, and I've got nothing to show for myself. But it just so happened that the day before I was supposed to leave, my suitcase arrived. I started calling everybody up, but nobody could see me, except for Makeup Effects Laboratories (M.E.L.,

Inc.). They had me come by to show them my book, and they said I needed to work some more on my technique, but I was headed in the right direction. They didn't have any work at the moment, but they told me they would call me.

So I flew back to Greece thinking that the whole trip was a failure. One month later, I got a call from Makeup Effects Lab, and they wanted to have me come work for them, and they were going to get me a Green Card, too. I couldn't believe I was finally getting my big break.

As he set out to make a name for himself for the United States, Tatopoulos was thrown right into the mix at M.E.L. and helped out on a few horror projects as he got his bearings at the shop.

My very first job was working on *The Blob* (1988), and I had to do vacu-form work, which was all new to me. Then, the next show I did after that was *C.H.U.D. II [Bud the Chud]*. I was mostly doing manufacturing stuff, not so much artistic things at first. There was this kid across from me that was sculpting a heart, and even though he had been working on it for a week, nothing was coming of it. So I gave it a shot, and everyone liked it, and because of that, I started sculpting more and doing more artistic projects.

Over time, I became more of a sculptor, a bit of a painter, and a bit of a mold maker, too. When they discovered that I was particularly good at drawing, they started to use me as a concept artist, and whenever a job would come in, I would do all the drawings, which I loved. My next job happened on *Beastmaster 2 [Through the Portal of Time]*, designing the witch, starting from the original concept of the character, all the way through the build. That's when I realized that I was really into being involved in the design process from start to finish.

Looking to continue to hone his craft and gain more experience in the realm of special effects, Patrick began finding work outside of M.E.L., but he didn't have to look far for new opportunities.

Across the street from Makeup Effects Labs was a company called Global Effects, which was run by Chris Gilman. There was a friendship between the two companies, so Chris started to give me work. We had been working a lot on *Star Trek: The Next Generation*, and one day they came in and asked me to play around with this creature for Michael Westmore for an episode called "Conspiracy." The creature was like the *Star Trek* version of a

Xenomorph, and Michael ended up getting an award for that episode, so that was my first connection to awards and things like that.

Around the same time, Chris was just starting on *Bram Stoker's Dracula*. A designer named Eiko Ishioka initially designed the armor, which was stunning. When she presented Francis Ford Coppola with the helmet, he didn't really click with it. Meanwhile, I was working at Chris' shop doing props like the inkwell and the top of the cane. Eiko called me up one day and asked me to do some drawings, so I ended up redoing the helmet for *Dracula*, which Coppola liked.

At that point, the production designer for the film, Tom Sanders, saw some of my drawings and told me to do the concept art for the castle and some other drawings. I never really got the credit for it, but I did end up doing the concept art for the chapel for Dracula, and Coppola ended up using that art for his wine label that year, too, so that was a neat thing to come out of it. And then things really started to change for me after that.

I was hired to be a concept artist for *Super Mario Bros.* in the art department, which is right around the time when I started to step outside of Makeup Effects Labs. I started to design the Goombas, and as I was designing these things, I was thinking about who could come in to build them, because I wanted to pay people back for all they had done for me – guys like Mark Maitre and Rob Burman. Mark ended up doing the little Yoshi creature, and Rob did a creature, too.

I know the movie had a lot of issues, but I got to do a lot of great work on *Super Mario Bros.* because I also did some designs for the sets in addition to the creatures. Also, if you look at the final stages of King Koopa inside that bucket when he's transforming, you'll notice something: in the last stage, when he almost deteriorates, he's almost like Godzilla. You know why? Because he's got something that has become my trademark in all my creatures: they all have chins. I don't know why I've always done that, but if you look at my work in *Independence Day* or *Godzilla (1998)*, they all have a chin.

Patrick had no idea that the very next project in his career would end up having the lasting impact that it did when he was called in for a meeting on an upcoming sci-fi project that would take the world by storm.

One day, I got a call randomly, and this producer asked me to come in and meet the production designer [Holger Gross] for a project called *Stargate*, which was being directed by Roland Emmerich. So, I went in and talked with

Holger for three hours. Two months went by, and I heard nothing, so I just assumed it didn't work out.

But then, I finally got a call, and the producers wanted me to come back and meet with Roland since he never got to see me that first meeting. I found out during that meeting that he had seen all of my drawings, even for Bram Stoker's *Dracula*. He liked the stuff I had done and asked me to come on board for *Stargate*. I started working as a concept artist on the village drawings and the desert stuff, but then Roland asked me to work on the creatures. So while he went to Germany, I drew three characters – Horus, Anubis, and Ra – then I painted them, and they were waiting for him on the wall when he came back.

Roland loved them all and didn't want any changes made, which was great. He asked me who we should have come in and build them, and that's when I offered to do it. I didn't even think twice, and obviously, this was a major moment for me in my career because I was stupid enough to say that I would do it. Roland agreed to it, and Russell Shinkle was my shop supervisor, and I worked with Jacob Garber, who was a creature sculptor, to build the creatures for *Stargate*.

During the making of *Stargate*, I had used some textures on a helmet that were part of an aesthetic that I was doing for all these different elements. When Roland saw it, he also wanted to use it on the pyramid and on a bunch of other things you see in the movie, so that one texture ended up having this huge influence on the entire movie. The reason I'm saying this is not to brag, but because my next movie with Roland, which was *Independence Day*, he asked me to be a production designer in addition to handling the aliens. And I think he saw that I could define the look of a film on *Stargate* and that impressed him.

And it was on Independence Day where Tatopoulos would find himself challenged in a variety of new and exciting ways.

I began working with another designer, Oliver Scholl, and right off the bat, we were working together on the production design of the film. What got me interested in *Independence Day* was mostly the alien world. I was more interested in the spacecraft, as that became more "me" than the other things I was doing.

As I was designing the spacecraft, the attack and the model ships too, one day I looked at the alien spacecraft, and I looked at the top of the alien head and realized that they were exactly the same thing. Do you think I did that intentionally? No, and that's okay. To me, design is an emotional process. It's never intellectual. For me, as a designer, I want to start with form. When I find a form that excites me, that's when I'll figure out everything else, because I like to be challenged. If you can imagine the way things move, articulate, how joints move, you can design these sometimes impossible things without needing to draw its core.

So I say all that because, when I started, I didn't think the alien head needed to look like the craft. It was just one of those organic, happy accidents that happened along the way as everything fell into place. It was a phenomenal film to work on, especially because I felt like I was part of the process, and *Independence Day* became a massive moment for me as a designer.

Tatopoulos would have the opportunity to collaborate with Emmerich on yet another sci-fi themed epic, the controversial 1998 Godzilla reimagining, which pitted the King of the Monsters against the Big Apple. Patrick discussed Roland's decision on taking the iconic creature in a bold new direction and how it once again raised the bar for him professionally once they had the approval from the heads of Toho.

It was when I was doing *Dark City* in Australia when Roland first called me about *Godzilla*. I was excited because I am a huge fan of Godzilla, so I knew this was going to be something huge. We talked about the direction he wanted to take with the monster, saying he didn't want us to do the traditional Japanese Godzilla. Roland wanted him to go 200 miles per hour charging through the streets of New York, which meant we had to start with a re-invention of the character. I knew going into it would be a controversial topic with fanatics of Godzilla (like I am), but it was an interesting challenge for me as an artist because it was a re-invention.

So I did two drawings, and the second one that I drew was the one that I felt really good about. At the end of *Dark City*, I went to France where Roland was at the time, shooting, and I showed him the drawings, he picked the one I liked, and that was it. I came back home and started to build the maquettes of Godzilla, and then we flew to Japan to show Toho, the production company, to get their approval. That was an important moment for us, especially with the detractors who say, "How could you dare to change Godzilla?" Toho had to approve it themselves, or it would have never happened in the first place.

I remember the meeting was in this big conference room with twenty different people from Toho, and when we unveiled Godzilla, they all stood up, and there was this big long discussion between everyone, and we didn't understand most of it. But they told us they were going to have to take the maquettes to Mr. Tomoyuki Tanaka, who was sick in his bed and passed away shortly after that. The next morning we got into the conference room, and I think we were both nervous, but then they told us that Tanaka had approved the maquette and said it was a great design, and it still had the spirit of Godzilla, even though it was a new take on the character, and that meant a lot to me.

When I got back to L.A., we had to immediately start building this thing, because it was such a massive undertaking. I was able to put together the biggest creature shop that had ever been assembled at the time. And it wasn't because I was cooler than anybody else, but it was because I had more choice as to who I could bring in, and I was lucky to have every great artist in town there at the time. Fortunately for me, I think when we started *Godzilla*, there was a bit of a gap where Rick Baker wasn't doing anything at the time. Stan Winston was probably in between projects, too, so it was the perfect situation for me in terms of putting together a brilliant crew.

We built a giant Godzilla, and a bunch of Godzillas that were all different sizes too, and working on this film was just the most exciting time for me ever since I had come out to Los Angeles. To be working on so many creatures at the same time, it was my paradise. I would walk in the shop every morning, and I could not believe how many unbelievable artists were also there, many who have either become their own shop owners or they've gone on to become these brilliant digital artists. It was incredibly exciting, and we even had to have security guards at the shop too, twenty-four hours a day, because of all the fans and the secrecy surrounding Godzilla.

There was this one surreal thing that happened during *Godzilla*. Out of the blue one day, Terry Gilliam called me up because he wanted to have a meeting with me for *Fear and Loathing in Las Vegas*, and he came out to my shop. As a European, and being a huge *Monty Python* fan, I was so pumped. But two days later, Roland came in with the idea that *Godzilla* was about a female Godzilla, and she's going to have seven babies, which meant we had to design and build these babies very quickly.

I ended up having to call Terry to tell him that I couldn't do *Fear and Loathing* after all. I was so disappointed, and because he's the most gentle guy on the planet, Terry sent me a letter that I still have framed today that says, "I hope we get to work together one day." That meant a lot to me.

Even though Tatopoulos had hit an enormous peak in his career with Godzilla, he would continue to flex his creative muscles on even more

science fiction projects, including both Pitch Black and The Chronicles of Riddick.

I can't remember how I met David [Twohy], but he wanted me to come on and design the creature for *Pitch Black*, and I was working on *Stuart Little* and *Supernova* at the time. It was a very instinctive design process on *Pitch Black*. We knew it had to fly, we knew it had to be a night bird that didn't have eyes, and we knew it needed to be fucking scary.

I decided that I wanted to do a creature that's very narrow from the front, so when you see it from the side, it's quite massive, but from the front, it's very narrow. I thought that was quite amazing, to be able to play around with a creature with that kind of design. I knew *Pitch Black* was going to be relying heavily on CGI, so I built a maquette of my monster, they scanned my design, and I was pleased with how it ended up looking in the end. I still think that creature is terrifying.

As soon as things started rolling on [*The Chronicles of*] *Riddick*, David brought me on board to start doing some concept designs. He wanted the sequel to be this big epic and also wanted us to rework the creature from *Pitch Black*, too, which I enjoyed because it meant that I got to play around again with a design that I loved. What's cool is that one of the creature designs that I had originally done for *Pitch Black* that didn't make the cut then was used in the latest *Riddick* movie. So I loved that my work on *Pitch Black* came full circle in some way.

During that time, Tatopoulos would reteam with Dark City filmmaker Alex Proyas for the big-budget sci-fi actioner I, Robot. Patrick discussed how he once again pulled double design duty, and how the project shifted once the film's star, Will Smith, came aboard.

When I first came on board for *I, Robot*, Alex had intended to make a very dark movie, like what he did with *The Crow* and with *Dark City*. Then, Will was hired to be the lead on *I, Robot*, and I love Will and have the best relationship with him, from working with him on *Independence Day*, and later, we would do *I Am Legend* together. But it is a fact that once he was on board, this was not the same movie we thought we were making. The movie completely changed, and it became a challenging venture for Alex. Not because of Will, but because a great filmmaker wasn't able to make the movie that he wanted to make.

The first thing I did on *I, Robot* was to design the look of the robot because I knew it was such a crucial visual element for the film. I went and visited with all these companies across America that built robots, and so many of them reminded me of the Mac computers that had come out ten years prior. Since our movie was supposed to be twenty years in the future from the day we made the movie, I figured that the computers of that time would be the look of the robots of the future. So I started looking at the current Macs and said, "That is it." It was an incredibly rewarding film to get to design for, but it was also another case of having to do two jobs at once, and it was completely draining on me too.

It was during the early 2000s when Patrick's involvement on Stargate would pay off yet again, as he was approached to take on the design of warring factions of vampire and werewolves for a then first-time director by the name of Len Wiseman who was just beginning to get the wheels in motion for his slick and stylish horror-action hybrid, Underworld.

The first time I worked with Len was on *Stargate*, as he had been doing stuff for the props department. He was also on *Independence Day* and *Godzilla (1998)*, too. So, one day I get a phone call from him, and he says, "I've got this movie called *Underworld*, and I'd like you to come work on it with me." He came by the shop, and we started talking about the creatures. He already had someone on board for production design, so I was coming in to do the vampires and Lycans. I think that overall, we spent about a month planning everything out.

The biggest thing we focused on for *Underworld* is that we wanted the werewolf to be completely different. In fact, the inspiration behind the final look of our werewolves was my homage to Rick Baker. When I first saw *An American Werewolf in London*, my favorite part of how that creature looks is not the final stage, it was the in-between stage. To me, that was very influential, and so I ended up building Len a maquette of it, and he thought it was great.

When *Underworld* came out, it wasn't a huge movie, so it took everyone by surprise, and we very quickly moved forward on a sequel. Len wanted me to design the décor too for *Underworld: Evolution*, in addition to the creatures, and I think that's when I realized I couldn't do both jobs anymore – not like I had been. It was starting to kill me, so I realized that I loved doing both production and creature design, but I also had a lot of talented friends who could build these things I was designing at their shops for me, so that's when I started to refocus my work at the time. I realized I could still do all the design work that I loved, and if I hired my friends to create them, then I was able to still work with all these great people that I enjoy working with.

I can't remember the exact timing, but I think it was shortly after *Evolution*, where I was offered the directing job on *Midnight Meat Train*, which I was attached to for a while. And then Len asked me to come and direct *Underworld 3 [Underworld: Rise of the Lycans]*, and I was excited about the chance to do something as a director for the *Underworld* series. In addition to directing, we also designed the new werewolf and worked on some new characters, too. But most of our focus was about the re-invention of the werewolf. That's what the film was about: *Rise of the Lycans*. So we took what we had and played around with it.

And the great thing about *Lycans* is that it was a $27 million movie, and we made $100 million worldwide. So it's not *Iron Man* or anything, but it did great, and I was very proud of that, especially as the film's director.

Tatopoulos continued to keep busy throughout the mid-2000s, designing creatures and monsters for Godzilla: Final Wars, Cursed, The Cave and Venom, and it was during this time that he would be given the opportunity to collaborate with one of his favorite filmmakers, Christophe Gans, on the big-screen adaptation of the highly popular Silent Hill video game.

For *Silent Hill*, I was familiar with the games before I got the call, and I was very familiar with the director, too. Christophe Gans is a Frenchman and one of my favorite directors – he's a very talented guy and the biggest cinephile in the world. All the walls in his house are covered with tapes and DVDs, and I don't think it's an exaggeration to say that he's seen everything. He used to be a critic, too.

For *Silent Hill*, we knew that we had to recreate this world and come up with these creatures and characters and make them scary for the film version, and we also needed to make sure we included all those iconic things about the game that fans would be expecting to see. There's a soul to the world of the video game, and that soul is organic and bloody. It's such an incredible video game that has such an incredible look to it, so we had to make sure we tried to capture that but also add something to it, too. But to me, what we did in the *Silent Hill* movie was closer to something like *Hellraiser* than anything else, because it's so hard to replicate a digital world like that.

We began looking at the CG characters from the game, but we had to find a way to blend them into our world. Christophe wanted to move a bit away from the CG effects, but at the same time, we had to match with the game, so we had to figure out how we could make this work practically. When you have a character like Red Pyramid, he's going to have to be on some kind of extension to give him the movements and size that he needs to feel in line with what you see in the game. He has to be able to play with the sword with that helmet on too. So we worked hard to get things like that right.

I don't know what it was, but *Silent Hill* had an aesthetic to it that I just really felt comfortable with. I'm super, super proud of it. Everything about it was harmonious. We had an incredible production designer on board, Carol Spier, and she was essential in defining the look of the movie. It was an amazing experience for all of us.

After Silent Hill, Patrick had the opportunity to collaborate with a series of then up-and-coming filmmakers, including The Pang Brothers on The Messengers, Michael Dougherty for the Halloween-themed anthology Trick 'r Treat, and The Ruins with Carter Smith.

The first time we met, Michael Dougherty immediately impressed me, and I found him to be an extremely knowledgeable guy. I didn't expect the movie to be as great as it was either, honestly, because I didn't know what Mike was capable of. But he just blew me away. Our collaboration together was on the werewolf sequence, and the budget wasn't huge either, but we worked hard to make it something special. *Trick' r Treat* as a movie was one of those things that came and went very fast, so it was a very brief project. That movie blew my mind, though, and it is good for only one reason: Mike. His work. Anyone else could have done it. But to me, that movie is what it is because of Mike and his creativity.

When *The Ruins* came along, Ben Stiller (who executive produced the film) called me up, and we met to talk about the project. I started to play around with the concept of the flowers. I knew the flowers were going to be important because they were going to kill all of those kids. My job was to come in and design the flower, which I did. We went through the process of the way the flowers would crawl, the way they'd attack, and we spent a good amount of time developing them. It was fun to design the flowers as a creature because one of the most difficult creatures to design is a flower creature.

I did something similar on *Justice League* – I created an alien flower. You go and try to design new flowers, but you can't design anything more alien than what's already out there. So, the challenge for that is, you have to do something that feels real, and you push it and push it until you get to a point where you're like, "Well, that's just fucking goofy," so then you have to pull it back.

What ended up making those flowers cool in *The Ruins* was the way they move, the way they do things; the choreography defined the creature. If I stand in front of an alien creature and it's not moving, it doesn't scare me. I believe "scary" is connected to a creature and its choreography and movement inside the frame of an image. If you try to make a scary flower by giving it teeth, you're going to lose. It can be gruesome, weird, or whatever. But it's what it does that makes it scary.

Over the last decade, Tatopoulos has continued to work steadily as both a production designer on films like Total Recall (2012), 300: Rise of an Empire, Batman v Superman: Dawn of Justice, and Justice League, and helped bring the monsters and creatures to life for Solomon Kane, Silent Hill: Revelation, Riddick and 2014's live-action Beauty and the Beast.

I've come to realize that regardless of whatever it is that I'm doing, what's important to me is that I want to be creating for the rest of my life, whether it's creating worlds or designing creatures. And the thing about production design is that it's a job that people still don't completely understand yet, which is a pity because it's an amazing job. You get to come in with the director at the beginning and define everything in that world.

And it's not just sets either. People think that when you are a production designer, "Oh, you build sets." No, it's not just sets. Construction builds the sets, and the designer designs the world, mainly. It's a tremendous job. And what I love about creature design is creating characters. When you've got a creature within its own world, suddenly it becomes interesting to me because suddenly that creature belongs to that world, uses that world, and plays with that world. The world emphasizes what that creature is. The mood, the spirit of that place emphasizes what that creature is, so when I get to bring all of that together, it is an indescribable experience.

Looking back on myself as a kid, I don't think he could have possibly understood what my life would become. Before I came to the United States, I didn't know what a movie really meant. I wasn't born a director. That "click" moment for me came later when I moved to Greece and started painting and stuff like that. But I do believe that the things that I got interested in during my youth and where I come from, that gave me everything that I needed to be successful in America.

I know that I overcame a lot of challenges, and I feel good about the fact that I positioned myself in the way that I have over the years. I came from a time when we used traditional tools: pencils, markers, materials like that, and now I'm working with a computer, just like everyone else. It's been an incredible transition. It's a very different world now than it was back when I started. Not in a bad way, just different. But I am glad that I came to Hollywood when I did because I relied on the fundamentals to get better as a designer and as an artist. I'm fortunate in that way.

SUPER MARIO BROTHERS - DESIGN FOR KING KOOPA

Independence Day

Independence Day

Godzilla (1998) Crew

Godzilla (1998)

Godzilla (1998)

Underworld

Underworld

Special Effects Makeup Artist

Predator (1987)
Gremlins 2: The New Batch (1990)
The Nutty Professor (1996)
Planet of the Apes (2001)
Hellboy (2004)

Hailing from San Jose, California, artist Matt Rose may have spent his formative years a mere six hours from the bright lights of Hollywood, but he had no idea that one day he'd be blazing his own creative path while contributing to some of the greatest horror and sci-fi films in modern cinema.

When I was growing up, it was a special time for movies. It was the '70s and the very early '80s, and my father really loved watching films of all varieties. I come from a large family, so we would have family night where we watched movies like *The Wizard of Oz, The Ten Commandments*, or the original *Planet of the Apes*, which immediately captured my imagination.

As a kid, I used to sculpt with clay a lot and make these Japanese monsters. My grandmother was a very religious woman, and she had me sculpt religious figures, so I was making this bizarre mix of religious figures, Japanese monsters, and *Planet of the Apes*. But once I saw *Planet of the Apes*, I realized I wanted to try to make what they were. As a kid, my dad explained them as "actors in makeup," but I didn't know exactly what he meant. I just understood makeup as colors you would put on your face; I didn't know how makeup could turn a human into an ape.

Eventually, I found some books about stage makeup and making rubber noses, but not much else. There wasn't much up north growing up that you could find, information-wise, other than the library, and all that stuff was pretty basic. But when I found the behind-the-scenes stuff on *Planet of the Apes* with John Chambers, that's what really grabbed me. I just knew I wanted to make masks.

As Matt explored his creative tendencies throughout childhood, there were many adults along the way who were kind enough to recognize his talent and provided him with the resources and support he needed the more he realized that makeup effects were something he wanted to pursue beyond just a hobby.

I was so lucky growing up, because all my teachers that I worked with, from elementary school through high school, were so supportive of what I was doing. My parents were supportive, too, even if they weren't sure what I was doing. But they always encouraged my art, and I was lucky in that regard. My ceramics teacher in high school really liked what I was doing, and said to me one day, "You must start taking pictures of your work. I know a fella up north, at a place called ILM [Industrial Light & Magic], who I think should see your work. Do you know about it?" Of course I knew about ILM, because what kid doesn't know about *Star Wars*? So, he sent the slides up to Phil Tippett and I just kept going on with my schoolwork and making masks and things like that.

I think it was in early 1983 when our phone rang at home, and my mom yelled, "Hey, Matt! Someone on the phone for you! It's Chris Wallace!" I was confused because there was a newscaster by that name at the time, so why would he be calling me? I picked up the phone and it turned out to be Chris Walas, not Wallace, who had been given my portfolio by Phil Tippett, and he wanted me to come out and interview with him for a movie he had coming up.

Of course, then it came out that I was still in high school at that point, so I couldn't actually do it, and then I found out later on that the film Chris was gearing up for was in fact *Gremlins*. That bummed me out for the rest of the year.

Even though he missed out on a prime professional opportunity on Gremlins, Rose's entrepreneurial spirit was soaring as he began selling his masks and making a bit of money for his efforts.

It was my mom who first suggested selling my masks. We took them to flea markets. Everybody was looking at them, "Oh, they're very nice," but nobody wanted to spend any money on those things. I don't think we ever sold any there, actually. But then, all of a sudden, friends of the family would want custom-made masks made for different occasions, and I'd make a little bit of money through selling those. Eventually, I tried going to different shops, but again, no one wanted to spend that much money.

Around that time, I ran into Steve Wang at my very first convention, and as soon as I met Steve, we hit it off because he loved masks beyond belief. He was just so cool. He's been a mask collector forever. He saw the masks that I was making, and we just became instant friends. We would meet up at his place and at first, we talked about making some short films and stuff like that— things to keep us busy. I think it was probably his idea that we work together to create a mask company, because he was much more sensible than I was. At the same time, my father, who was so supportive, offered up his shed and told us that we could clear it out and turn it into a little shop for us. That's where Steve and I started working and where our small mask company was born.

We pretty much sold everything we made, too, and we made tons of stuff. I think we ultimately broke even, so it was a good time. And by working with each other, Steve and I both were learning a lot of stuff we could take with us once we started working professionally in the industry.

After the heartbreak of not being able to work on Joe Dante's Gremlins (1984) due to the fact that he was still in high school, Rose made the trek down from San Jose to Hollywood to check out several of the leading effects studios at the time, not realizing how soon he'd find himself employed at one of them.

I came down to Los Angeles in 1984 and visited some of the shops, just to get a sense of everything. I was blown away by what I saw during those visits. I had no idea how things worked, so it was all very eye-opening. I visited Stan Winston's studio when they were working on *The Terminator*, but I didn't know that's what it was at the time. I do remember seeing Shane Mahan sculpting a mechanical skull, because that was when they were working on the giant, mechanical skeleton. It was so amazing, fascinating, and beautiful, and again, I didn't even know what movie it was.

As I met with all these different people, they kept saying, "Well, if you get ready to move down, give us a call." And that's what happened next. I got a call from Bob and Denny Skotak over at L.A. Effects Group. They were doing all the model work on *Aliens*. So, it was myself and Mark Williams who were hired to sculpt lava and then resculpt a derelict ship for the scene that was ultimately cut from the beginning of *Aliens*. But it was wonderful seeing things getting made, and to be a part of it, too.

From there, we found out Stan Winston was hiring for *Aliens* as well to do the creature effects, so I went over there and started to do some work, just because they were about to move everything to England. And I think just after that is when Steve came down and we worked on *Invaders from Mars* together.

Matt felt as if his first few productions were a prime example of trial by fire, considering that he and Steve Wang were working on multiple sci-fi projects at the same time over at Stan Winston's studio. Before he knew it, Rose would find himself employed by another legendary talent in the special effects world: none other than Rick Baker.

When we were on set for *Invaders from Mars*, there was a call going out that Rick was hiring for a movie called *Harry and the Hendersons*. We didn't know that's what it was at the time, but everybody wanted to go work for Rick. So, we were all lined up outside of the production trailer that had the only phone on the set, to set up our interviews. It was myself, Steve Wang, and some other fellas who got a chance to go work on *Harry*, so we rolled right into that, which was great. It was such an interesting variety of work to experience one right after another—to go from *Aliens* to *Invaders from Mars* to *Harry* was wild.

I stayed on at Rick's, too. I was working on a Michael Jackson video that was put on hold for a while. I didn't work on it again until around two years later, and then this movie called *Hunter* came through and Rick had me start on a maquette, only for it to be gone the next day, as it went to Boss Film Studios. But then, it eventually became *Predator*, and went over to Stan's. So, Steve and I went over there and we worked on both *Predator* and *The Monster Squad.*

We were working on The Creature for *The Monster Squad* when *Predator* came back in. Steve was the engineer of the whole thing. My God, the suits are so incredible because of him. That was the case for both films. Steve is one of the biggest fans of The Creature out there. So am I, but his love runs really deep. That Creature suit was made so beautifully, and it was due mainly to him. In our industry, we had never made suits like that, so doing The Creature suit really prepared us for what we had to do on *Predator.*

The Predator suit engineering was, once again, done all by Steve Wang. I remember this one day when Steve was concerned about the paint job on the Predator's armor. He couldn't quite figure it out at first. He didn't want to make it silver, and he didn't want to make it just gold, either. It had rained, and we were walking over to a roach coach, and he just stopped and said, "That's it!" I looked down and saw this oil stain in a puddle, and that's what helped Steve crack that design.

There's an interesting story to the Predator's helmet, too. If you look at it closely in the first movie, you'll notice some battle damage, like a small dent. You know why it's there? Because I screwed up the mold. I accidentally hit it because we were moving so quickly, and I messed it up. When it came time to show Stan, I told him how I thought that the helmet should have some damage, to sell the idea of this creature being a warrior, and he said to me, "Wow, that was a great call. Good thinking—I love it." Had he known the real story, he might have fired me, but I covered it up well. We also ended up having to kill Bill Duke's character a lot, too. I think it took six or seven times to get that head explosion right, and we put Bill through a lot that day. But he is such a lovely guy and we loved working with him.

As he continued working during what would become known as the Golden Age of Modern Makeup Effects, Rose enjoyed the assortment of shops, talent, and films he'd have the opportunity to experience during that phase of his career.

It was a really chaotic time to be an independent contractor because of all the different shows that were going on at that time. For instance, during 1987 and 1988, I worked on a bunch of different movies within a very short time span. I went from *Beauty and the Beast* to *Coming to America* to *Gorillas in the Mist* to *Fright Night Part 2*, then *Beetlejuice* and *Outer Heat*, which became *Alien Nation*. We even did *Amazing Stories*. I eventually went to Japan for three months for a project out there, and when I came back to the States, Rick told me that he was going to start working on *Gremlins 2*, and I stayed on at Rick's for over fifteen years from there.

With Matt having to miss out on being a part of the first Gremlins film, joining the effects crew of Joe Dante's ambitiously over-the-top sequel was truly a dream come true for Rose.

I was so excited to be a part of the sequel. When Rick called us all in, he started off with a smaller group of people, but it grew very quickly. It was extremely exciting, because it was always in flux. It was probably the first time we were involved with writing parts of the script for a film, in creating characters and everything. We'd come up with a type of Gremlin, and Joe would come up with a scene to do around it. We used a lot of Warner Bros. cartoons for our inspiration.

Most of our ideas didn't make it in, but we did a lot of maquettes during the planning stages. Then, when they got a script together, we had to narrow the list of Gremlins down immensely. It was so massive. But we all had individual characters we were told to supervise and follow through with, not just their Gremlin versions, but their Mogwai versions as well.

We just built like crazy. It was such a lengthy process. In the end, most of us were puppeteering all those Gremlins as well. The one scene at the end, where all the Gremlins are in the lobby and are being soaked right before they get electrocuted, we all had a Gremlin on each arm and a helmet Gremlin that was stuck to our heads. It was incredible. I still think the best Gremlin in that movie was the Mohawk Gremlin, because his design was so cool, and he turned into a spider, which was actually a scary creature.

As he steadily worked over at Rick Baker's Cinovation Studios over the next few decades, Rose enjoyed how one project seemed to roll right into another, even if there were a few hiccups along the way.

When I was at Rick's, somehow another project would always be just on the horizon waiting for us. It was so interesting, and I now realize how lucky I was to be there at that time. At the same time, there were a lot of things we worked on that never got made, or effects that got cut for silly reasons. We did a version of *The Creature from the Black Lagoon* and *The Mummy*, and we were even working on the effects for a movie called *Isobar* that was very close to getting made by Roland Emmerich. There was also a dinosaur movie called *Rex* that eventually got made by a Japanese company.

On *Batman Forever*, there was a giant bat that we worked on that was really awesome, but it got cut out of the movie. I think they released the footage for it over the years, but it was cut out of the film, which was a real shame. Mark Roemmich came up with this incredible wing design that actually gave this bat a hurricane-like effect. As it came down at you on a dolly, it was frightening as heck. The wingspan was massive; it was over ten feet wide, so it was very imposing. That apparently scared McDonald's, who was putting up toys for the film, so they said, "You have to cut that from the film."

I was sad to see that go because I thought it was a great scene. But in this business, you never know what is going to happen with any production, or what kind of script changes are going to come along, so you just have to be ready for anything.

During the early 1990s, Rose experienced an eclectic variety of film work that came his way at Cinovation, including The Rocketeer, Wolf, the aforementioned Batman Forever, as well as Tim Burton's delightfully entertaining Ed Wood, in which Rick Baker was tasked with transforming legendary actor Martin Landau into one of horror's most iconic performers of all time: Bela Lugosi.

Rick did that makeup for Martin; I only did the detail work on him. I have to admit that when I first heard that they wanted Martin Landau to become Bela Lugosi, I just didn't see it. I didn't know how Rick was going to make it work, but he did this brilliant mock-up, and there it was. I could finally see it.

By the way, Martin Landau is one of the nicest guys on the planet. In my experience, I don't always like actors, but I do love watching them perform, if that makes sense. Martin Landau just knocked me out by how kind and cool he was to all of us. I am a huge fan of his, from *Mission: Impossible* to *Space: 1999*. I grew up watching him and always loving his work, but I never saw him as Bela Lugosi. I couldn't see it until Rick was able to put it all together. I still think that it was an incredible makeup, and when he was in the makeup, Martin was really into it. I could tell he loved every bit of it. He was always playing around once he became Bela. If that's not the greatest thing in the world to get to experience, I don't know what is.

Matt also got to experience another cinematic titan undergoing a transformative makeup effects process when comedian Eddie Murphy underwent heavy prosthetics to become the titular character (as well as a few family members) in the 1996 remake of The Nutty Professor.

One of the cool things about working at Rick's studio was that I usually got to wear every makeup we made during all the different tests. I loved it, too. The original *Nutty Professor* test makeup was done on me, and I had a blast. On that one, I also did the "Mama Klump" makeup on Eddie Murphy, and I had worked with him previously on *Coming to America* and had really enjoyed that experience.

Eddie always blew me away with how he'd wear makeup, too. He just loved it, and his enthusiasm would show through those performances. Everyone else would just make a character, but Eddie could make them feel real. It was just incredible. And when I was doing *Nutty Professor*, he was so into everything, but the "Mama Klump" makeup made him nervous because he'd never done a female character like this before.

Honestly, it was the weirdest thing to see Eddie Murphy nervous. He's performed on specials with millions of people watching, so this seemed easy in comparison. But once the makeup was done, it was like a light switch went on and he went right into the character. If you watch his performance as Mama, it's quite moving, actually. Not because of the makeup, but because of him and his performance.

After The Nutty Professor, Rose had the opportunity to undergo another makeup-fueled metamorphosis on Tim Burton's 2001 remake of Planet of the Apes.

I was insanely thrilled about doing it. It all started around 1995, with Peter Jackson's version. All I really heard about it at that time was Rick mentioning it, because he had just finished working on *The Frighteners*, so they had become friends. How I remember Rick describing it was that Jackson had wanted to create a Renaissance-style world in his *Planet of the Apes*.

Rick did a sculpture with himself as a gorilla, and then he created the makeup. There was an orangutan makeup test that was supposed to be done on me, but as Jim McPherson was finishing up that makeup, all of a sudden everything got shut down. I don't know what the reason was exactly, but everything shut down, and all those designs got put in a box.

Eventually, the project went ahead with Tim Burton some time later, and Rick wanted to use Jim's original orangutan makeup, which was still packed away, on me for the makeup test. Everything was still good, but the foam smelled like cat pee. Even though it smelled awful, I just went for it anyway because I knew we needed to get it done. It looked great and I remember asking Rick to make me a beautiful red beard to put on top of the makeup. It looked incredible, although I was dreading the next part.

See, I've done makeup for a long time, and I've worked with people with lenses, but I cannot put lenses in my eyes myself. I have this reflex reaction where if you come near my eyes with anything, I will just blink repeatedly to try and avoid anything going in. Of course, because I didn't want anyone to know, I didn't really mention it to anyone because I knew they were going to have to put lenses in, so I was just quietly dreading it and hoping I could do it.

And then, they told me that they wanted to do two layers of lenses, with a set of the eyes we created for Jack Nicholson in *Wolf* on top of the sclera, and I was freaking out in my head because that sounded even worse. It took a few tries, but when I finally had both sets of lenses in, they looked like the coolest things ever. It was like somebody had cut my head off and put a monkey's head on top of my body. When we were in the mix of everything, we were all so excited we were going to work on a new *Planet of the Apes*, that we just plunged right into everything. The film itself ended up not being all that good, but the makeups in it were top-notch, and I stand by our work.

Rose would eventually go on to collaborate with another visionary filmmaker, Guillermo del Toro, for the 2004 adaptation of Mike Mignola's Hellboy comic book series, although he found the road to getting that film made was even more bumpy than what he experienced on the Planet of the Apes remake. His patience and perseverance would pay off, though, as he took home the Saturn Award for Best Make-Up during the Academy of Science Fiction, Fantasy and Horror Films annual event.

My partner in crime, Chad Waters, and I had been working together on a bunch of different films for a few years, like *The Nutty Professor*, *The Ring* remake, *Batman & Robin*, and we worked together on Mikey for *Men in Black*. One day, he told me about this project he had heard about called *Hellboy*, and I don't follow comics that much, so I didn't really know what it was. But Chad did, and he showed me the first big *Hellboy* comic series, called *Seed of Destruction*. When I read it, I just fell in love with the character and Mike Mignola's world.

Now, this was back in 1999, and that's when he told me that Guillermo del Toro was going to make it into a movie, and we both knew we needed to work on it. Chad and I had worked on so many things together, we knew we had to do this one together, too. What's even more amazing is that as we were both thinking about this character, we only thought of one actor to play Hellboy: Ron Perlman. Even back then. That's all I saw when I read the comic. I don't know why, but that was it.

So, Chad and I went off and did two maquettes of Hellboy. We used colored clay, so we could do the character without painting it. Then, from Rick's basement I grabbed a bust of Ron Perlman, from his days working on the *Beauty and the Beast* TV series, so we could finish sculpting all the details. And we eventually got to meet with Guillermo. I didn't really know him very well, but he had visited the shop back when we were working on *Gorillas in the Mist*, when he was still doing effects. I didn't talk to him a lot, but I remember he was a little bit kooky, but just an all-around enthusiastic person who loved movies.

It all just came together between the three of us, and as it turns out, Guillermo had been thinking of Ron for the role, too, but everything kept getting pushed around for almost four years. There was a lot of pushback from the studio because they didn't think that Ron Perlman was a marketable enough name. It was absurd. But Guillermo would always push back, saying, "No! It has to be Ron Perlman!" They ran through so many names, and finally they agreed to do the project with Ron Perlman, but I think at half the budget.

So, it all worked out eventually, and Chad and I got to spend six months in Prague working on set. And truthfully, Ron and I did not hit it off right away. I think he had hoped it would be Rick doing his makeup, because that's how it worked on *Beauty and the Beast*, but once we got through the tests, he began to trust me. We did an incredible amount of work on *Hellboy*. There were ninety days of shooting, and each makeup took at least five appliances, plus the body, the arms, the tails, horns, and hair pieces. It was outrageous the amount of effects that went into just that one character.

But every single day, Ron would just embrace all of that makeup, and he always had a smile on his face throughout the process. I was blown away by Ron in that film because he never once complained about everything he had to endure each and every day. He really brought that makeup to life, and I don't think any other actor could have done it better.

Throughout his career, Rose has been a part of many memorable films featuring some of the best practical effects work ever committed to celluloid, and after more than thirty years in the industry, he still remains grateful for every opportunity he's received, but what he's most appreciative of is the fact that he's been able to work alongside some of the greatest artists in the realm of modern practical effects.

I love this industry. I love the craft. I love everything about it, but the best thing out of my career is knowing all of my colleagues. I really mean that. Even if you have arguments, there is still this sense of camaraderie that we all share. We have all been in the same battles together, and we understand the importance of being supportive for each other, even if we don't always agree 100 percent on everything.

There is really something special about being a part of this industry, and I've been so fortunate to not have only met so many wonderful people, but I've been able to work with so many amazing and talented artists throughout my career. How wonderful is that?

There was a time when I hit a low point in my career, though. I was feeling overwhelmed by the digital stuff taking over practical effects, and I was almost going to retire and just toss my tools into the Los Angeles river. And by chance, I was visiting with my friend Chad Waters. He was doing some sketches of this one character, and I just felt compelled to sculpt him. So, I went home and stayed up all night, sculpting this character. It was almost like I was chasing the sun.

But I finished it and showed Chad the next day, and then asked him to draw me another picture. And he did. He did about four of them and he was the one who got me going again. I felt like the Tin Man, or something like that, where you're dormant until someone comes along and revives you. Since then, we have kept working together like this, and any time I get morose or something like that, Chad helps me shake the tree and get it all going again.

When you're an artist, you have to be solid and stay solid, regardless of any doubts. It's worth it. You will never know going in if you're going to ever be completely successful. I know it sounds crude, but I always tell aspiring artists to just jump in, even if you're frightened. The risk will be worth it, if you're able to do what you love for a living. I'm lucky that I've been able to spend my entire adult life loving what I get to do each and every day. Some days are better than others, but I wouldn't have wanted it any other way.

Sadly, Matt Rose passed away on Friday, January 25, 2019 at the age of 53, nearly a year after this interview was conducted. He will be greatly missed by all that knew and loved him. May his creative spirit live on forever.

Matt Rose playing around with one of his creations

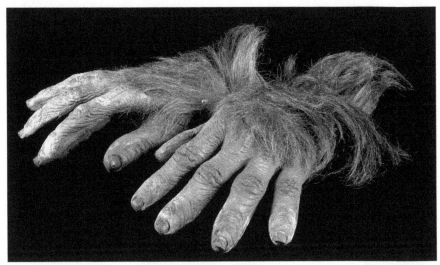

Harry and the Hendersons

Harry and the Hendersons - Makeup Crew

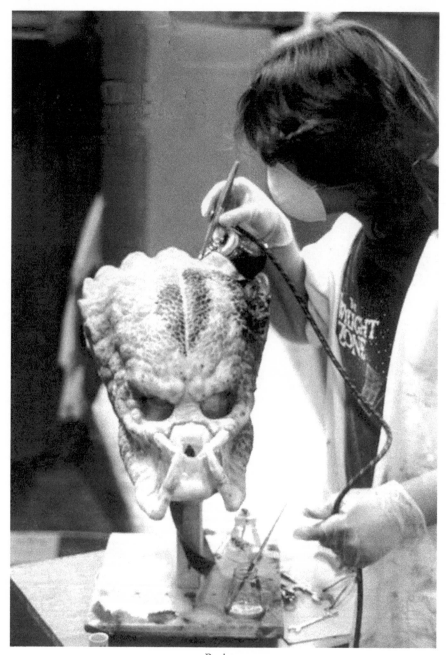

Predator

Predator

Predator

The Monster Squad

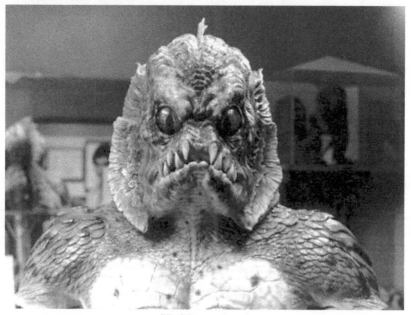

The Monster Squad

The Monster Squad

The Monster Squad

Hell Comes to Frogtown

Hell Comes to Frogtown

Moonwalker - Michael Jackson Robot Head

Moonwalker - Michael Jackson Robot Head

Gorillas in the Mist

Gremlins 2: The New Batch

Gremlins 2: The New Batch

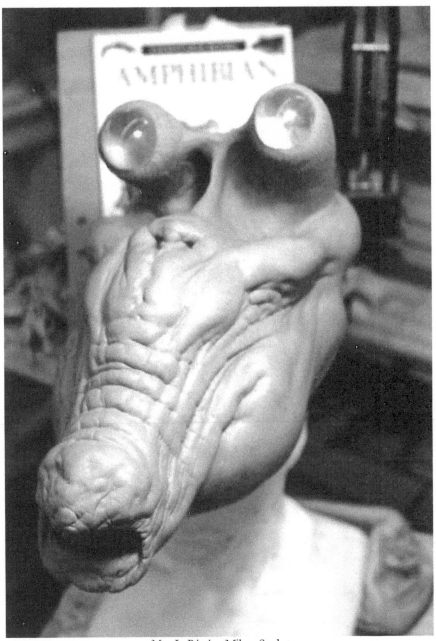

Men In Black – Mikey Sculpt

Planet of the Apes – Sculpt

Hellboy - Matt Rose Sculpt

Hellboy – Sculpt

Hellboy – Ron Perlman

Hellboy - Shots with Ron Perlman

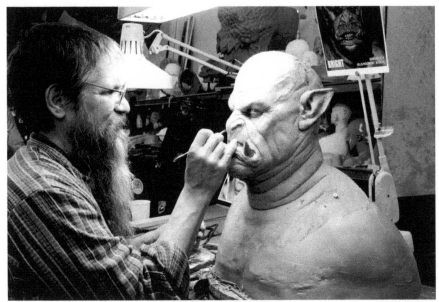

Bright - Sculpt

Bright – Sculpt

Conversation with...
DOUG DREXLER

Oscar and Emmy Winning Special Effects Makeup Artist

Starman (1984)
Poltergeist III (1988)
Dick Tracy (1990)
Star Trek: Generations (1994)
Star Trek: First Contact (1996)
Battlestar Galactica (2005-2009)

As a multi-hyphenate artist, Doug Drexler has done it all in his career: practical makeups, sculpting, graphic design, illustrator, visual effects, and scenic arts. He's worked with some of the biggest on-screen talents in modern cinema, and he got his start in the industry under the tutelage of one of the greatest talents ever, the legendary Dick Smith.

Dick Smith has always been the guy. He didn't have a crew of forty people. He worked out of his basement and I always admired the hell out of that. Rick Baker's done incredible work, but I don't get all googly-eyed over him. With Dick Smith, I did. If it wasn't for Dick, I'm not sure what would have happened to me career-wise. He gave me my start. If you were an aspiring makeup artist, Dick would do anything to help you out.

I remember back when I was working with [John] Caglione [Jr.]. There were a couple of kids from Italy who were visiting the North Carolina Film Studio. They wanted to be makeup artists. Carlo Rambaldi came over to us and said, "There are two Italian boys looking for information and tips. Don't tell them anything. We need to protect our jobs." John and I were both shocked, because we came from the Dick Smith school. Dick was one of the most generous artists, with both his time and his knowledge, and anyone who ran with Dick Smith never tried to keep secrets. Dick was never about that. So when we did meet those kids, we gave them everything we could.

Before meeting Dick Smith, Doug did his best to try and find any and all information that he could as a kid enthralled with practical effects growing up on Long Island, and New York City.

It was really hard to get any kind of information back then. There were very few makeup books. There was Richard Corson's book [*Stage Makeup*], which is still on my shelf to this day. That was the book that got me going, and where I discovered Dick's work. There was a whole section of him doing the makeups for *Little Big Man*. That blew my mind.

I studied those, and enlarged the pictures using a projector to try and read the labels on the cans to figure out what everything was. Lee Baygan had a couple of books as well. He was the head of makeup at NBC at the time. But to show you what kind of guy Dick Smith was, if you wrote him, he had mimeographed pages he'd send you—things like how to put on a bald cap or what his formula was for his Marlon Brando old-age stipple that he invented for *The Godfather*. You just couldn't get that stuff anywhere else.

I showed some of my first works to a friend who wrote for various cinema magazines. He had just interviewed Dick and gave me his telephone number. I couldn't believe my good fortune. It took me two weeks to build up the courage to call him up, and he was amazing. Dick kept me on the phone for a couple of hours, forking over information. Three months later, he offered me my first job. It was on *The Hunger*, which was a huge job, with many stages of old age makeup for David Bowie. There were Change-O-Heads, crumbling mummies, and full body mummy suits. It was the most amazing job to start a career on. It was my college of prosthetic knowledge. It was surreal. One minute I'm studying those pictures of Dick at work in his lab, and the next minute I'm sitting at that very desk. That was the first of many "pinch me" moments in my career. It was all I wanted to do from that moment on.

Even though he found his professional calling in the realm of special makeup effects via Dick Smith, Drexler had originally set out at an early age to follow an entirely different creative path.

When I was a little kid, I was always drawing, and I remember that the first thing I ever wanted to be was a comic book artist. I was a first generation Marvel fan, and watched all of those characters being born. I was a huge fan of Stan Lee, Jack Kirby, Steve Ditko and Don Heck. I realized that most of these guys lived in the New York Metropolitan area, and started looking in the phone book for them. It turned out Don Heck lived a half a mile from me and for two summers, Don let me come over and he mentored me. He'd throw tracing paper over my sketches, and show me where I went wrong.

That was the beauty of growing up in New York. I could visit *Mad Magazine* and chat with Al Feldstein and Bill Gaines, or visit Marvel, and sit with Stan Lee in his office. Stan was always gracious and very funny, too. I didn't meet Jack Kirby until much later. He invited me to his home in Thousand Oaks, and that was unforgettable. But mark my words, once I retire, I am planning to do a graphic novel, and finally lay that longing to rest.

Another big influence was Forry Ackerman and his magazine, *Famous Monsters of Filmland*. That may have been my earliest exposure to makeup artists like Jack Pierce and Lon Chaney. I loved the classic Universal Monsters, but I never considered being a makeup artist until I was about twenty-three. I was a late bloomer.

In 1980, I was working at an architectural supply in Manhattan, called Charette. The company had a big Halloween party that year. I was determined to take first prize. I'd collected all kinds of how-to articles on effects from sources like *Cinemagic* magazine, back when it was still a fanzine. There was a terrific article on how to do a *Planet of the Apes* makeup, so I dove in. It hooked me, the entire process. The mold making, the sculpting, running foam latex. That was the start of it. I spent the next few months finding all the books on makeup that I could get my hands on.

That's about the same when I found out that Dick Smith lived in Larchmont, which is only about fifteen minutes north of New York City. And not even a year later, I was working with him on *The Hunger*. I still remember when Dick called and asked me if I would come to work with him, I had been mixing a bucket of plaster. When I came back to that bucket, it had set. It had solidified, along with my life. So, I keep that bucket of plaster in a case in my living room to this very day.

Even though he was very much the "new kid on the block" in Dick's shop, Drexler found an immediate family while working alongside several other talented artists who would all go on to enjoy illustrious careers, much like Doug has done for decades now.

During that time in my career, I was falling in with a bunch of guys who would become close friends of mine for decades. Guys like Carl Fullerton, Kevin Haney, and John Caglione Jr. Caglione and I became like brothers, and we had some crazy adventures over the years. A book in itself. So, to be up at Dick's with those amazing guys, it was like jumping head first into a whole new universe.

Dick Smith always had his own way of doing things. It was just a cornucopia of data for me to take in. I still have my notebooks from those days. I was so excited to be a part of *The Hunger*, getting to watch Dick sculpt all those makeups. It was *Little Big Man* times five. The mummy suits were a big deal. They all had to be built up by hand. We had spandex suits fit to the actors, made two-piece plaster bandage molds of their bodies, and poured rigid polyfoam forms to put the spandex suits on. We built on top of that, spatulating uncured foam latex, adding rib cage appliances and the tops of shoulder blades, and so on.

We even had to make our own makeshift ovens using space heaters, where we'd hang the suits in a room with the heaters, close the door and cook them. But it was on that show that John Caglione [Jr.] came up for a visit, and we hit it off. And that chance meeting kickstarted another phase of my career.

Getting to work alongside another rising talent like John Caglione Jr. provided Drexler with a new set of experiences, opportunities, and of course challenges through their various early collaborations such as Amityville 3-D and C.H.U.D..

John called me in for *Amityville 3-D* to come and work with him in his basement, and of course I was thrilled for the opportunity. Then, he asked me if I wanted to go to Mexico City for four weeks, so I was really excited. The thing about going on location to shoot is that you have to learn to be resourceful and take care of yourself. Production isn't really going to take care of you, but that was part of the challenge. I loved the idea of going to another land where they spoke another language, and figuring out how I was going to get by. It taught me how to roll with the punches.

Amityville 3-D was directed by Richard Fleischer, who had directed *20,000 Leagues Under the Sea* and *Fantastic Voyage*. His father was Max Fleischer, who founded Fleischer Studios, which was the main competition with Walt Disney back in the 1930s. They did all the old wonderful *Superman* and *Popeye* cartoons that we still marvel at today. It was a thrill to work with Richard. Just mind-boggling. We were working at the Churubusco Studios in Mexico City for *Amityville* and Mexico City was quite the adventure. The dollar was worth a lot there, so I could get a cab and keep it all day. We had loads of fun.

The second picture I did with John was *C.H.U.D.*, and I'll be perfectly honest, I didn't even put that on my résumé for a long time. But as the years went by, I realized there were a lot of fans of *C.H.U.D.* out there, including Homer Simpson, and now, I'm rather proud to be associated with it. We did *C.H.U.D.* out of John's little house on Long Island. We had a big oven that we'd bought for *Amityville 3-D*, to cook that big demon suit in, so we knew that we could go right into *C.H.U.D.*

I fondly remember that Kevin [Haney] was someone who would get carried away during production meetings. His imagination would just run wild. He had this wacky idea for the C.H.U.D. where it's neck would stretch through the apartment looking for Kim Greist. John and I were exchanging glances, thinking about how much extra work was being added. Rolling his eyes, John said to me, "He's going to have to do it himself, because he was the one who promised it. He's on his own."

It was really late into production, and we were running out of time, so I jumped in and helped. We made the head with a super elasticized, stretchy skin-flex neck. There was a ramrod that would push the head forward, stretching the neck. Kevin did a real nice job finishing it off, but we were exhausted. The morning of the shoot, the stretching C.H.U.D. head was on its stand, finished, and looking great, but Kevin sat there with a Dremel tool, endlessly sharpening the monster's teeth.

All of a sudden we hear this blood curdling scream. The drill he was using caught the lip of the C.H.U.D. and spun everything around like spaghetti on a fork. It was a mess. I think Kevin had checked out at that moment. But Caglione, ever the man of action, scooped the entire project into a big cardboard box, put Kevin under one arm, the torn C.H.U.D. under the other, heading for the van waiting to go to set. John said, "It ain't over until I say it is," and I'll never forget that. That filled me with admiration for John. His survival instincts just kicked in, as they would do many more times in the future during our partnership.

Drexler continued to collaborate with John Caglione Jr. over the next 12 years while still working for Dick Smith from time to time, two entirely different types of experiences.

When you were working with Dick, you were working with God. He knew he was God, you knew he was God. But with John, he was a young guy just starting out, so we were like a couple of kids who were always goofing off in a basement. It was a lot more relaxed, and there was a lot more laughing, although Dick had quite a sense of humor himself. Although not everyone knows that. But John and I worked together supernaturally well. We had a shorthand. We were a great team. We used to play good cop/bad cop with the production, where they would try to split us up, make us contradict one another in order to get their way. So, we would always have these plans in place on how to defeat them.

I remember on this one film, production was using Walkie-Talkies, and it just hit me one day that I could pick up a police scanner and cut into their line of communications. I made friends with one of the PAs [production assistants], asked him if I could see his Walkie-Talkie, feigning excitement about the latest model Motorola, and he would hand it right over. I took it around the corner, used a screwdriver to pop open the case, and the frequencies were printed inside. And I'd program those into my scanner.

In the makeup room, using my scanner, we could hear everything they were saying. They thought that we had ESP [extrasensory perception]. We did eventually get hilariously caught. The first AD [assistant director] and the director came in the makeup trailer, and they were giving us a hard time about something. Just then I noticed that the AD was keying his mic. Every time he keyed his mic, he saw my transceiver stop. I had forgotten to hide it. He looked up at me, and I was smiling like the cat that ate the canary.

But I've had a lot of fun partnerships during my career, and I've met a lot of great people over the years, but John was a significant force in makeup for me. We looked out for each other, and since he knew more than I did about makeup in the beginning, he enjoyed teaching me stuff. I learned a lot from him. If I was intimidated to do something, he would just blow it off. He'd go, "Come on man, don't give me that." That's the way he was, and that personality dynamic that we shared made us a great team.

For as much as he loved collaborating with his now longtime friend Caglione Jr., Doug was always happy whenever his mentor Dick Smith would ask him to come aboard new shows. It was on John Carpenter's Starman where Drexler really had the opportunity to connect with the effects legend.

Starman is one of my favorite John Carpenter movies, and for me, it was a really important film on a personal level because it's the show where I really got to know Dick Smith. I was his right-hand guy on that job. Up until then, he had mostly used Carl Fullerton and Kevin Haney as his go-to guys to help him work stuff out. But they weren't available for this one, so when he asked me, I was totally blown away that he would even consider me.

He invited me up to Larchmont for dinner so we could break the ice, because this was a new dynamic for both of us. Dick used to do this thing after dinner where he would take Saltines, spread some butter on them, and eat them. I'm sitting there, with the bar of butter on the table, trying desperately to sound smart. I'm gesticulating with my hands, when my pinky finger hooks the bar of butter, and flips it up in the air. Dick and I both watch it go in slow motion. It came down in Dick's lap. He looked at me slack jawed, I looked at him slack jawed, and that was it. I just totally burst out laughing because it was so ridiculous. As soon as I started laughing, he started laughing, and we had a great guffaw. It was all perfect after that and I was never nervous around him again.

Back when we did *Starman*, there were no computers yet. The type of stuff we were doing on that film, in six months, we could easily do now over lunch time. But back then, we had to use replacement animation. For the head morph we had to make 140 heads of the kid transforming into Jeff Bridges. It was just fraught with unknowns because there was no way to really test anything; no way to play it back. You had to just dive right in and hope to God that it was all working together. One wonders how Ray Harryhausen did it.

We had made something like three or four rubberized Change-O-Heads that were the boy at different stages. There was a structure underneath that was articulated where the neck, shoulders and the face were cut into numerous mobile pieces. You could crank each one up a little bit so that he'd start to stretch. We'd lock it, make a mold of that, take it out of the mold, crank everything up a little more, and make another mold. There was a mountain of molds by the time we were done. I think that's why my thumbs are shot now. Mold-making is hard on your hands, but it was worth it.

Since there was no way to know if it was really working, it was pretty scary. I knew Dick was nervous about it as well. *Starman* was a pretty tense experience, but it was a big moment for me, my career, and my friendship with Dick Smith. In a way, we became brothers on that job.

Drexler faced even more new challenges when it came time to work on Michael Mann's Manhunter, as he was tasked with handling the practical makeup effects for a film by himself for the very first time.

John didn't want to go to North Carolina, so he told me that I was doing it. I was scared to death. I am almost positive that it was the first time I'd gone on a job alone to put makeup on an actor. The thing that I learned on *Manhunter*, because I was by myself, is that you have to be aggressive. You have to ask to look through the camera. You cannot be afraid to stop the roll if you think something is wrong with how your work looks. But you've got to be pretty damn sure, or it could get you into some trouble.

Michael Mann loved that I did that, though. I was looking out for him, and myself, of course, and he knew that, so he never gave me any trouble. One funny thing I recall is that Michael would pick up buzzwords—like "stipple." It was a makeup word. You'd stipple some color over something. He didn't know what it meant, but he'd use it all the time. He would call me over and say, "I think that Francis [Dolarhyde, played by Tom Noonan] needs some stipple." I'd look at him and I wouldn't know what he was talking about, but Dick always taught me that if you're dealing with someone who does that, what they're really looking for is reassurance. So, whenever Michael would say, "Someone needs some stipple," I'd go out with a sponge and put on a show for him. And then he'd go, "Perfect!"

Michael Mann could be a taskmaster though. They had built Dolarhyde's house in the middle of the woods in North Carolina in a bog, and they were racing against time, because it was sinking an inch every day. Dino De Laurentiis had given him an ultimatum, where Michael had to have the movie finished in the next few days or he was going to pull the plug on the picture.

Manhunter was a non-union shoot. Everyone was hungry to work, no matter what. People were tired and just wanted to finish the job. Michael gave us a speech and told us that he needed everybody to sign away their overtime in order to get the movie done. I called up John in New York, and I remember he said, "Well, guess what? That means the makeup crew is getting on an airplane and coming home tonight. How about that?" So, it ended up that we were the only ones on the crew getting overtime in the end, and I don't feel too guilty about it either.

But to make things worse, the physical effects guys quit on the very last night. Now they had no way to do bullet hits, and that's what the last night was mostly about. I remember I said to Neal Martz, who was there working with me, "You know that any minute now, they're going to come in and ask us to pick up where the physical effects guys left off." We didn't want to get involved. We knew we could do it. The other departments figured that out and begged us to. No one wanted to have to come back. It was improvisational makeup from then on.

We took a bunch of eggs, blew out the yolks, painted them black, and filled them with blood. They were like blood hand grenades, and they made a nice shotgun hit. There's a scene where Dolarhyde shoots a cop in the face and the back of his head comes off. We borrowed a hair piece from the hair department, bobby-pinned onto the guy's head, got some monofilament line and stuffed jam and blood in there. When Dolarhyde fired, the cop would jerk his head back, and I'd yank the line. It looked like the back of his head blew clean off. We actually made it all work. *Manhunter* was tough, but it was the show where I really learned how to be myself, and roll with the punches.

While working a few years later on Gary Sherman's Poltergeist III, Drexler faced some new challenges, and disappointment as well, when one of the effects he was most proud of was never fully captured for the film the way he intended.

I remember having to do a lifecast of Heather O'Rourke, and it was the most terrifying lifecast that I've ever done. I flew out to Los Angeles, and borrowed Mark Shostrom's lab. This was not that long after those horrific accidents on the *Twilight Zone* movie, so they sent someone out from Child Welfare to watch over me working on Heather. She was this teeny tiny little girl. Her nostrils were the size of baby peas, so if you're putting alginate on her, you've got to keep those itty bitty airways open, working delicately around the nostrils. It all came out, but I was a nervous wreck the entire time. I don't think anyone knew though.

The reason for the life cast was that there was a scene where Heather has to face the demonic character, Kane. That turned out to be a great moment for me. Dick just couldn't see how it was going to work, but I just knew it somehow. I took the Kane lifecast, and I took Heather's lifecast, just to see what I could do, and I nailed it. I was very proud.

Dick was impressed, too. When he saw it he got excited, and asked to sculpt the final appliances. It turned out to be an amazing makeup. The awful thing is that if you watch the movie, there's not a single close-up of that makeup whatsoever—in the whole freaking movie. When they were going to reshoot the ending of the film, they came out to our lab. I put this 8x10 picture of Heather in the makeup on the wall, with a sign that said, "This makeup did not get one single close-up," where I knew Gary Sherman could see it.

After *Poltergeist III*, Drexler's life changed big time after he and John Caglione Jr. were hired by Warren Beatty to create the stunning, and eventually award-winning makeups for Beatty's 1990 adaptation of the popular comic strip *Dick Tracy*.

That film brought us to L.A. We always knew that Los Angeles was 'movie town,' and John and I knew that we would eventually end up there, but we didn't want to come out unless we had something substantial lined up. Then *Dick Tracy* happened, as natural as can be.

Basically, Warren Beatty changed my life. I wouldn't have met my future wife, Dorothy, if it hadn't been for Warren Beatty either. He's a much different kind of a guy than John and I were. Most of his career was rooted in reality, so *Dick Tracy* was so far outside his realm. I think that's what appealed to him, and it was the reason that he wanted to do it. I remember reading about *Dick Tracy* in *Variety* a year before it started, and John and I just looked at each other and said, "Well, whoever gets that job is going to get an Oscar." There was no doubt in our minds because it was the perfect character makeup job.

One day, we got a call from [*Dick Tracy* co-producer] Jon Landau saying that he had mentioned us to Warren. Apparently, Beatty met with Rick Baker, Rob Bottin, and a few other Los Angeles people, and just wasn't sold on them. We happened to be out in L.A, working on a TV movie about Liberace, and Jon asked if we could come up to Warren's house to meet him. So, we drove up to Mulholland Drive and his assistant told us to go down into the screening room and Warren would be down shortly. We waited there about twenty minutes, and then, all of a sudden, there's Warren Beatty in a towel, dripping wet, like he just stepped out of the shower.

He sits down on the couch, looks at John and I without even saying, "Hello," and says, "What can we do?" We didn't know what he meant, "What do you mean, what can we do?" And he says, "How can we make it better?" And that's when we realized Warren was talking about the script. We had never had anyone ask us how we could make a script better before, because most people don't want our opinion on that.

So we chatted with him for a while about the script, shook hands, and left. I guess it was during that meeting when he decided we were the ones. I do remember that when we first got *Dick Tracy*, Dick Smith said that due to union rules, we would never get the chance to lift a brush on stage. But Dick underestimated Warren Beatty. Beatty got us in, and the union president, Howard Smit, personally drove our paperwork out to our lab. It was pretty incredible.

Dick Tracy was really way ahead of the wave, in terms of comic book movies. Chester Gould wrote and drew *Dick Tracy* for half a century, and I remember reading it as a kid. They were these amazing oddball stories that would sometimes be really far out, and it was all because of this one guy. I grew up reading *Dick Tracy*, so it meant an awful lot to me. The movie story-wise was really not much like the comic strip. The art department, makeup department and wardrobe all nailed the looks perfectly though. But I thought as far as the story went, it was very ordinary and flat. I missed the oddball, far-out stories of Chester Gould.

In an early production meeting Warren gave a speech about how everything we were doing with *Dick Tracy* was new for all of us, because all of their previous films were reality based. So this was a big departure for everyone. Of course, it really wasn't new for the makeup team, but Warren and his other department heads needed to get themselves into a comfortable position in this fantasy world, so they could understand what the film needed.

Vittorio Storaro, the DP [Director of Photography], had been planning on how he was going to light *Dick Tracy* for years, but he didn't know anything about makeup. He didn't even consider it, which made for a rather big monkey wrench. Makeup is a camera trick, especially the kind of makeup where you're using foam latex. Light doesn't diffuse through it, and if you light it with a red light, or a green light, half the details are going to disappear. And that's exactly what happened.

In the early tests, the makeup looked horrible. It was those primary colors. They were killing the paint on the appliances. When we explained the issues, Vittorio's answer was that he was, "The author of the cinematography." John and I knew we were in trouble, because Vittorio was an established genius.

Thankfully, another genius stood up for us: production designer Dick Sylbert. He said "Vittorio, how come that door that I painted green looks black?" Warren got up, smiled, and said, "We have to allow Vittorio the right to be wrong once in a while." The very next day Storaro came into the makeup trailer with lights outfitted with a range of gels on them so he could see the effect that they had on the makeups. And life was good from there on.

***Dick Tracy* would prove to be one of the biggest and most challenging projects of Doug's illustrious career in film, but it's a time he looks back on fondly and can tell stories about for a lifetime because of his involvement with Beatty's daring approach as a director, as well as the fact that Drexler and John Caglione Jr.'s efforts earned them an Academy Award in 1991, much like they had predicted.**

Warren was working in a new arena on *Dick Tracy*, but he was never overwhelmed by it. I'm sure he was stressed, or maybe not, you wouldn't know, because he always maintained an even strain. One day, when we were doing a complicated scene where Sam Catchem [Seymour Cassel] is coming down the hall, and there is all this dialogue overlapping, and people are crossing the frame in front of him, and Warren shot it forty-two times.

I was standing next to Dick Sylbert watching in amazement, and I let out a low whistle. Dick explained that there were suits from Disney on set, and this was Warren's way of showing them that this was his picture, and that he would do it his way. Dick told me, "This is nothing. You should have been on *Reds*. He did seventy-two takes once." That was his message to any producer who tried to interfere with his work: I'm Warren Beatty, and I'm going to do exactly what I want.

Thinking back, just getting *Dick Tracy* was more of a longshot than winning an Academy Award. We shouldn't have gotten it. With guys like Greg Cannom and Rick Baker already out in Los Angeles, why hire us? It was a miracle. Warren just had a good feeling about us. When we did the first makeup tests for Steve the Tramp, Warren took one look and said, "You guys are getting a statue. You are definitely getting a statue."

After Dick Tracy's release, John and I went to the makeup bake-off down at the Motion Picture Academy. That's an event where you go to show off and explain your work that is under consideration. As we were leaving, Warren stepped out from behind a curtain to pat us on the back. He actually came down to the Academy to support us. We were touched by that. I think we all felt—Warren included—that if we didn't win the Oscar that year, then something was definitely wrong. But you never know. There were some great makeups, but nothing that really compared to *Dick Tracy*. It was a makeup tour de force.

After we won, I remember thinking back to when I was a kid, first deciding that I wanted to do something creative. My father thought I was crazy. He was from the generation that grew up during the Great Depression. He was in World War II. He'd say, "Get your head out of the clouds and plant your feet on the ground," because to him, nobody really does this type of work for a living. I think it was when John and I got nominated for the Oscar that he finally took it seriously. Up until then, it was, "Oh, are you still doing that makeup thing?" But to this day, my dad jokes that if I need advice, I ask him first, and then do the opposite.

It was right around the fourteen-year mark of his career when Doug decided to change things up with a transition to new filmmaking arenas due to his deeply-seated desire to work in the Star Trek universe. Drexler got his wish, spending the next seventeen years of his career being a part of a variety of Star Trek television properties, including Star Trek: The Next Generation, Star Trek: Deep Space Nine, Star Trek: Voyager, and Star Trek: Enterprise, as well as four different Star Trek films: Star Trek: Generations, Star Trek: First Contact, Star Trek: Insurrection, and Star Trek: Nemesis.

After *Dick Tracy*, I knew that I had to work on *Star Trek*. The first thing I did was go and see Michael Westmore at *Star Trek: The Next Generation*. I knew him, but we weren't pals yet, and I literally begged him to let me come in and work on the show. He couldn't understand why I wanted to move on from doing features to working in television. I explained to him my obsession, and that it was *Star Trek* that got me going as a kid.

Back in 1968, at the age of 14, I read *The Making of Star Trek,* and it was an epiphany. *People actually made a living doing this!* I was 14 and reading call sheets, production memos, and budgets. That book was a career-maker for me. It just took off from there. I was at the very first *Star Trek* convention in New York City in 1971. They expected a couple hundred people to attend and over 2,000 showed up. I remember Gene Roddenberry himself ran the projector when showing the *Star Trek* blooper reel.

Fast forward to 1986 when I read that they were going to do *Star Trek: The Next Generation.* My head exploded, and it was with original producers Bob Justman and Gene Roddenberry. I idolized them. I couldn't believe it. John [Caglione Jr.] said to me one day, "You're a professional. Why don't you just call Bob up on the phone right now?" I remember incredulously replying that I couldn't just call Bob Justman on the phone, just like that. But then I stopped myself. Well, why couldn't I? So, I got on the phone, called the Paramount switchboard and told them that I wanted to speak to Robert H. Justman at the *Star Trek* production office. And I had Bob on the phone – just like that.

We struck up an immediate friendship that continued until Bob passed many years later. He invited me out, and I visited Paramount while they were first gearing up. They didn't have a makeup artist yet, but there were union problems that would prevent me from working on the west coast. On my second visit, Mike Westmore was already hard at work. That's when I first met him, and he would become a lifetime friend.

Even though he set out to work in the makeup department of Star Trek: The Next Generation, Drexler was able to stretch his creative muscles in other ways for the long-running series, as well as on several other Star Trek television properties in the future.

When you're on a continuing television show like *Star Trek*, it becomes one big family. Every department knows every other department, so you look out for one another. Motion pictures are a different animal. It's nomadic. You work together for a few months, and then it's on to the next job, and a completely different crew. On *Star Trek*, sliding sideways into another department is always possible. I had been spending long hours on board the

Enterprise marveling at the production design, and the art department was calling me. So, it felt like fate.

I worked eight years in the *Star Trek* art department as a graphic designer, eventually as a senior illustrator, and then onto visual effects. Being a part of *Star Trek* opened up all these other creative opportunities for me. I had been doing makeup for fourteen years, but there were just so many amazing things happening all around me, how could I not stretch my legs? Most people find a career, and that's it for 40 years. To me, that's strange. Most of my friends do, and that's fine. That's their passion. When I got out here to L.A., and got to work on *Star Trek: The Next Generation*, it was just like one big candy store. I wanted a taste of it all.

When *Star Trek: Deep Space Nine* came along, I made the jump to the art department, thanks to Mike Okuda, the show's scenic art supervisor. We'd help design sets, interfaces for consoles—everything you saw, we probably touched. I was in the art department for seven years on *DS9*, and I was having a great time doing something totally different. I was in heaven. After *Deep Space Nine* finally wound down after seven years, visual effects beckoned. The art department and VFX worked hand in hand, and naturally I got to know those guys really well. I picked up the CG program they were using, and learned it.

So, when *Deep Space 9* ended, and *Star Trek: Voyager* started up, Ron Thornton at Foundation Imaging brought me to work on it as a CG artist, where I stayed for two years, until *Star Trek: Enterprise*. When I came on, they were having trouble nailing down the ship. Mike Okuda suggested to Herman Zimmerman, the show's production designer, that they bring me in with my new computer design skills. And we were breaking new ground as we were designing the ship because it was probably one of the first times it had ever been done in a television art department.

Instead of drawings, we were building the design explorations of the *Enterprise* in the computer. It was revolutionary. We could see a design from any angle, in any kind of lighting and even see it in motion. Today, that's all routine. But to get to design a *Star Trek* ship was crazy to me – I was so lucky.

In the mid-2000s, Doug would have the opportunity to become part of the filmmaking family on yet another prominent science fiction series, the SyFy Channel's re-imagining of the original Battlestar Galactica, which ran from 2004 to 2009. While on the air, it garnered countless accolades and awards, including four Primetime Emmy nominations for the series' outstanding visual effects, and two wins, with Drexler, as CG

Supervisor, being a large component of the show's success on that end of the creative spectrum.

I knew *BSG*'s visual effects supervisor, Gary Hutzel, from my *Star Trek* days, and we had always enjoyed being around one another. He had gone on to work on the new *Battlestar Galactica* after *Enterprise* had been cancelled. I remember thinking that I'd probably never work again, and that after 17 years on *Star Trek*, I was sure I had used up my stash of good fortune. As soon as I got home from that last day there, I stepped in the front door, and Dorothy was waiting for me. "You have a message from Gary Hutzel. He wants you to call him right away." And that was when he asked me to jump to *Galactica*.

This new *Battlestar Galactica* was more of a descendant of *Star Trek* than it was of the original *Battlestar*. It was more adult, and those actors on this new *BSG* were on another level. They were allowed to run with a scene. We'd watch dailies, and be absolutely blown away. Plus, the actors were allowed to improvise. Edward James Olmos and Michael Hogan, who played [Colonel] Tigh, had a scene, just the two of them sitting in a bar talking. They ran with it for hours. On *Star Trek*, if they wanted to change two words, someone from the front office would have to come down and approve it. Ron Moore, the showrunner, didn't want *Galactica* to be like that. He wanted it to be more malleable. That posed some challenges for visual effects, because the show continued to evolve in editorial.

But because we had an in-house VFX team, we were able to address those challenges immediately. Editorial was just down the hall, and we could cut in our shots within minutes, and with no additional cost to the production. The new *Galactica* was unique because of the behind the scenes dynamic that grew from our days on *Star Trek* together. There were things in hindsight that maybe were mistakes for *Trek*, that we were able to spin in a different direction for *BSG*, and I think that was one of *Galactica*'s great strengths. It was an amazing experience.

Drexler has continued to stay busy since his Battlestar Galactica days, lending his talents to a variety of television and film projects, including Caprica, Drive Angry, Battlestar Galactica: Blood & Chrome, Defiance, and Beyond. He attributes his ability to still be thriving in an industry that can be unforgiving to a solid business sense, a keen ability to adapt, and the desire to constantly push himself as an artist.

I've always had a good understanding of the business. I knew that it was constantly changing, and I realized that the way to keep busy was to be able to branch out. Expand your horizons. If you're only doing makeup, what are you going to do when there is a lull in makeup driven projects? And I'm someone who actually likes getting out of their comfort zone. I'll jump head first into something that I know nothing about, because I found the joy in having to adapt. That's something I always found exciting about working in this business. One of the very first things I learned when I first set out as an adult, was that you have to know yourself. You have to figure out how your brain works, and how you think, and then determine how to use that to your advantage.

One thing that I recommend to anyone who wants to get into a creative business is to spend all your free time practicing and being creative. Draw with a pencil, sculpt with clay, paint anything and everything. Do as many things as you can, because when you're talking about creativity, one discipline informs the other. Create as much as you can, whenever you can.

Working in the film business takes an attitude, and a studied toughness. There are going to be times when being creative isn't going to be enough. You have to be ready to take criticism, you have to be ready to be a team player, and you have to be ready to fail. Failure goes hand in hand with success. You will never get better without failure. Fail as much as you can, and as often as possible. In order to be successful, you have to understand that it's not about the destination. It's all about the journey. Everything else will take care of itself.

The Exorcist - Regan Dummy

Leonard Nimoy and Doug Drexler

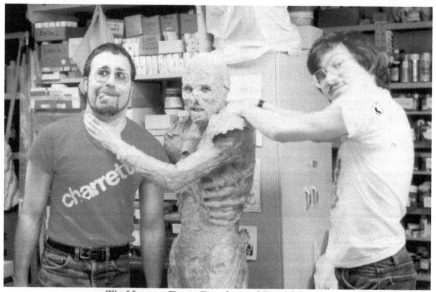

The Hunger - Doug Drexler and David Smith

Amityville 3-D

C.H.U.D.

F/X - Jerry Orbach Puppet

Liberace: Behind the Music - Saul Rubinek

Poltergeist III

DICK TRACY

Dick Tracy - The Gang

Dick Tracy - Al Pacino and Madonna

Dick Tracy - Doug Drexler, Al Pacino and John Caglione

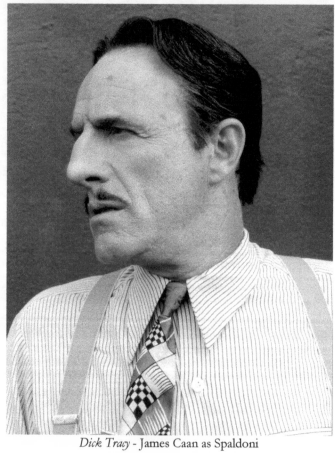

Dick Tracy - James Caan as Spaldoni

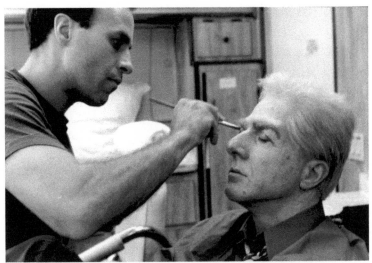

Dick Tracy - Doug Drexler and Dustin Hoffman

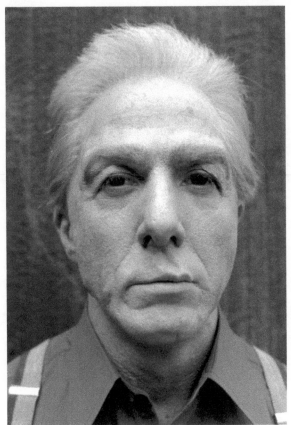

Dick Tracy - Dustin Hoffman as Mumbles

Dick Tracy - Paul Sorvino as Lips

Dick Tracy - William Forsythe as Flattop

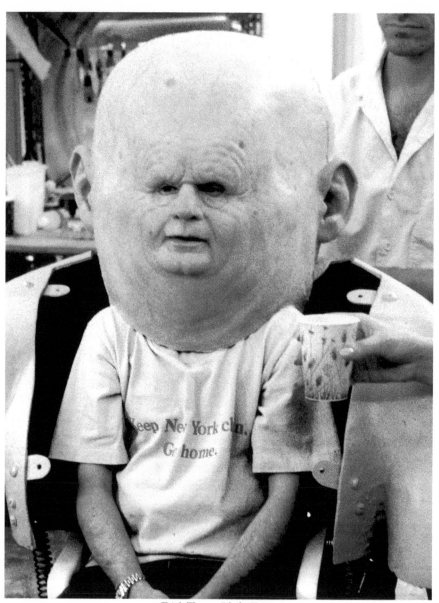

Dick Tracy - Little Face

Dick Tracy

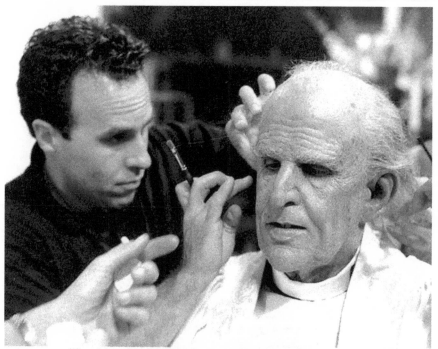

Three Men and a Little Lady - Doug Drexler and Ted Danson

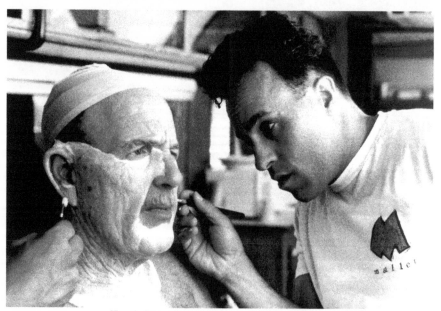

For the Boys - James Caan and Doug Drexler

Star Trek: Voyager – U.S.S. Voyager

Star Trek: Enterprise – NX-01 Ship

Star Trek - Doug Drexler on the Bridge

Doug Drexler

Emmy Nominated Special Effects Makeup Artist

RoboCop (1987)
Fright Night Part 2 (1988)
It (1990)
Gremlins 2: The New Batch (1990)
Captain America: Civil War (2016)
Avengers: Infinity War (2018)

For nearly 40 years now, Texas native Bart J. Mixon has paved his way in the world of special effects, tirelessly lending his talents on over one hundred films and more than twenty different television series since 1980. A multiple Emmy Award nominee, Mixon has helped to create compelling and unique makeups for almost every cinematic subgenre in horror and science fiction, overseeing crews on some of the most ambitious productions in modern film history.

I guess I've always been artistic. I started collecting comic books when I was about five or six. My brother, Bret, and I would draw our own comics and that sort of thing. I was always interested in comic books, monster movies, science fiction, and that's how I learned about makeup and stop-motion stuff. There was a member of this comic book club in Houston I was in that knew a little bit about makeup, so he would give me pointers on how to do things. Not that they were necessarily the right ways, but it was at least something that made me familiar with things like how to make a mold or how to pour latex into it.

There was also the *7 Faces of Dr. Lao*, which was the first makeup-type movie I can remember—there was one actor playing all these various characters, and I realized there was a makeup artist that was behind it all. Then there was *Planet of the Apes*, which fueled my interest in makeup even more. I started making my own Super 8 movies, where I was trying to do makeup effects and stop motion, but it was pretty difficult because I didn't have the proper cameras and equipment. But I was able to sculpt and mold, and I was pretty good at making masks and prosthetics. I just didn't know where that would all lead me.

Where it all changed for me, though, was reading about Rick Baker in *Famous Monsters of Filmland* sometime around 1970. Seeing him in there made a career as a makeup artist seem a little more attainable. Before, you'd always see guys like John Chambers and Jack Pierce in articles, but they were all these older guys. Rick Baker was eighteen, essentially still a kid, so it was like, "Well, if this guy can do it, maybe I can, too." Of course, the hurdle of living in Houston still had to be overcome, but at least the dream felt like it wasn't a complete impossibility.

The professional world of makeup effects became even more attainable for Mixon in the late 1970s when he discovered an annual comic book and sci-fi convention in Houston. That's where Bart met Rick Baker in 1977, striking up a friendship that would continue over the next forty years.

When I met Rick, I had done a few things, but nothing very good and, quite frankly, most of the stuff I had to show him was pretty bad. I'm surprised he even talked to me in the first place. He gave me his address and phone number and invited me to correspond with him, and I used to send him a list of questions and a cassette tape. Rick would sit there and record his answers and mail the tape back to me, because that would be easier for him than writing everything out. So that was a huge help to me as I was figuring things out.

A funny coincidence: the same convention where I met Rick was the very same one where both Steve Johnson and Matthew Mungle met Rick, too. In fact, Steve grew up a half hour from me but I didn't know him until then.

Baker wasn't the only contact Mixon made early on in his career as an aspiring artist in Houston. In fact, he found a few legends who weren't all that far from his very own backyard.

I knew Ernie Farino, who lived in Dallas, and he was doing stop-motion effects up there. He ended up becoming the effects coordinator on *The Terminator* and worked on *The Abyss*, too. I made a few more contacts in the area and then I started working on local projects, not that there were that many. I was still going through *Famous Monsters* as my resource, and I came across a photo for *The Alien Dead*, which was done by Fred Olen Ray. He was living in Florida at the time, and I tracked him down and contacted him and ended up doing a few projects for him while he still lived in Florida. When Fred moved out to L.A., I kept in touch with him, too. Basically, I kept looking under every rock that I could while I was in Texas to try and find what little work there might be out there.

But Ernie was great. When he moved out to Los Angeles to work for New World Pictures, I was sending him pictures of sculptures and makeups and whatnots that I was doing, and he must have shown them to John Carl Buechler, who was heading up the makeup department on *Forbidden World*. I remember getting a call that they needed some extra help, so I flew out for basically a week of work. It was two weeks before I was supposed to get married, so I couldn't stay out there any longer even if I wanted to, but on that job, in addition to meeting John, I met [R.] Chris Biggs and Mark Shostrom, who was the main contact. I stayed in touch with him and even did a few projects with him over the next couple of years.

I did a show for him called *Raw Courage* in 1983 out in New Mexico, and then in '84 I drove out to L.A. and worked for him on this project called *The Supernaturals*. At this point, my twin brother, Bret, had already moved out there and was doing animation effects at Fantasy II [Film Effects, Inc.], working for Ernie Farino. While I was out there, Ernie had me work on *The Terminator* a little bit and Mark brought me out a year later so I could work on *A Nightmare on Elm Street 2*.

A Nightmare on Elm Street 2: Freddy's Revenge became Mixon's first taste of a real Hollywood production, a monumental occasion in his up-and-coming career that he still relishes to this day.

Nightmare 2 was definitely the biggest show I had been involved with at that point, and to some extent, it was my first real movie. We were all certainly aware that we were doing a sequel to *A Nightmare on Elm Street*, and that it had become a big deal with horror fans and audiences everywhere, so there was some pressure on us, and there was some apprehension, too.

There were two effects teams on *Nightmare*. One was led by Mark and the other was led by Kevin Yagher, and it happened early on in his career, too, so we were all pretty much at the same level experience-wise. Going into it, the producers told Mark that he had to make a choice between either doing all the Freddy makeup or doing the transformation where Freddy rips himself out of Jesse's [Mark Patton's] body. Mark's thinking was that because Freddy had already been done and was somewhat established, that transformation was going to be the showstopper moment in *Nightmare 2*. In that respect, I think he was absolutely right. I was very happy with the work we did on it, too, and that transformation scene ranks up there alongside *An American Werewolf in London* as one of those really cool moments in effects history.

And if I can toot my own horn for a moment, the one thing I was really proud of on *Nightmare 2* was the shot where Freddy's eye is in the back of the throat, because that was my idea. It wasn't in the script, but I thought it could add something to that whole idea of Freddy being inside someone. What's funny is that decades later I worked on *Insidious: Chapter 3*, and they did the very same gag on that, too—although theirs was done digitally and ours was 100% practical.

Also, I couldn't believe that when we were prepping *Nightmare 2*, the producers came super close to not bringing Robert Englund back. They thought they could just get a stuntman because Freddy was wearing all this makeup, so why would they need an expensive actor for the role? Thankfully, they realized that Robert brought more to that role than just being a guy beneath the makeup, and they brought him back again and again.

Seeing steady effects work coming his way in the mid-1980s, Bart decided it was time to make the leap towards becoming a full-time artist.

It was 1986 when I basically quit my regular job in Houston. I had been working at an oil tool company as a technical illustrator where I would do their tech manuals. But when I got hired to come onto *The Texas Chainsaw Massacre 2*, which was being shot in Austin, I knew it was time to make the leap.

I was just happy to be working on anything, but the fact that it was a sequel to the first *Texas Chain Saw* was very cool. Because my brother had already moved out to L.A., I had known a lot of the guys on the crew secondhand, like John Vulich, Mitch Devane, and Shawn McEnroe, who was an old Rick Baker guy. I was trying to get on the crew with Tom [Savini], and I was calling, but he was always very non-committal. John Vulich finally said to my brother, "Tom is never going to hire Bart until he meets him face to face," so I got in my car and drove to Austin to meet Tom. And John was right, because I started working a day or two later.

It was great working with Tom. By the time I came on, they had already been prepping it for a couple of weeks, so everything had pretty much been assigned already. Mitch Devane was doing the Leatherface mask, Shawn McEnroe did Chop-Top, and John Vulich was doing Grandpa. There was a severed hand that I got to sculpt, but it never made it into the movie. We did it on an amputee and the guy had recently lost his hand. I remember when I was taking the mold off his stump, I asked him, "Hey, are you sure you're going to be okay with this?" He said, "Oh yeah, it's going to be great. I mean, it's *Chainsaw 2*, so this is going to be so cool!" So we thought everything was great.

But then, on the day we had to shoot the effect, John Vulich was doing the makeup on him and as he applied blood to the stump, the guy freaked out and he just bolted. We never saw him again. And I was like, *Ah, great. There goes one thing I sculpted for the entire movie and now it's not even going to be in there.*

But I did do a lot of lab work on *Chainsaw* [*Massacre 2*] and ran a lot of foam latex, too. I remember one last-minute thing that came up was when Chop-Top was beating the guy at the radio station and Tobe [Hooper] wanted some hammer wounds on the guy's head. It was a spur-of-the-moment thing, so we didn't have anything prepped for it. I just had to do stuff out of the kit very quickly. Thankfully, Tobe was happy with that, so I was happy I was able to give him what he wanted right there on the spot.

The one thing that I will always remember about that shoot was how Tobe told me that I looked just like Stephen King, which I took as a compliment (and hopefully he meant it that way).

As it turns out, quitting his day job to pursue makeup was the right call for Mixon. Shortly after completing work on The Texas Chainsaw Massacre Part 2, he was contacted to come on board what would become one of the most iconic sci-fi films of its era, Paul Verhoeven's RoboCop.

Shortly after *Chainsaw 2*, Rob Bottin called me to work on *RoboCop*, which was shooting in Dallas. We had met years prior through Rick Baker, and Rob knew that I lived in Texas. So when an opening came up last minute on *RoboCop*, he reached out to me. I remember that he called me up at midnight on a Saturday night, I flew up there on Sunday, and started working by Monday, so it all was a very quick process for me.

With *RoboCop*, it had all been built in L.A. and shipped out to Dallas, so what we were working with was all this finished stuff, and all of it was so cool. The suit that Rob Bottin designed was brilliant, and he had already done *Legend* and *The Thing* (1982), so he was the biggest-name effects guy that I had worked for at that time.

I remember on the first day, I was helping suit up Peter Weller, and the suit itself was a little tricky to put on. You had to do certain things in a certain order and it was a very different process for me. Peter didn't know what to make of me at first, but by the end of the week, I was the only guy that he wanted to suit him up. I also think it was because I was the only one with the upper body strength to get him in there properly, too.

RoboCop was also the first time I had ever applied prosthetics on set. Stephan Dupuis was doing the right side of Peter's face and I was doing the left, and I remember on the first makeup test it was Stephan on one side, myself on the other, and then Rob's face was right between us the entire time. It looked like the opening of *The Three Stooges* or something, where you've got the three heads lined up. But there was a little bit of pressure with Rob watching me as closely as he did that day, and I would have to say that *RoboCop* was a really great learning experience for me. *RoboCop* also ended up being a career highlight for me, so when the film turned out as well as it did, it became a good calling card to use when I moved out to Los Angeles shortly after that.

In March 1987, Bart decided it was time to take his career to the next level, which meant he needed to get himself out to Hollywood to be in the mix of everything happening in the makeup industry. Having already established relationships with many of his peers (and legends in the business who were running their own shops back then), Mixon was able to find work rather quickly after transitioning to the West Coast.

Within two weeks of moving out here, I was working during the day at Rick Baker's [studio] on *Gorillas in the Mist* as extra help in the mold shop. I was just doing whatever menial stuff they needed done on that show. I thought it was great, as I didn't care what kind of work I was doing; I just wanted to keep working. At night, I was working at the Chiodos' [Stephen, Charles and Edward's] shop, which was literally around the corner from Rick's shop. They were busy prepping for *Killer Klowns from Outer Space*, and I worked over there for a few days on an oversized hand gag they were using in the movie. I would come in at night and I sculpted up a couple of generic skin texture shapes, then I molded those and ran a lot of latex skin pieces that I applied to the hand so that it was ready for painting.

At that time, my brother was still working over at Fantasy II Film Effects, which is Gene Warren Jr.'s company, and Gene knew that I was a makeup effects guy. They had been doing mostly opticals and miniatures, so he thought I could help them out by doing some practical effects. There was a show called *Dracula's Widow*, where I made a plaster head that we rigged with a chamber behind it to pump blood out of it on cue, that could then be matted onto the vampire's face. It was a quick job, but I enjoyed working with Gene. And because of him, that's how I ended up working on *Fright Night Part 2*.

When *Fright Night Part 2* came along, Gene had put in a bid for the visual effects, and I think he went to the producers and asked to do the practical [makeup] effects as some kind of package deal. Initially, there were some debates about who was going to handle certain aspects of the effects, but the feeling was that because Greg Cannom had just done the *Werewolf* TV show, it made sense that he do the werewolf character that was in [*Fright Night Part 2*].

I'm not sure how Greg ended up with the bug guy [Brian Thompson's character, Bozworth], but I think he was something that came along later on. I ended up with the rest of the characters on *Fright Night 2*, which was mainly Julie Carmen's Regine character and her various incarnations, as well as the androgynous roller-skating vampire [Belle, played by Russell Clark] and Charley's friend Richie [played by Merritt Butrick], who becomes a vampire.

Fright Night 2 also ended up being the first show that I supervised on, too. I was still under Gene, but he wasn't applying the makeup or anything, so he mostly just let us do our thing. That was certainly a huge stepping-stone for me, and a lot of responsibility, too, especially since I knew our work was going to be on-screen next to Greg Cannom's. Those are some high standards to have to meet, and I feel like I assembled a great crew with Brian Wade, Norman Cabrera, Aaron Sims, Joey Orosco, and Matt Rose, who did a little bit, too. I'm sure I'm forgetting some other people, but our team created some amazing effects on *Fright Night 2* that were of a comparable caliber to the fine work that Greg did, so it's a show I'm still very proud of.

After Fright Night Part 2, Mixon spent the next few years contributing to several other notable sequels, including A Nightmare on Elm Street 4: The Dream Master, Predator 2, and Gremlins 2: The New Batch, which provided him with another opportunity to flex his creative muscles in an advisory position.

Rick [Baker] brought me onto *Gremlins 2* as the shop foreman, and I think we had a crew of seventy-five people on that show. I did the initial script breakdown, which was very involved because of the amount of work we had to do on that show. Usually, Rick would just have one guy running things, but for *Gremlins 2*, he had three—one in the office, one in purchasing, and me on the floor in the shop.

There were a lot of headaches on *Gremlins 2*, and I remember that I'd wake up sometimes at two or three o'clock in the morning, thinking, *Well, what are we doing today? Are we going to get this done? We can't forget about that, either.* I was constantly going back over our schedules. It was a lot to keep track of and sometimes I had to be the one to make the unpopular decisions, like moving from an eight-hour workday to a ten-hour day. We had the best people in town working on *Gremlins 2*, and I brought all my *Fright Night 2* people over that weren't already working for Rick themselves.

When it came time to create the Gremlins themselves, we were all following Rick Baker's art direction. On the first *Gremlins*, it's all a standard design other than Stripe, so they all came from the same mold. One of the things that Rick wanted to do with this one—which, obviously made more work for us—was to create eight distinctively different Gremlin looks even before you got into the genetics lab, so we started having all those wild designs of Gremlins: the Vegetable Gremlin, the Bat Gremlin, and all those crazy creatures.

Rick's inspiration came from a project he almost did back in the early '80s called *Night Skies*, which was being produced by Steven Spielberg, and Ron Cobb was going to direct it. It was based on a famous UFO case in the 1950s, where some guy on a farm was supposedly terrorized by aliens for a weekend after a UFO landed nearby. John Sayles wrote it and Rick was building the aliens for it. While he was prepping it, Spielberg was off doing *Raiders* [*of the Lost Ark*], and he decided he didn't want to make an evil alien movie, so he came up with *E.T.* [*the Extra-Terrestrial*]. So, when he got back from *Raiders*, he said, "We're not going to do this *Night Skies* thing anymore. We're going to do *E.T.* instead." And Rick knew all those designs for *Night Skies* wouldn't work for *E.T.*, either. But then Rick got onto *American Werewolf* and had to quit working on *E.T.* because he didn't want to screw [over Director] John Landis.

The point of bringing that up is that he had one basic alien he had created for *Night Skies*, and then there were, like, six different designs, so when you would look at them, you knew, *'This is the smart one, that's the mean one, that's the stupid one,'* and that brought out their characteristics. So that's what Rick ended up doing with *Gremlins 2*, where you had your basic Gremlin look, but then you've got the George Gremlin, the Daffy Gremlin, the Mohawk Gremlin, and other than Lenny, they're all the same body. So I just thought it was interesting that Rick hung on to that idea for eight years. We probably ended up making four to six different puppets just of those initial characters, which was around fifty puppets right there. Once all the other Gremlins took over, *Gremlins 2* became a huge undertaking, where I would say we ended up making something like five hundred puppets on just that show alone.

Even though the final version of Gremlins 2: The New Batch boasted an unprecedented amount of practical effects, there were several ideas that were scratched during production.

Because [Director Joe] Dante was so open to ideas, I remember he was always fielding our suggestions for gags we could do in the movie. I had storyboarded out a transformation sequence that I thought would be interesting story-wise, where there was a cocktail of something in the genetics lab that would turn a Gremlin back into a Mogwai. I did a shot-per-shot sequence based on the *American Werewolf* transformation, where a Gremlin is horrified that he's turning back into a Mogwai, with all the same angles and all the same cuts as [*American*] *Werewolf*.

I remember Dante asked me, "So, what would he drink that would make him change back, then?" I honestly had no idea. I guess that maybe I didn't pitch it enthusiastically enough, or maybe I should have based it on *The Howling* transformation, but he didn't go for the idea I presented. I thought it was a pretty good idea, though, even if it would have been an enormous amount of extra work.

Recently, I found these storyboards that I had forgotten about involving the Spider Gremlin. We had played around with the idea of having this little tag at the end of the film, where the husk of the burned Spider Gremlin would burst open and his abdomen would split like an egg. It was going to be filled with little Mogwais that would spill out, almost like spider eggs. There was something discussed where it would be implied that fire would turn them back, but because they were in the movie theater that burned down in the first *Gremlins*, I don't know if it made much sense with the mythology. I don't remember if we ever even showed that to Dante or not.

After surviving eighteen months on Gremlins 2: The New Batch, Mixon moved on to another project that was ambitious, albeit for very different reasons, as he was tasked with bringing to life the nightmarish world Stephen King's best-selling novel IT (1986).

When you're in this business, it's nice if you can get one character that truly becomes your calling card, and Pennywise became mine. Working on *IT* in that respect was very gratifying because it's something that has endured with fans to this day. Go to any horror convention, or any store that sells Halloween stuff, and Pennywise's face is everywhere.

I was certainly aware going into *IT* that it was so popular, but I honestly wasn't a huge Stephen King fan myself. I didn't dislike his stuff, but I hadn't read a lot of his books up to that point. I had read *Pet Sematary* and one of his short story collections, but my twin brother, Bret, was a huge fan, and he helped get me familiar with the book. Then I decided to read *IT* for myself, and between Stephen King's vision and what we were given in the script, I had to find the best way to represent the character of Pennywise. Story-wise, the clown is an illusion; it's not a real manifestation. So, to me, it made sense that it would look like a friendly clown, especially since he was trying to lure in little kids. I almost wanted him to look like a live-action cartoon, and at one point, we were going to do blue contact lenses that would almost look like an animation drawing.

I was also thinking of giving him pure white teeth that would match the clown-white paint on him. I just wanted to see him pure white, because a lot of clown makeup goes gray since you can often see the skin tone underneath it. The colors had to be real stark, and I wanted to use primary colors like the red and yellow against these clean lines. I just thought that would all be horrific to see as It brought about suffering on these innocent kids.

My intention was to have two looks for Pennywise: the clean version, because that makes sense when you're dealing with kids, and then a monstrous version that is there taunting them as adults, because they all know at that point that he's a monster. Originally, I had wanted to continue using the battery acid look, where half of his face is disfigured, but for different reasons, Director [Tommy Lee Wallace] didn't want to go that route.

One of the more interesting "what if?" scenarios on Stephen King's IT (1990) concerned the miniseries' casting of its now-iconic villain. Looking back, Mixon reflected on how it was down to three brilliant actors for the role, and how much he enjoyed collaborating with Tim Curry, who would end up playing Pennywise.

Originally, Tim Curry, Roddy McDowall, and Malcolm McDowell were the three names that were mentioned to me when I first came on. It was going to be a three-part, six-hour miniseries, too, which I don't think a lot of people know, either. Any one of them would have been a very cool Pennywise, but Tim really made this character his own. Just coming up with the Pennywise makeup was certainly a collaborative effort between Tim, me, and Tommy. They both would give me their feedback on my drawings or sculptures, and I would fix anything they didn't feel was right.

Tim was so great to work with, too. What I liked about him was that you could do a clown makeup on him and he could look like a nice, friendly clown, and then with just his eyes or a twitching of his mouth, he suddenly looked evil. It was so subtle. I do remember that there was some controversy surrounding the battery acid look of Pennywise, though. It was decided at that point in the script that he would get that disfigured makeup, but when we shot the movie, we ran out of time up in Vancouver and we never got to the battery acid look. They just kind of shot around the kid spraying Pennywise, and then Pennywise jumping in the drain. They never did Pennywise's reaction shot, so I figured they would just be picking that up on inserts later on.

But we had to make a miniature of Pennywise for the shot of him going down the drain. It's an eighteen-inch stop-motion puppet, and up until the time that I molded it, they weren't going to use the disfigured look for whatever reason. So I said, "Well, all right. Sculpt it with the normal face." And literally the day that I molded that half of the puppet—the front half—they came and said, "All right, we decided Tim's going to wear the disfigured makeup, so now we're going to shoot that sequence." What that meant was that I then had to make a little miniature prosthetic to put on the stop-motion puppet to change its appearance to look like the disfigured one. I'm so grateful they finally changed their minds and that Tim was willing to wear that piece, because that sequence would have played out very differently had Pennywise just had a normal face.

Also, the sequence where they hit Pennywise in the head with the silver and it punches a hole in his head where the deadlights shine out originally played out differently in the script. It was supposed to be spider hairs sticking out of his head, and to me it just seemed too literal because the spider isn't what he really looks like, either. It's the deadlights that are the true representation of what this character is. So at least Tommy agreed with that and they ended up rewriting the script. Dynamically, I thought it would be more interesting to present it that way, and I think that scene turned out great.

Right around the time that he was wrapping up on Stephen King's IT (1990), Mixon also did some work on James Cameron's Terminator 2: Judgment Day making models and a stop-motion puppet of Arnold Schwarzenegger. While the writing on the wall regarding the need for computer-generated imagery (CGI) in modern filmmaking was becoming slightly apparent on that project, he explained how it was Jurassic Park a few years later that sent many of his peers into a frenzy.

There was this feeling once *Jurassic Park* came out that it was all over for special effects. Everyone went into this doom and gloom mode, but I realized that there were just certain things you were never going to be able to afford to do with a computer, so I wasn't panicking myself. Besides, look at all the big special effects shows that still came out during that time: *Men in Black*, *The Grinch*, *Planet of the Apes*, *Hellboy*, or even more recently, you have movies like *Oz the Great and Powerful* or *Guardians of the Galaxy*, where almost every character is under some type of makeup. Things may have slowed down, but makeup effects weren't going anywhere, at least in my mind.

Mixon was right. Throughout the 1990s, he continued to stay busy working on a number of films, including Ernest Scared Stupid, Return of the Living Dead 3, Necronomicon: Book of the Dead, Ed Wood, Fargo, Men in Black, and How The Grinch Stole Christmas. In 2000, Bart reconnected professionally with Rick Baker when the effects legend hired him as a Project Supervisor on Tim Burton's remake of Planet of the Apes.

I think every single person on our crew was influenced by the original *Planet of the Apes*. There's no denying the historical significance of the original film, so it was cool from that respect to be involved. Plus, with Tim Burton directing, that aspect of it had its own potential, too. What made this something of a dream project to me was just Rick Baker himself. Nobody does apes like Rick, and him being the guy to create these apes made it all that much cooler. One thing I do admire and appreciate in the new [*Planet of the*] *Apes* was that previously, whenever someone would do an ape or a monkey type of character, they would do it just like [makeup artist] John Chambers did in *Planet of the Apes* [1968]. Nobody was really looking at it and trying to rethink it or improve it in any way. It was just an industry standard.

But Rick was like, "No, we can definitely do something to improve upon that look," and he came up with the idea of using dentures where the teeth were to push the lips so far forward that the actors were able to manipulate the lips in ways that they couldn't do in the original *Planet of the Apes*. It was an innovative way to take that classic makeup to another level. I can remember doing a press event for *Planet of the Apes* over a weekend, and everyone kept remarking that the makeup looked so great because of all the advancements in the technology that had occurred since the original *Planet of the Apes*. I had to point out that our approach was all foam latex, hair, and dentures—stuff that has been around since *The Wizard of Oz*—so it wasn't anything with technology. It was all due to Rick Baker's art direction.

The makeups were originally designed to have contact lenses to complement the look, so we could get bigger, more ape-like eyes because their irises are larger than a man's. But production didn't want to spend the extra money to have a couple of lens technicians on set to handle all the contact lenses, so that was a design element that got dropped early on. I know there are a couple of test makeup photos floating around that *Make-Up Artist Magazine* had in one of their issues featuring the makeup with the contact lenses, and they really just take it that much further.

Something else that elevated the work we did on *Planet of the Apes* was the fact that we had a great group of actors behind the makeup who put in the extra effort with their performances to make it all look so believable. I remember Paul Giamatti was watching the Roddy McDowall interviews for the original [film] to help with his performance, and that extra effort shows. There were some guys on *Apes* that really embraced their look, and it shows when you go back and watch it now.

The same thing happened when I did Michael Chiklis as the Thing on *Fantastic Four* [2005]. On the first day we put him in the prosthetics, he sat there in front of the mirror for a half hour and just explored what it took to make the face do what he was imagining it was doing. He saw that he had to exaggerate certain things, and it's always great when you have an actor that really embraces the makeup like that. It doesn't always happen.

While Mixon spent several more years collaborating on other Baker-led makeup movies, he was also forging a creative relationship with the likes of Rob Zombie and fellow effects artist Wayne Toth, who hired Bart to come on board the musician's directorial debut, House of 1000 Corpses, and would also bring him back for several of the rocker-turned-director's subsequent cinematic projects over the next fifteen years.

I thought *Corpses* was fun just because Rob was trying to do something different at the time, and he's always trying to do that with all his movies. You can debate whether or not it's successful, but at least he's trying. I like that with every film, he firmly puts his own unique stamp on it. I've had great experiences on all of them with him, and with Wayne Toth, too. Wayne had created a lot of the stuff for Rob's stage shows, and for *Corpses*, he brought me in to help apply the burn makeup to Tiny, who was played by Matthew McGrory. I was only on most of the days that he worked, so it was low pressure. There was a lot of pressure on Rob on that one because it was his first film, so I didn't really bother him much on *Corpses*.

But by the time they did *Halloween II* (2009), which was his fourth film, he was more comfortable as a director and I was there for the whole show, working with Wayne. I was in the inner circle by that one. I was in our makeup trailer that Zombie would come hang out in when he couldn't stand all the crap, so he would just come in and sit down and hang. I got to know him and his wife [Sheri Moon Zombie], and what's funny is that after the *Paul Blart* movie came out, they both would call me "Blart" instead of "Bart." The cool thing about Rob is that he's a fan and he's always open to everything. There aren't a lot of directors who are as open as he is.

We were talking one day when we were working on *31*, looking at all his tattoos, and on one of his wrists he's got a tattoo of the Jack Kirby version of the Thing from *The Fantastic Four*. That meant a little bit more to me because Kirby's my favorite comic book artist and Kirby did my favorite run on *Fantastic Four*, so that was an extra level of cool to me.

And Wayne and I have been friends for a while. He's one of a handful of guys that whenever they call, if I'm available, I'm there. It's always fun to work with either of those guys, and I've enjoyed our working relationship over the years.

Shortly after being a part of Zombie's House of 1000 Corpses, Bart got the opportunity to work with another passionate filmmaker making his mark on the landscape of horror and sci-fi cinema: Guillermo del Toro. While working for Rick Baker on How The Grinch Stole Christmas, Mixon was brought into the creative mix as del Toro was beginning to gear up for his adaptation of Mike Mignola's cult comic book series, Hellboy.

We had our first meeting at Rick's back in 1999 when I was doing *The Grinch*, and that was about four years before we got around to actually doing it. Coincidentally, when Matt Rose did his first clay sketch of Hellboy, he just went into Rick's archive and pulled out a Ron Perlman bust because he thought, *Oh, this guy has got a good face.* So he picked Ron completely independently and without any direction from Guillermo. As it turns out, Guillermo and Mike Mignola were talking about who they would want for the character and they both, at the same time, said, "Ron Perlman." So I always thought it was interesting that they all came up with Ron on their own.

The main reason the *Hellboy* films are so great is because you have Guillermo at the helm. He's a real fan of the source material, and he's also a fan of makeup effects, because that's the world he used to work in. He's a guy who knows when to be practical and when to be digital, and both *Hellboy* movies were good examples of how to properly marry the two techniques.

Hellboy was a passion project for everyone involved, too. Rick was doing *The Haunted Mansion* at the time, and he just took *Hellboy* because Matt and Chad [Waters] were so passionate about it. In fact, I quit *The Cat in the Hat* to work on *Hellboy* because I was a *Hellboy* fan. I remember I was prepping *The Cat in the Hat* over at Steve Johnson's, and people on the crew were jumping ship to go work on *Hellboy* because they were so excited. The great thing with the *Hellboy* films was that Guillermo was the only guy that you had to make happy. He had the final word on everything. Other shows, you usually have to run the stuff up the ladder, but with this, it all began and ended with him.

On the first *Hellboy*, I got to do Ron's makeup for a couple of days, but I was mainly doing the photo double, who was wearing the same prosthetics. On the second film [*Hellboy II: The Golden Army*], I started co-applying Hellboy's makeup with Mike Elizalde. Early on, the guy that was doing Luke Goss' makeup quit kind of unexpectedly, so they were scrambling around trying to find somebody who could take over Luke, and so I volunteered for that. That schedule was twenty-seven days long, and I ended up doing him like fifty-three times. It was pretty crazy.

I also remember going by Spectral [Motion] when they were sculpting all this stuff for Luke's character [Prince Nuada], and I saw how thin the appliances were, so I was like, "Man, am I glad I'm on the Hellboy team." Then, a few months later, here I am working on Luke. Should have kept my big mouth shut, right? But Luke was just cool and we got along great on *Hellboy II*.

Throughout a career that now spans over four decades, Bart Mixon has been a part of over one hundred film projects, has more than two dozen television credits to his name, and he has no plans for slowing down just yet. When asked about the secret to enjoying longevity in such a demanding profession, Mixon credits his willingness to always lend a hand as a big factor in why he's stayed so busy over the years.

I don't want to say, "Oh, I'm a great guy and people love me," but there are a lot of very talented people that burned their bridges for whatever reason over the years. So a lot of it comes down to not being a jerk and just being the guy who always wants to help. You have to be a team player in this industry. There's no way around it. I'm sure there are a number of factors behind my career, but all I really know is that I've been very fortunate. I'm grateful I got to work with guys like Rick [Baker] and Steve Johnson, and I'm thankful that people continued to hire me and still hire me today.

When I was a kid, all of this seemed like a million miles away because I was out there in Texas. When I was first even thinking about doing effects, it was like, *Ah, what are my chances?* But then some smaller projects came my way, which led to some very high-profile, memorable projects, and then suddenly I'm getting to work on films like *RoboCop* or *IT* or *Gremlins 2*. I've gotten the opportunity to apply a Rick Baker makeup for the main villain in *MIB³* [*Men in Black 3*]. There's a part of me that thinks about that and it still makes me giddy. The fan in me is still excited about the work and getting to be a part of all these incredible movies. I grew up loving all this stuff, and now, to be able to do something like create the Thing for *Fantastic Four* [2005], or work on *Planet of the Apes* [2001], or even create Vision for *Captain America: Civil War*—how cool is that?

I don't know if there's a real secret or anything, but I'm very thankful for all I've done. I'm happy that I can just hang on in this world for a little longer. It's been a great ride.

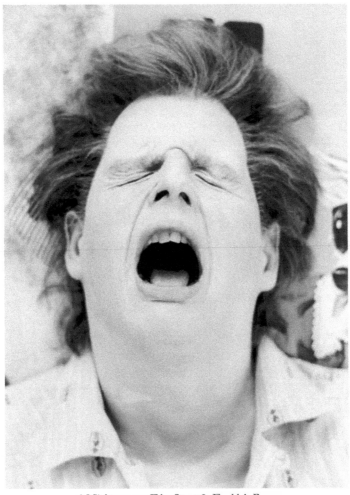

A Nightmare on Elm Street 2: Freddy's Revenge

A Nightmare on Elm Street 2: Freddy's Revenge

RoboCop

Fright Night Part 2 – Regine Monster and Bart Mixon

Fright Night Part 2 – Regine Monster and Set Team

Fright Night Part 2 - Corpse

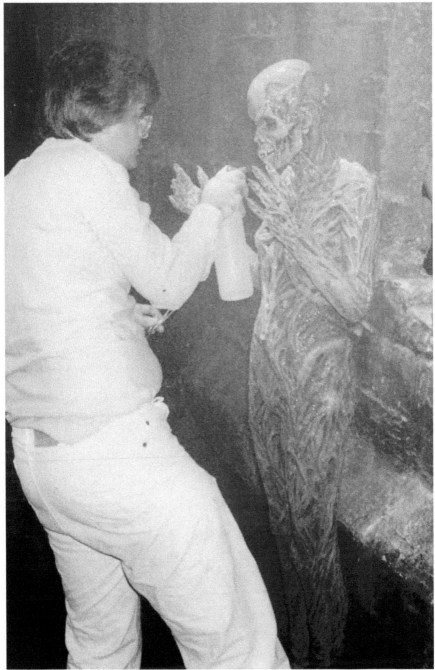

Fright Night Part 2 – Bart Mixon and Corpse

It (1990)

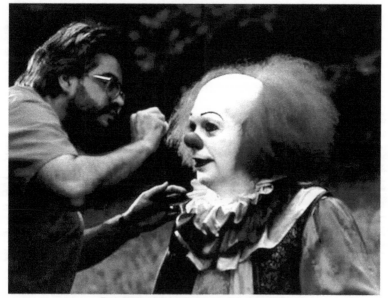

It (1990) - Bart Mixon and Pennywise

It (1990) - Bart Mixon and Spider

Necronomicon: Book of Dead - Bart Mixon and Melting Man

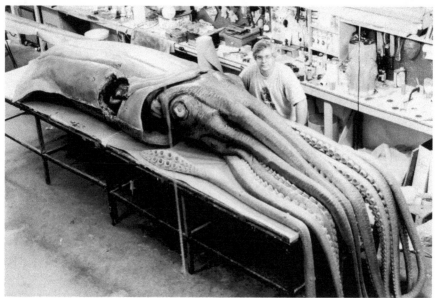

The Beast

Hellboy – Ron Perlman and Bart Mixon

X-Men: The Last Stand – Bart Mixon and Kelsey Grammer

Fantastic 4: Rise of the Silver Surfer – Bart Mixon and Michael Chiklis

Conversation with…
DAVID LEROY ANDERSON

Oscar and Emmy Winning Special Effects Makeup Artist

The Serpent and the Rainbow (1987)
The Nutty Professor (1996)
Cinderella Man (2005)
Star Trek (2009)
The Cabin in the Woods (2011)
American Horror Story (2014 – 2019)

For two-time Oscar-winning artist and co-owner of AFX Studio David Leroy Anderson, his journey to becoming a prominent special effects creator in the industry is quite unconventional in comparison to many of his peers.

Most people who work in effects usually came to it through horror movies or magazines. For me, it happened by surprise. My dad, Lance Anderson, was an electrician, a general contractor, and we lived in Venice until I was 10. He would leave for work at six in the morning and come home at five o'clock, so we were a working-class family, not exactly blue-collar, though. More like a white t-shirt family, as I recall.

After we moved to Malibu, my dad continued working as an electrician. He was driving back into Santa Monica every day while we were living in a trailer on a dirt lot and building our house for two years. I started to realize that our neighbors did different things than the other neighbors I was used to. On one side of us was Mick Fleetwood, who was cutting the album *Tusk* and playing the drums in his bedroom, which was right outside my bedroom window. And on the other side of my house was Barbra Streisand's compound, and she was in there editing *A Star is Born* when we first moved in. That's when things started changing pretty quickly for us.

It was 1976 when I started sixth grade at Point Dume Elementary School. One of the first friends that I made was Carlos Estevez, or Charlie, as he liked to be called. He was in the Philippines for the first two months of the semester while his dad was shooting *Apocalypse Now*. When he came back, we were in the same classroom and drafted onto the same little league team, and we became fast friends. When my parents would be sitting on the bench at my games, they'd be there with Martin Sheen and Janet Sheen, as well as with a lot of other celebrity parents who also had kids in my school, and that was very surreal to me.

By being around all of these filmmakers, as kids, we were inspired to make our own Super 8 movies. I remember this one time where I was making a movie with my neighbors, Christopher Peters and Jason Gould, and I had to ask for help from my dad because I needed a bloody nose for a scene. We were sick and tired of ketchup, it just stunk, and after you've got ketchup on you for a while, you don't ever want to smell ketchup again. Dad willingly drew a bloody nose on my upper lip with my Mom's red fingernail polish. He put a white liquid paper highlight dot right in the middle of the bottom of the drip, and it looked great. I couldn't see straight from the fumes off of that fingernail polish.

Coincidentally, it was that weekend when my dad saw an ad in the back of the *L.A. Times* for the Elegance School of Makeup, and he decided that he was going to start going to night school to become a makeup artist. After 20 years, he was tired of being an electrician, and the effect of all these creative people around us had inspired him and freed him as an artist.

He took a liking to the courses and was using my mom, my sister Joni and myself as guinea pigs to work on his effects. Before that, he had no interest in makeup effects, and before that, I did not know about makeup effects either. His career took off immediately, and in 1980, he opened Lance Anderson Makeup Designs, with his first solo Job as a shop owner being *Captain EO*.

As David got older, he found himself connecting more with his creative inclinations, which led to his decision that after he graduated high school, he would pursue art school after getting his grades back on track at a nearby community college.

It was during high school that I found art. Lamonte Westmoreland was responsible for that. He was my high school art teacher and was the first person that told me I was an artist. It was something that I enjoyed doing, and probably the only reason I graduated. I was even voted 'Most Artistic' in my senior year at Samohi. That's when I started thinking about going to art school, but I decided I should go to junior college for two years first because my grades sucked in high school. Then, I would transfer.

I moved out of my folks' house, moved to Santa Monica and went to SMC [Santa Monica College] to study for two years. I soon realized art schools were very expensive and the reality was that if I went to art school, this was going to be my burden for a long time. My dad was busy at his shop, making a name for himself in Hollywood, and one day, he just made me a flat offer. He told me that working at his shop may not be exactly my cup of tea, but he knew I needed a job, and he wanted to put me to work.

At the time, he had just started up on the remake of *The Twilight Zone* television series, and he had three or four episodes of work to get done. It was 1985 when he brought me in as the lowest man on the totem pole, and I started out sweeping floors and things like that. But it was on my very first day when I realized that this was exactly what I wanted to be doing. When I walked into the building, my dad treated me just like he treated everyone else, and that was nice. He also introduced me to the artists working there that would become my professors over time. That's when I realized that I didn't need to pay for art school because I was going to get everything that I needed right here at his shop.

So, being in the shop was my education in painting, sculpting, and mold making, which was something I didn't have any understanding of at all. When I discovered mold making, I thought it was the most exciting aspect of all this new information I was getting because it helped me understand the world of effects. I became very passionate about mold making, and that happened because the person that taught me how to make a mold was Gunnar Ferdinandsen, a legend in the industry. It was Werner Keppler who taught me how to make appliances, and Jim Kagel, as well as my dad, taught me how to sculpt. All three of them were close to my dad and had a very similar work ethic. They were so good at what they did and were such generous teachers. Looking back now, I realize how lucky I was to get to work with those guys.

And after a few shows, it became extremely easy and very natural for me to dive into all aspects of the process of creating a makeup effect. Because of them, I realized I had a passion for the whole production process, and the ability to make something from nothing motivates me every day. There's nothing more exciting and full of potential than a box of clay and a bag of plaster.

As he continued to settle into his new career in the special effects industry, David ventured outside of his father's shop and ended up working for another legendary artist in Hollywood, none other than Stan Winston.

I first worked for Stan Winston on *The Monster Squad*. Our families had been close ever since my dad got out of school. We were out at dinner one night, and my dad put it out there that he thought that I was ready to go out and do more work, so Stan offered me a job.

The thing I remember most about that experience was that Stan asked me what I would like to make and I said I told him I would be happy with whatever he was paying. Stan then gave me the most memorable speech that I have ever been subjected to in my professional career; it was a little harsh, but he was right. What he told me was that in this industry, you have to know your worth, and you should never let someone else out there define what your value is. That left a big impression on me, and I have never made that same mistake again.

While he may have had some initial jitters about working over at Stan Winston Studio, Anderson discussed how he just did everything he could to put his best foot forward and keep up with the demands of the workload at hand.

I remember that first day I did my best to find my place there and did everything as best I could so that I would never have to experience Stan yelling at me again. Plus, I also wanted to make my dad proud. We were doing a ton of lifecasts, and I guess I was doing a great job, because both Alec [Gillis] and Tom [Woodruff Jr.] were very complimentary to me, regarding how I was making the positives for their lifecasts. The pace back then was feverish, and the pressure to be consistently productive was high.

We were all showing off to each other and feeling each other out to see who had the goods. It was an amazing group of artists to be around, and I'm still friends with all of those people, too. When I think about it now, I don't think there's anyone who was there at Stan's at that time who isn't still in the industry currently, and doing well in this business. It was an extremely charged room of very motivated artists. Even though I was only there for about four months, I took so much away from that experience.

That's around the time when my dad called me back to his shop and offered me the opportunity to go on location for him. So I seized that opportunity and put in my two-week notice at Stan's, and then got ready to go to Haiti for *The Serpent and the Rainbow*.

Directed by Wes Craven, production on The Serpent and the Rainbow was a remarkable and terrifying experience for David, as it required the cast and crew to head to the embattled country of Haiti in 1986 as it was reeling from economic issues, socio-political turmoil as well as the AIDS epidemic which had run rampant throughout the small country during the early 1980s.

Honestly, *Serpent* was very surreal for many different reasons. At the time, I was very young, and I had never been on location and only out of California one other time. My dad said to me, "You're going to represent Lance Anderson Makeup Designs on set, you're going to be the key special effects makeup artist on this show, and I'm going to send you to Haiti." Initially, I thought he said Tahiti, so I had no idea what I had gotten myself into. My dad and Wes were friends, and it wasn't a secret that at the time, I was green, so this was a whole new level of responsibility for me. Every day after work, my dad would teach me how to do basic makeup effects like cuts, scrapes, and bruises, so that I was prepared.

Thankfully, the work we were doing for *Serpent* fell somewhere in-between makeup effects and props, so I was comfortable with a lot of the more prop-like elements we were building. I was nervous about going on location to Haiti. I flew there by myself, and I arrived at night when Haitian Mardi Gras was going on. We took this funky bus ride from the airport where I met a couple of other crew members and started driving out into the country, into the blackness of night.

We drove through these little villages that were lit by fire and candlelight, and then all of a sudden, our bus was attacked by people in masks with torches. They were just partying for Mardi Gras, but I was terrified. I had no idea what I had gotten myself into, and I was overwhelmed. Tim Pershing, the key grip on *Serpent*, who was way more seasoned than I was because he had been in the industry for a while, did his best to comfort me.

Things had been bad in Haiti for a while, but production had found a three-month window of calmness after 'Baby Doc' had been run out of the country. So we snuck in and did our thing. But, as it turned out, what I was worried about the most on *Serpent* was keeping continuity because that was something that I hadn't done before. My dad had walked me through how he handled continuity, so I just did my best to follow his lead, and it was a full trial by fire experience for me.

Luckily, Bill Pullman was an incredibly warm and wonderful guy, and we immediately got along. So, between him, the makeup department head Michelle Bühler and the hair department head Robert Hallowell, they taught me everything I needed to know. So by the end of Serpent, I was a semi-pro, and in retrospect, I think I did a pretty good job. The best part was that I think I made both Wes and my dad proud, too.

We were run out of Haiti, though, with people throwing rocks at us. We were filming the big procession scene with a thousand Haitian extras, and that's when they decided to revolt because they weren't going to be paid enough money. We all ran to get on these buses and went straight to the airport, with the plane engines running when we got there. We didn't even go back to the hotel to get our bags or anything. They flew us to the Dominican Republic, and our bags showed up the next day, and we finished filming there then made our way home from there.

The best part for me was the wrap party for *Serpent*, as that was where Wes' assistant Marianne [Maddalena] introduced me to Heather [Langenkamp], and we've been married for 30 years now, and have raised two amazing children, Atticus and Isabelle. We have also worked as partners at AFX Studio since the early '90s. She is the greatest, smartest, most beautiful woman I have ever met and the reason myself and AFX have had so much success.

To be partners in love and business takes a special relationship. Neither one of us would say it has all been easy, but we both would do it all again if given the chance. Now that we are empty-nesters, Heather is still running things at AFX, but she is also acting a lot more, too. Recently, Heather also produced and directed an outstanding short film called *Washed Away*.

After The Serpent and the Rainbow, David returned to Stan Winston Studio to work on the feature films Alien Nation and Pumpkinhead before heading to Maine to head up the onset effects for Mary Lambert's adaptation of Stephen King's best-selling novel, Pet Sematary.

When dad got *Pet Sematary*, he sent John Blake and me to location as co-makeup effects artists, and we did all the onset stuff for him. John and I hit it off immediately. He was so much more accomplished than I was at makeup at the time, and so I learned a lot on that set, where he was gracious enough to split the work with me as I was learning.

It was a very collaborative and exploratory makeup experience for me because we would do these characters half and half. That meant that I would be on one side of the face, and John would be on the other side. We did Fred Gwynne's makeup like that, and we did Victor Pascow's makeup like that too. When we started working the makeups out, neither one of us were ever satisfied with how they came out. So each time we would figure out how we could do everything a little better, a little smoother, and a little faster. I think John and I had a very similar unreasonable desire for perfection, which is why we worked so well together. My favorite quote from John was, "It's perfect. It'll have to do," which is a mantra we still use to this day at AFX Studio.

My first fatherly hackles came out on *Pet Sematary*, too. I wanted to protect Miko Hughes, that beautiful little blonde baby, because of the things they were asking his parents to make him do. I was so concerned about the scene when Miko had to bite Fred's neck. Everybody was playing around with it as if it was this joke, but I was concerned. Miko had to bite this thing off of Fred's neck, and that's when it was going to start bleeding everywhere. There was no rehearsing that setup because it was going to make a mess everywhere. I wasn't there when they shot it, but I heard that Miko had some trouble with that scene, so even in my core as a future parent, I knew my concerns were legitimate.

The great thing about *Pet Sematary* was that there were no cliques. It was just everyone hanging out together in this little hotel called the Ellsworth Inn for the first month. I think that led to all of these extremely strong relationships between all of us that grew over time. Everybody from the assistants to the caterers to the actors and all of our department heads, we were all on this adventure together, and we all had a great time.

At the time when David began working on Shocker for Wes Craven, he was riding high, as he continued to establish himself in the realm of special makeup effects, and was enjoying great success in his personal life as well.

When we started *Shocker*, I will admit that I was slightly oblivious to everything else around me at the time. I was living the dream because Heather and I were engaged in 1989, we had just bought a house together, and I was having the time of my life. I remember that during *Shocker* Wes was dealing with some professional issues because of the studios and the whole business of getting movies made, but he was still as focused as ever.

But it was on *Shocker* where I started to feel my own independence, as I had been doing more onset work, so my confidence as a makeup artist was growing. I hung out a lot with Pete Berg and Mitch [Pileggi], and there was a lot of silliness that went on between us. The highlight for me on *Shocker* was that Heather was an extra in it and has a credit on *Shocker* as "The Body." But something else that I remember was that if you look closely, I signed my initials in the blood on Camille [Cooper]'s forehead in one of the scenes. There's a flash when her character Allison looks in the mirror, and if you look closely, you can see DLA written backward so that it looked correct in the reverse.

As the 1980s were drawing to a close, Anderson found another teacher and mentor by the name of Jeanne Van Phue who would introduce him to an entirely new world in the field of makeup.

My old friend, Charlie Sheen, asked me if I was interested in doing his straight makeup for his brother Emilio's production, *Men at Work*. I told him that I was an FX guy and that I wasn't interested in straight makeup, but he convinced me that I had to do it and that I had to meet Jeanne. So, I met with Jeanne, and she took me under her wing and taught me everything I know about straight makeup, as well as how to be a professional in this business. She had an incredible gift of making everyone feel included. Whether it was Mick Jagger sitting in her chair, the craft service person, an extra, a studio executive, or your mom for that matter, Jeanne had this ability to make us all feel like equals. Very sadly, we lost Jeanne this year after a hard-fought battle with cancer, but her legacy lives on in all of us who were blessed to know her.

And it was with the skills acquired from Jeanne that David went on to work as a personal makeup artist to his longtime friend Charlie Sheen on several films over the years, and even created the old-age makeup for Emilio Estevez on Young Guns II. Eventually, David found himself back at work for Stan Winston on Tim Burton's suburban gothic fairytale, Edward Scissorhands.

I wasn't at Stan's very long, but I was excited to go back because it was his new shop where they eventually made all the effects for *Jurassic Park*. I went right into the moldmaking department, and I ended up being paired up with Eileen Kastner-Delago, who was an up-and-coming makeup artist at the time. We were making molds for all the scissors and blades for Edward's hands, and instantly, we became great friends. We were even guests at her parents' house in Austria at one point. So even though my time on *Edward Scissorhands* was short-lived, I ended up making a dear friend from that experience.

In the early '90s, David found himself working for his dad on Death Becomes Her, and enjoyed hearing the stories and soaking in the expertise of the incomparable Dick Smith, who was assisting the elder Anderson on the project as a consultant. And it was around the same time that David and his wife, Heather, found themselves in desperate need of a reprieve of their lives in Los Angeles, and it was a call from Studio ADI to come work on Alien 3 that helped them out of a tight spot.

The opportunity to go work on *Alien 3* was something that happened as a result of Heather and I begging the universe for a reason to get out of town. There was a bad situation here, and we knew we just needed to get out of town for a while. It was Alec [Gillis] who called me up, and he said to me, "You're never going to want to do this, but I wanted to see if you would like to move to England for a year to work on the new *Alien* movie." We just jumped at the opportunity, packed our bags immediately, and were on a plane the very next day.

So we moved to England with a whole group of Americans and set up shop there, and we were doing pre-production on it for six months, up until Christmastime. As Christmas approached, we realized that Heather and I were expecting our first child, and we decided to experiment with the doctors in England in her first trimester. We ultimately decided that we wanted to go home to our regular old doctors so that we could have our first baby at home. So, we cut our ties and left during the holidays.

During pre-production, I did a bunch of sculptures, and even though I never got to set foot on set, it was still a fantastic experience. In fact, in all of my career, *Alien 3* was the only time where I was hired mainly as a sculptor, and that was such a gift from both Alec and Tom [Woodruff Jr.]. I took full advantage of that experience, and had the best time and probably sculpted the best things I've ever sculpted in my career. I can call myself a sculptor, but I don't get to do it as often as I would like, so I am still grateful to have been called in to work on *Alien [3]*.

Another highlight was a competition that Alec and Tom arranged between all the artists to design the embryo Alien for the poster art. We made our sculptures, and it was my design that won, and became the iconic poster image. It was a throwback moment for me to these stories I heard when I was a kid, about how my dad won Stan Winston's design competition that he had set up while they were working on John Carpenter's *The Thing*. It was his design of the Dog-Thing that won, and he got to puppeteer it in the movie.

Those rough personal times that David and his wife Heather were contending with during the early 1990s ended up providing some of the inspiration behind Wes Craven's return to the Nightmare on Elm Street franchise. The Master of Horror utilized a meta-narrative involving certain real-life elements of the Andersons' life at the time for the story of what would be the final entry in the series, New Nightmare.

When Wes first approached Heather about this concept, I was very put off by the whole idea. I thought it was crazy, but somehow or another, I got talked into being okay with it. Heather did have many conversations with Wes, where we would hash things out at night then she'd go back to him the next day to let him know if there were things we were not comfortable with.

There were several things that we made them change because it wasn't even a case of things hitting too close to home; some moments were straight up like a mirror reflecting things that had happened to us. But there was a certain point where we were like, "What do we have to hide? There's nothing to be ashamed of, Wes wants to do this, and we owe him a lot, so let's do it." And Heather just went for it. Part of our plan, as being parents in the entertainment industry, was that we were never going to accept a job at the same time. Nowadays, Heather and I work together, but back then, when she was acting a lot, I was a full-time dad, and vice versa.

But *New Nightmare* was a very demanding job for her, and I think it was also the ultimate experience for Heather because she had always dreamed of having her name at the top of the call sheet. So, she had an amazing time working on it. Plus, they had Miko Hughes, who I knew from *Pet Sematary*, playing the character of our son, so I felt even more protective of him after *New Nightmare*. I still do think it's one of the best things that Wes has ever directed and it also features one of Heather's best performances, too. Although it is still pretty weird to me that, essentially, I get killed in *New Nightmare*. And I die while singing R.E.M. of all things – and I've never even liked R.E.M.

David was also involved in Craven's next directorial effort, *Vampire in Brooklyn*, but he came aboard that project through Bob Kurtzman at KNB EFX who needed Anderson's expertise beyond his makeup effects skillset.

I had done a string of movies as Charlie Sheen's personal makeup artist over the years, so I had a reputation for being able to work with "particular" actors. Bob had decided that I would be the right candidate to apply makeup on Eddie Murphy. I was terrified, but I told him I would do it.

I was there for the very first test makeup, and Bob Kurtzman was with me. I hadn't met Eddie yet, but as soon as he walked in the trailer, I was suddenly more nervous than I have ever been before in my entire life. He sat down in the chair, looked right at me, and asked, "How long is this gonna take?" I told him it would be about two hours because it was just a test, and he put his head down, looked back up at me, and said, "You've got 45 minutes." And at that very moment, sweat started shooting out of my pores. There was no way I was going to be able to do it in 45 minutes, so Eddie was setting me up to fail.

Kurtzman and I just decided that all we could do was try to get it done. I was shaking, and I remember that feeling of being confident in one moment and then just completely shattered in the next – there was so much pressure at that moment. So, we started doing everything, and I can't remember how long it took exactly, but it was more than 45 minutes. And I remember that those last few minutes were pure torture. I didn't know if Eddie was going to jump up and leave, and I had no idea what was going to happen at the end of those 45 minutes. I just figured I was going to be fired and that was that.

I don't know what happened, but it felt like Eddie relaxed a little bit, and we were able to get the test done. Over time, I think I gained his trust, and I did the rest of the show with Eddie. Honestly, I didn't think I would ever see, let alone, work with Eddie ever again, but lo and behold, shortly after that, that's exactly what happened for *The Nutty Professor*.

Anderson's journey in Hollywood would lead him back to reteaming with Murphy on the aforementioned Nutty Professor remake, but it was his work on another film that would be the reason he got hired to take on the highly ambitious makeups.

After *Vampire in Brooklyn*, I went and did *The Arrival* for Charlie [Sheen] down in Mexico. When we came back into town, I was a full-fledged journeyman in the makeup union, which meant I had health insurance and had to keep up my hours. So, I put myself on the list and got a call to come in as a background artist on *Batman Forever*.

On my very first day, they pulled in all these makeup artists for this dance scene and filled up a whole stage with tables so we could work on all the background players. I was nervous as hell, and I felt like I stuck out like a sore thumb because I wasn't as honed as these other artists I was working with. But we all started talking, getting to know each other, and one of the artists was named Sylvia. Our stations were close, and on the next day a group of us were talking about kids and life and our families and ended up talking a lot more than we were working. I realized later that the whole time we were having these conversations, Sylvia was sizing me up to help Rick decide whether or not he should bring me on for *The Nutty Professor*.

At the end of the day, Sylvia handed me this tiny, torn piece of paper with Rick's number on it, and she says, "I'm Rick Baker's wife, and Rick would like you to call him right now." So I stepped outside the stage, got in a pay booth, and set up an appointment to go into Cinovation and meet Rick. The day of the interview, I got to Cinovation early, so I decided to go to a park nearby so I could relax and breathe and get ready to meet Rick. I somehow fell asleep, and I woke up in a panic with only three minutes to get to the studio. I made it in time and sat in the waiting room for what seemed like an hour. Finally, Rick invited me into his office, we started a conversation, lost track of time, and suddenly, it was three hours later.

We had this incredible connection, and at the end of the meeting, he asked if I was interested in working on *Nutty Professor*, and the rest was history. When I was working on that film, I knew immediately that it was one of the greatest makeup effects ever created. The work was so clean and perfect, and it was all done before I had even come into the picture. In fact, it would have been nearly impossible for me to fuck it up. And within a couple of weeks of being Rick's assistant, he looked at me and said, "You need to find an assistant because you're taking over my position."

So, I asked Toni G. to join me as she was a new acquaintance and together, we did 84 applications of the Sherman makeup, as well as all the other family members. It was an extremely challenging makeup for Eddie, and the fact that he was able to withstand it all was incredible, so I have nothing but respect for Eddie Murphy.

That whole experience of working with Rick and Eddie, and then winning Academy Awards with Rick back-to-back on *The Nutty Professor* and *Men in Black*, was very overwhelming because it happened so fast. I went from zero to 100, and I was so young that I felt this whiplash effect. Everything was different, and everyone was treating me differently, and if I walked into someone's shop, everyone would be whispering and treating me differently, and I did not like it. It felt so bizarre, and I had a lot of doubts which took a toll on me.

It was at that point in his career where Anderson decided he wanted to pursue other creative endeavors outside of the industry to challenge himself in new ways as both an artist and as a businessman.

I felt like I was losing my independence as an artist. So I decided I was going to quit the industry, and I pulled out in '97 to reinvent myself as a jewelry designer. I got this wild idea because there was this wave of very successful designers coming out of Malibu that I went to school with, who were now becoming these superstars in Japan for their silver jewelry designs. I didn't know anything about it, but it involved all of the things that I had been taught in the lab, so I thought I could figure it out.

So, I created this line of jewelry called DLA Silverwear and went into Maxfield in Beverly Hills after making a cold call. When I met the buyer, we hit it off immediately. She told me if I was serious about this, the first thing that I needed to do was to flesh out the line more. Six months later, I came back, and they took me on as a client, so I had a little shelf in Maxfield with my jewelry on it. I also did a jewelry trade show in New York. We spent nearly all of our money trying to make this happen, but it felt like we couldn't get anything going.

About a week or two went by after the trade show, and I got a phone call from a Japanese buyer who had seen us in New York, and they wanted to come over and talk. So, within a couple of weeks after our trip to New York, I had a deal with five stores in Japan and this large order. I was doing the jewelry work full force through '97 and into '98, and I was still doing some film work from time to time. Out of nowhere, there was a big financial setback in Japan, and I learned that a bunch of people that I was involved with were getting stiffed. People had to walk away, and there was a lot of debt floating around, so I got really scared. And when the Japanese economy tanked in 2002, that's when I decided I was giving it up.

But even though that happened, the whole experience benefited me a lot. I needed to be creating something that was all mine again, rather than to be doing work that I felt like it had just "happened" to me. I needed to express myself as an artist again, and I felt like I did just that. I had overcome this challenge and started the new business, created this whole line of jewelry, and it helped me a lot. I felt like I had legitimized myself again. I have every intention of doing it again full-time when I retire from the film industry because it has become my passion. It's what keeps me sane in this business of doing all these crazy things for all these different companies and producers and directors. It's the one constant in my life, and as an artist, I always fall back on it.

But after the economic bubble burst in 2002, I called up James Brubaker at Universal. He had previously reached out to me about several projects that I had turned down when I was making jewelry. I apologized to him for having to say no in the past, and I mentioned that if anything comes up in the future, I would appreciate being considered again. James ran the Universal physical production for a while, but he also ran the Teamsters too. And even though he could be a real hardass, Jim was also the sweetest man, and he taught me a valuable lesson about loyalty. And as the popular saying goes, Jim was keen to remind me: don't quit your day job.

As he was fully transitioning back into the world of special effects, David wouldn't have to wait very long for a monumental opportunity to present itself. Brubaker called him in to take on a brand new remake that Universal was gearing up for at the time, Zack Snyder's *Dawn of the Dead*.

Honestly, when Jim called me, I could not believe it. This wasn't just a job for me; it was going to be the biggest show I had ever done and on a scale that I couldn't even wrap my brain around. We started pre-production here in Los Angeles, had a few meetings with Zack, and then we packed it all up and went to Toronto. We built our studio up there in an old mall.

We hired a bunch of Canadian artists and brought a bunch of American artists up there too so that we could crew ourselves up to the gills. Heather was the producer for our department, so we went up with our kids, Atticus and Isabelle, and lived in Toronto for a while. *Dawn* was an amazing reintroduction to the industry for me. Because I had my confidence back, I was excited about every single day we worked on that film, and it became a life-changing experience.

It was the hardest job I've ever done, though, and the scale of it was ridiculous. The number of people we were putting in make-ups was beyond anything I had ever done before. It was incredibly empowering and satisfying when we saw it in theaters, and to top it off, I loved the movie. Even looking back on it now, I still can't believe it actually happened. I'm so proud of our work.

After experiencing a great amount of success with the work that he and his team were able to create on *Dawn of the Dead*, David found himself taking on an entirely new set of challenges for Ron Howard's boxing biopic, *Cinderella Man*, alongside his father, Lance. The duo's realistic makeups created for the sports drama led to them being nominated for an Academy Award, and it became yet another huge turning point in Anderson's career.

When *Cinderella Man* came up after *Dawn*, it was the complete opposite of the experience that I had just had. This was going to be a high-profile job with Ron Howard, and instead of thousands of zombies, we had to create the character of Jim Braddock out of Russell Crowe. I was ready for it, and I don't think I could have done *Cinderella Man* at any other point in my career. I also hired my dad, because I realized that not only did I have to do Russell's makeup, we were going to be responsible for the other fighters and their makeups. So, I brought my dad on to be my second, and he was going to handle all the makeups for Jim's opponents. We had such a blast working together, and it was an incredibly memorable experience for both of us.

When Academy season was starting up, I realized that I was going to be involved in one of the selection meetings for the nominations because I was a member of the Academy. I was so nervous about how that would go and how I was going to present it, present myself, and present the work. When we got to the meeting, they went down the list alphabetically, and then they got to *Cinderella Man*. A few people in the room had seen it, and they were like, "Yes, it's a beautiful movie, but there's no makeup in it." And at that moment, I got very excited because the whole room was discussing the fact that there was no makeup in the film.

That's when I began to explain that in every frame of *Cinderella Man*, Russell has a fake nose, fake ears, a fake tooth, and a fake widow's peak. They couldn't believe it. As everybody got up from the table to look at this presentation book that I had brought with me, it was apparent that I had fooled them. Regardless of whether we got the nod or not, that particular moment in that room with my peers was the moment I had been working for throughout my whole career.

Plus, having my dad on the ticket with me made it feel even more special. It became his swan song in the industry. To show my gratitude and make his retirement official, I gave him a Rolex when we got our Oscar nomination. This nomination was my third, and it was a very different experience for me. We didn't win that night, but it didn't matter. The moment I won was the moment when I was acknowledged by the people that mattered the most in my professional world. It was the greatest compliment and my greatest achievement.

Anderson continued working on a series of high-profile studio films over the next few years, including Evan Almighty, Get Smart, Frost/Nixon, Angels & Demons, Cirque du Freak: The Vampire's Assistant and Mission: Impossible – Ghost Protocol. But it was in 2011 when he'd find himself taking on yet another ambitious genre project called The Cabin in the Woods for director Drew Goddard.

Cabin was a hell of an opportunity. It was also a good example of how you never know who's watching and you never know who you are going to cross paths with. The reason that I got *Cabin in the Woods* was because of Dan Kolsrud, who had been a producer on *Cirque Du Freak*. We ran into some troubles during production, but we figured out how to get through it, and I made a friend in Dan by helping to keep production moving along. He told me when we wrapped if he could ever pay it forward to me, that someday he would.

One day, he calls me up and tells me that he's running things at MGM and they were getting ready to make a movie called *The Cabin in the Woods* and he wanted me to do it. So, I went in, and I met with Drew [Goddard] and Joss [Whedon], and I was pinching myself the entire time. I couldn't believe it. I knew nothing about it walking in, and when they told me that they wanted to do an old-school monster movie practically, I thought they were joking. But it was exactly what they wanted to do. There was this incredibly challenging list of practical effects, and there were a lot of variables that were going to make the job very difficult. We only had three months for pre-production, so we had to build everything in Los Angeles, and then take everything up to Canada.

Because this was such a gigantic show, I was going to need everyone from town, and I was going to need to work in a room with the best of the best. Lucky for me, there was nothing else going on in L.A. at the time, and every single artist that I called jumped on board. We were all working together in this giant lab that I rented called "The Bat Shop," which was over by the Burbank Airport. Apparently, Warner Bros. had built a fully-functioning makeup effects shop for *Batman* and then just left it there. So, we took over this building for four months, and it was perfect.

About two and a half months into the build, I left and went up to Canada, so I could start setting up our satellite shop up there, and we were off and running in Canada. I brought a whole bunch of people from Los Angeles up there, and we all had the best time that any of us have ever had. Every day was just another opportunity to do the most insane things, and we couldn't believe what we were doing every day. It was a total free-for-all where we were using every trick in the book when it came to doing all these practical effects.

The one thing about *Cabin* where I kicked myself in the ass for was not making a stink at the Academy when it came time to consider it. Now they're starting to consider more horror-type films, but they weren't taking horror movies seriously back then. But we did every single type of makeup you could do, everything from the oldest makeups straight out of the kit to these practical/digital effect hybrids. There's always a focus on these Academy types of projects, but as I see horror movies being considered more these days, it makes me realize I should have fought harder for *Cabin in the Woods*. Especially because so many artists poured their hearts and their souls into those makeups. It was a massive community effort.

When David was presented with another tremendous opportunity to create the special effects on Star Trek: Into Darkness, circumstances weren't that great for him, both professionally and personally.

When we had come back from *Cabin*, the industry was beginning to slow down a lot in L.A., and we were having a hard time getting another show going. This opportunity to get involved with *Star Trek* came along, and I did every possible thing that I could do to get that job. I danced and sang because we needed it badly. It had been months of nothing in the shop, and there's always that time in-between projects where you are nervous because you don't know what's next.

At the point when *Star Trek* came along, I dove into everything with 100% conviction. Deep down, though, I was terrified because, and I shouldn't admit this, I wasn't ever a *Star Trek* fan, so I wasn't sure if it was going to be a good fit. I got the job in the end, but the conditions that I got the job under were not ideal. I was told that my position was to realize all of the designs done by someone else. This type of arrangement was a first for me, but I went along with it.

Then my life changed in an instant during one of the pre-production meetings. I was in a tone meeting with J.J. Abrams and all the department heads when my cell phone rang. I answered it, and it was my son who had just gone to Berlin to study abroad. I could tell immediately that something was wrong. His voice sounded very weak, and he told me that he had had a seizure, he was in the emergency room and that they had done a scan on his brain and found a mass. I just collapsed to the ground. And so began the hardest period of any parent's life.

Somehow, Heather and I managed all these things on *Star Trek* while we as a family tried to figure out how to help my son. When we finally got through *Trek*, I wanted nothing to do with anything of that scale ever again. It was so difficult to do, trying to deal with production demands while trying to figure out which hospital my son was going to have brain surgery at. Once we got through the surgery, and the follow-up procedures, and he had a clean bill of health, Atticus immediately returned to Stanford and completed his studies. He graduated with his class having never missed a beat. For me, I just knew that we didn't need to take on any other giant shows like that ever again, and we needed to focus on family first.

We struggled for a while and took these smaller opportunities that came our way. There were a few other makeup artists who knew what my family was going through, and they sent some work our way to AFX to help us out. Doing those jobs, I could have a normal 9-to-5 job here at the studio and still go home at the end of the day. But after a while, it wasn't going so well, and then I was given the opportunity to work on set for *American Horror Story* by my dear friend Eryn [Krueger Mekash]. I needed the hours badly, and just in the nick of time, I was sent out to New Orleans. I just rolled my sleeves up, dove in, and worked my ass off with my friends Chris Nelson, Jason Hamer, and Mike Mekash.

Because I had so much built-up frustration and pain and sadness in me from my son's situation, I was just glad to be somewhere where someone was going to tell me what to do, and I would just do it. To quote my grandpa, "Just tell me who to shoot and where they fall," so I couldn't have been happier. I guess all of my hard work impressed somebody because it wasn't too long after I had come home that Eryn called me up about doing the next season of *American Horror Story*. It was the exact job that I needed at that point in my life because it allowed me to prioritize my family.

Plus, it provided us with enough work to keep the shop going full-time. Between *American Horror Story*, *Scream Queens*, *American Crime Story* and some other side projects that Ryan [Murphy] did over the years, we retooled AFX Studio to be a fully-functioning makeup effects lab for television, and we changed the whole method of how we were doing things here.

Beyond all of that, Eryn and Ryan allowed me to have a very secure situation, where I could still be with my son, and be with my family every day. In fact, Atticus became an employee at AFX, where he brought his engineering skills to help us. He learned to sculpt, he got to make molds, and he even had the opportunity to go to set. When we were working on [*American Horror Story:*] *Hotel*, Atticus was even sculpting appliances for Lady Gaga, and was mentioned in several magazines for his work.

Atticus was my date at the Emmys for the year we were nominated for [*American Horror Story:*] *Freak Show*, which he also had worked on. We won that night, which was also a huge highlight for him. I've never heard anyone scream louder in my life when they called our names. He was so proud, and so was I.

Unfortunately, Atticus ended up having a relapse amidst all of the successes that AFX Studio was enjoying at the time. But fate intervened in an unusual way which allowed David to be able to have more time with his son during what would become his final year of life.

Atticus was dealing with major health setbacks, and he had another brain surgery right before we were going to the Emmys in 2017. That year, I took my daughter, Isabelle, with me, and I had booked a room at the Ritz Carlton. As we were checking in at the counter, it all just hit me out of nowhere. I remember saying something to my daughter and the concierge about having some weird déjà vu feelings. Then I just passed out and hit my head hard on the marble floor. My daughter was terrified.

They ended up taking me to the hospital in an ambulance, and it was just an awful experience. I was suffering from terrible vertigo and side effects that were affecting my hearing and vision, which made me pretty useless at work. So while it was a terrible thing to have to go through, what it did was make me the person who could stay with Atticus day in and day out. It was the most beautiful thing that could have happened to me.

It gave me time with him that I wouldn't have had otherwise if I had been working full-time. That's something that no one can ever take away from me either. It's another example of these moments that become signposts for your life. You can't predict the reasons for these things happening, or how meaningful they will be in the bigger picture of things.

Atticus got sicker and sicker, and he ended up passing away in our home with Heather, Isabelle, and myself by his side. The employees here at AFX have become our family, and losing Atticus has affected them too. We've all been doing our best to get through our sadness by remembering to live life as Atticus did. By adopting his love of life and sense of adventure, we are navigating life, one day at a time and living every moment to the fullest.

Quality of life is always the motivation now. Despite everything we've recently been through as a family, I have to say that I've had a beautiful family and life, and I've had a wonderful career. Even though it's been a difficult six years, I think we're all turning around now finally, and I'm very excited about some of the things on the horizon. I'm starting to find myself inspired again, and I'm so grateful for that.

Opportunities have been coming back and presenting themselves to myself, to Heather and to my daughter too, and I think that's a sign that everything is connected. We've been trying to put ourselves back together over the last year. And now, I believe with Atticus by our sides, and in our hearts, we are finally beginning to heal.

Losing Atticus is something we will never get over, and the pain will never go away, but my whole family and my extended movie family are devoted to living in his honor and doing as he did. My son's favorite quote was, "Make cool shit," so that's what we've been trying to do and that's what we're going to spend the rest of our careers here at AFX doing. It's all about making cool shit again because that's what Atticus wants us to do.

The Serpent and the Rainbow - David Leroy Anderson

The Serpent and the Rainbow - Bill Pullman

The Serpent and the Rainbow - Bill Pullman and David Leroy Anderson

Pet Sematary - Fred Gwynne and David Leroy Anderson

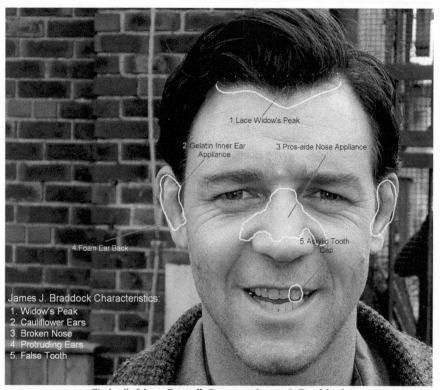

Cinderella Man - Russell Crowe as James J. Braddock

Cinderella Man - Russell Crowe and David Leroy Anderson

Dead Silence - Lance Anderson and David Leroy Anderson Creating Billy the Dummy

Dead Silence – Judith Roberts and Billy the Dummy

Dead Silence - Billy the Dummy

Film: Evan Almighty
Actor: Steve Carell
Character: Evan Baxter
Notes: Stage 5 - Sc. 132 thru 182
"NOAH" - combed

Date: 1-30-06

Evan Almighty - Steve Carrell

Frost/Nixon - Frank Langella as Richard Nixon

The Cabin in the Woods - David Leroy Anderson and Doll Faces

The Cabin in the Woods - The Sugarplum Fairy

The Cabin in the Woods – Buzzsaw

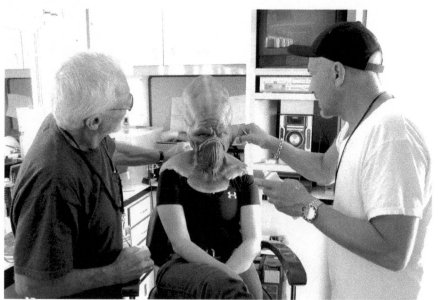

Star Trek Into Darkness - Lance Anderson, David Leroy Anderson
and Heather Langenkamp as Moto

Star Trek Into Darkness - David Leroy Anderson and Heather Langenkamp

Star Trek Into Darkness - Zachary Quinto as Spock

Star Trek Into Darkness - Zachary Quinto as Spock

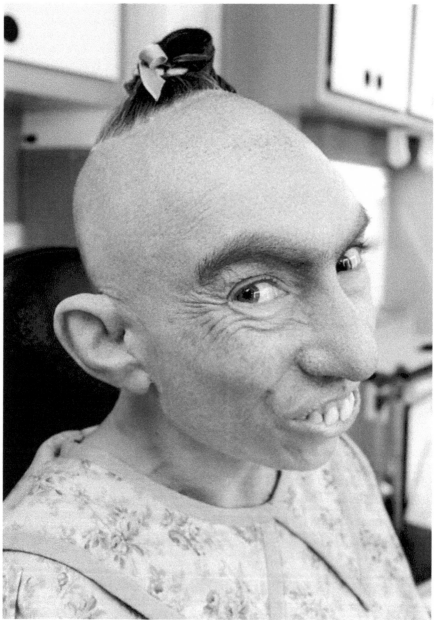

American Horror Story: Freak Show – Pepper

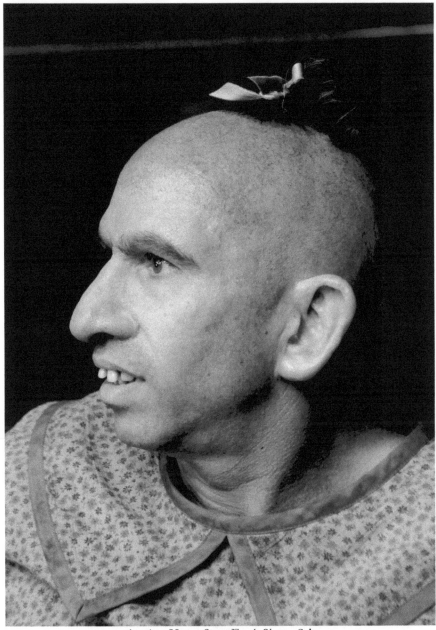

American Horror Story: Freak Show – Salty

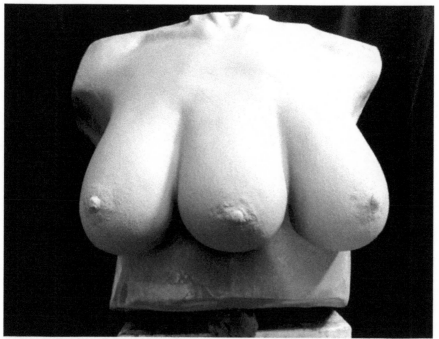

American Horror Story: Freak Show - Desiree Sculpt

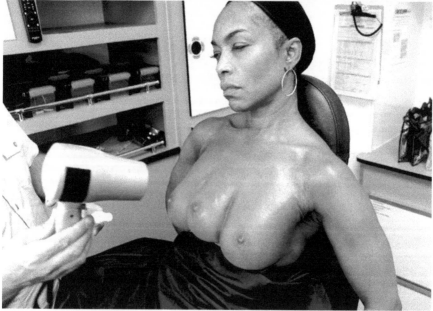

American Horror Story: Freak Show - Angela Bassett

American Horror Story: Freak Show - Angela Bassett as Desiree

The AFX Crew

Father and Son - Lance Anderson and David Leroy Anderson

Conversation with…
EVERETT BURRELL

Emmy Winning Special Effects Makeup Artist

Harry and the Hendersons (1987)
Night of the Living Dead (1990)
Babylon 5 (1993)
The Dark Half (1993)
Pan's Labyrinth (2006)
Prometheus (2012)

Growing up in Riverside County, California, artist Everett Burrell had no idea that he would become part of the Hollywood special effects scene, but he knew it was something he wanted to pursue after he fell in love with a variety of creature features, and the magazines that stoked his endless imagination.

One of the first things I remember watching that got me interested in movie monsters was the 1970s reissue of *20,000 Leagues Under the Sea*. That was pivotal. Our local station, KTLA, had a horror host called Seymour and he would show horror films on Saturdays, like the original *King Kong* (1933), *The Brain That Wouldn't Die*, and the original *Night of the Living Dead*.

I also used to watch the *Thunderbirds* and all the Ray Harryhausen stuff, too, which became a huge influence on me as a kid. I knew the monsters were fake and that's when I began to realize that they were created by artists and technicians, so I became obsessed with this idea of "How did they do that?" I already had stacks of *Star Log*, *Cinemagic*, *Famous Monsters [of Filmland]*, and *Cinefantastique* in my room, but when *Star Wars* came out in 1977, I was 12 years old and that just blew the lid off everything. I just knew this was something I was going to do.

I spent a lot of time making characters as a kid—sometimes on myself, sometimes on my friends, or sometimes I would even make puppets. I was also a huge fan of Tom Savini and I wanted to really be part of that world that Tom created in *Dawn of the Dead* (1978). I got his book when I was in high school, so it was really great that I eventually ended up working for the guy. When you work for your heroes it can either go badly, or it can go well, and sometimes, it can be a little in between. And for me, working for Tom was a huge turning point.

Once he graduated high school, before he'd get the chance to collaborate with one of his heroes, Everett found himself at a crossroads. He had to decide whether or not he should pursue a formal education, or begin his professional career in Hollywood under the guidance of one of the greatest low-budget filmmakers of all time.

I applied to CalArts [California Institute of the Arts] in 1982, the year before I graduated, and when I went in to interview with them, I brought a bunch of short films and props that I had made with me. They said that they saw that I had promise because I was doing techniques on my own that weren't even being taught there at the time. They offered me a scholarship, but it was a really expensive school. It was $10,000 a year back in 1983, and it was only a $3,000 scholarship, so my family had to come up with the rest of the money. I was going to have to get student loans and work a lot the summer before school began.

A good friend of mine was working for Roger Corman, and I got a job helping out at Roger's lumber yard in Venice doing some low budget horror films. I remember as I was walking in the door, Jim Cameron was walking out the door to go do *The Terminator*, and it was really exciting to be part of that kind of a rough-and-tumble crew. Working in that environment teaches you humility from a variety of aspects. Sometimes, you have to go get everyone lunch, and then when you're done, you have to jump in and help sculpt this giant gorilla head, then you need to sculpt a zombie or do a life cast of Erin Moran or make some tentacles, and then it's up to you to clean up the shop and go buy beer for everybody for wrap. We did everything, and we all looked out for each other too. We had a really good club of people over at Roger's for a long time.

One day Roger came up to me and said, "I heard you're going to college next year. Why don't you work for me for a year, and I'll train you, so that you'll never have to go to film school because you'll learn everything you need to learn from me." I took him up on it, so that was the beginning of my education. And I've had a great career that isn't slowing down anytime soon. I've worked really hard, made a ton of great friends and done really well financially over the years, but there is still a part of me that wishes I'd done that discipline of going to school for four years. There's so much that I've learned that I never would have learned in school, but it still chaps me that I don't have that degree to hang on my wall.

After his time under the tutelage of Roger Corman, Everett began working on several films for another scrappy production company, Empire Pictures, which was run by home media pioneer and filmmaker Charles Band.

After Roger, I went to work for John Carl Buechler, and I think the first movie we did was *Ghoulies*. I met some really amazing artists on that film – Mitch Devane, Bob Cantrell, Cleve Hall, and Chris Biggs. We ran John's shop for probably a good three or four years when they were doing all those Empire shows.

Ghoulies was definitely cheesy, and we could sense that it would be cheesy when we were working on it. God love John, but the puppets are pretty bad. He had a great imagination but had no real technical sense of how to make things work. John could sculpt and paint, but he just didn't have the sense or understanding of how to make a puppet work, so we were always trying to help him. Whenever I watch the film, I cringe because the back of the Ghoulies' throats are just like little pieces of rubber and you can see my fingers sticking through at least three or four of the puppets trying to puppeteer them. John did have a really good go-to spirit and tried really hard, but creatively, he didn't have the most refined techniques always.

But a lot of great artists started their careers at Mechanical and Makeup Imageries [MMI], John's shop, and we got a lot of opportunities to do some really cool shit too, because all bets were off. We all had a lot of fun there, and it was pretty much party city over there every night after John would go home for the night.

One of the next projects to come through MMI was Stuart Gordon's cult classic Re-Animator, but Burrell only had a chance to work on set for the reshoots (it was an experience he summarized as "an absolutely wild day of shooting"), as he had been busy collaborating with his aforementioned hero Tom Savini on the George A. Romero sequel, Day of the Dead (1985). And while it may not be his favorite from the Master of Horror's original zombie trilogy, it still provided Everett with a great opportunity to work with some of the very best talents in the effects industry, and have a hand in bringing one of the most iconic zombies to the silver screen.

Everyone loves Bub. He's great. I do think in some ways though that his look was greatly inspired by the Nazi zombies in *Shock Waves*. John [Vulich] used those textures of the Nazi zombies for Bub, so it's a blend of that design and Howard Sherman's face. And Howard was such a great and patient guy, too. John must have made him up like 30-to-40 times during the shoot, and I don't think he ever complained once.

In the script that George had initially written, the zombies were starting to heal themselves, as whatever disease had wiped out humanity was slowly recycling itself, which is another reason why Bub looks the way he looks, and acts the way that he acts. I don't know if it was explicitly expressed that way in the language of the final film, but I do remember that was some of the inspiration behind Bub. And it was almost like he was a dog in some ways, where he was affectionate and sought out love, too. I do think those scenes with him are some of the best stuff that George had ever directed in his career. The gag where he starts shaving was inspired. We all loved that moment.

After contributing to a few more films over at MMI—Trancers, Troll, Hard Rock Zombies, and Eliminators—Burrell had the chance to transition over to another premiere shop and work for another legendary talent in the industry, none other than Stan Winston.

I had the chance to interview with Stan back when you still had to bring your portfolio with you everywhere, to show people what you could do, and you had to have all those iconic creatures in there—a mummy, a werewolf, a zombie, a Frankenstein—things like that. A bunch of us used to get together and make each other up, so that way we had what we needed for our portfolios.

But Stan was very sweet, and the interview went great. He told me to come in the very next day to start work at 8 AM. He said to me, "Don't get here at 7:40, don't show up at 8:15, just be here exactly at 8 AM, or you're fired," and then proceeded to hand me the script for *Aliens*. I went home, and read the whole script, and I don't think I slept at all that night. I was just so nervous. I woke up at 6:30 AM, and got there early, so I got breakfast at Denny's first, and walked in the door promptly at eight. Just like Stan said.

Burrell immediately settled in and worked hard at Stan's, doing a variety of jobs ranging from sweeping to prepping molds to fabricating. He reflected on the day that the original Alien Xenomorph suits showed up at the studio, which wasn't nearly as cool as it initially seemed.

I was excited when I heard they were sending us the original *Alien* suits. But then, the crates from Fox showed up, we got the crowbars out to open up those crates, and it smelled like they had dead corpses inside. They never washed the suits after *Alien*, so the suits were just taken off the actor and put into a box for 10 years to basically rot. No disinfectant, no anything—they just had sweat and whatever other fluids happened to be in them.

We had to clean out all of those suits out and then we had to set them up on mannequins. We analyzed all the molds and everything that [H.R.] Giger had done. What was interesting is that he was an amazing artist, but his techniques in film were amateurish. He really didn't know how to make professional-grade props or suits, so the Xenomorph suits were very roughly put together. He even sewed them together, as opposed to molding the pieces of the suit together, and I had never seen that before. So, we made molds of all the original parts and did our best to maintain the original Giger designs.

Something else that struck me about those original *Alien* suits was just how rough the work looked in person. They definitely translated much differently on film, so I could see just how important something like lighting was in relation to how effective practical effects look in a movie. If you looked at these things outside in the daylight, they looked like shit. But in *Alien*, when they were all wetted down and lit properly, these suits were fucking terrifying. They ended up shooting *Aliens* over in London, but I stayed here in the States, and basically sculpted monsters for four months since I had this amazing shop mostly to myself.

Burrell also kept himself busy during that time at the Stan Winston Studios on another science fiction project that had come their way—Tobe Hooper's 1986 remake of Invaders From Mars, whose creatures presented their own unique challenges to the crew.

I worked on all the different aspects of the creatures for *Invaders*—fabricating, fine-tuning, puppeteering—and they were a disaster. I think they look pretty good in the film, but in reality, they were just terrible. That was a challenge, right there. And Tobe was a bit of a handful, too. I think he was going through some rough times, but he showed up to set every day wearing his hat that held two Dr. Peppers, and he'd pretty much go off the rails daily.

Everett continued to branch out professionally after his time at Stan Winston Studios, working with the likes of Kevin Yagher, Greg Cannom, and Rick Baker, on a wide variety of films that ranged from straight horror (Trick or Treat, A Nightmare on Elm Street 3: Dream Warriors, The Hidden) to comedic vampire films (The Lost Boys and Vamp) to family-friendly creature features with Harry and the Hendersons.

I think the first of those to come along was *Vamp*. That was with Greg Cannom, and he was a lot of fun to work for. Keith Haring, who did Grace Jones' body painting in the film, was great, and I remember he died just a few years after we made the film. It wasn't my first time working with Greg, but I always thought it was interesting that he would do these two different vampire movies back-to-back.

Greg had a very distinct style that he used in both movies, so they couldn't be any more different from each other. I do think *The Lost Boys* was the better-looking design though, but Greg did a great job on both films. *Vamp* was a really crazy set though—Grace Jones was always on something, and just doing her life cast was a total trip. The whole cast was kind of nuts, in a good way though. It was just hard to get them to sit still whenever we needed to get our work done. And we were shooting in some really weird areas too, so the whole experience had this surreal vibe to it. Which I guess fits the film. But we all had a good time on *Vamp*.

It was rough at times, being a freelance artist. Because, while you were getting to work alongside some great talents, which was invaluable, the job uncertainty could take its toll, plus you had to worry about things like insurance and your 401k. Very few shops had permanent positions, so I treated every opportunity as my way of getting to work towards the best, eventually landing at Rick Baker's. Once I wrapped up on *The Lost Boys*, that's when I started working with Kevin Yagher for a few years off and on.

Kevin and I had a very rocky relationship. I love Kevin, and he's incredibly talented, but we had very different work ethics. I remember when I was doing *Glory* for him, I just hit a wall, so I called John [Vulich] up and said, "John, we have to find a way to do this for ourselves." And that's how Optic Nerve got started.

Prior to officially opening the doors on Optic Nerve, Burrell had the chance to collaborate once again with both Tom Savini and George Romero on Monkey Shines, which was being produced by Orion Pictures.

Tom called [Greg] Nicotero, Mike Trcic and me up to work on it out in Pittsburgh, and we had a blast. I think it was *Monkey Shines* (1988) where Tom realized he could trust us, and I can't say for sure, but I feel like that's how we ended up getting involved with *Night of the Living Dead* (1990).

A remake of one of the greatest horror films of all time comes with its own baggage, but Burrell realized early on that being a part of Savini's new take on Romero's classic film would provide him with a chance to

create unique makeup approaches to this new iteration's zombified monsters.

John [Vulich] and I did a bunch of makeup tests that Tom was really fascinated by. I think Tom really loved John, and he really loved John's mind. Tom loved me too, but I think it was more because I was great at problem-solving. But that makeup test got us the job.

The thing is, we were trying to do something very different, very new and unique, with the zombies and I still stand by what we did. We tried very hard to break out of the box and John and I did some really interesting things, even though not all of it shows up in the film. We really looked into what made those original *Dead* films scary, and we realized that what made *Night of the Living Dead* work so well was that the zombies weren't gory, and they weren't over the top either. Those effects were a subtle look, so we went to a morgue in Pittsburg to take reference photos of all these dead bodies.

John got literally sick at the door. He couldn't make it through the door, so I took a thousand photos of all these dead bodies, and the coroner explained everything, and I noticed how it looked the opposite of the filmic bullshit Hollywood stereotype of what a zombie looked like. We adopted everything that we learned into the film and created these very subtle wounds on yellowed skin with this fog over the eyes, because when the blood gets drained out of your body, you don't turn grey, you turn this weird beige yellow color.

But there was so much that Tom wanted to do that just never made it into the film unfortunately, through a combination of politics, schedule issues and budget problems. When we had a break, Tom, John and I literally would sit in his house, have an amazing bottle of wine, put on every great horror film and we would smoke a giant joint and just really analyze all kinds of horror films for twelve hours at a time. To be invited into the king's castle like that was amazing, and those years in the business were great.

Burrell continued working in the Romero universe after Savini's Night of the Living Dead remake, as he was part of the effects team on Two Evil Eyes, a collaboration between George and fellow Master of Horror Dario Argento, that brought to life two tales of terror written by Edgar Allan Poe. Everett was brought in on Tom Savini's team, and he recalled the whole experience being one of the most fun projects he had been involved with at the time.

Tom [Savini] had been contracted to do the effects for both Dario and George's segments, so we had a lot of fun with them both. Dario was amazing; oh my God, he was super fun to be around. And George was in really good spirits, so that was a really fun film and we tried a lot of fun things on it too. It felt like the whole gang was working with us too—John [Vulich] was there, of course, and then there was also a bunch of the old timers from the Pittsburgh school of makeup effects, too. I have been a huge fan of Dario Argento's for such a long time, and we got to ask him every question in the world on that movie, and he answered every single one with his great Italian flair.

One day, he [Dario Argento] came to Tom's shop during our life casting session with Harvey Keitel, and he talked about *Suspiria* (1977) for quite some time, explaining certain plot points, his color choices and it was really fascinating. We were all playing around too, where we made a Dario Argento movie with my video camera, and he was so into it. We did this funny shot where I flew the camera into a barrel of a gun that was actually made out of cardboard tube, and he thought that was great. But Dario loved Tom, and he loved our work too.

When he signed on for another Romero helmed production, The Dark Half, Burrell found that film to be a much different experience than he'd had on previous projects due to some clashes between the director and star Timothy Hutton, who just did not gel creatively.

The Dark Half was much more of an intense experience because of Timothy. Timothy had to be both parts, but trying to come up with a subtle makeup, like a subtle Dick Smith makeup, to differentiate the two was really hard. It was hard on George especially, because I don't think Timothy really got it. It was really frustrating for George and he kept trying to tell Timothy to tone it down, to back off and play it more real, and he just kept going bigger and bigger, and it just became a war. Things blew up on several occasions on set. I just don't think they were ever on the same page.

John [Vulich] had to try and figure out how to cover Timothy's face for the alternate character, and we went through multiple tests. Timothy had all these ideas and all George wanted to do was to try and really differentiate those two characters with prosthetics. But the heavier we went with the makeup to hide Timothy, the more he hated it. Tim just kept making us back off and back off and back off, until it was such a subtle makeup that was really hard to blend.

It was just really hard on John, too. He did it like forty times, and he just got so fed up with Tim that I had to take over.

Although The Dark Half wasn't necessarily an enjoyable production, Everett explained that the work he did on the film lead to his involvement on Tim Burton's highly anticipated superhero sequel, Batman Returns.

Mike Fink was the VFX advisor on *Batman Returns*, and he was the one who brought us on. He found out about the birds we made for *The Dark Half* and asked us if we could make bats. So, we made the bats that attack the Penguin and the Christmas Queen, and Tim Burton loved them. That film had the coolest sets I had ever seen, and both Michael Keaton and Danny DeVito were great. Danny even knew George [Romero], too.

In the early to mid-nineties, the world of cinema saw the rise of visual effects in modern filmmaking, which of course had an immense impact on the practical effects industry. And while makeup was his first love, Burrell saw the impending changes as an opportunity more so than something that would hinder his ability to continue working in Hollywood.

John [Vulich] and I had been doing this type of stuff since 1989. We both had Amiga computers and we were doing very rough design work using a program called Deluxe Paint. This was way before Photoshop. We liked to scan photos of actors and do designs on top of those pictures. That's what we did for *Night of the Living Dead* and *The Dark Half*, and it was a really great creative tool. John and I used that as our trademark device as we moved into designing, and once we saw *Jurassic Park*, we knew all bets were off. But I was very excited about moving into the digital realm.

While we were doing *Babylon 5*, I was very heavily into Video Toaster and Lightwave, and I became more fascinated with that side of designing creatures. Then, I had an opportunity to join the team at Universal for *Hercules* and *Xena: Warrior Princess*, and I wanted John to join me. I had wanted our company, Optic Nerve, to be both CG and makeup effects, but John got very offended and we had a break up in 1995 where it all just ended badly. Ultimately it all worked out, as we became friends again five years later, but for a while, it was like a bitter divorce. We were truly creative brothers, though, and we loved each other to the very end.

Looking back, I feel we definitely thought differently than most of our competitors, and to this day I'll stand by our work. But I knew this transition to digital effects was an important one to make, especially back then. I just knew it was the perfect time to do it because nobody knew what the possibilities were, including myself.

Burrell knew that these new frontiers he was traversing would come with a lot of trial and error, but he relished the endless possibilities that this new form of creature design provided him as an artist. He kept busy on a variety of television and film projects over the next few years, including **Castle Freak, Mighty Morphin Power Rangers: The Movie, Dracula: Dead and Loving It,** *and* **Mortal Kombat: Annihilation.** *One of his biggest challenges from that era in his career came by way of Stephen Norrington's* **Blade,** *where he was tasked with digitally destroying hundreds of vampires and bringing the film's ambitious Blood God finale to life.*

Blade happened because of Steve Johnson. A good mutual friend of ours introduced us and we hit it off immediately. Steve's an absolute genius; he's a little crazy but we've always had a good time working together.

With *Blade*, they were in a real trouble situation. They didn't have a visual effects company that could solve the problems they were having. And if we couldn't crack these issues, there wouldn't have been a movie. So, I helped solve a lot of the issues they were having both technologically and creatively. We did a lot of the vampire disintegrations and we did a lot of weird other shit too.

The biggest issue came with the big [Deacon] Frost puppet in the finale that was a whole other challenge in itself. There's some of it on the deleted scenes on the DVD, but so many companies came in and failed, so *Blade* was a real struggle for a lot of people. But Steve kicked ass, and I was glad we could come through because that film is really great and is exceptionally directed.

While he may not have had the chance to collaborate with the director of **Blade II** *on that sequel in particular, Everett was able to come on board a different film that Guillermo del Toro was producing in the late 2000's,*

J.A. Bayona's The Orphanage, which led to him working on several other projects for the modern genre master.

Getting to work with Guillermo was incredible. I came in late on _The Orphanage_, because another company had been on that show, so we had to come in and help out because there were some big problems. I was working at a company called Cafe FX at the time, and we worked on a few of the big scenes like the girl who would light her hand on fire or the demons. I had done some work on _Hellboy_ but _The Orphanage_ was the first time where I actually met Guillermo, and we had so much fun together that I got to do _Pan's Labyrinth_.

Regardless of what he's doing, Guillermo is always the same guy he always has been. He's the hardest working guy in show business, and he's in the trenches whether we're at the Four Seasons eating filet mignon on the balcony or we're laying in a shithole ditch in Spain getting covered in mud. He gets the power of filmmaking, and to me, out of all the directors I've ever worked with, Guillermo is the most respectful to the old traditions of drawing and painting and great artist illustrators who really inspired us like Ray Harryhausen and Dick Smith.

There was a lot of creative energy on the set of _Pan's Labyrinth_, and even though we had a lot of fun, it was still quite a challenge, especially because it was Edward [Irastorza] and I, two Americans who barely spoke Spanish, out in the middle of the woods for most of the time.

As visual effects continued to get more ambitious, technology advanced and opened up even more digital possibilities and Burrell found himself embracing new techniques and environments, particularly the use of green screen stage work on a variety of projects like Sky Captain and the World of Tomorrow, the Spy Kids series and Robert Rodriguez's big screen adaptation of Frank Miller's Sin City.

I remember our very first conversation with Robert was him telling us to rent every film noir movie we could find and spend the next two weeks just watching all of these films. He wanted us immersed in the look of those films, and it really helped us understand how the key light and fill light ratios affected the atmosphere in various shots. When we started doing all these tests, Robert was really impressed.

We worked on the "The Big Fat Kill" episode, and we asked if we could see how the other episodes were progressing, but Robert told us no. For him, every episode was unique so he wanted our work to be strictly our vision, and not be influenced by anyone else's work. I still think it's incredibly cool how all those episodes blended together in the end. Everything about *Sin City* was so experimental and creatively, it ended up being one of the most satisfying experiences of my career.

After that, we got to do all the *Spy Kids* films, and I became very bored of the technique very quickly. Shooting on green screen is definitely both a blessing and a curse.

These days, Everett finds new and exciting ways to challenge himself with his digital art, whether it's working in tandem with practical effects teams or creating new cinematic landscapes and worlds.

One of my favorite things is to be able to add to something that already exists. If there's an amazing set that I can add onto, that to me is a great challenge to have, especially if I can make that aesthetic unnoticeable and just extend everything to meet a production designer's wishes. I love making worlds feel bigger.

When I came onto *Prometheus*, those sets were amazing as-is. They were huge and epic and cool, but they still weren't big enough, so it was our job to extend them. WETA brought me in to be a guest supervisor, so I wasn't responsible for the whole film, but I was certainly there for a lot of it and I had a great time having all these conversations about different ideas with Ridley [Scott].

I thought it was interesting that on *Prometheus*, sometimes he would just go off and spend two or three days just doing creative stuff that probably didn't make any sense to anyone else, but it certainly made sense to Ridley. He was all about very unorthodox filmmaking, but because he's Ridley Scott, he can do whatever he fucking wants.

There were two big things I remembered about *Prometheus*. The first was that back when I was in high school, 20th Century Fox donated the MU-TH-UR computer room from the first *Alien* film to a nearby high school science center. So, I went and unpacked all the crates and set everything up when I was only like 15-years-old. I took a photo after I was done, and I brought that photo onto set to show Ridley and it blew his mind.

The other thing I remember involved Charlie [de Lauzirika] who does a lot of Ridley's behind the scenes things, and we had all been told that we couldn't take any photos in front of the space jockey in *Prometheus*. I did have permission to take reference photos for visual FX, so when I got in there, Charlie was in there doing some interviews with Ridley. When Ridley left, we started taking turns taking photos of ourselves pretending to do work in front of the space jockey just so we could get photos of us in front of the space jockey. It was hilarious, even though we weren't sure if we were going to get in trouble or not. I don't think we cared really, because we were too busy geeking out on that set.

Even though his artistry primarily revolves around digital effects at this stage in his career, Burrell is still driven by his boundless imagination and has found that the same things that drew him into the practical effects industry still inspire him to this very day.

I think the same fascination I had with clay and Ultra Cal and making molds is similar to whenever I'm trying to figure out which computer chip I should buy, what software I should get. For me, I've always had this inquisitive nature of how to bring these creatures, monsters and worlds to life—whether through clay and plaster or through CG bits and bobs.

I never thought I would have gotten this far. Never in a million years. I have made so many amazing friends, and I learned so much. The gifts that I've been given from guys like Dick Smith, Rick Baker, John Vulich, or Mitch Devane and all these other really talented artists that I have worked with have made a huge impact on me, and on my career. I either need to start writing down everything that I've learned over the years, or I need to start teaching my kids or my dog.

The business can be hard, though. I think the politics of filmmaking are always really difficult, and people just have to understand that sometimes you win and sometimes you lose and there's just nothing you can do about it. You can't let the bullshit get you down. This industry has always been tough, but we were all so lucky just to be in the game at the height of all these amazing moments in special effects. I look back at my career now, with all my masks and monsters sitting around me in my office, and I can see just how lucky and fortunate I was for all those years. I got to work with and make so many great friends, and I also got to be a part of the golden age – the 1980's and 1990's – of monsters, too, and that is something I will always be grateful for.

Creepshow 2

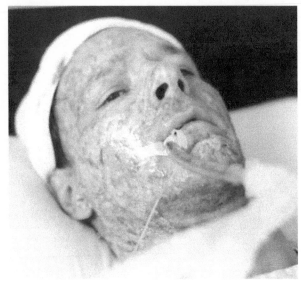

The Hidden

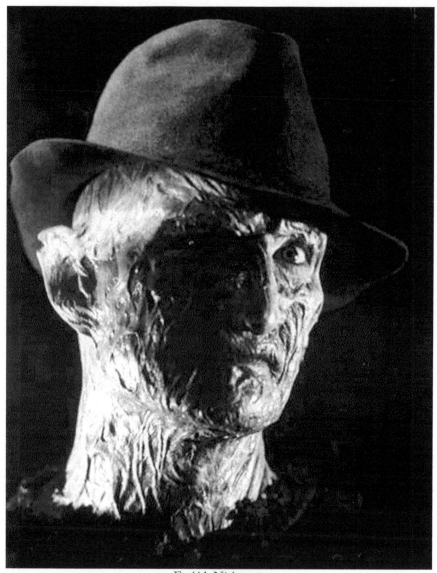

Freddy's Nightmares

Hot Shots! Part Deux - Charlie Sheen and Everett Burrell

Hot Shots! Part Deux - Saddam Hussein Figure

Unreleased *The Fantastic 4* - Dr Doom

Unreleased *The Fantastic 4* - The Thing

Babylon 5 - G'Kar

Conversation with…
PAUL JONES

Special Effects Makeup Artist

Hellbound: Hellraiser II (1988)
Nightbreed (1990)
Blade (1998)
Ginger Snaps (2000)
Silent Hill (2006)
Resident Evil: Afterlife (2010)

Artist Paul Jones has been an integral figure in the filmmaking community of Toronto for over 25 years now, contributing to an array of genre classics like Hellraiser, Wishmaster, Nightbreed and Hardware, and recent horror hits, including Ginger Snaps, Blade, Bride of Chucky, Silent Hill, and the Resident Evil series. Paul's journey to the world of special effects first began during the 1980s when he was just growing up in a small town in Northern England, never realizing he'd become a part of this industry.

My background in effects comes from being a young kid making masks in my bedroom and then doing horror makeup for my friends at fourteen and fifteen. The film industry never seemed like something I'd be part of, because it seemed so far away. Because I lived in Northern England, it was a very working class and a non-Hollywood lifestyle. But I had a hobby that I was dedicated to, and I was constantly building stuff.

I was in art school at the time, doing foundation courses for a year and a half, mainly because I didn't know what else to do, and a friend of a friend said, "Hey, there's this guy who works at Shepperton Studios, you should send him photographs, he might give you a job. He does the same thing that you do." His name was Bob Keen. So I sent Bob a bunch of pictures, and he hired me a week later.

I went down to London, and the first job I did for him was a wallpaper commercial, where we built a bunch of animatronic ducks. I was the shop person, so I did a bit of molding, a bit of painting, but nothing really that important. But at the end of the job, it was a huge conflict for me because I had never been away from home, I had never had a job before and I had never thought about moving to London, so it was a bit of a culture shock all happening at the same time. After two weeks I said to Bob, "I don't think it's for me, I think it's a bit too much excitement." He said, "Well go home, sort yourself out, and if you ever want to come back, there will be a job waiting for you."

I went back home that weekend and as I got off the train, it felt like my big town was now one house in a field. It felt so small. I realized that London was where I actually wanted to be now. So, I sorted some stuff out and moved to London, and I started working for Bob in 1987.

Ultimately, Paul spent the next seven years working with Bob Keen, on a variety of horror films that helped shape his burgeoning talent for

special effects and continued his passion for film in general.

I started off working on *Waxwork, The Lair of the White Worm* and *The Unholy* with Bob, and then we switched gears to *Hellraiser II*, and that moved us to Pinewood Studios. When we were working on *Waxwork*, there was very specific input from Tony (Hickox), but he was also very hands off. It was mostly a case of, "Hey, you guys like monsters, make me some cool shit." Bob, being from the background he had, that was kind of the modus operandi: "Let's make Frankenstein. Let's make monster brides. Let's make all of the stuff we grew up with in the '70s." That was *Waxwork*."

And with *White Worm*, it felt like the same movie to me in terms of the work we were doing, because the process was very similar. I'm a pragmatic makeup guy—I'm always thinking about how it's going to work, not how it's going to work in a scene. As I've matured, I've thought about what the character motivation is, and that would drive the design aspect. But when I started, it was a case of, does this have to go on an actor? Okay, let's make it so it's safe. Does it have to catch fire? Let's make it flame-retardant. Does it have to be translucent? Is it going to be foam? Is it going to be silicone? I try to take a practical point of view. So the art side of it, I used to leave that to the directors. So *The Unholy, Lair of the White Worm*, and *Waxwork*, they were all just projects I worked on, and that was it.

Having said that, there was definitely a different atmosphere on Tony's set as opposed to *Lair of the White Worm*. Ken Russell's directing style was completely different from Tony's. It's the same product, where they're both essentially doing a campy Gothic horror, but from two very different points of view. With Ken Russell, I was second from the bottom on the credits, so I didn't have any direct interaction with him on the movie except for one day when I was on set and I was just given a gag of a hand being cut off and it was supposed to be Amanda Donahoe's arm. I was sent to set, and I was to pump the blood and I had to talk directly to Ken and to the AD.

From one point of view, it was great for Bob to give me that opportunity, but now I'd be terrified. I had seen *Altered States* and I had seen *The Devils*, and I had watched all of Ken's work. Being from a small town, you look at the guy in front of you and they don't connect. You go home at night and watch a movie, and you go to work the next day and you don't associate the two. One is real, and the other is fantasy. I grew up loving movies, that's what I enjoy doing, but I still have trouble associating the two. You have to have a suspension of disbelief when you work in the film industry, so when I work on a project, I can't watch it as a movie. I find watching my own work really hard, and I only enjoy watching movies that I didn't work on.

When it came time to start work on Hellbound: Hellraiser II, Jones never really felt the pressure of having to follow in the successful footsteps of Clive Barker's original shocker, simply because it was a film he hadn't seen prior to his involvement with the sequel.

To be perfectly honest, when I interviewed with Bob, I hadn't even heard of *Hellraiser*, so there wasn't any pressure in that sense heading into *Hellbound.* I think that's why my first interview went so well, because I wasn't intimidated by the amazing work they had created for that first film. But for the second film, we started building and Tony (Randel) had said, "I want to go in a different direction and I want to have this play out on a much bigger scale." The first movie was more intimate, set in basically one house, and the sequel takes you into a different realm of existence.

So basically, it was like, "Just tell us what to do." I didn't have any input in how anything was going to be done on this one, but it was fun to see similar effects being done from a different point of view. Pinhead was Clive's invention and Clive (Barker) was the designer, but the use Tony had for him was a totally different thing entirely.

And in those days, there wasn't an option to fix things digitally in post, so we were looking at doing everything in-camera, which, considering the level of work we were doing on *Hellraiser II,* was a challenge. I think there might have been a few optical effects added in, like lightning bursts, but there was certainly no digital blood or edge removal to help us out. That kind of frees you up to be more enthusiastic, they had to give us the time to get it right. If we were doing *Hellraiser* now, it would be different. You want to do the best job you can and if you're not allowed to do it because of time, you start to get demoralized.

That's the one thing that bums me out about effects these days. I look back fondly at all the things I did—all my work in the eighties and nineties, which was considered the heyday of film effects—because they gave you the time to do it until you got it right. Nothing's really changed about the industry, though.

"The effects we were doing back during that time are essentially the same effects we're doing now, only with much more photorealistic materials. It's the same blood tubing, the same cables, the same animatronics, but we're not given the time to get it right anymore. It's still practical, it's not a magic trick. Just because you get a convincing skin on a puppet, it's still a puppet. You have to take the time to cajole things into working the way that you want them to.

After wrapping Hellbound: Hellraiser II, Jones found himself once again working in the realm of Clive Barker's wildly evocative genius for Nightbreed. Because of the film's ambitious number of creatures (and effects in general) there was a lot that Keen's team were tasked with throughout production. But it was one fateful afternoon where Paul decided to start tinkering around that opened up his effects career in an entirely new way.

I think what really helped us out was that Clive was very careful in his casting. He knew what he wanted for a role before the character was even designed. Usually—especially with monster movies these days—the creature is designed, they come up with a "look," and they find an actor to fit the look, rather than the other way around. Clive knew that Doug Bradley, Nick Vince, all those guys were going to be in it, and because he knew their strengths and weaknesses, Clive knew what would work on them and what wouldn't. The makeup was designed to fit the actors, and not the other way around.

Lylesberg was one of the characters Mark Coulier created that I was able to apply the makeup for a couple of times, but my main job on the movie was creating the Berserkers. I was given those from the get-go, because I figured out how to do the animatronics. A lot of the other guys couldn't do the animatronics, and believe it or not, animatronics was something I never had an interest in either. I loved sculpting, I loved painting, I loved doing makeup, I loved bladder effects, I liked doing hair work—I really like punching and hand-laying hair—but animatronics never appealed to me until I started working at Bob's.

All of a sudden, I was working around guys who had worked at (Jim) Henson's, who had worked on *Labyrinth* and *The Dark Crystal* and things like that. One weekend, we had finished our work on *Nightbreed* for the day and we had started a couple of other things. I said to Bob that I wanted to play around with animatronics at home, and asked to borrow some cable, glue and acrylics. He told me to help myself. I went home on the train to my parents' house that weekend and built an animatronic face. It had eyebrow movement, it had lips and a jaw—the whole thing was about five inches from chin to forehead, it wasn't very big at all. But I came in on Monday, and Bob was like, "Wow, this is great. Who helped you with this?" I told him nobody helped me, that I just made it at home over the weekend.

Because of that, I got the Berserkers job the next week. To me, once you understand the principles, it's really just a matter of learning how to cut and bend metal, and learning about radio controls. The first thing I learned about Servos is that different Servos have different strengths. You can't just buy a Servo to make something move, you have to buy a certain kind of Servo to make a certain kind of movement. You can't make a head move on a little plastic-geared tiny hobby Servo, because it'll break. But at the same time, you don't want to put a wheelchair Servo inside an eye blink. It's just the practical application of the techniques. In my eyes, there wasn't some great mystery to doing animatronic work anymore.

Paul continued working with Bob Keen for several more years, but an influx of work in other parts of the world began to take him outside of the U.K., which ended up having far more of an impact on what was to come in his career than he realized at the time.

We ended up getting a couple of small movies that were being shot in Toronto. At this point I was supervising at Bob's. I had worked my way up to that level because I was fairly proficient in everything, so any job that came in, he was able to put me to work on it and not have to worry about bringing in a specialist. That's why I was able to stay at Bob's for the longest amount of time among so many other people.

I remember Richard Stanley's *Hardware* came in, and my involvement in that film was pretty small, to be honest. There were a couple of exceptionally talented guys working on that from the start, Paul Catling and Chris Cunningham. I consider them two of the most talented guys I've ever met, never mind worked with. They could do everything. These are guys who can sculpt, who can apply makeup, who can do animatronics—if you got these two together on a movie now, it would be the most perfect duo of effects people.

Then, when it came time for us to do *Hellraiser III: Hell on Earth*, we shot in North Carolina. It was basically a bunch of English guys straight off the boat, working in North Carolina with a bunch of stuff that we had started building in England. It wasn't finished, so they set us up in a mobile home, kind of a *Breaking Bad* situation, parked on the lot and we converted it into a crazy workshop where a lot of the work was finished. Pinhead's costume was finished in North Carolina. Two of the characters that weren't originally intended to be

Cenobites were turned into Cenobites in North Carolina, too.

For instance, Camerahead, Barbie, and CD Head—those were just victims, those characters were never intended to reappear as Cenobites. We had just built masks for CD Head and Barbie; they were just going to be pullover masks we were going to cover them in blood. Camerahead was just going to be the camera guy found dead in his apartment. We just finished building the make ups and we were packing everything to leave, and Tony (Hickox) says, "Hey, we're doing a re-write and we're thinking that there aren't enough Cenobites in this *Hellraiser* movie. So we're going to make these three guys Cenobites, see you in a couple of days and we'll talk about it." And we were like, "WHAT?" So, when we got off the plane and brought everything into the makeup room, we knew we had to immediately figure out just what we were going to do.

That's when Tony told us that these characters were going to turn up and walk down the streets of Raleigh, North Carolina, and this and that. We thought we could make the heads work, but we didn't have costumes. So we turned to Bob, who decided to change the way we built costumes. Pinhead was originally an elaborate, all-leather costume. Bob decided—really, to save money—that he was going to sculpt Pinhead's costume. We took a body cast of Doug (Bradley), and sculpted his costume in clay to look like it was made of leather, then we ran it in foam latex and painted it black. It was a much cheaper way of doing it, and that's how his costume was done. If you look carefully at *Hellraiser III*, his costume looks a bit different because it's foam latex and not leather like it had been before.

But Bob realized that with this mold, we could run more skins out of it and take them to North Carolina with us, so we could chop them up and essentially hybrid the pieces into these three brand-new costumes. Not only were they foam latex costumes chopped up, but we went to Wal-Mart and bought thermal underwear, black paint, dog harnesses and a whole bunch of other stuff, and then brought it all back to the shop, and created these brand new costumes with all this other stuff. That's why those costumes look so similar, even though they have different elements to them.

After his time on Hellraiser III, Jones returned to England while his boss headed back to the States.

Truthfully, Bob and I needed a break from one another at that point, so I came home, and he went to Los Angeles to drum up some more work. The guy that was in charge of his workshop at the time, Gary Tunnicliffe, he had a couple of projects, and asked me to do animatronics and makeup on them in the meantime. But when Bob got *Warlock 2 (Warlock: The Armageddon)*, he pulled me right back into the shop for that and within a week, he and I were like best mates again. That was the first job back, and that was the last job that me and Bob worked together on the set.

Warlock 2 was great because he had set up a small garage workshop in Pasadena and they shot all over L.A., so he'd go all over the place while I worked in the shop, and he would come back and work in the shop while I'd go to the set. Then we did a smaller movie called *Little Devils: The Birth*, which was terrible, but it was a great experience for me while I was working in Toronto. Then I did a little TV movie with Meatloaf called *To Catch a Yeti*, and Toronto became a place to be.

I came back to Toronto for a TV series that was the worst of all, called *The Mighty Jungle*. It was a sitcom with talking puppets, but it was on that show that I met my now ex-wife. We got married and I said, "Do you want to move to England?" and she said, "Not really." So I moved to Toronto, and that's what brought me here.

As he began to set up his new life in Canada, Jones didn't anticipate that he'd be also setting up his very first shop in Toronto as well, Paul Jones Effects Studio, Inc., which has been going strong for over two decades.

All these skills that I had gained by working for Bob for all those years had given me the grounding to be able to start my own company, but when I first moved to Toronto, I never intended on running my own company. And honestly, I still would prefer not to, and I say this as someone who has been doing it successfully for over twenty years now.

When I first came to town, there were two guys I met who were working here. One was Gordon Smith, and the other guy was a guy named François Dagenais. François was originally from Montreal and he had worked in L.A. for a bunch of guys under the table. He worked for John Beuchler and Tony Gardner, and he moved back to Toronto and worked on a few TV series, but he was essentially one guy in a garage. Gordon Smith, on the other hand, had a different setup.

He was an artist, he didn't really hang around with other "effects guys," as he considered himself kind of above all that. I interviewed with him, and even with all of my experience and all of my credits, he wasn't interested in hiring me. I think it was shortsighted in the long run, because within two years

I was taking shows off him. Every job that was offered to me was also offered to Gordon Smith. We'd go in and bid on the same project, and I would say six or seven times out of ten, I was awarded the project because, essentially, he was too expensive. Cut to twenty-three years later, and Gordon's retired now because no one would hire him.

It wasn't because he wasn't good, it was because he wasn't willing to compromise. He was very much set in his ways. Toronto doesn't have the luxuries that Los Angeles does. We're not a hub of filmmaking, we're a service town. So what that means is, you bring your project here, you make it, and you leave. Everything here is about the bottom line. Toronto has talent, great facilities, and great infrastructure for filmmaking, but it doesn't have the history that Hollywood has for filming projects. At the end of the day, producers come here because it's cheaper, and that's the bottom line, so you have to be able to haggle. And I could.

Things were definitely starting to change in the industry at that time, but I didn't really see it as a problem. I think you'll find that whenever any new technology comes out, initially people are going to have a knee-jerk reaction to that. They're going to only see the negative because they're only looking at it from one point of view. I look at technology as a tool, I don't see it as a replacement. Filmmakers and directors are generational and the filmmakers from ten years ago are not the same filmmakers now.

The young guys directing now grew up with monsters, and feel like they're missing the boat. They'll come to set and say, "Hey, we want to build a creature," and I'll say, "That seems like something you'd do digitally." But most of the time, they really do want something practical and just want to add something digital to it. What happens there is that you end up doing the same job for the same money, with half the pressure. It's about communication. The bottom line is that I'm making a very good living building stuff, but I don't have the arrogance to think that if you don't film it, that I should get angry about it.

Paul continued to pave his path of independence in the realm of special effects throughout the 1990s, all while lending his talents to fellow artist Gary Tunnicliffe's shop on several memorable horror movies from that era, including Robert Kurtzman's Wishmaster and Blade from another effects artist-turned-director, Stephen Norrington.

My involvement in *Wishmaster* was at an arm's length, really. The movie was awarded to KNB EFX Group and to my old buddy Gary, who had a shop in Los Angeles at the time. He basically brought in all of his friends to help him out. I built some animatronics for him and built some puppet rigs, and he had some other people come in to do some other stuff. We all flew into L.A. and handed it over to him. I asked him if he was feeling the pressure, because he was doing effects for a director who really understood special effects, and he said, "Yes and no. I'm feeling the pressure because I'm the new guy in town, but Bob basically said to do something cool, and he just completely gave me the trust to do it, so I feel like that means I can have some fun." And I think the work we did was really good.

But *Blade* was one of those happy accident movies. Originally, the entire movie was given to Greg Cannom. Greg and Steve (Norrington) had known each other for years. When Steve got the project, it was going to be shot in Los Angeles, and he couldn't afford Stan Winston, and he probably couldn't afford Rick Baker either. So, he went with his old friend Greg. They shot the entire movie with Greg's work, and there were a couple of extra gags that they needed to shoot that Greg wasn't able to provide. At the time Steve called Gary, I was in between projects in Toronto and was working in L.A., and we ended up making a lightweight dummy of N'Bushe (Wright) so Wesley Snipes is able to carry her up the stairs like it's nothing. We did a fully articulate dummy that he could pick up and it would just look like her unconscious in his arms.

When we finished that, Steve was happy with our work, and he finished the movie up with Greg. But when *Blade* needed a whole new ending, he called up Greg, but he was busy with another project. So, Steve called up Gary Tunnicliffe, and he came back on board. That's when he did the whole exploding (Deacon) Frost body at the end, with the EDTA darts. That was all added months after the movie was finished. It ended up being one of those fun little movies that I love because I didn't have that much to do with it. I went on set for one day, but I wasn't there every single day, so I can still enjoy it as a movie and separate myself.

It was right around this time when Jones would find himself working on a film that would help relaunch one of the greatest franchises in horror history—Bride of Chucky—and reintroduced a horror icon to a new generation of fans at the same time.

This one was very exciting because it was one of those projects that I knew all about before going into it. I knew about the puppets, I knew about the first three movies, and it was all just very iconic. So, what could little old me add to this series?

David Kirschner, who is a producer of the Chucky movies, called me up and said, "Hey, we're doing this movie, *Bride of Chucky*. Do you know the *Child's Play* movies?" And of course I did. He talked to me about how they wanted to change things up this time, because usually these movies revolve around the puppet and a lot of blood. For *Bride*, they actually wanted to show the victims more and to do more visceral, more operatic deaths than they had ever done in the past. This time, they wanted to make all of it feel more theatrical, and David asked me to design some of the deaths.

One of those deaths was John Ritter. Obviously, I knew who John Ritter was, because he was an icon in his own right. So I started off by creating a little maquette of John, just pushing nails into it and it reminded me of something else. I said to Ronny (Yu), the director, "You guys know there's a comparison to this and *Hellraiser*, right? Because the guy has pins in his head like nails, and obviously ours is more abstract in the positioning and stuff, but you do know I worked on *Hellraiser*, right?" They hadn't even thought of that. So when Chucky says, "That reminds me of something," when he's looking at John after he kills him, that's a direct reference to Pinhead they decided to put in there.

But working on John (Ritter) was a dream. I spent one of my best two hour makeups in a trailer with him, and he was just the sweetest, most gracious guy in the world. We did that makeup twice on him; the first time was just me, John, and an assistant gluing on the makeup, where he was just telling us stories about Hollywood. The next time we did it, he had a set visit from an old friend of his, Peter Bogdanovich. John and Peter just sat next to each other in the trailer for two hours, just talking about all kinds of Hollywood stuff. It was fabulous. Those moments are the payoff for the other times when it's not quite so fun.

As a new century was approaching, Paul would find himself challenged greatly while working on coming-of-age werewolf movie, Ginger Snaps (2000), as director John Fawcett's unconventional idea for the lycanthrope designs was extremely difficult for him—and anyone, really—to achieve.

Ginger Snaps is something that has this whole history with me in itself. When I was first approached to do the movie, I knew John Fawcett socially. We had mutual friends, but we had never worked together. When he got his producing team together and they were coming up with a budget, he started to shop around to all the effects guys. John had a very specific image in mind— he wanted an albino hairless werewolf. I will say this much about that decision: I challenge any effects company to pull something off that's convincing, where you have these two things—hair and being dark in their coloring is what werewolves are historically known for, not being the two major contributing design factors to the design. It was like a curse.

Whenever a director thinks they should make their creature albino, I really try to get them to reconsider. To me, creatures only work when they're dark, because you should be shooting them in the shadows. And if it's a white creature, it's really hard to shoot in the shadows. I understand aesthetically why you might want to have a white creature, but from a practical point of view, it's not going to work the way you might think it would, especially in a horror movie. And basically, John was having none of it.

He asked every guy in town to do a maquette for him, offered to pay for a model of what we thought it would look like, and offered the job to the company that made the best maquette. I refused to meet for it, because John was so specific in what he wanted, which means you're going to have four identical models. That money could go on screen instead of in a bunch of little things you'll put on a shelf. Why not just interview with people and see what works? So they ended up interviewing everybody, and they awarded it to me purely on that fact, because they thought I could give them what they wanted without compromising John's design. And the very first thing I did was try and compromise John's design.

John's background is not in monsters, it's in art films. When it comes to the creature, you can't make it white and you can't make it hairless. So right up until the day we were filming it, we were still arguing about the creature. I said to him that this guy can't be a guy in a suit, this has to be a puppet. It's just not practical, and a puppet would give him way more leeway, especially the way John wanted to shoot it. But he wanted a suit. I tried to get him to understand we shouldn't make the creature completely white, it needed to have more colors and veins and you have to try and make it look sickly. He said, "No I want it white, I want it to look albino."

I tried to get him to realize we needed to have some hair on it, and he was like, "I don't want to have any hair on it, I want it completely hairless." I tried to explain to him that nobody would be ready for that, and that the audience is going to be so shocked that it's not even going to read as a werewolf. Wolves are hairy, and this is going to look like some kind of weird facsimile of a creature, instead of a werewolf.

In the end, the only reason there was any hair on the creature was because I needed to hide zippers on its legs and belly; the rest was a one-piece suit. But he just fought me on everything. The movie came out and some people loved the wolf, and some people absolutely hated it. I thought I did the best I could, but the same criticism came along: it just looked like a guy in a suit. Well, that's because it was. So I just let it go. Then, I read an interview with John a couple of months after the movie came out and somebody asked him, "So you did an original design on the werewolf, and a lot of people have not liked that design. Can you explain your thought process on that?" And he basically threw me under the bus, saying that we felt what Paul gave us wasn't what we wanted, so we had to shoot around it because it didn't look that good on camera. I was not happy. So that was what happened with *Ginger Snaps*.

What's interesting is that I have gotten hired over the years because of *Ginger Snaps*, and I have also had to go into job interviews and defend that movie before I was hired for something. The movie itself was a very good piece of filmmaking, I thought it was an intelligent film, and I am proud of the work I did, but I am not proud of what it became after the fact. It seems like twenty years later, it's still a sore point for me. I think the majority of criticism it did get was because it was so different, not because it was essentially a bad piece of effects work, it was just stylistically such a departure that people didn't like it because of that.

Paul ended up having a much more positive experience when he collaborated with effects legend, and hero, Stan Winston on the backwoods horror movie Wrong Turn in the early 2000s.

That was a fun project because Stan was a producer and the deal was that Stan was going to do all of the effects. Executive producer Don Carmody called me up about *Wrong Turn* and I didn't think I could do the show. That's when he told me that he wasn't asking me to do the effects – because he had "a guy named Stan Winston doing them" and so they were looking for someone to come in and glue makeups on. And the experience was everything I wanted it to be.

They always say to never meet your heroes, and that was definitely the case with me and another one of my heroes, Rick Baker, who I had been waiting something like thirty years to meet, and it just went badly. So when I had this chance to work with Stan, I just kept hoping in the back of my head that he would at least just be nice because I really wanted it to work out. And as it turned out, Stan was the most gracious professional I've ever had the chance to work with. He really was just frigging awesome, and I loved the experience. I have a picture of Stan Winston and I gluing on a makeup, and it's one picture that I still look at today and think to myself, "That moment right there has been worth everything I've gone through in my entire career."

Shortly after working on **Wrong Turn,** *Jones was asked to meet with the team behind the first* **Resident Evil** *movie, as they were gearing up for a sequel, and needed a team to take on their ambitious effects which included the oversized villain,* **Nemesis.** *During the first meeting, Paul found himself once again going to bat over his work on* **Ginger Snaps,** *which he found to be a rather unexpected experience.*

When I went in to bid on *Apocalypse,* Jeremy Bolt sat me in a room with the other producers and said, "Okay, Paul, *Ginger Snaps.* Tell us about *Ginger Snaps,* because I hate the werewolf. I think it's terrible." I said, "Well, frankly, Jeremy, if you have an issue with the werewolf, you should speak to John Fawcett." Jeremy had just done a movie with John Fawcett, and he replied, "Really? Isn't it the effects guy's job to tell the director what's going to be best?" I was like, "Seriously? Have you ever tried to talk to John Fawcett? It's like trying to get water from a stone. So, hire me or don't hire me, but don't ever put me on the spot like that. You don't like it? That's fine, but don't make me defend something with no relevance to the project in front of us." And when he asked for a quote on the whole show, I initially said no.

To me, *Apocalypse* had two elements: makeup effects, and the Nemesis, which meant they needed two companies working on this. Anybody in Toronto at that time couldn't do this movie as a whole and give them what they needed. So, I agreed to do Nemesis and I was hired on the spot. Eight weeks later, we're on set, Nemesis is in the hallway, he bashes through a stone wall, lifts up a machine gun, and fires three hundred rounds down a hallway while this big roar is coming out of his mouth with steam. The director, Alexander Witt, shouts, "Cut! Print! Amazing, moving on," and then I hear Jeremy shout from the back of the stage, "*Ginger Snaps* is all forgotten, Paul. Well done!" So, that's how I stayed working with those guys, and it just proves that sometimes you have to stand your ground as an artist.

The next two *Resident Evil* movies I worked on, I did the zombies. At that point, I had a bigger crew, I was more established, and I was able to take on more work. But when they were getting ready to do the third movie, *Resident Evil: Extinction*, we found out that they were going to shoot it in the States, and they ended up using Patrick Tatopoulos, who I later worked with on *Silent Hill*. But when they came back for the fourth one (*Afterlife*), it was literally, "Hey Paul, we're doing another *Resident Evil*, you on board?" I didn't even hesitate because even though I had only worked with them once before, there was no hassle whatsoever.

Afterlife ended up being a much easier project too because I didn't have to prove myself, and that freed me up from a design point of view. We knew we needed to make the Axe Man come to life, and we really needed to work on these zombie dogs because the dogs had always been difficult to achieve. They did the first movie out of England with animated extras, and *Apocalypse* had some techniques that they used, but the producers still weren't happy with any of those. So they asked how I was going to do the dogs, and I told them, "I'm going to make zombie suits that the dogs are going to wear. We're going to zip them into a suit, and they will walk around with bits of meat hanging off of them." They had no idea how I was going to do that, but it was my job to figure it out.

So, they bring in the dog trainer and the first question I asked was, "Have these dogs ever worn suits before?" and he said, "Yeah, they wear winter suits all the time to keep them warm." He gave me one of those suits and I broke down the pattern, and recreated a little padded suit for a dog that was incredibly lightweight, breathable, and made of foam parts rather than silicone. We made a couple of suits and had the dogs wear them every day while they were being trained, so by the time the day of shooting came along, they had already been wearing their costumes for two weeks.

The only thing we added to them that day was a smearing of edible KY jelly and blood. it was just another day, but Jeremy and Paul (W.S. Anderson) were both dreading it. We get to set, the suits are on the dogs, they come in and do a rehearsal and Jeremy says to me, "These dogs don't know they're wearing suits." I said, "It's because they've been trained to wear them every day, so it's completely normal." He thought it was amazing, but it just seemed obvious to me to not add things to a dog in little pieces, just do the whole thing in one big suit and let the dog be trained accordingly. It worked out really well.

Jones had the opportunity to be a part of bringing more characters from the world of video gaming to life when he came aboard Christophe Gans' big screen adaptation of Silent Hill. When he met with the director, he

immediately connected with Gans and his admiration of the Silent Hill universe, and was thrilled to be asked to come aboard.

Silent Hill, ironically, was one of the only video games that I've actually played all the way through. I'm not a huge gamer, and I own all of the consoles, but I don't get the time to play video games. I just see a new video game come out, I play it for an afternoon, and then I don't touch it for six months until another game comes out. But *Silent Hill* came out right when I was in-between projects, and a friend from England was really into it. He was always twenty percent ahead of me, so I already knew the world, the atmosphere and what the game was all about.

When I first went into my interview, there were a lot of effects on the movie that they wanted done locally. I went in and met the director, and all we talked about was the game and how we got through certain levels. We never spoke about the script once, just the video game. I've never before or since had that kind of a conversation with anybody, so it was a perfect moment. I was hired, and it was an easy project for me, because Patrick (Tatopoulos) had done all of the heavy lifting already. He had designed the Red Pyramid's helmet, the prosthetics on Roberto (Campanella)'s body, the nurses' faces, the armless guy and the gray child.

But there were a few crossover things that hadn't been addressed. The first issue was the costumes for the nurses. They originally offered those to Wendy Partridge, who was the costume designer, who said, "I can do those, no problem." But after two weeks of R&D, she said, "I don't want to do these, this is too much." She had tried to create them as patchwork quilts, and right off the bat she had realized that that wouldn't work, because the costumes were so tight that the way she was doing it wouldn't have had the integrity to hold up to all that tension. So, two weeks before shooting, they gave it to me, and we had no choice but to do it as quickly and as simply as possible. It was very similar to how we did the Cenobite costumes for *Hellraiser III*, because latex is such a versatile material.

Around the same time, they told me that Red Pyramid needed a skirt, so again, we sculpted it to make it look like it was made of multiple pieces and it was really just one piece of latex and some Velcro. If you look at the movie, that skirt is just the same latex you'd make a mask from. I do remember that the stuff Patrick sent up for production may not have been the most practical way of doing things, but his painting and sculpting was just fantastic. The Red Pyramid was originally a prosthetic that took about four hours to do, which didn't seem very practical, but when it was all on, it was an outstanding piece of work.

Then, when *Silent Hill: Revelation* came along, I was told that Patrick would be involved from a design point of view, where he was going to send some drawings, but they wanted me to build everything for the movie. That meant I had to essentially redesign the nurses and Red Pyramid from a practical point of view, all without changing any of the aesthetics. The first time around, Red Pyramid was a prosthetic glued to Roberto, and I figured out that we could just make a skintight prosthetic bodysuit instead, because the neck went up into the helmet and the cuffs could blend into the wrists. It doesn't need to be glued on, we just needed to make it like we would a costume.

So, we took Patrick's sculpture and converted it from individual pieces to one big upper-body suit. The first time we applied it to Roberto and got him to set, it only took forty minutes. Artistically, he looks the same; we just changed how it was applied because I had the experience of doing it one way the first time to be able to re-jig the process the second time around. It's just nice to be able to do sequels sometimes, because you can consider the first movie as R&D, since you're often just scrambling to get these things on camera. The second time around, you've already done the molding and the sculpting, so now you can just play with the materials and that's what I really enjoyed about the work on *Silent Hill 2*—getting to play around a bit.

With well over 100 film and television credits on his resume, and showing no signs of slowing down anytime soon, Paul Jones attributes his longevity in the special effects industry to a variety of factors.

The first one is enthusiasm. Even though I've been doing this work for over thirty years, I still have a child-like enthusiasm for my job. I make monsters for a living. How could I possibly ever get jaded? I've been doing it longer than most people have had entire careers, but I still get the same thrill of opening molds for the first time or doing sculpture for the first time. I think producers and directors pick up on the fact that I have an enthusiasm that is infectious. And directors want somebody around them that seems to give a shit as much as they do.

They don't want somebody who's just going to come in for the paycheck, and I never treat any of this like a job. I treat it like a hobby that I get paid for, and I think that comes across in my job interviews all the time. I've been lucky to have been offered projects that have become iconic. I did

Pinhead for *Hellraiser III*, I did *Ginger Snaps*, I did *Silent Hill*, I did *Resident Evil*. In the horror world, these are projects that are held in high regard. So when a director or a producer wants to hire you, your work speaks for you.

And if it wasn't for prosthetic effects, I undoubtedly would have ended up in a much less fulfilling career. I just can't imagine doing anything else. Now I'm a dad, and moving into that world puts things into perspective. Being a father is definitely way more special to me than making monsters, but monsters are a very close second.

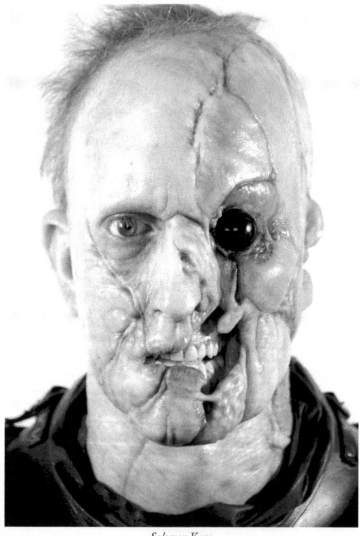

Solomon Kane

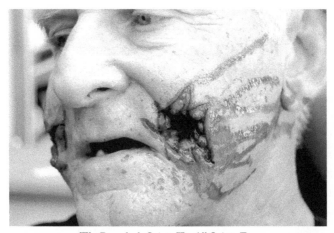

The Boondock Saints II: All Saints Day

Resident Evil: Afterlife - Nemesis

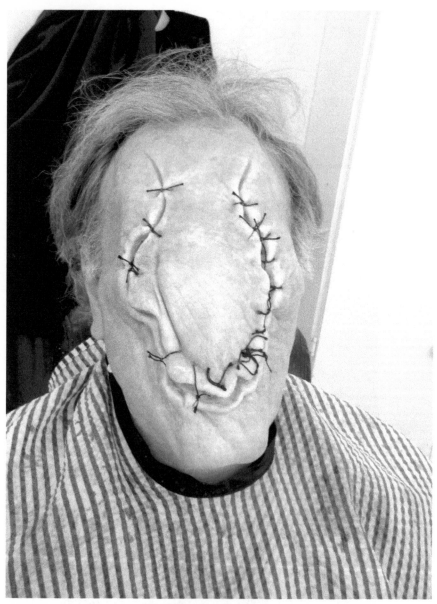

Silent Hill: Revelation

Documentary Now! - Bill Hader old age makeup

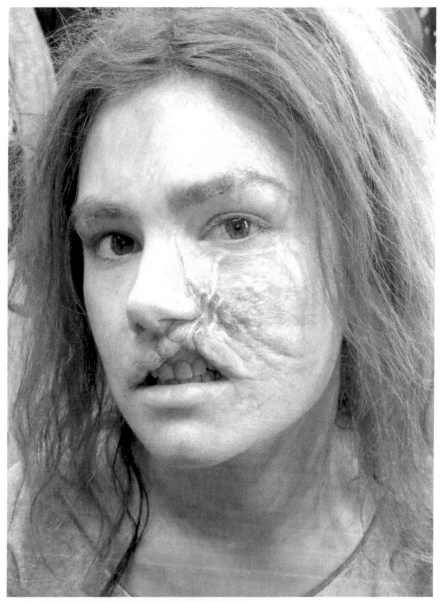

Reign TV Series

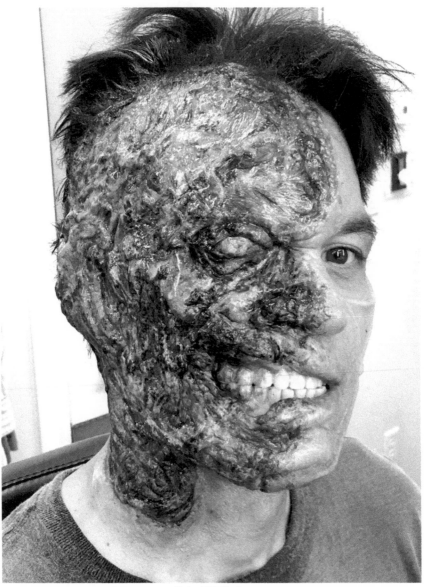

Reign TV Series

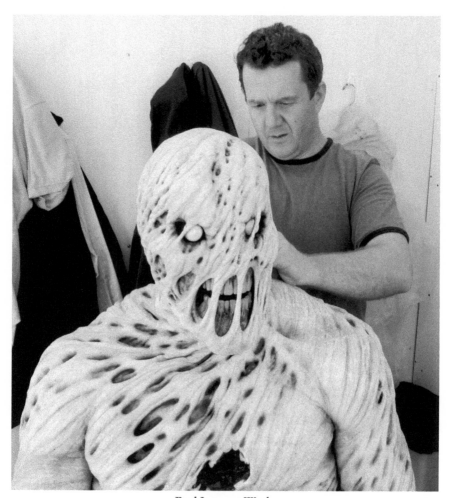

Paul Jones at Work

Conversation with…
GABE BARTALOS

Special Effects Makeup Artist

Spookies (1986)
Brain Damage (1988)
Darkman (1990)
Leprechaun (1993)
Godzilla (1998)
The Cave (2005)

For more than thirty-five years, artist/director/writer/producer Gabe Bartalos has been leaving his imprint on the filmmaking world at large in very unique ways. Not only did he help bring to life the now-iconic Leprechaun character that has terrorized horror fans for decades, but he has also been a frequent collaborator with boundary-pushing filmmakers like Frank Henenlotter and Stuart Gordon, and he recently worked with visionary artists David Byrne and St. Vincent. For Bartalos, this wild ride of a career was born out of his love of Japanese monster movies that began at a very early age.

When I was a kid, I can remember taking out my dad's Super 8 camera and making horror films. It's interesting, because back then the biggest influences I had were the Japanese monster movies I'd watch on television. Then, I saw some of the Universal Monsters movies, and then *Planet of the Apes* came along, too. Looking back, I was probably at the perfect age during that Golden Age of Horror and Splatter in the late '70s and early '80s, when there was an explosion of films celebrating makeup effects with Dick Smith and Rick Baker at the forefront.

As I was making these homemade movies, I realized that someone had to do the effects if a head was being chopped off or someone was getting cut, so I was doing that, too. It was through that process where I began to realize that for as much as I loved cinema, I also loved art. And it was during that period when there was a new awareness, through publications like *Famous Monsters [of Filmland]* and *Fangoria*, that this is a real profession. That's how I learned about Tom Savini and Rick [Baker], and Tom was this important force in the business because he was so charismatic and a big character who was always ready to talk. I've been fortunate to know Tom, and getting to work with him was amazing because he was a really good person to help lead the charge of this new art form of special effects.

Because I grew up in New York, I had access to Dick Smith and was able to visit him from time to time. He was very open with his technical advice and that was exciting. Then, I met makeup effects artist Arnold Gargiulo and I worked at his studio, first as part of an internship. I got to go on sets at a very young age under Arnold, too. As I was learning about the business, it was a much different landscape than it is now, as there was a real destitute of information back then. It was very hard to get information on anything, but I quickly understood from Dick Smith to take pictures of everything I was working on and use that as my way of building a portfolio.

One of the films that helped establish Bartalos' career as a professional artist was Spookies, a low-budget cult classic burdened with complex production issues (it is still debatable whether or not the film even received a proper release in the mid-1980s). For Gabe, though, it was a chance to prove himself at the young age of seventeen.

I came on *Spookies* with Arnold, but he had some creative differences with the production and left the project. We were already into filming at that point and the producers said they would be happy if I just took everything over, and with Arnold's blessing, I did just that. That was the first project where my work that was being built would be on the screen, so that was exciting. The history of *Spookies* is a little sad, though, and I think the foundation of the film, why it still works, probably comes from the original directors, Tom Doran and Brendan Faulkner. If they would have finished the film the way they had wanted to, especially now, looking back at the films coming out at that period, they would have had a pretty good film, maybe above average because of the monster count.

During post[-production], they got into difficulties with the British financier, who panicked, withdrew them from the project, and brought in a new director [Eugenie Joseph] from the adult entertainment world. The film was never the same. I remember when it came to the Muck Men, these big creatures I had created, the new team added this flatulence to them, which I always thought was a little weird. They thought it was hilarious, and there it is in the final version of *Spookies*. They came back and shot all this extra stuff with the wizard and this girl running around, which didn't make much sense, and they brought in other effects people, too, just to fill it all in. In the end, it just seems like one big confusing movie to those of us that were there.

Despite all of that, I still got to create the Muck Men, and there's a mummy with a Ouija board that I also got to do, which was very exciting to me as a teenager. I got to do the shriveling head of actor Peter Iasillo [Jr.], too, which was my homage to what Chris Walas did in *Raiders of the Lost Ark*. His shriveling head just blew me away, and then here I was calling him up at seventeen, and for two hours he described the entire process—how to do it, what I was going to run up against, everything. So being a part of *Spookies* was a very special time for me in my career for a lot of reasons, even if the film itself turned out to be inconsistent in tone.

While he had already enjoyed a fair amount of success on the East Coast as an up-and-coming effects artist, Bartalos began to realize that if he wanted to continue following his dream of creating the kinds of monsters he grew up loving, he was going to have to take the leap and move to Los Angeles.

One thing I started to realize was that a lot of makeup artists in New York, when they were not doing special effects makeups, they would be doing straight makeup instead. That was their foundation to survive, but I wanted to do special effects makeup every day, and I understood that in order to do that, most of that work was consistently happening in Los Angeles. And so, at nineteen, I decided it was time to move out here.

Gabe found his cross-country transition an easy one to make, as he quickly landed work and has stayed busy in the world of special effects ever since.

As soon as I came to L.A., I got an interview at John [Carl] Buechler's studio, MMI [Magical Media Industries], and he hired me that day. John quickly recognized that I had already been running crews and was great at organizing projects, so he made me the makeup supervisor on *Dolls*, which was a Stuart Gordon film.

It was funny, but actually we prepped *From Beyond* first, and it had a huge workload with various studios working on it. During that process, *Dolls* got pushed to shoot first, so we had to change gears to give *Dolls* our full attention. *Dolls* is a really interesting film to me because it firmly has its foot in two different worlds, where part of it is a kids' fairy tale and the other part is a dark genre film, and both succeed. The film is actually a really good example of Stuart, because he has many sides to him. It was fun to watch Stuart at work because this was coming off the success of *Re-Animator*, and we had a great time.

Then I was quickly off to Italy, working on a parallel film called *Crawlspace* with Klaus Kinski, so that was really a fun way to start off a career in L.A., collaborating with talent like Stuart Gordon and Klaus Kinski. While working, I was always very focused on trying to find an expression for my imagination, so I was constantly sculpting and designing. There was so much to learn in proper mold techniques, proper fiberglass techniques, and proper foam running that at every shop I worked at, I was given all these great learning opportunities. I still really appreciate that to this day.

After working on those films at John's, I started working for a company called Reel Effects. They specialized in creating physical effects like explosions, rain, and wind effects. But there was a period when they were taking on makeup effects just to see if more was better, and we did *Friday the 13th Part VI* [*Jason Lives*], which was significant for me. The original *Friday the 13th* was the first splatter film I saw that had no apologies, and Tom [Savini]'s work is amazing in it. To get to work on one of the sequels years later? I was all over it.

I got to make the Jason masks and I think we made thirteen, because at that point ripping off the masks from the set was a big thing because the franchise was in full swing, and producers knew that people were going to steal them—how weird. I also got to work on the scene where Jason cuts off the guy's arm with the machete, and we had to design a really interesting mold that would come apart. There were fun little technical challenges among all of the bloodshed, including the sheriff's death, where Jason breaks him in half. We had just done a body breaking in half for a film called *The Outing* [a.k.a. *The Lamp*], so we used that same rig when the sheriff got cracked, and it worked great.

But every trip was an adventure, and while I was working on *The Lamp*, Savini called me up and said, "Oh you're in Texas? We're doing [*The Texas*] *Chainsaw* [*Massacre*] 2, come on over and help out." So I went over to Austin for that. My career at that point was a lot of fun because these were the people I had read about and respected, and now I was getting to work for them. I began a relationship with Frank Henenlotter around that time while I was on the film *Brain Damage*, and we've worked together many times since then.

Throughout his career, Henenlotter has always been a director looking to push horror into some rather bold territory, and for over twenty years, Bartalos has helped him do just that, creating the special effects for the aforementioned Brain Damage (1988), Frankenhooker, Basket Case 2, Basket Case 3, and Bad Biology.

Frank is just great, and his sense of humor is outrageous. On *Brain Damage*, what was so cool is that the three heavy effects in that film—Aylmer the parasite, the gore effects, and the withering effects of the old couple—those alone would be a dream on any one film, but the fact that all three of those were in one film was so much fun. That film is one of my favorites of Frank's, and it was great because that's where we got to know each other. There's nothing more personal than shooting a film and being in the trenches.

Frank is also a real taskmaster, but it's in the quest of this ultimate vision, and he's amazing because he knows exactly where he's going. Coming from the low-budget world with *Basket Case*, *Brain Damage*, and [so] on, he's learned how to make sure every cent goes on the screen. We hit it off and we had fun, so when he got the deal for *Frankenhooker* and *Basket Case 2*, he asked me back. Looking back, it was at a great time, because my imagination was just exploding at that point, and he must have sensed something way in advance with the amount of freedom he gave me.

He was probably like, "Well, let's exploit Gabe; he's crazy, his energy is boundless, and he will always give me a bunch of monsters." He was really smart in tapping into what I had to offer, because it just makes him and the film look good, and someone who is excited about the work is the best employee. My imagination and taste tend to go towards the surreal anyway, so it was a very easy fit to collaborate with Frank.

I also think being very young, to have a director recognize your talent is completely liberating, and it is a huge confidence builder. Looking back at that time, it was an incredibly healthy atmosphere to be working in, and I was lucky that it was someone like Frank, who had enough confidence in himself to allow everyone else the chance to rise to the occasion.

Around the same time he began his longtime working relationship with Henenlotter, Bartalos was called to join Bart Mixon's crew to work on Tommy Lee Wallace's Fright Night Part 2.

Bart had been working at a studio within Fantasy II [Film] Effects, which had been known more for visual effects at that time, but they began to find themselves working a lot with miniatures and makeup effects, so they wanted to just do it all under one roof. *Fright Night 2* was fun because everyone got different effects to do. I got the scene where the vampires go bowling with the guy's head, and I got to make the head.

Bart was a great guy to work for. He let everyone run with their own effect, so at the end of the day you could say, "I did this," or "I did that," and it made you feel like you had ownership of the work, which was nice. It doesn't always happen that way.

In the late 1980s, Bartalos was given the opportunity to work alongside one of his heroes when none other than Rick Baker brought him on board to contribute to Gorillas in the Mist.

Gorillas being the first project with Rick was so cool because in the years of reading about him, I learned that his biggest professional pursuit was to build the ultimate gorilla suit. And now, he was going to have the budget and he was very aware of the challenges ahead of us. He said, 'You know, this isn't a fantasy ape and this isn't a gorilla on its own. Our stuff has to be able to cut in with the real stuff.' And when you think about that, it becomes a really challenging prospect.

Rick was pushing everything that he had learned to another level on *Gorillas*. It was a great time because he got the pre-production period that he wanted to get the job [done] right. It was a very small crew, especially compared to where Rick would go in the following years, but for this film, there were only eleven of us. Rick built a prototype suit on himself first, and the idea was that any complaint or problem that would come up, Rick would know about it first and would completely understand how to fix it.

So the suit was put together almost to completion on Rick, and then we began on John Alexander, who played Digit. I started in the mold department and when the molding and fabrication were done, I got pushed to the paint department as the crew got smaller and smaller. When there were only a few of us left, I was moved to the hair department, and it was really nice to watch all these components come together all the way to the end. Still, to this day, the work we did on *Gorillas in the Mist* is some of the best work that I've seen, and Rick's Digit became the benchmark for gorillas in film.

Gabe would also join Rick on another ambitious project shortly after wrapping on Gorillas in the Mist: Joe Dante's ambitious sequel, Gremlins 2: The New Batch. To take on the formidable amount of special effects the production would require, Baker insisted on a key stipulation before coming on board the project.

Rick turned down *Gremlins 2* so many times because the studio initially wanted to follow in the path of the first *Gremlins* and go the same route with the Mogwais and the Gremlins. Rick told them he would only do it if he could make them into individualized characters, and when they agreed, that's what finally sold Rick on it. There was a really fun period where, for six weeks, we were just designing all different types of Gremlins. Some were just a free-for-all of different styles, and there were others that Rick was specific about. Rick gave me the Vegetable Gremlin because it was just my kind of crazy. Again, it was nice to have that one character you know is your own up there on the big screen.

Gremlins 2 took a massive turn once the characters were picked and we had to make all the versions. As Rick does on every job, there is a hero, there's a backup, there's a stunt double, there's one to fly through the air, and there's a hand-puppet version of every type of creature. Suddenly it was like, *Holy smokes, we're going to do eleven versions of twenty-eight characters?* It was a massive amount of work. It became a bit of a factory line then, where instead of characters, there were tables of ears, there were tables of teeth, and all the other parts, too.

Rick, to his credit, built everything on *Gremlins 2*, which was a huge project, with the same quality and care that he would use if he were doing a smaller show, where he could handle [things] personally for the entire show. It was very impressive to watch and to be a part of. There were so many cool sculptures being generated, and then there was some standout mechanical work happening on the Spider Gremlin and the Brain Gremlin, too.

I think why Rick Baker is so admired by many, and what really impressed me, is that when he is hands-on, he is one of the best designers and craftsmen out there. Then, when he has a project like *Gremlins 2*, where it was impossible for him to do it by himself, he hired a good team and insulated us from the drama that every production has, and let us focus on our art. Rick made me feel proud to be a member of his crew.

What is really cool about Rick is that sometimes you get close to your heroes and it's not so great. When I got to work for Rick after looking up to him for all those years, he was a gentleman, he was funny and caring, and he was more than I could have ever imagined. Rick actually took the idea of hero worship and made it even better.

As Gabe continued to establish himself as a special effects technician, he realized it was finally time to put his official stamp on the industry and opened Atlantic West Effects, which is still running to this day.

Starting my own company was a pretty organic process. I continued to take on small jobs while working for Rick, like a friend's play or a photo shoot, and so I turned my apartment's dining room area into a little studio, where one side was sculpting and the other was mold-making. I was working on a film called *Wild About Harry*, a werewolf film for HBO, and my friend Dave Kindlon and I decided that we should go get a space because we were tired of trashing our apartments. We found a raw space in Sylmar, and right around that time, *Basket Case 2* happened. That deputized the space with a real job.

It wasn't like I hung my name on the door, cracked my knuckles, and said, "Okay, now I have to go find work." I basically hit a point where I said to myself, *I can't run all this through my personal accounts anymore, and now I need to hire people to help with everything because I can't keep up on my own.* As more demands of work came, it made sense to become incorporated as Atlantic West Effects.

We were fortunate to get a big rush of work early on, like *Leprechaun* and this film I did for [Roger] Corman called *Dead Space*, and then I worked with [*Jason Lives* Director] Tom [McLoughlin] again on *Sometimes They Come Back*, which was a TV movie. It was nice of him to call me back on that. [Robert] Rusler was just great to work with as he went through the head cast process, and we designed this elaborate makeup for his character. What's interesting about *Sometimes* is that Tom had us build 100% graphic stuff, but because this was a TV movie, he knew he was just going to show it in bits, and if those bits weren't fully realized, it might not have had the impact that he knew he wanted.

That was interesting, because as time goes by, you realize how different directors handle your work. This was a good lesson for me. If we didn't build it full-on, it wouldn't have sustained just a few frames. He was also working for television, so he knew what he needed to get through the shoot because he knows the medium very well.

Considering Bartalos was always fond of breathing life into vivid cinematic characters that he could take some ownership of, in the early 1990s, he was given a huge opportunity to create one of the most iconic modern movie monsters to ever grace the silver screen: the titular baddie from Leprechaun, portrayed by Warwick Davis. In fact, Bartalos had the rare chance to continue overseeing the handling of Davis' killer character as he worked on all of the subsequent Leprechaun sequels as well (although he had nothing to do with the remake Leprechaun: Origins).

What my vision of a leprechaun had been reduced to at the point I was hired for *Leprechaun* were these ridiculous images from traditional fairy tales and a cereal box. None of those images were all that interesting to me, so the direction I took the character was almost like my way of saying, "F you." You have to embrace the absurdness of the concept and then just jackhammer it into a very bold conceptual area. The punch line to all of this was that they had Warwick, who is an amazing actor and treated the role with an incredible sense of seriousness. That, to me, was the cherry on top.

I remember listening to the producers early on discussing what they thought they wanted. They had done two sketches, and one of them had a clover hanging off a derby hat he was wearing. I didn't want to go in that direction at all, because if that's your monster, which is going to forever brand this character, you have to make that interesting. I realized the producers weren't going to see it that way, so I quietly pushed their artwork aside as I started to design him.

I did a full miniature body sculpture right down to the little Irish straps in his shoes. I thought, *If this is a real creature, it has to swing the pendulum in a very tough direction.* I sculpted the Leprechaun with an ultra-aggressive sculpted brow and chipped tooth just to give him that edge. In *Leprechaun*, there are actually three different stages of makeup. If you look at the first images of the Leprechaun in the movie and again at the end, you can clearly see it. But because we cross-pollinated the pieces with three different stages, he looks like he has almost six to eight guises in the film. By the end, his final look is what they kept for the rest of the films.

The professionalism of Warwick added so much more to the character beyond just the makeup, and it was cool how *Leprechaun* became this Holy Grail for the studio, because they wanted a monster franchise and they got it. I don't think they would have had it not been for Warwick.

As he continued to work throughout the 1990s and 2000s as an effects artist and a leader in his industry, Bartalos realized he had other creative itches that needed to be scratched.

Because this all started with me making films, that feeling just never went away. As a makeup artist, there is nothing worse than turning a prosthetic character over to wardrobe, and ten minutes later they come out with a bad Carol Burnett scissored-up outfit. That can be so frustrating. You begin to understand that you can't control a lot of aspects in a film when you come on as a hired gun makeup effects artist. You're just not in a position to challenge that world. It made me realize that I wanted to go back to the world of filmmaking so I could explore that feeling again and have a chance to realize more things the way I first envisioned them.

That's what *Skinned Deep* [Gabe's 2004 directorial debut] became. I thought, *Let's not just sculpt the characters, let's sculpt the entire world. Let's build the sets, let's make our own reality and create a dream and then film the dream.* Putting together your own film that you're writing and directing allows as much of your imagination to get in that you want to try and get on the screen. That's what I find really fun about the process. The fact that these are homegrown projects that are lucky to find a release means there isn't a responsibility to a studio yet, so I can be as absurd and playful as I want. When they do land in a good place, that's great. It allows me to really clean out my head and get it all out there on the screen.

It also puts a different light on your responsibility as the makeup effects artist after you've directed, because you really can respect the fact that the director is managing an entire film, and here you are just worried about your precious little effects.

A few years ago, Gabe had the chance to work with another purveyor of the strange and surreal, musician David Byrne, who hired Bartalos to help create the image manipulation for the cover of his album with St. Vincent (a.k.a. Annie Clark), Love This Giant.

David totally embraces the underbelly of intellectualism through art. At my first meeting, it was such a subtle modification that he was looking for on him and singer Annie Clark that, while I really didn't want to talk myself out of a job, I told him that it sounded like what he needed was just a digital tweak. David said, "No, I want to go through a face cast, I want to see the sculpture, and I want to wear a thing." He wanted to celebrate the art of prosthetic application, and the fact that it was so subtle is what really got it exciting for me as a challenge. It's much harder to hide a subtle nuance.

When the makeup was done, we had a photo shoot with large monitors. As they were taking the first shots, I heard this hilarious laughing that came out of the room where David was, and Annie, who was sitting next to me, said, "Oh, I think David is happy." He loved that what we did to him was just so subtle that fans were going to endlessly sit there and stare at it just to figure out what was different. Annie's look was more severe, where I broadened her nose bridge and made the left side of her jaw look broken.

But David was great, and he loved the process of wearing the makeup and going through it all. Once we had wrapped the shoot, I took the castings we did of their teeth and faces, as well as the extra vacuform pieces, and sent those to them as a "thank you." As it turned out, I ended up solving their inner artwork problem. So, on the album and on the CD, it's all the teeth and the face mask. He put all of those pieces to use. I thought that was really cool and very gratifying as an artist.

Throughout his decades-spanning career, Gabe Bartalos has been fortunate to work alongside some of the greatest talents in the effects industry and collaborate with a vast array of filmmakers who helped shape the landscape of modern horror. Gabe has even been able to leave his own imprint in the world of genre cinema through his very own directorial projects as well.

I think that I'm really lucky to have gotten into it when I did. There was a foundation laid by those we still consider great, Rick Baker and Dick Smith being the biggest two, so there was a lot of excitement that fueled the industry to the point where it just exploded. That gave room for all of us.

Now, once a big bang like that happens, every star is up to its own trajectory and [must] find its own orbit. I was lucky that all directors that I've worked with, and my fellow artists that have supported me, all came with a real love and a real honoring of creatures. We don't wink and nudge at the work we are doing. To all of us, this is really special stuff. Monsters and creatures are a wonderful byproduct of our fallacies and insecurities. They are fused to us and we wear it like a coat of arms. It's such a cool thing.

Then, when you take it further to the arts, when you push yourself to consistently make things better and you work with people who inspire you, it can allow you to find an amazing community of really good people. There are a lot of people in the film business for the wrong reasons, so if you are lucky enough to work with directors like Frank Henenlotter, Kevin Tenney, Tom McLoughlin, or Stuart Gordon, all these guys really love this stuff, and that helps you get through the dry spells and the more frustrating aspects of your job. I don't think I could have possibly gotten any luckier than I did in my early career.

Friday the 13th Part VI - Jason Mask Buck

Friday the 13th Part VI - Gabe Bartalos

The Texas Chainsaw Massacre 2 - Gabe Bartalos and Bill Johnson (Leatherface)

The Texas Chainsaw Massacre 2 - Gabe Bartalos and Bill Johnson (Leatherface)

The Texas Chainsaw Massacre 2 - Makeup Crew
Including Gabe Bartalos, John Vulich, Bart Mixon and Tom Savini

Frankenhooker

Talking Heads David Byrne and Gabe Bartalos

Talking Heads David Byrne – Album Cover Makeup

St Vincent (Annie Clark) and David Byrne
Love This Giant Album Cover

Gabe Bartalos with his Lion Sculpture for the
"Abhorrence and Obsession" Art Installation

Sometimes They Come Back

Saint Bernard

Saint Bernard – Gabe Bartalos

Rusty Truck Band - *Rattle Trucks* Music Video Sculpture

Rusty Truck Band - *Rattle Trucks* Music Video

Special Effects Makeup Artist

A Nightmare on Elm Street Part 4: The Dream Master (1988)
Casino (1995)
Men In Black (1997)
House of 1000 Corpses (2003)
Transformers (2007)
Halloween II (2009)

For artist Wayne Toth, monsters have always been a way of life, and as he got older, he was able to parlay his penchant for cinematic creatures into a career that has now spanned over four decades in the special effects industry. That passion also became the framework for a string of successful retail businesses launched by Toth in Southern California and provided Wayne with endless opportunities, including contributing to nearly every horror franchise and collaborating alongside some of the greatest genre storytellers as well.

Loving monsters and loving monster movies was so natural to me, I can't remember a time where they weren't a part of my life. My brother and I were always obsessed with monster movies, and I think *Frankenstein* was one of the first ones that really got me when it was on TV. Our mom would wake us up at night when the monster movies were on too, so ever since we were little, little kids, I had an interest in it and started drawing all the time. It was always monsters and King Kong and all that kind of stuff. I even tried to turn myself into Frankenstein using a shoebox on my head once. It seems to be this thing that you're just born with, where you start so young you don't even realize it that it's happening.

Luckily, our dad was also into Super 8 movies, so we always had cameras around the house. That led to the next step for both of us, which was filming stuff. We would do all kinds of stuff with silly putty, sometimes even putting it on our face, or making stop-motion animation movies with Play-Doh people and eventually, action figures. Even on a rudimentary level, making those movies as kids was beneficial for both of us, especially later on, when you're trying to come up with in-camera gags, and you need to have an understanding of all those camera tricks to pull off an effect.

Halloween was a big holiday for our family too, and back when we lived in Denver, we would always do a little haunted house or a haunted walk-through in our backyard. I kept wanting to do more, but when you're in a different state where there aren't a lot of movies being made around, there's no way to learn anything other than some theatrical makeup books. I got lucky because in our local mall, we had a magic shop that had Halloween masks, and a couple of them struck me as being different.

I learned that they were made by a fellow in Denver, Ed Edmunds of Distortions Unlimited. When I was around 12 or 13, my dad took me over to visit him. He was making those masks in his basement and selling them at local stores, but now, he's gone on to become one of the biggest Halloween prop manufacturers in the world. He even had his own TV show for a year or two.

Ed's a great guy, and he was nice, giving me some basic sculpting and molding pointers. I was fortunate, in that sense, to live near Ed and that he was kind enough to start helping me get a little more of a leg up on effects.

Once Toth finished up high school, he was unsure of what his next steps were, even though deep down he knew he wanted to find a way to continue honing his skills and making monsters. Ultimately, Wayne decided it only made sense to enroll in a makeup program in California so that he could begin to pursue his dreams of working in the world of big screen monstrosities and iconic characters.

When I was 18, that's when I moved out to California to live in this cheap, horrible apartment so I could go to makeup school. It was a six-week course that covered some beauty makeup and some prosthetics. I knew half of the material that was being taught just based on what I had done as a kid, but it was still helpful. Now, that I look back on it, it was such good timing because it was the heyday of effects at that time. And somehow I went from watching Freddy Krueger movies in high school to, a year and a half later, working on one. How do you even begin to register something like that?

The first place I worked was John Buechler's MMI shop, right out of school. It was a very slim crew, and a lot of us were new. One of the first things I worked on was *A Nightmare on Elm Street Part 4*, and I also worked on *Halloween 4* at that time, too. John's shop was great because you could do just about anything you wanted to if you were capable of it. It wasn't as departmentalized as things are now. That's what was fun to me, and it made me a well-rounded artist. I was in every department, working my way up through shops: I have been a mold shop supervisor, I have been in mechanical departments, supervising shows, going to set, and doing makeup. I could do a little bit of everything, which just kept everything more interesting to me, and I believe that's what the creative process should feel like.

I still remember how funny it felt to me that working on a movie, and being in the middle of everything, was so different than when you'd go and see a movie in a theater. It was hard to get a sense of it when I was right there in the middle of everything because it was just doing my job. However, to go from never being on a film set before to seeing Robert Englund and you're working on him, or around him, and that was mind-blowing. We were working all the time, sometimes off the clock, doing Freddy's chest of souls and the soul pizza, but we didn't care because we were having so much fun.

Wayne continued working at MMI through several more filmic projects, including To Die For, Indiana Jones and the Last Crusade and Brian Yuzna's Bride of Re-Animator.

Indiana Jones was a side project, as it was basically a gag that someone else had built that we had to augment. *Bride of Re-Animator* was a much bigger show for us, and I was co-supervising that for MMI with Mike Deak. I know I was young, but we were the ones doing most of the work. I was super excited to be working on a sequel to *Re-Animator* too, and it was so wacky, just coming up with solutions and ways to achieve those effects of Doctor Hill and the bat. Working with Brian was great too, because that was the first time I had to communicate that much with the director, and he is a very creative and interesting filmmaker.

As Toth continued to establish himself in the realm of special effects, he began working with an assortment of talented shops and artists outside of MMI.

After *Bride*, I don't remember exactly what happened, but John probably didn't have a project coming in at the time. But, because I had met the KNB guys [Robert Kurtzman, Greg Nicotero and Howard Berger] on *Bride of Re-Animator*, they were getting ready to start on *Tales from the Darkside* and invited me to come over and work with them. I didn't have to show them a portfolio or anything, and it was my first exposure to working in a different shop. For *Tales*, I didn't go to set for that as I was mainly doing shop work, like sculpting, molding, and I did some mechanics, too. But I had a great time working with them.

I think it was right at that time when I realized that you couldn't live in a creative bubble as an artist, especially when you're working in a creative field that encompasses so many techniques and skills. In some instances, you might have to come up with the entire gag; from the concept of how it's going to be filmed and shot to how to achieve it. Then, it's up to you to figure out all the steps to take to bring it to life. And a big part of that is gaining different experiences on different teams. It's the only way to broaden everything that you're learning because every shop is different.

I worked over at KNB EFX for a long time. KNB was doing so much stuff at that time so you would work on a little bit of everything. There would be somewhere around 10 to 12 films a year, but I wasn't heavily involved in all of them. A lot of cool shows came through the shop though, like *Freddy's Dead: The Final Nightmare* and *The People Under the Stairs* for Wes [Craven], where I worked on the makeup for the boys in the basement during the reshoots.

When we did *Army of Darkness*, there were so many gags in that movie with the skeletons, so I was heavily involved in all of that stuff which was so much fun. We had such a large crew, and we were all there in the trenches every day and trying to figure out how to do whatever Sam would come up with. One day, the skeletons could be carrying a ladder or the next day their marching and playing a bone flute. That movie was an absolute hoot.

During the early 1990s, Toth was also part of the crew for a then up-and-coming writer and director by the name of Quentin Tarantino who was putting together his first feature, Reservoir Dogs, which ended up catapulting his career and became a landmark moment for the independent film scene to boot.

I know most people know this story, but I still think it's pretty cool. Bob Kurtzman, from KNB, had a story idea for a movie but he had never written a script before. He met Quentin before Quentin had done anything at all. Somehow, those guys met and made a deal where Bob asked Quentin to write this script for him and, then, if Quentin were ever to do a movie, KNB would do the effects. So, for *Reservoir Dogs*, he took Bob up on that deal. The work mainly consisted of setting down tons of blood and a couple of gags. The slicing off of the ear was a gag that Kurtzman designed and sculpted, but they sent me down to apply it, which was great.

We had no idea at the time that *Reservoir Dogs* was going to be a big deal or that Quentin would go on to be one of the most revered filmmakers of all time. The next thing we know, Quentin's a huge deal, and now Bob has a Quentin Tarantino script to work from. So, Bob's silly vampire movie he'd been talking about for years became this big movie with Harvey Keitel and George Clooney, and all these amazing people.

KNB had an ongoing relationship with Quentin, and I believe that they have done all of his movies. I worked on a couple of them along the way, too. For *Pulp Fiction*, I did Uma Thurman's needle in the chest gag and a few other gags, too. Around the same time, that's when *Jason Goes to Hell* came in, which was great because I got to sculpt Jason for that one. And if you're going to work on a *Friday [the 13th]* movie, that's one of the best things I think anyone who loves these movies could work on. I felt spoiled.

But after *Jason Goes to* Hell, that's when I got a call from Mike Deak because he was going to be heading up the makeup set shop for Charles Band's Full Moon. I felt bad leaving KNB at the time, but there were no hard feelings or anything like that. I just had this other new opportunity that I wanted to pursue with Mike which, again, was great. That began another big period in my life.

While working at Full Moon with Mike Deak, Wayne was given the opportunity to sow his creative oats while creating the effects on several of the production shingle's Puppet Master and Subspecies sequels and the H.P. Lovecraft-inspired Lurking Fear (1994).

Working at Full Moon was a lot of fun, and it gave us many opportunities to do some cool stuff that we both had always wanted to do. Mike ran the shop but, creatively, it was just a couple of other guys and us. We didn't have to answer to anyone either, so we had a lot more freedom. They were Charlie Band-branded movies, but the director was the only one you had to please, which is always the best-case scenario in making movies. We didn't have a ton of money, but on a creative level, it was a very satisfying time for me.

I did end up going over to work on a few other projects for KNB around that time too. There was *[Wes Craven's] New Nightmare*, which a few different shops were on, there was *Lord of Illusions* with Clive Barker – who was such a nice guy to work with – then there was *Darkman II [The Return of Durant]* and *Vampire in Brooklyn*, but that one I didn't end up going to set for.

We also got to work with Martin Scorsese on *Casino*, which was a huge highlight for me. We did the whole sequence of Joe Pesci getting killed, the guy who gets his eyeballs popped out of his head in a vise, and when De Niro smashes a guy's hand with a hammer. To me, Martin Scorsese is one of the top filmmakers of our time, so to just be involved with that was unbelievable. In fact, it was Martin who introduced me to Robert De Niro. That was one of those, "Is this really happening?" moments.

But probably my favorite project I got to work on over at KNB was *From Dusk Till Dawn*. I sculpted Quentin's vampire makeup, and Howard and I applied it on set. The amount of work we had to do on that show was staggering. I wouldn't say something like that wouldn't ever happen again, but the number of makeups and effects that we had to do daily, you probably wouldn't see all of that happening together again. We had a big crew for it, and we filmed all those interiors in an old Lawry's meat-packing plant, where KNB's effects room was this huge meat locker. It was just nonstop fun, even though we were all exhausted. I don't think I have ever worked that hard in my entire life. It just can't be compared to anything else I have ever done.

Having Tom [Savini] around too, was pretty great. A lot of those guys had worked with Tom, like Nicotero and Gino Crognale, so even though he wasn't doing effects work, it still felt like we had another effects guy around. I remember, Tom had this bullwhip in *From Dusk Till Dawn* and he was getting pretty good with it. He was always trying to get people to hold a Styrofoam cup, and he would whip it out of your hand. He tried me to get me to do it at one point, and there was no way I was going to do it.

When we did the reshoots, Robert asked a bunch of us effects guys to work in the vampire suits, so we got a chance to become monsters, which was pretty cool. Robert also had a lot of us do these little cameos in the bar during the scene when Savini was fighting off all the vampires. I remember we had rehearsed the moves, and I forget exactly how the action was supposed to go, but at the end of it, I'm supposed to be coming straight at Tom, and he's backed up against the bar. So, when we shot that moment, I came at him and he just full on kicked me in the chest. I went flying back a few feet, and I could see him laughing as I went flying. It was one of the best experiences I've ever had.

Toth continued to stay busy as part of the KNB throughout the '90s, but he also began to get more and more projects collaborating with numerous rock bands and musician over the years, including The Ramones, Motorhead, Danzig, Alice Cooper, and Rob Zombie, which would lead to Wayne teaming up with the former White Zombie frontman for his directorial debut, House of 1000 Corpses.

My work with different musical artists started very early on in my career, and then I just kept doing more over time. During my early days at John Buechler's shop, I met Kirk Hammett from Metallica, and then, Greg Nicotero connected us again. So, I knew Kirk, and he was good friends with Glenn Danzig, and because of Kirk, I wound up doing the wings for Danzig's *Her Black Wings* video which was a long time ago. And it just all kept going from there. I feel like heavy metal and horror movies pretty much go hand in hand, so when you start to get to work with those people, it's just as incredible as working with these bigger filmmakers. Danzig was my first exposure to doing this type of work, and I still do stuff for Glenn to this day. It's probably one of my oldest working relationships by far, I would say.

With Johnny Ramone, I met him around 1990 when he visited the set of *Bride of Re-Animator*. We stayed in contact over the years, and he even had me make a new Pinhead mask for The Ramones' on-stage mascot. Johnny had become friends with Rob Zombie, and at one point, Rob commissioned me to make a gag Christmas gift sculpture of Johnny, which was an in-joke that they shared.

But when Johnny was diagnosed with terminal cancer, he and his wife Linda began planning a memorial for him and approached me to create a full-size bronze statue based on that small statue I had done. Bronze was a new avenue for me, but I was honored to be asked of course, and took on the task. And the statue resides at the Hollywood Forever Cemetery in Los Angeles and gets hundreds of visitors every year, and it felt great to create something to honor Johnny with something that will be in place for a long time.

For Rob [Zombie], I had worked on a couple of his music videos with a friend that had been doing them. Then, I wound up doing most of the work on *House of 1000 Corpses*, which was the first time I worked with him extensively. It was just a match made in heaven. It's such an easy working relationship. He's just super creative, and he is also an outstanding artist, where you have a guy who can illustrate his own ideas. What better starting place can you get than that? Sometimes you'll have to work with a director where you have to keep doing something over and over again because they don't know what they want at all. Rob is someone who always knows exactly what he wants.

It felt pretty natural, seeing his progression from music to directing both *Corpses* and [*The Devil's*] *Rejects*. On *Corpses*, we did reshoots, which made the movie in the end. Many people may not know how much work we'd done after the fact, because it was a Universal film when it was shot but, right as it was finishing up, editing and everything, the Columbine shootings happened. Universal didn't want anything to do with controversial violence at all, so they dropped the movie, and it was in limbo for a couple of years. In the meantime, Rob just wanted to keep working on it.

So, he'd come up with some ideas, and we would just go shoot it ourselves. We shot stuff in his basement at his house. We built sets in my shop and shot scenes on those sets on 8mm video cameras, and the way that Rob was able to edit and stylize the footage, no one could tell the difference.

By the time we did *The Devil's Rejects*, I knew that everyone would be surprised by how different it felt than *Corpses*, but because I had gotten to know

Rob, I knew the types of films that inspire him creatively. So, to me, *Rejects* was just Rob doing another type of project that he himself would enjoy from a fan's perspective. Plus, he's not the type of guy who is going to do the same thing over and over again either.

In 2006, Dimension Films announced that Zombie would take the helm of their planned remake of John Carpenter's Halloween (1978), and for Toth, it was one the first times he felt any real pressure heading into a new project.

I think there was immense pressure on us from the minute it came out that Rob would be doing it. I mean, the first *Halloween* was, obviously, one of the best horror movies of all time, and it will never be topped for what it is. Everybody knows that. So, to remake it, I can't imagine the pressure Rob had on him because you had to be faithful to it in a way because you're dealing with a franchise of legend.

The pressure that was on me was the fact that there hadn't been a good Michael Myers mask since the original *Halloween II* (1981). I knew whatever we were going to do with that mask was going to be put under the microscope by everyone. So, when I started working on it, I wanted it to resemble the original, but it didn't have to be an exact duplicate of the original, because it was aged and weathered. I made my first version, and Rob loved it, so that was it. One thing that I have figured out over the years is that your first instincts are usually the best instincts that you can have as an artist. And I am proud of our Michael Myers. I think he's still really cool.

When we came back for the sequel, it felt like we pushed things even further. For example, there's Octavia [Spencer]'s death, which for some reason, many fans found it to be extremely horrifying. I think it was the slice across the face because it was so subtle, then all that blood started pouring out, and Michael stabs her in the back of the head. Also, Octavia was so nice about all of it too. She took it all like a champ, and it felt like she was having fun with everything.

Another scene that people ask me about a lot is when Danielle Harris gets killed in the bathroom. In the script, Laurie finds her, and the only description was that she's cut up and dying. So, Rob just told me to figure out what I could do with it. So, we took Danielle to the trailer, and we were using a bunch of generic appliances that we had, and I was trying to take it to the next level, especially, with Rob. He's not a guy that is easily shocked, but when he saw Danielle when we were done, he was totally and completely shocked. I was really proud of that.

When it came time for Rob to put his own spin on the world of witchcraft for The Lords of Salem, the project got Wayne's creative juices flowing since Zombie was taking his story in a very surreal direction, which meant he had a lot of room to experiment.

I've worked on a lot of great projects, but from a creative standpoint, *Lords* was one of the most fun shows I have ever done because we had to make a lot of bizarre, surreal and scary stuff to go with Rob's vision. It was tough, too, because a lot of those elements in *Lords* were so hard to try and nail down ahead of time.

So, a lot of what you see were things that we just made up as we went along, which wasn't easy. We also had to make things weird, but they had to look natural too, which was another challenge for us. I like the stuff to look as organic as possible, and it was hard to make stuff that doesn't actually exist. I loved the look of our Satan too, because it was something very unique and different than we have seen before, and for me, that's the ultimate goal in what I do as an artist. I want to make something different that people haven't seen before, but it still has to look cool, and it's not always easy to find that balance.

Another big component to *Lords* was Meg Foster in that full-body makeup. It took a good amount of time, and we ended up having to do it for a few different days during production. It was brutal. Meg was such a trooper, about the process, too. She was completely naked, standing in this cold warehouse while we had to put makeup on every square inch of her body. We had to work fast because we didn't have a ton of time on that one, and Meg was amazing about everything.

When I look back at everything we were able to achieve on *Lords of Salem*, I'm still very proud because we got to do lots of cool stuff, and we didn't have a ton of time or resources, so it really pushed all of us to rise above those limitations and do our best work possible.

Even though Wayne has been able to enjoy a long and fruitful career in the special effects industry, he's been able to branch out in other ways over the years too, with his imaginative creations that he's conceived over the years for the haunt industry as well as his successful Halloween and horror-themed retail stores located in Burbank, California.

It was during the late '90s when I started noticing that the haunted house industry was pretty big. Actually, it was [Tom] Savini that had mentioned to me when I was working on *From Dusk Till Dawn* how big the industry was getting. I had a couple of ideas that I thought would serve that industry pretty well, and for a few years, I would take my different creations to the Halloween industry trade show. It was during that second year I attended the show that I had come up with these things called "Stalkarounds," which were these big, oversized costumes with mechanics inside that can turn you into this eight-foot-tall creature. They ended up becoming a big deal, and I took so many orders for them that I think I had to stop working at KNB so that I could fill all the orders.

I still sell those "Stalkarounds" to this day, and over the years, I came up with some other props and fun haunt items like that, which is just another fun aspect of my career. It's not a big part of what I do all the time, but it does keep me busy here and there.

At the time all this haunt stuff was taking off, the company my wife was working for went out of business. She'd been in human resources for years, and she didn't feel like doing that anymore. Because we had gotten this exposure from the trade show, that's when we started to decide to try opening a Halloween store, and we called it Halloween Town.

We didn't have this big business plan when we set out either. We just started all on our own, on credit cards, and that was 18 years ago. Now, it has turned into the massive thing it is today, where we even have multiple locations. I could never have imagined that it would have taken off like it has. However, at the same time, it is so much work, and we kill ourselves just trying to keep up sometimes, but it is completely worth it.

And I think that ties into something that has always driven me my entire career: you have to love what you're doing because it is so much work. When it comes right down to it, you have to be a hard worker because it's not easy. For me, this is what I always loved, so I always knew I was going to have to work hard at everything that I've done. Doing creative work always comes down to being passionate about your work, and taking the time to enjoy who you're working with too. I'm so lucky to have worked with so many great artists and directors over the years who have all made a huge impact on my career.

From Dusk Till Dawn - Quentin Tarantino

From Dusk Till Dawn - Wayne Toth as Vampire

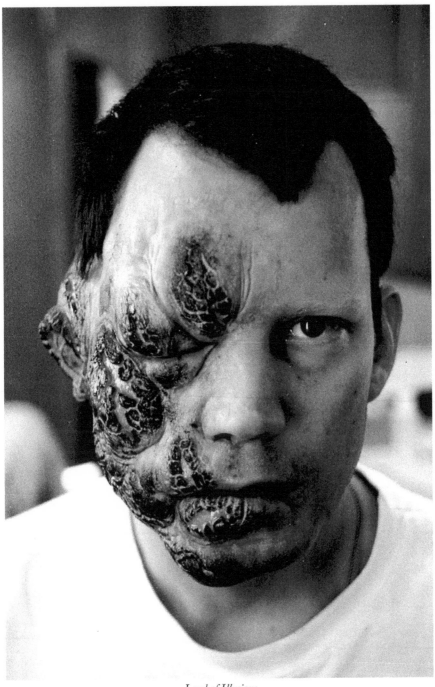

Lord of Illusions

House of 1000 Corpses - Bill Moseley

House of 1000 Corpses – Rainn Wilson transformed into "Fish Boy"

House of 1000 Corpses – Dr. Satan

Halloween - Asylum Mask

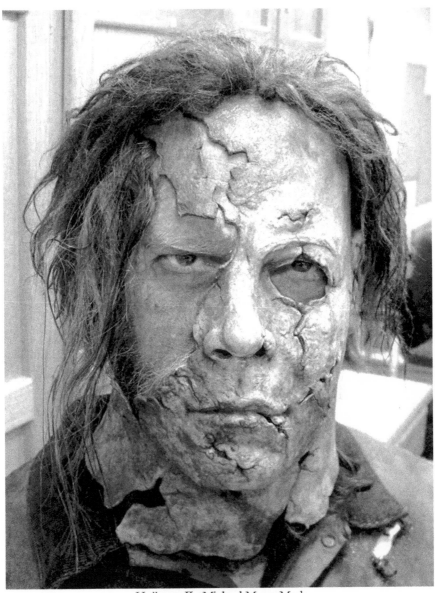

Halloween II - Michael Myers Mask

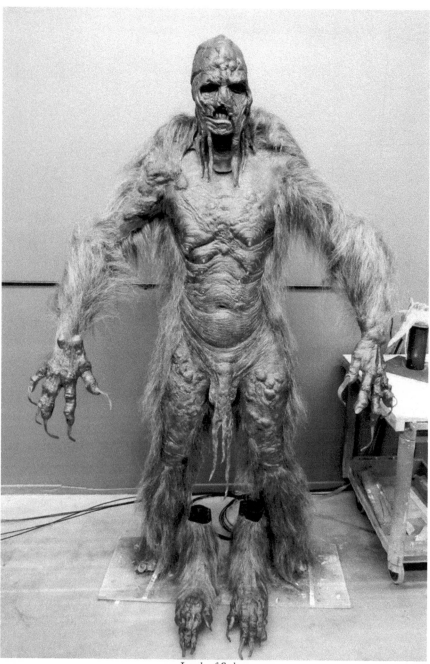

Lords of Salem

Alice Cooper - Stage Prop

Danzig - Stage Prop

Danzig - Stage Prop

Misfits - Stage Prop

Wayne Toth - Creating the Johnny Ramone Memorial Statue

Johnny Ramone Memorial Statue - Hollywood Forever Cemetery

Johnny Ramone Memorial Statue - Hollywood Forever Cemetery

ACKNOWLEDGEMENTS

Five years ago, I set out to do something different and provide a platform to a group of artists that I grew up loving and admiring as a lifelong horror fan. I wanted to share their stories with the world, celebrating their work and their legacies, and I never could have imagined how incredible this entire journey would be for me, both personally and professionally. I have been very fortunate to have been given the opportunity to live out my own dreams for the last 14 years of my career in the world of horror journalism, and while I am incredibly proud of my entire body of work, these interviews contained within the *Monsters, Makeup & Effects* book series are what I am most proud of because I get to share the stories of all these amazingly talented people with all the fans out there who admire and appreciate these artists just as much as I do.

First and foremost, I have to thank the artists from *Volume 1* who were gracious enough to share their time with me, and allowed me to share their stories in these books: David Leroy Anderson, Lance Anderson, Gabe Bartalos, Howard Berger, Thomas Burman, Bari Dreiband-Burman, Everett Burrell, Doug Drexler, Tony Gardner, Alec Gillis, Joel Harlow, Paul Jones, Jim McPherson, Bart J. Mixon, Ve Neill, Matt Rose (who I wish was still here with us to see the release of this book), Screaming Mad George, Patrick Tatopolous, Wayne Toth, and Tom Woodruff Jr.

Also, a huge thanks to my main editor, Derek Anderson, for taking on the unenviable task of cleaning up hundreds of pages of my writing, as well as Kathryn Morris who also provided me with some additional edits as well.

To every single person out there who helped me out with transcribing, I cannot thank you enough for taking on such a tedious task, and I would not be here without your help and I owe you so much for your kindness and time. My transcribing heroes include: Bryan Christopher, Rob DiCristino, Zena Dixon, Mariesonn Florendo, Sarah Jane, Nolan McBride, Elise Middlespoon, Moxie McMurder, John Pavlich, Emily von Seele, Anya Stanley, and Jerry Smith.

I'm also grateful to all my friends, family and co-workers who have been extremely supportive of this endeavor over the course of the last five years, and I appreciate all the love and support you have given me along the way. Without your kindnesses, I know I would not have made it as far as I have and I am forever in your debt.

Above all, I must thank my partner, Brian Smith, for being my biggest champion and cheerleader throughout this entire process. Every single day I get to spend with you is a gift and there's no way that I would have been able to embark on this journey in the first place without your love and encouragement along the way. You are amazing and I can never thank you enough for always believing in me and in my work.

Also From

Available in Print - eBook - Audiobook

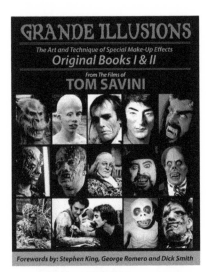

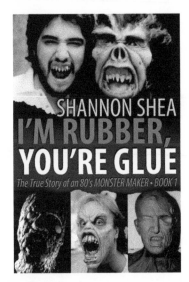

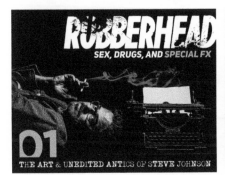

Also By Heather Wixson

Available in Print - eBook

Monsters, Makeup & Effects 2

Conversations with Cinema's Greatest Artists

VOLUME 2

Heather Wixson